William Penn

AND EARLY QUAKERISM

WILLIAM PENN

AND EARLY QUAKERISM

———————————————

MELVIN B. ENDY, JR.

———————————————

PRINCETON UNIVERSITY PRESS

LCC: 72-7798
ISBN: 0-691-07190-x

This book is composed in Linotype Janson

Printed in the United States of America
by Princeton University Press

For Susan

THIS STUDY of William Penn's religious thought was begun in response to the needs of a seminar in American religious history. Attempting to determine the influence of Quaker thought on the founding and structuring of the colony of Pennsylvania, I soon learned that no comprehensive study of Penn's religious thought could be found among the many works on Penn and his colony. Indeed, it became obvious that most of the biographies and monographs on Penn and the histories of the early colony were incomplete, and in some cases misleading, precisely because of their authors' lack of familiarity with Penn's theological writings and with the thought of early Quakerism in general. My reading in Penn's works and a growing acquaintance with interpretations of early Quakerism also indicated that Penn's relationship to other early Quaker writers constitutes a fascinating problem and that there are important differences among historians of the Friends' thought concerning Penn's place in the movement. These differences are in turn related to disagreements over the fundamental nature of early Quaker theology and its connections with contemporary intellectual developments. Accordingly, my study of Penn's religious thought and its influence on his political and social life has necessitated an attempt to relate his thought to early Quaker thought in general and to contemporary ideas and movements having superficial or genuine affinities with Quaker doctrines.

As the path of my research became broader and my study grew from a seminar paper to a dissertation to a monograph, I have become increasingly grateful for the multitude of fine works by predecessors and contemporaries on seventeenth-century English religious thought, especially those on puritan and nonconformist materials. Among studies of

vii

Quakerism and its immediate background, the works of Rufus Jones, Geoffrey Nuttall, Frederick Tolles, Hugh Barbour, Maurice Creasey, Howard H. Brinton, and Gary Nash have been especially useful. The staffs of several libraries have been most helpful: the Chester County Historical Society, The Quaker Collection at Haverford College, the Historical Society of Pennsylvania, and the Beinecke Rare Book Library at Yale University. I am particularly indebted to Barbara Curtis and Edwin B. Bronner of Haverford College, the trustees of the Albert Cook Myers Collection at the Chester County Historical Society, and Hannah Benner Roach of the Papers of William Penn project at the Historical Society of Pennsylvania. A Margaret Bundy Scott Fellowship from Hamilton College and grants from Hamilton College and the Ford Foundation were of great assistance. At various stages of progress my work has been read by and discussed with Hugh Barbour, John F. Wilson, and Sydney Ahlstrom, and it has been immeasurably improved as a result of their assistance. I am especially indebted to Sydney Ahlstrom for fostering my interest in puritan and American colonial studies and for serving as a very helpful guide and critic through several stages of the study's development. Sanford G. Thatcher of Princeton University Press has provided excellent advice and much encouragement, and Mrs. Arthur Sherwood of the Press has done much to improve the clarity and style of the manuscript.

TABLE OF CONTENTS

William Penn

AND EARLY QUAKERISM

INTRODUCTION

WILLIAM PENN is best known to both schoolchildren and scholars for his political thoughts and activities. To the former he is the wise and gentle founding father—a quaint, portly gentleman standing under an elm tree, peace pipe in hand, bargaining earnestly with a group of trusting Indians.[1] More advanced students of colonial America learn from a host of historians that Penn's colony, the "holy experiment," rapidly became a prosperous center of trade and a vital experiment in constitutional government. Although the economic and political vitality of Pennsylvania have been attributed to a variety of factors, the important role of the founder has not been neglected. Many students of the era have written of the firm political foundation established when Penn, drawing on his extensive knowledge of political theory, provided the colony with an enlightened frame of government designed to preserve the fundamental rights of men.[2]

Penn's interest in political affairs developed largely because of his desire to achieve toleration for England's religious dissenters. His ideas on religious freedom and his pleas for toleration have accordingly been portrayed as crucial to the development of his political thought and of utmost importance in the struggle for religious liberty in Restoration England. Moreover, Penn knew that the English government could not be persuaded by treatises and speeches alone either to stop interfering with dissenters or to give Pennsylvania's merchants and citizens the autonomy they needed. Scholars have not failed to note that the growth of

[1] The reference is to Benjamin West's famous painting, "Penn's Treaty with the Indians."

[2] The selected bibliography includes a guide to the most useful of the kinds of studies referred to throughout this introductory discussion.

3

toleration in England and the relative autonomy of the colony owed as much to Penn's energy and influence as a politician as to the persuasiveness of his pen.

Although it is not inappropriate that Penn has become associated primarily with political history, the almost exclusively political concerns of students of his thought have left us with a truncated view of his mind. From at least the time of his conversion to Quakerism at the age of twenty-three, Penn observed himself and the world about him through the peculiar perspective of a twice-born saint. As one of the foremost leaders of the newly risen Quakers, he believed that the world was ready for a harvest of souls that would transcend national and cultural barriers and lead to the eschatological events foreseen since the beginning of Christianity. Although it would be misleading to portray Penn as a man whose thoughts and activities stemmed exclusively from a few basic religious assumptions, we cannot understand his life and works—including their political and colonial aspects—without a knowledge of his religious hopes and ideals. For the first half of his career Penn was primarily a Quaker preacher, writer, and spiritual guide devoting virtually all his time and energy to a movement that he believed would culminate in the world-wide triumph of "Spiritual" religion. One of the early Quakers' most prolific theologians, Penn wrote both to convince and encourage the sympathetic and to refute the Quakers' many detractors. A large majority of his more than 150 published writings were either religious exhortations or theological treatises, and his correspondence with Quakers and leading puritans and Anglicans of the day provides much insight into his own religious thought and into the nature of early Quakerism.

Penn's more than forty biographers have not been unaware of the central place of religion in his life or of his prominent position in early Quakerism. Indeed, many of them were inspired by a reverent regard for a man they believed to be among the great saints of modern history. From the accounts of such writers we gain a full appreciation of the religious ardor that motivated Penn and of the importance of his activities within the Quaker movement. We look in vain, however, for more than the barest summaries of his religious thought. This is not surprising when we consider the extraordinary amount of ground to be covered in chronicling Penn's long and active life, as well as the absorbing drama of his shifting roles as gentleman, Quaker, Whig, proprietor, courtier, and accused traitor. But the problem is not primarily one of space; it is, rather, that Penn's life has not attracted writers with a significant interest in Quaker theology or in the intellectual and religious thought of seventeenth-century England. Most of Penn's biographers could have subscribed to the judgment of William Hull that "in a century when theological argument was regarded as the chief end of man, Penn yielded to the prevalent fashion of striving to unscrew the inscrutable and indulged in the futile custom of dogmatizing about the unknowable."[3] Accordingly, they proceeded on the assumption that, in the words of the biographer Samuel Janney, controversial theological material "is seldom interesting or edifying to succeeding generations, especially when tinctured with party zeal, or imbued with the prejudices of the age."[4] We learn from a few of Penn's biographers the occasions of his major writings, the names of his theological correspondents, and occasional summaries of works, but we find no comprehensive account of his beliefs, few indications of the tenor of his mind or of his basic assumptions, and still less analysis of the relation of his thought to the intellectual currents of his era.

As William Braithwaite noted in his monumental history of early Quakerism, Penn achieved greater heights as an activist trying to turn Quaker visions into reality than as a theologian.[5] Nevertheless, although no study of Penn's religious thought has appeared, students of seventeenth-century

[3] *William Penn: A Topical Biography* (London, 1937), 166.
[4] *Life of William Penn, with Selections from his Correspondence and Autobiography* (2d edn., rev.; Philadelphia, 1852), 44.
[5] *The Second Period of Quakerism* (2d edn., rev. by Henry J. Cadbury; Cambridge, 1961), 211.

Quakerism have generally considered Penn one of the most important and articulate exponents of early Quaker thought. Ernst Troeltsch no doubt overstated the case in his reference to Penn as "the greatest of the Quakers, who expressed their ideals in their purest form."[6] But historians of Quaker thought have linked Penn with George Fox, Isaac Penington, Robert Barclay, and Samuel Fisher as one of the most important of the Quaker writers of the seventeenth century. Not infrequently Penn and Barclay are portrayed as the writers who most effectively distilled the visions and experiences of Fox and his "First Publishers of Truth" into the theological language of the times.[7] Others, especially since the revival of puritan studies and emphasis on the puritan roots of Quakerism, have granted Penn's importance but have seen him as a transitional figure of the second generation with a message fundamentally different from that of George Fox and the First Publishers of Truth.[8]

This study is an attempt to go beyond the political historians, the biographers, and the historians of Quakerism to provide a comprehensive account of Penn's religious thought, its influence on his political thought and activity, and the significance of his life and thought to the early Quaker movement. The development of the last-named topic has led to a broader pattern of research and, I hope, a more substantial contribution to the understanding of early Quakerism than I had originally envisioned. My attempt to assess Penn's place in the Quaker movement, and especially the relationship between his thought and that of other lead-

[6] *The Social Teaching of the Christian Churches*, trans. Olive Wyon (2 vols.; New York, 1960), Vol. II, 782.

[7] *The Beginnings of Quakerism* (2d edn., rev. by Henry J. Cadbury; Cambridge, England, 1955), 286; Rufus M. Jones, *The Faith and Practice of the Quakers* (Garden City, N.Y., 1928), 32-33; Howard Brinton, *Friends for 300 Years: The History and Beliefs of the Society of Friends since George Fox Started the Quaker Movement* (New York, 1952), 31.

[8] See especially Hugh Barbour, *The Quakers in Puritan England* (New Haven, 1963).

6

ing Quaker writers of the seventeenth century, has led me to an understanding of the movement that differs in certain respects from the recent tendency to stress strongly the puritan origins and relationships of the Quakers. The Interregnum Quakers appear to me to be part of what I have called the spiritualist movement of the 1640's and 1650's and must be clearly distinguished in several respects from the puritans. This interpretation, in turn, has led to a somewhat distinctive understanding of the relationship between the thought of Interregnum Friends such as Fox, Burrough, Nayler, and Penington and Restoration thinkers such as Barclay and Penn. Because of the revisionist nature of this interpretation, as well as my conviction that early Quaker thought has never been adequately explored in its relationship to its intellectual milieu, I have developed my study of Penn into a vehicle for an analysis of early Quaker religious thought and its social and political implications.

ONE

THE PREHISTORY OF QUAKERISM:
PURITANISM AND SPIRITUALISM

The Puritan Background

When in 1649 George Fox began lifting his leather breeches from "steeplehouse" benches to contradict the tepid deliverances of "hireling" ministers with his own fulminations, most of his listeners quickly diagnosed the malady: another case of the sectarian fanaticism that had reached plague proportions. As early as 1641 Ephraim Pagitt published his *A Discovery of 29 Sects here in London all of which except the First are divelish and damnable*. By 1646 Thomas Edwards, scouring all of England, turned up 199 religious sects for his *Gangraena*. Although several groups of Seekers who were later to be part of the Quaker movement were already meeting together by this time, when the Quakers congealed as an identifiable entity several years later the proliferation was still proceeding apace. The Quakers were among the innumerable religious groups that emerged from the religious, political, social, and economic turmoil that England experienced in the revolutionary decades of the Interregnum. The sectarian tendency of the 1640's, in turn, had its roots in earlier reformist developments in England, and the Quakers could trace back to the sixteenth century the impulse that led to their appearance.

Penn often discussed Quakerism as the culmination of the movement for reform of the English church that had begun in the sixteenth century with the Marian martyrs and the "Puritans." Pagitt and Edwards could easily explain such claims by "enthusiasts" as the result of the self-serving deception typical of heretics, but we may imagine that they would be greatly perplexed and not a little disgruntled to

8

find a whole generation of later, more professional, and presumably more objective historians in substantial agreement with Penn. Historians in general since the revival of puritan studies in the 1930's have emphasized the puritan roots of most of the Interregnum sects, and the most significant studies of Quakerism as a religious movement have been especially emphatic about its links with the earlier movement for reform of the English church.[1] Richard Vann has reminded us that the different levels of objectivity achieved by Penn and later historians is, after all, a relative matter by pointing out that emphasis on the puritan roots of Quakerism has come to the fore "in a theological climate of revived Calvinism."[2] My own reservations about the insistence in some recent scholarship on the similarity and continuity between puritan and Quaker theology will be evident throughout this study. The origins and nature of the Quaker movement, nevertheless, are understandable only when they are studied in relation to puritanism.

As scholarly studies of English religious history of the sixteenth and seventeenth centuries proliferate, it becomes increasingly difficult to justify applying the single label "puritan" to the various reforming tendencies and movements that appeared between the times of King Edward and Queen Elizabeth and the Restoration. At least, it may be essential to distinguish Edwardean, Elizabethan, Stuart, and Interregnum puritanism and then nonconformity.[3] In addition to the difficulty of finding characteristics that are applicable to all the reforming parties in that time-span, there is

[1] Barbour, *Quakers in Puritan England*; Geoffrey Nuttall, *The Holy Spirit in Puritan Faith and Experience* (Oxford, 1946) and *The Puritan Spirit: Essays and Addresses* (London, 1967); Henry Cadbury's notes in Braithwaite, *Beginnings of Quakerism*.

[2] *The Social Development of English Quakerism: 1655-1755* (Cambridge, Mass., 1969), 31, n. 56.

[3] See Everett H. Emerson, *English Puritanism from John Hooper to John Milton* (Durham, N.C., 1968), 1-46; C. H. George, "Puritanism as History and Historiography," *Past and Present*, No. 41 (Dec. 1968), 77-104.

9

the problem caused by the tendency of widely influential scholars such as William Haller and Perry Miller to focus almost exclusively on religious and theological characteristics in defining puritanism. Christopher Hill, Katherine and Charles George, and Michael Walzer have pointed to the widely varying uses of the term in the seventeenth century, many of them based on social and political characteristics, and Hill and Walzer have emphasized anew that economic, political, and social, as well as religious and theological, forces led to the imperfect unification of the elements of the populace in opposition to church and court in the seventeenth century, and that the secular forces help to account for the appeal of the religious doctrines and practices.[4] Moreover, the student of Quakerism desiring to stress the relation of the Friends to puritanism must be especially careful of broad definitions. It is not readily apparent, for instance, that the apocalyptic spiritualists who gathered around George Fox, James Nayler, Richard Farnsworth, and others in Interregnum England were in any way dependent for beliefs or inspiration on the Elizabethan presbyterian movement led by Thomas Cartwright.

There is, nevertheless, some significance in the fact that many Quakers, despite their insistence on the newness of their dispensation and a tendency to set themselves over against all Protestants, acknowledged their English religious predecessors' accomplishments, beginning with the Marian martyrs' individual witnesses and carrying on in the presbyterian, separatist, baptist, and spiritualist movements. Sometimes the acknowledgment was made in a backhanded way, as when Edward Burrough lamented the increasingly dangerous because ever more subtle and impure—that is, mixed with truth—errors one found as he moved left on the Eng-

---

[4] Christopher Hill, *Society and Puritanism in Pre-Revolutionary England* (New York, 1964); Charles H. and Katherine George, *The Protestant Mind of the English Reformation: 1570-1640* (Princeton, 1961); Michael Walzer, *The Revolution of the Saints* (Cambridge, Mass., 1965).

lish religious spectrum.[5] More common was Penn's commendation of the increasing spiritual concerns of each new religious party.[6] The sense of continuity with all English reformers dissatisfied with Anglicanism is no doubt attributable in part to the fact that most Quaker writers had travelled "from vessel to vessel" through at least parts of the Protestant spectrum on their path to spiritual religion. The feeling of affinity with English reformers of a hundred years earlier was also related to their familiarity with Foxe's *Book of Martyrs* and their belief in the religio-nationalistic myth concerning England's role in God's plan for the reformation of the world. Each successive reforming development in English religious life was another link in the chain of events leading to the end-times.

If we define puritanism in the broadest and most ecclesiastical sense, then, we must include the Quakers among those men of the sixteenth and seventeenth centuries who were so dissatisfied with the incomplete reformation of the English church and nation that they either actively sought their further purification or condemned them and formed a purer church. Many changes of emphasis and doctrine came to the fore at various times among the reforming parties, and after the 1590's the object of their efforts, the Anglican Church, also began to change, but throughout the period from 1559

[5] "A Trumpet of the Lord Sounded forth out of Zion" (1655), in *The Memorable Works of a Son of Thunder and Consolation* . . . [London, 1672], 104-109.

[6] Letter to Viscountess Conway (Oct. 20, 1675), The Papers of William Penn (hereafter cited as PWP), a photo-reproduction collection at The Historical Society of Pennsylvania (hereafter cited as HSP), Philadelphia, Pa. (A.L.S. in the British Museum). Documents in the PWP collection are in chronologically ordered folders and can be located by date and, in most cases, by title or description on the folder. Hereafter the location of the original—or the contemporary or later copy if the original can no longer be located—will be noted in parentheses after PWP or after the citation of the other major collection used, the Albert Cook Myers Collection (hereafter cited as ACMC), a photo-reproduction and transcription collection, Chester County Historical Society, West Chester, Pa.

to 1662 the fundamental minimal program of the more conservative reformers was remarkably constant and pointed the way for more radical innovators. The Presbyterian address to King Charles II in 1660 was largely made up of recommendations that had appeared in the reform program in the 1560's, the Millenary Petition of 1603, and the Directory of 1645.[7] Baxter summarized the essential demands as matters of church government, liturgy, and ceremonies.[8]

It was, of course, precisely the constancy of the program of conservative reformers that distressed the more radical reformers and sectaries of the Interregnum. Many of them, including the Quakers, had a progressive view of religious history and thought it rather late in the day for offering mild reforming measures that had been good beginnings "for their day" generations earlier, and they opposed supporters of such measures as strenuously as they did Anglicans.[9] Moreover, the Quakers no longer believed in church government, liturgy, or ceremonies, in the strict sense of these terms. There was, nevertheless, an essential continuity between the conservative perspective on these matters and the position of the Friends. The dissatisfied Anglican's or presbyterian's desire for at least suffragan bishops, better ministerial training, and congregational discipline was the conservative way of expressing a concern for a more godly nation and a church similar to that of the New Testament, and the Independents, Baptists, and Quakers shared that concern. The presbyterian objection to Anglican liturgy reflected an insistence on a more Biblical, Word-centered, and Spirit-directed worship that was echoed in the more startling demands from the left. The distaste for the surplice, sign of

[7] E. C. Ratcliff, "The Savoy Conference," in Geoffrey Nuttall and Owen Chadwick, eds., *From Uniformity to Unity: 1662-1962* (London, 1962), 100-104.

[8] *Reliquiae Baxterianae*, ed. M. Sylvester (London, 1696), I, ii, par. 96.

[9] See, e.g., John Saltmarsh, *Sparkles of Glory, or Some Beams of the Morning-Star* (London, 1648), 53-55, 73-77.

the cross, bowing at the name of Jesus, kneeling at communion, and observing holidays, among other ceremonies, extended across the reforming spectrum. It stemmed from a combination of rabid anti-Romanism and a suspicion about the dangers of overemphasis on the corporeal in religious affairs that was inherited from the Swiss Reformed movement and was reflected in statements of reformers from the Convocation proposals of 1563 to Fox's "declaration" against "images and crosses, and sprinkling of infants, with all their holy days (so called) and all their vain traditions. . . ."[10]

Having related the Quakers to this broad background, however, we must move on to point out that the proper focus for understanding the background to the events that produced the Children of the Light in the 1640's is Stuart puritanism and especially the "spiritual brotherhood" described by William Haller and the preachers' many lay followers.[11] Beginning in the late 1580's several developments in English life led to a change in emphasis in the reforming movement that had begun after the Marian exile and to the formation in the seventeenth century of a kind of spirituality that influenced important segments of the populace and contributed to the growth of a fundamental cleavage in English society. These included the effective suppression in the 1590's of presbyterianism and separatism, the deprivation of many reforming preachers by Archbishop Richard Bancroft, the decline of Calvinist theology among a small but influential minority of Anglicans, the rise

---

[10] *The Journal of George Fox*, ed. John L. Nickalls (Cambridge, 1952), 35. All references to Fox's *Journal* will be to the Nickalls edn. unless otherwise noted. On the usefulness of linking the diverse groups of English reformers, including the Quakers, see Nuttall, *Holy Spirit*, 9-10; Anne Whiteman, "The Restoration of the Church of England," in Nuttall and Chadwick, *From Uniformity to Unity*; and Alan Simpson, *Puritanism in Old and New England* (Chicago, 1955), 1-2.

[11] *The Rise of Puritanism* (New York, 1938). See also Norman Pettit, *The Heart Prepared: Grace and Conversion in Puritan Spiritual Life* (New Haven, 1966), chap. 3.

among this same minority of divine-right episcopacy and "Romanist" liturgical influences, and King James's decided opposition to reform of church and state.

IN RESPONSE to these developments many of those who had hopes of reforming church and society were drawn in new directions, or, rather, devoted all their energies to activities that had previously simply shared their time. Since it was obvious late in Elizabeth's reign and early in James's that the changes desired could not be brought about through official channels in Convocation, at court, or even in Parliament, most of the reformers who had not separated had to limit their efforts to preaching, teaching, and writing. Involved in this change was the necessity of attempting to live more or less quietly with the official polity, liturgy, and ceremonies of the church while modifying them in practice where episcopal oversight was either lax or supportive. At the same time the reformers to a certain extent minimized concern with these focal points of much Elizabethan reform and turned toward theology and ethics. As a result of these partly unconscious shifts there came into being early in the seventeenth century a "spiritual outlook, way of life, and mode of expression" that, although dependent on a series of Elizabethan teachers, only now began to define itself over against the influential Anglican innovators.[12] On the clerical side William Haller has listed and described the thought of the central figures of the "Puritan order of preaching brothers" held together by educational, ecclesiastical, and personal ties. The founders of the movement in the sixteenth century were Richard Greenham, Henry Smith, and Richard Rogers. The main body included, to name only the most prominent leaders, Laurence Chaderton, Arthur Hildersam, John Dod, William Perkins, Paul Baynes, Richard Sibbes, John Preston, William Gouge, John Cotton, and Thomas Goodwin. These men and the many preachers and lecturers they trained and

[12] Haller, *Puritanism*, 9.

influenced became prominent—mainly by holding lecture-
ships—in many parts of England but especially around London, for James's hostility to presbyterianism and to the puri-
fying urge in general was combined with an unwillingness
to impose strict enforcement of church canons on parishes.
This was especially so during the archbishopric of George
Abbott from 1610 to 1628.

The puritan preachers became astoundingly popular,
mainly in urban areas and among the lesser gentry, yeomen,
merchants, and prosperous artisans. For a variety of reasons
that have been discussed by Christopher Hill and Michael
Walzer, the preachers' experiential theology of conversion,
their sermonic dramas about pilgrims and spiritual warriors,
and their personal and social ethical teachings about family,
vocation, personal discipline, morality, and Sabbath and holy
days had a strong appeal.[13] Many of the policies of King
James and especially King Charles were inimical to the economic and political as well as the religious interests of these
classes, and the decade of absolutism and ecclesiastical suppression beginning in 1629 solidified the opposition to major
policies in church and state. It is to this clerical movement
beginning in Elizabethan times, expanding and developing
its peculiar emphases in Stuart England, and then split-
ting into Presbyterianism, Independency, and the Baptist
churches that I shall hereafter apply the term puritanism.[14]

[13] Hill, *Society and Puritanism, passim*; Walzer, *Revolution of the
Saints*, chaps. 3-7, and "Puritanism as a Revolutionary Ideology," *History and Theory*, 3 (1963), 59-90.

[14] For a very different interpretation of this era of English religious
history, see K. and C. H. George, *Protestant Mind*; C. H. George,
"A Social Interpretation of English Puritanism," *Journal of Modern
History*, 25 (1953), 327-342; and C. H. George, "Puritanism as History
and Historiography." For an answer to the Georges' insistence that
the term "Puritanism" is a meaningless abstraction as used in much
scholarship, especially in the period 1603-1640, see Walzer's review
essay in *History and Theory*, 2 (1962), 89-96. We can view Haller's
study of the prerevolutionary movement as a perceptive description
of the thought of a distinctive and important group of men without

The distinctive mark of this reforming movement is what Sydney Ahlstrom has called its combination of "an unprecedented emphasis on the need for an inner experience of God's regenerating grace as a mark of election" and "a concern for drawing out man's duties in the church and in the world."[15] It was, then, a form of *spirituality* or a concern for the reactions that the objects of belief arouse in the religious consciousness, rather than doctrine, or the beliefs themselves, that was the distinguishing feature of the loosely unified party.[16] This psychological concern is what led Richard Sibbes to call the Book of Psalms the heart of the Scriptures because they provide "the anatomy of a holy man" and "lay the inside of a truly devout man outward to the view of others."[17] The spirituality of the preachers had an effect on their doctrine, but as late as 1660 the Presbyterians attested to the continuing doctrinal unity of the main body of puritans and most satisfied Anglicans when they noted the "firme agreement betweene our brethren and us in doctrinall truths of ye Reformed Religion."[18] The developing Arminianism of some Anglicans induced some puritans to emphasize their adherence to Reformed tenets on occasion, especially after the king outlawed preaching on predestination in 1622. At the same time, the preachers' desire to draw their hearers on to the path of regeneration

---

going along with his simplistic views of the products of puritanism, such as his belief that these men were "the immediate spiritual and intellectual begetters of the Puritan revolution" (p. 79). Norman Pettit's important study of the experiential theology of most of the men studied by Haller develops their distinctive strains in a way that backs Haller's categories.

[15] *Theology in America: The Major Protestant Voices from Puritanism to Neo-Orthodoxy* (New York, 1967), 27.

[16] The definition of spirituality is that of Louis Bouyer, *The Spirituality of the New Testament and the Fathers* (New York, 1963), viii, cited by Pettit, *Heart Prepared*, 5, n. 6.

[17] *The Soul's Conflict and Victory Over Itself by Faith* (1635; rpt., Phila., 1842), 2.

[18] Whiteman, "Restoration," 54.

led to the development of a doctrine of preparation that stood out in contrast to the Reformed emphasis on man's bondage and his total passivity before divine grace and had apparent similarities to Arminianism.[19] The slow growth of ceremonialism and sacramentarianism that culminated in Laud's program, in combination with their own increasing concern with the Spirit's direct operation on man, induced some of the puritan preachers to second Sibbes's advice to "shut out of your hearts too much relying on any outward thing," but they continued to believe that God normally touched man indirectly through secondary agents that became known to the faculties through the senses.[20]

By analyzing the inner experience of men as they received God's regenerating grace, the spiritual brotherhood produced a veritable theology of conversion outlining the myriad paths one could follow. Many saints could expect to learn the depths of despair and then receive a sudden overpowering sense of newness. For others the rebirth might be a process drawn out over a long period and, in unusual cases, have no recognizable turning point.[21] Because of their belief that a man could begin with a "weak faith" and strive to recognize and capitalize on God's spiritual dealings with him, a group of preachers and writers developed the idea of preparation for conversion.[22] This concern for the inter-

[19] Pettit, chaps. 3 and 4.

[20] Sibbes, *Complete Works of Richard Sibbes . . .*, ed. A. B. Grosart (6 vols.; Edinburgh, 1862-1864), IV, 295. On the puritans' Zwinglian suspicions about overreliance on the physical and their concern for distinguishing between the operation of the Spirit and its vehicle, see Nuttall, *Puritan Spirit*, chap. 10. On the Aristotelian epistemology of an over-lapping group of puritans, see Perry Miller, *The New England Mind: The Seventeenth Century* (1939; rpt., Boston, 1961), 281.

[21] See Edmund Morgan, *Visible Saints: The History of a Puritan Idea* (New York, 1963), 4-12; A.S.P. Woodhouse, "Notes on Milton's Early Development," *Univ. of Toronto Quarterly*, 13 (1943-1944), 73-74.

[22] Pettit, *Heart Prepared*, includes Greenham, Rogers, Chaderton, Hildersam, Dod, Perkins, Sibbes, Preston, and Ames, among English puritans, and Thomas Hooker, John Cotton, Thomas Shepard, Peter

action between God and man in conversion contributed, along with Continental influences and their Old Testament preoccupation, to the puritans' extensive development of the covenant idea.[23] It also led to an unprecedented focus on the workings of the Holy Spirit.

Although an explicit doctrine of the Spirit did not come to the fore until the 1640's, and although most of the puritan preachers were more biblical than mystical, their psychological preoccupation with the inner experience of regeneration, when combined with a continuing insistence on God's initiative in confronting man, made it inevitable that the Holy Spirit would be increasingly prominent in their theology. The craving for an experimental knowledge of God through the indwelling Spirit and the campaign against deadness of heart and "notionalism" became more and more noticeable in the 1620's and 1630's, especially under the influence of the most popular puritan preacher and writer of the period, Richard Sibbes. According to Sibbes, true religion begins when "the Holy Ghost slides and insinuates and infuseth himself into our souls."[24]

Bulkeley, and John Davenport among those who came to Massachusetts.

[23] See Michael McGiffert, "American Puritan Studies in the 1960's," *William and Mary Quarterly*, 3d ser., 27 (1970), 47-50; John von Rohr, "Covenant and Assurance in Early English Puritanism," *Church History*, 34 (1965), 195-203; Richard L. Greaves, "John Bunyan and Covenant Thought in the Seventeenth Century," *CH*, 36 (1967), 151-169; C. Conrad Cherry, "The Puritan Notion of the Covenant in Jonathan Edwards' Doctrine of Faith," *CH*, 34 (1965), 328-341. Perry Miller's belief that the covenant served to modify the Calvinism of puritans and lead them toward a "hidden rationalism" has given way to the recognition that "the covenant theology grew out of the strain of Protestantism that made an experimental faith the basis of the Christian life. . . ." David Hall, "The Puritans versus John Calvin: A Critique of Perry Miller, *The New England Mind*," unpubl. paper read to Am. Hist. Assoc., Toronto, Dec. 30, 1967, cited by McGiffert, 49.

[24] *Works*, I, 24. See James Fulton Maclear, " 'The Heart of New England Piety Rent': The Mystical Element in Early Puritan History," *Miss. Valley Hist. Review*, 42 (1956), 621-652.

Following regeneration, the "new man" was to strive to take on the life-pattern of the saint. The preachers embellished and combined the old Christian images of pilgrim and warrior and taught their hearers to view themselves as spiritual soldiers struggling through enemy territory toward the promised land. In gratitude for having been lifted by the grace of God from the ranks of the Devil, the saint was to fight ceaselessly against sin wherever he found it. The first place he looked was his own breast, and there he found the occasion for many of his fiercest battles. Puritans were normally more confident than most Lutherans and Calvinists of their ability to gain control over the Devil within them, but at the same time they knew, with the Continental Reformers, that the cause of their election was God's free decision to justify through Christ and not their own sanctification. They also expected the inner struggle against sin to continue as long as they remained in the world. For this reason they developed the discipline of self-accusation, self-trial, and self-denial. A strict daily regimen of Scripture, prayer, self-examination, moral seriousness, and hard work; a family life in which husband and wife sought the good of each other in the sight of God and provided a nursery of piety to "inform and reform their children in the fear of God"; a vocation devoted to the greater glory of God: these were the marks of a godly life.[25]

The puritans, however, did not become the scourge of England simply by beating the Devil in their own souls. They were convinced that *all* men should walk according to God's law and were involved in what Woodhouse has called "a determined and varied effort to erect the holy community."[26] John Foxe had taught Englishmen that they were living in the fifth and last era of history and that they were an elect nation that would experience a reformation

[25] Richard Greenham, *The Workes . . . Revised, Corrected and Published . . .* (London, 1612), 279.

[26] *Puritanism and Liberty: Being the Army Debates (1647-9) from the Clarke Manuscripts with Supplementary Documents* (London, 1938), 37.

under a godly prince and bishops. The later years of Elizabeth and the reign of James I tarnished these hopes, but in
the seventeenth century the eschatological speculations of
Hugh Broughton,[27] Thomas Brightman,[28] and Joseph Mead[29]
kept them alive. Indeed, as several scholars have emphasized
recently, puritanism had a markedly eschatological streak
in the seventeenth century, especially in the 1630's and early
1640's.[30] Brightman's attempt to revise Foxe in the light of
the failure of the godly prince and bishops to materialize
fitted in with the general shift in reforming sentiment, after
the turn of the century, away from structural changes. By
the time of Laud's repressive regime Brightman's identification of episcopacy and Antichrist provided a framework for
puritan self-understanding. Most of the clerics had more
difficulty finding their monarch among the Satanic forces
of the Book of Revelation and Daniel, but the signs of the
times in the 1630's nourished their hopes for a transformation of English society as a prelude to world reform. Although the developing preoccupation with Revelation and
Daniel fed the apocalyptic sense of the discontinuity between the present deteriorating scene and the new era, most
reformers who indulged their eschatological hopes retained
the view of Brightman and Mead: the new era would arise
from the events of seventeenth-century history through the
intervention of God working by means of his human agents,
both the elect and reprobate.[31]

[27] *A Revelation of the Holy Apocalypse*, 1610.

[28] *Apocalypsis Apocalypseous*, 1609, with edns. and transs. in 1612,
1615, 1616, and 1644; *A Most Comfortable Exposition of the Prophe-
cie of Daniel*, 1635 and 1644; and others.

[29] *Clavis Apocalyptica*, 1627, 1632, 1643, 1650; *The Apostasy of the
Latter Times*, 1641; and others.

[30] John Wilson, *Pulpit in Parliament: Puritanism During the Eng-
lish Civil Wars, 1640-1648* (Princeton, 1969), chap. 7; William M.
Lamont, "Puritanism as History and Historiography: Some Further
Thoughts," *Past and Present*, no. 44 (Aug. 1969), 133-146; Walzer,
Revolution of the Saints, 290-294.

[31] See Wilson, *Pulpit in Parliament*, 214-223.

PURITANISM IN THE 1640's

When the Civil War began, the puritans sided overwhelmingly with the Parliamentary forces. The alliance between the Commons and the reforming clerics and their followers that had been consolidated in the previous decades made the ministers the logical spiritual leaders and ideological interpreters of the upheaval. Analyzing the sermons they preached before Parliament between 1640 and 1649, John Wilson has shown that the eschatological millenarian streak in the movement led to fundamental disagreements among the clerics in their interpretations of the significance of the civil struggle. Most of the preachers, at least in the early 1640's, still emphasizing the continuity between the present and the future, interpreted their times in terms of a prophetic eschatology. Viewing England as an elect nation in covenant with God, they saw her troubles as attributable to her failure to carry through the reformation of church and nation, and counseled Parliament to repent on behalf of Englishmen and then to instigate the required reforms. Others, more attuned to the apocalyptic literature that had come to the fore in the preceding years, sensed as early as 1642 and 1643 that they were witnessing the enactment of God's foreordained plan for the end-times. This perspective became increasingly prominent as the war dragged on, bringing in its wake unprecedented religious, social, political, and economic upheaval. The apocalyptic interpreters sensed that human agents were not in control of events and took solace—in the face of increasing turmoil—in the belief that God was in control and would shortly intervene openly to establish his kingdom.[32]

Wilson, noting the correspondence between the apocalyptic perspective and the rising Independents among the spiritual brotherhood, has suggested that "through the Independents this speculative and apocalyptic exegesis of the scriptures, with the derivative millenarianism, moved from

[32] *Ibid.*, 200-214.

the background to the foreground of Puritanism as the differentia of a party within the movement," and that this split made possible the more radical divisions to the left.[33] Although the rise of apocalyptic millenarianism cannot in itself account for the sudden splintering of puritanism, the strength of this approach to the revolutionary period lies in the fact that it provides the most appropriate background for understanding the sudden force given to the centrifugal tendencies that had always existed within the movement and helps to explain the spiritualizing thrust of the proliferation process.

Although most of the clerical disciples and lay followers of the spiritual brethren remained in the Anglican fold before 1640, constituting a more or less unified party, their ecclesiastical unity both with contented Anglicans and among themselves was precarious. The experiential piety that distinguished the movement was at the same time a source of disunifying tendencies that had spun off separatist and semiseparatist bodies into several orbits. With the exception of the nonseparating congregationalists, these groups were small and rather insignificant in the religious life of England before the 1640's, but the fact that each separatist urge since the first prominent one of Robert Browne in 1581 had included leaders drawn from or directly influenced by the main clerical party was a foreboding of future ills if separatism should ever become a less costly option or strange events and unsettled times produce an aura of spiritual speculation.

The 1640's saw the arrival of both developments in quick succession. With Laud impeached and episcopacy on the defensive and finally abolished, the puritan "outs" no longer had an "in" party to unite against. In 1641 the Commons, attempting to anticipate and control the religious stirrings, passed a law allowing all parishes to have lecturers if their minister was a "dumb dog," but already, with the High Commission and the other repressive machinery of church

[33] *Ibid.*, 223, 198.

and state on the way out, unauthorized "mechanicks" were free to gather unauthorized congregations and to publish their views for all to read. Separatism had clearly become an option. At the same time, the events of the decade were bizarre enough to raise religious imaginations to new heights. Englishmen were living through what has been called "the most profound civil disturbance in their turbulent history."[34] The public executions of rulers in church and state that began with the Earl of Stafford in 1641 and ended only with Charles himself in 1649 were startling reminders that the most exalted men were but puppets in the great divine drama of history. The striking success and the political effrontery of Cromwell's army of commoners as it captured nobles and kings, debated its commanders, and purged Parliament was seen, by way of contrast, as a foreshadowing of the eschatological exaltation of the lowly. The economic turmoil of the time, though apparently bracing for the economy as a whole, produced a heavy burden and heady visions for those elements of the population already dreaming of God's dramatic intervention to right the wrongs of history.[35]

It is not surprising that in these troubled days the glue of puritanism came unstuck. Interpreters of the movement have often pointed out that puritan thought was a precarious balance of Biblicism, a "hidden rationalism," and a mystical or spiritual side focused on longings for direct communion with God.[36] To the extent that this somewhat abstract approach to puritanism is helpful, it enables one to see how the brotherhood that had held together the Biblical Gouge, the rational Preston, and the mystical Sibbes gave way, in the absence of Laudian restraints, to the conflicting messages of John Bastwick, Richard Baxter, and William Dell. Looking more closely at puritan thought we can detect several

[34] Vann, *Social Development*, 7.

[35] See Margaret James, *Social Problems and Policy during the Puritan Revolution* (London, 1930), chap. 2.

[36] See, e.g., Maclear, " 'Heart of New England Rent,' " 623.

themes that had led to separatism even at the cost of exile or death and that would increase the impulse to sectarianism a hundredfold in the freer and more eschatological world of the Revolution.

One such theme was the prominence of the concept of sainthood—the conviction that all men must be reborn and then lead a life of combined separation from and struggle against the world. As long as the preachers insisted on an "experience of conversion which separates the Puritan from the mass of mankind and endows him with the privileges and duties of the elect," they could be certain that some men would glory in their separation and sense of superiority.[37] Others, like Robert Browne, Henry Barrow, John Smyth, John Robinson and Hanserd Knollys, would sooner or later come to the conclusion that they could no longer worship with unconverted men still using more or less Romish and non-Biblical rubrics. As the sense of the imminence of the end grew, so did the itch for purity.

Another aspect of puritan thought explaining the centrifugal tendency was its implicit affirmation of faith in the individual as the ultimate authority in the interpretation of his religious life. The preachers' message was that one could not afford to accept his faith from someone else: it must be a firsthand experience. One who did not scour the Bible regularly for himself and who had not been led by the Spirit operating through Scripture to an experience of conversion and a continuing confrontation with the Spirit was no saint but simply an "implicit" Christian—no better than a Roman. The stress on the use of Scripture and on experience inevitably produced a strong thrust toward religious individualism. This was in theory balanced by the belief that preaching and spiritual guidance should be limited to trained intellects who could apply grammar, logic, and rhetoric to the interpretation of God's Word, but the preachers' conviction that "notional" or secondhand faith was their main enemy, and their earnest desire to lure as many as possible into the path

[37] Simpson, *Puritanism*, 2.

toward regeneration, forced them to stress the clarity of Scripture for serious inquirers and the necessity of being one's own spiritual guide. It was natural that, in the confusing days of the Revolution, the listeners themselves forgot about the need for trained guides to help them interpret Scripture and understand the patterns of conversion. In the words of Thomas Hobbes, "every man became a Judge of Religion and an Interpreter of the Scriptures to himself." The dynamics of puritan faith had outrun the restraints of puritan discipline.[38]

Related to the tension between individualism and church authority are other points of divergence in puritan thought about the process of conversion that were accentuated under the press of events in the 1640's. Their saturation with the Old Testament and their pastoral experiential bent caused the puritan ministers to develop the concept of a covenant as the framework for understanding man's relations with God. This enabled them not only to speak of a kind of personal interaction between God and man in the regeneration process but to treat the baptized children of regenerate or covenanted parents as though they contained seeds of covenantal grace that they could "improve" by seeking earnestly to enter fully into the covenant. On the basis of this covenantal approach many of the ministers combined their doctrines of predestination and prevenient grace with a belief in the possibility of "preparing" oneself for conversion during a period of prolonged introspection. Seeking to escape from the idea that a man is wrenched by the law and its terrors into a state of salvation and to introduce a more voluntaristic attitude toward conversion, they said that a man should desire to change, look to God with expectation, and hope for a reconciliation with God before the moment comes.[39]

[38] *Behemoth: The History of the Civil Wars of England* (London, 1680), 28. See Haller, *Liberty and Reformation in the Puritan Revolution* (New York, 1955), *passim.*

[39] Pettit, *Heart Prepared*, 17, 217.

Although none of the preparationists explicitly modified his adherence to orthodox Calvinism, individual theologians were encouraged by the very nature of their introspective endeavor to develop the ideas in their own ways, and tensions developed in the thought of the brethren. If one approached the covenant, with Hildersam, as an arrangement according to which "we may ourselves do much in this work, yea . . . we must be doers in it ourselves or else it will never be well done," he gave the impression that it was a pact imposing real obligations on both parties. Others, such as Perkins, who insisted that regeneration was a "creation" and that "no sinner can prepare himself to his own creation," despite his own modest hints at preparatory procedures, made clearer the position that the covenant was a promise or testament leaving no room for human freedom or initiative.[40] Similarly, there developed differences between those who made much of preparation and tended to view conversion as a long process involving human initiative and certain predictable steps but without any necessary seizures or empirical feelings of gracious influence, and those who insisted on the variety of conversion experiences or on seizures of grace and assurance of salvation.[41]

There were numerous pitfalls for preachers and theologians in such an attempt to combine the rigors of Calvinistic orthodoxy with a pastoral desire to "console the fearful, convince the hesitant, set aright the erring, guide the unsure, and above all bring assurance of salvation to the Elect."[42] Not only one's personality and more or less limited pastoral experience but even ecclesiastical and social position could exercise an enormous influence on such idiosyncratic theol-

[40] Hildersam, *The Doctrine of Fasting and Prayer, and Humiliation for Sin* (London, 1633), 110-111; Perkins, *Works* (3 vols.; London, 1626), I, 733. See Pettit, *Heart Prepared*, chap. 3.

[41] Although they differed much among themselves, Preston, Hooker, Shepard, and Hildersam fit the former description, Perkins and Cotton the latter.

[42] Ahlstrom, *Theology in America*, 27.

ogy. With the Laudian controls gone and the social perspectives of the puritans increasingly varied, the brotherhood split into several at least partly opposing theological schools. In part the differences stemmed from what seem to be pastoral and theological concerns. Theologians most involved in covenant thought carried the emphasis on divine-human cooperation rather farther than the prerevolutionary preparationists had gone. Because of their belief that God communicates with man in a way that respects his reason and will, they wrote of the rationality of Christianity and developed somewhat uncharacteristic puritan apologies for the faith, but their sharpest debates stemmed from their thought on the doctrine of justification.

Making no sharp distinction between nature and grace, men such as Richard Baxter, John Ball, Thomas Blake, Stephen Geree, Anthony Burgess, and Samuel Rutherford tended to see the covenant as a pact involving conditions of faith and repentance that in a real sense had to be fulfilled by man before he was justified.[43] Baxter's *Aphorisms of Justification* (1649), which his later thought modified only slightly, referred to faith, works, and obedience as "part of the condition on which Christ's righteousness becomes ours." He was also wary of the tendency of sinful men to claim righteousness on the basis of Christ's righteousness while making no efforts to serve God better.[44] Some of the moderate Calvinists also modified the doctrine of election by introducing a conditional election and general redemption even as they rendered them useless by insisting that in an "absolute" sense election and redemption pertained only to certain men.[45] The theologians who wanted to stress man's ability to cooperate with God naturally viewed the law as a helping hand that God had extended to enable men

[43] Richard Greaves calls these men "moderate Calvinists." "John Bunyan and Covenant Thought," 152.

[44] Cited by William Orme, *The Life and Times of the Rev. Richard Baxter* (2 vols.; Boston, 1831), II, 38-39, 48.

[45] See Orme, *Baxter*, 64.

to help themselves. The law was portrayed as a means of grace and as a guide and test for the regenerate Christian, who presumably could roughly estimate his place on the route to salvation by his success with the law.[46]

John Owen was convinced that such attempts to modify the received Calvinistic truth, however slightly, were invariably simply the first steps down a slippery path, since one who compromises on the least particle of truth raises tumults and ends moving to the party he tried to accommodate.[47] Owen is representative of many writers who insisted on a sharp distinction between nature and grace and viewed the covenant as a testament or promise or even, with John Saltmarsh, questioned the usefulness of the whole idea of a covenant. Justification, they said, had no conditions attached to it and preceded faith and repentance on the basis of the election decree, the covenant between God the Father and the Son, and Christ's righteousness.[48] The argument between the moderate and the strict Calvinists, with the latter including Owen, Samuel Petto, and John Goodwin, was focused in large part on the significance of the law as a means of grace. Although the strict Calvinists allowed that the law had a necessary place in the life of the Christian, they emphasized the powerful ability of the Holy Spirit to bring one the assurance of new life, and they warned of the inevitable disappointment one would experience if he attempted to measure himself by the law rather than resting on Christ's righteousness. The position is seen in Owen's

---

[46] It should be pointed out that although men such as Baxter carried the modification of predestinarian theology further than puritans had in the past, they like their predecessors—with the exception of a very few Arminians such as John Goodwin—continued to view themselves as Calvinists and accepted the judgment of the Synod of Dort and the Westminster Confession and Catechism.

[47] "Vindiciae Evangelicae" (1655), *Works of John Owen*, ed. William H. Goold (1850-53; rpt., 16 vols.; London, 1965-1968), XII, 49.

[48] *Free-grace: or, the flowings of Christs blood freely to sinners* (London, 1645), 153; Owen, *The branch of the Lord, the beauty of Sion* (Edinburgh, 1650).

statement that when he speaks of justification by faith alone, "Alone respects its influence unto our justification, not its nature and existence. And we absolutely deny that we can be justified by that faith which *can be alone*; that is, without a principle of spiritual life and universal obedience, operative in all the works of it, as duty doth require."[49]

There were also those who went beyond the position of the strict Calvinists to insist that the reborn Christian was totally beyond the law and should cling to the Christ within him and his own assurance of salvation and avoid the temptation to test and prove himself. The men who took this position, including Tobias Crisp, John Eaton, Paul Hobson, John Saltmarsh, and Walter Cradock, have been termed antinomians. In radical opposition to the tendency among certain puritans toward a kind of synergism, these men espoused a divine-human dualism. In their view the distinction between law and gospel was total; regeneration came in a powerful experience in which Christ came to dwell in man and mystically to replace the "old man"; and the reborn Christian was not to be exhorted to perform duties or to measure himself by the outworn law.

Most of the antinomians moved rapidly in the direction of a conception of religion in which all acts of worship and individual witness had to be directly dependent on the guidance of the Holy Spirit. This often represented an extreme development of another aspect of puritan thought that provided fruitful ground for the divisive impulses of the 1640's. Geoffrey Nuttall, among others, has insisted on the centrality of the Holy Spirit in puritan faith and life as a result of the movement's concern for direct communication with God and the violence of its reaction against Roman Catholic ceremonialism and sacramentarianism. The English reformers, according to Nuttall, received from the Continental Reformed movement a philosophical-theological tendency toward separating the physical and the spiritual and

[49] "The Doctrine of Justification by Faith . . ." (1677), *Works*, v, 73.

a violent reaction against a form of Christianity in which physical mediation through priesthood, saints, and sacraments was central. "In Puritanism, what religiously and theologically springs from concentration on the doctrine and experience of the Holy Spirit may be seen more philosophically and theologically as a concern with immediacy, as an insistence on the non-necessity of a Vehiculum or medium."[50] It was this that brought about the movement's focus on the inner experiential aspect of the Spirit's work, its growing concern for the direct guidance of the Spirit in worship and prayer, and its willingness to de-emphasize the sacraments and even to forego them for long periods.[51]

Before 1640 there were extremists around the edges of the spiritual brotherhood, such as John Smyth, Roger Brierly, John Everard, Giles Randall, and the more radical among the Lincolnshire followers of John Cotton, who were teaching listeners to rely on the immediate witness of the Holy Spirit rather than the formal life of the "external" church with its liturgies, ceremonies, and ordinances; especially after 1640 the opportunity to follow one's spiritual whims in worship immediately led to widespread experimentation. As some puritans began to rely on extemporaneous prayer, Spirit-inspired sermons by both clergy and laity, simplified and improvised liturgies, and Spirit-possession rather than confrontation with grace through the sacrament, others, who believed for a variety of reasons in the necessity of unity and decorum, as well as in controls on the Holy Spirit's meanderings, pulled back in alarm.

UNDER the impact of these several developments, with their disintegrating effects, puritan discontent produced a diversity of sects. In 1614 the Englishmen who could be classed as presbyterians were united only by their Calvin-

---

[50] *Puritan Spirit*, 102-103.
[51] Nuttall, *Holy Spirit*, chap. 7 and *passim*. See also Maclear, " 'Heart of New England Rent' " and "The Making of the Lay Tradition," *Journal of Religion*, 33 (1953), 113-136.

ism, a vague opposition to bishops, and possibly a desire for changes in ceremonies and the Book of Common Prayer. They had no very clear-cut ideas about polity.[52] There had been, however, as early as the presbyterian movement led by Thomas Cartwright, something of a hiatus between many of the essentially conservative English reformers and the experiential theologians who moved more firmly in the direction of the priesthood of all believers and who were willing to allow this principle to have constitutional implications for the church.[53]

Under the influence of the Scots and Parliamentary pressure, the sense of responsibility engendered by the duties assigned them at Westminster, and their own dour perceptions of a social and religious scene increasingly plagued by chaos and disunity, the men of a conservative bent inevitably pulled back from the radical implications others saw in puritan thought. Developing the conservative possibilities in covenant thought, they said that conversion was to be viewed as a process fitting certain prescribed rules and requiring the guidance of trained interpreters of Scripture and spiritual psychology. This could be done much better in a church in which old ministers, rather than congregations of laity, made new ministers and in which a hierarchy of judicatory bodies could ensure uniformity by providing rules for the church and working out the patterns by which the rules could be enforced by church and state.[54] It is well known that the term "Presbyterian," as used in the 1640's, identified a political position more than a religious one, but nevertheless the beginning of the Restoration body made up of strict Calvinists and some moderates of the Baxter type,

[52] See Ethyn Kirby, "The English Presbyterians in the Westminster Assembly," *CH*, 33 (1964), 418-421.

[53] See Maclear, "Making of a Lay Tradition," pp. 121-122.

[54] On the crystallization of the Presbyterian party and its division into "Irreconcilables" and moderates, see Wilbur K. Jordan, *The Development of Religious Toleration in England, From the Convention of the Long Parliament to the Restoration, 1640-1660* (Cambridge, Mass., 1938), 267-346.

and differentiated from its nearest Protestant neighbors by virtue of its views on ministerial ordination and control of membership and by presbyterian polity, lies in the 1640's.[55]

The term "Independent" was also as much a political as a religious label in the 1640's, but even when we isolate the religious positions to which it was applied, we find that they constitute "less a sect than a loose confederacy of radicals, the growing edge of Puritan division and fragmentation."[56] Men as different in theology and ecclesiology as the Dissenting Brethren of the Westminster Assembly, on the one hand, and what George Yule has called the "radical" independents of the New Model Army on the other, were united only by their belief that presbyterianism was at least as bad as episcopacy and by their related espousal of religious toleration.[57] The Dissenting Brethren, however, did form the nucleus of what became the Congregational sect. Its ancestors can be traced back to the indigenous separatist movements of the sixteenth century, beginning with the London congregations in the 1560's, or at least to the separatists of 1592 who moved to Holland and gathered there the nucleus of the Plymouth Brethren, as well as to the technically nonseparating congregationalists traceable to Henry Jacob. All believed with the later Congregationalists in the "gathered church" of saints and stressed the autonomy of individual congregations.

The Congregationalists of the Interregnum believed that each congregation formed by a covenant was to elect and call its pastors, teachers, elders, and deacons and was to control church membership, admitting only those who were

[55] The Presbyterians also differed from the Congregationalists on certain political positions relating to the Interregnum. See C. E. Whiting, *Studies in English Puritanism from the Restoration to the Revolution, 1660-1688* (London, 1931), chap. 2; Gerald R. Cragg, *Puritanism in the Period of the Great Persecution 1660-1688* (Cambridge, 1957), chaps. 1 and 2.

[56] Maclear, "Lay Tradition," 123.

[57] *The Independents in the English Civil War* (Cambridge, 1958), 11-19.

"visible saints" according to the congregation's standards. Theologically the Congregationalists were covenantal theologians but strict Calvinists in accordance with the views of their most eminent spokesman, John Owen. Their opposition to the Baxter approach to the covenant, with its emphasis on human ability, is probably as much a product of their apocalyptic millenarianism as of their pastoral concerns. While the "prophetic" Cornelius Burges could ask Englishmen to stir themselves and take hold of God to prove themselves worthy covenantal partners, the Congregationalists, with William Sedgwick, in a more apocalyptic vein, saw the Tabernacle of God descending and counseled men to "continue praying, waiting, labouring, believing, God will at last establish, and make Jerusalem a praise in the earth."[58]

Next to the Congregationalists there came into being in the Interregnum a sizeable group of Baptists. The earliest English baptist group is normally traced to John Smyth's secession from the Amsterdam separatist church in 1608 and his formation of a congregation, in 1609, differing from the Amsterdam body in its belief in adult baptism, its freer and more spiritual worship, and its rejection of the Calvinist position on election, free will, and original sin. Smyth shortly renounced his anabaptism and joined the Waterlander Mennonite Church, but part of his congregation returned to England in 1612 under the leadership of Thomas Helwys and John Murton. Several congregations of these General Baptists sprang up and lived a largely underground existence in London, Lincoln, Sarum, Coventry, and Tiverton until the Interregnum, when they began to spread and to expand rapidly.[59] Ecclesiastically the General Baptists were congre-

---

[58] *Zion's Deliverance and Her Friends Duty* (London, 1642), 53-54, cited by Wilson, *Pulpit in Parliament*, 210. On Congregationalist origins and thought, see Geoffrey Nuttall, *Visible Saints: The Congregational Way 1640-1660* (Oxford, 1957), and *Puritan Spirit*, chap. 7.

[59] See Robert Barclay, *The Inner Life of the Religious Societies of the Commonwealth* (3d edn.; London, 1879), chaps. 2, 5, 6; Louise

gationalists, with each congregation selecting its officers and setting the terms for admission of visible saints, although the sect also had a missionary orientation in the 1640's and 1650's that depended on the labors of travelling elders.

The General Baptists had apparently been influenced by the Dutch Mennonites, and they retained many of the peculiar customs of the Mennonites relating to speech and dress. Even more evident was the Mennonite influence in their theology. In addition to their similar positions on original sin, free will, and predestination, some Baptists were influenced by the Christological position of Melchior Hofmann that Menno Simons had bequeathed to the sect. With the Mennonites, they were also wary of scholastic theological language and of making creedal tests of membership. Aware of the inadequacies of orthodox definitions, they insisted on sticking to Scriptural formulations on controverted and apparently non-Scriptural doctrines such as the Trinity and the substitutionary atonement.[60] Another distinctive characteristic of the group was its spiritualizing tendency. John Smyth's final confession of faith said that "the new creature which is begotten of God needeth not the outward Scriptures, creatures, or ordinances of the Church. . . ."[61] There is evidence that this emphasis on the Spirit was retained in England and that many believed that a third dispensation of the Spirit would shortly follow those of the law and the gospel.[62]

A second group of Baptists, adopting adult baptism but

Fargo Brown, *The Political Activities of the Baptists and Fifth Monarchy Men in England During the Interregnum* (Washington, 1912), 3. The recent effort to separate English Baptists completely from Continental influence is, in my opinion, no more successful than similar efforts on behalf of Quakerism. See, e.g., W. S. Hudson, "Baptists Were Not Anabaptists," *The Chronicle*, 16, 171-179.

[60] See Whiting, *English Puritanism*, 89-93, and William Tallack, *George Fox, the Friends, and the Early Baptists* (London, 1868), 72.

[61] It is reprinted in full in Barclay, *Inner Life*, appendix to chap. 6.

[62] See Rufus Jones, *Studies in Mystical Religion* (London, 1909), chap. 17.

retaining the Calvinism of the main body of English reformers, came into being in the 1630's and also prospered in the
next twenty years. The earliest congregations were the results of separations from the nonseparating congregationalist
church at Southwark over the issues of adult baptism and the
legitimacy of the Anglican Church. They remained in essential agreement with what became the Congregationalist positions in theology and polity.[63]

THE SPIRITUALIST MOVEMENT

The apocalyptic millenarianism of the 1640's not only
formed the background for the breakdown of puritan unity,
accentuating disintegrative forces already present; it also
helped to determine the direction taken by the splintering.
Many of those who left the Church of England and joined
the Presbyterians, Congregationalists, or Baptists did not
stop for long within the fold they entered but moved on in
search of a more suitable religious experience. It is overly
simplistic to understand English puritanism in the Interregnum as a spectrum consisting of conservative to radical
"denominations" possessing distinctive theologies as well as
ecclesiologies. Nevertheless, it is true that many of those
who became dissatisfied with the English church during this
period entered upon a similar religious pilgrimage that took
them from the Anglican Church to the Presbyterians, then
to the Congregationalists, and then either to a Baptist congregation or beyond that to the Seekers, the Family of Love,
the Quakers, the Ranters, or some other body on what was
viewed as the lunatic fringe. It seems likely that the impend-
ing sense of momentous religious developments in an eschatological setting had much to do with the tendency to move
from sect to sect, going from the more stable and traditional
bodies into relatively uncharted spiritual areas. Moreover,
the most evident theological or religious trend in the move-

[63] See Whiting, *English Puritanism*, chap. 3; Brown, *Baptists*, 4-6.

ment from Presbyterians to the Familist and Ranter groups was toward a greater concern for and reliance on the Holy Spirit. Such a pattern of religious change is a natural product of eschatological hopes.

The millenarian influence produced two rather distinctive tendencies that led to similar forms of religious expression and ultimately coalesced. A rapidly increasing number of individuals in the 1640's and 1650's who could have been classed as puritans in 1640 travelled from sect to sect until, profoundly confused and disgusted by the numerous conflicting claims to the true key to Scripture's theological and ecclesiological directives or a monopoly on the power of the Spirit, they came to the conclusion that God's Spirit had withdrawn from the visible churches. They had been left with no key to Scriptural interpretation and no authoritative or even valuable ministry, worship, or ordinances. Those who came to this shattering conclusion believed that God would again establish his church on earth, but in the meantime they could do little but wait and pray. They were known as Seekers, a term that was used loosely of a variety of groups and individuals of unsettled religious life, but it was probably this group waiting for the reinstitution of the visible church to which the term was principally applied.[64] Although not an organized sect, they replaced their sectarian religious life with a variety of substitutes. Some, according to a contemporary, John Jackson, kept up a private prayer life and collected and dispersed alms by means of a meeting once a week in which they also asked to be made instruments to stir up the grace of God once again.[65] Others began to meet together in total silence to pray and wait for

[64] *The Great Plot for Restoring Popery*, a pamphlet written anonymously in 1663, listed six kinds of "Seekers." Cited by Whiting, *English Puritanism*, 271-272. In addition to those of the "waiting" variety, the term was most commonly given to those who gathered for spiritual worship in the belief that the age of "outward" worship had ended. See below.

[65] *A Sober Word to a Serious People* (London, 1651), 3.

the reappearance of the Spirit among men. In some of these groups the Spirit moved individuals to make utterances and even to preach. What united these men and women, in addition to their common decision to forego "visible" churches and their belief that God would re-establish his church in its pristine form, was their millenarian hope that God would act in the near future by sending prophets or apostles and by authenticating their authority through their miraculous powers.

The waiting Seekers were nothing new under the sun. Similar individuals and groups had arisen on the Continent in the sixteenth century in response to the incompleteness and diversity of the magisterial Reformation. Small and obscure groups of Seekers also existed in England probably in the late sixteenth and surely throughout the early seventeenth century. Some were known as the Scattered Flock and looked forward to a prophet who would arise to set up the church once again.[66] These underground movements mushroomed, however, at the time of the Revolution. In 1646 John Saltmarsh wrote of them as the fourth substantial group after the Presbyterians, Independents, and Baptists, and Thomas Edwards feared that their impetus was such in 1646 that in a few years they would swallow up all of England.[67] In addition to their increase in prominence, the waiting Seekers of the 1640's seem also to have differed from their predecessors in their openness to spiritual religion. Their focus on the re-established visible church was apparently combined with a sensitivity to spiritual influences coming apart from "outward" ordinances, since vast numbers of them ceased waiting and accepted the early Quaker preachers as their prophets when the latter claimed that a new era had replaced that of visible churches with set ordinances.

[66] Champlin Burrage, "The Antecedents of Quakerism," *English Historical Review*, 30 (1915), 78-90.

[67] Saltmarsh, *Smoke in the Temple* . . . (London, 1646), 6-13; Edwards, *Gangraena*, II, 13-14.

The second thrust beyond the confines of the more or less orthodox sects in the apocalyptic era was in the direction of a wholly spiritualized religion. Many individuals agreed with the waiting Seekers' assessment of the Anglicans, Presbyterians, Congregationalists, and Baptists as bankrupt sects but did not share their nostalgia for the apostolic church in its primitive form. Theirs was a progressive *Heilsgeschichte* with a line of development from external to internal, from formal and ceremonial to spiritual religion. According to John Saltmarsh, "And the great and excellent design or mind of God in all these things is only to lead out his people, Church, or Disciples from age to age, from faith to faith, from glory to glory, from letter to letter, from ordinance to ordinance, from flesh to flesh, and so to Spirit, and so to more Spirit, and at length into all Spirit...."[68] The nature of the times encouraged frenetic scouring of Daniel and Revelation and convinced many that the events of the Revolution were ushering in that final "Spiritual" age. The first four monarchies were ended, exulted William Dell, and "the time of the restitution of all things makes haste upon us, and we hope is even at the doors."[69] Saltmarsh warned the waiting Seekers that the transition from an outward to an invisible church was at hand and that Christians were to look no more toward "grosse, carnall, visible evidences and materiall beams, as gifts and miracles."[70]

For some the new age was about to begin; for others it had already begun but had clearly not reached its culmination. All these agreed, however, that the church was no longer to be "any outward or visible society," for the Spirit

[68] *Sparkles of Glory*, 54-55.
[69] "The Stumbling Stone, or a Discourse Touching that Offence Which the World and Worldly Church do take against Christ Himself . . ." (1653), *The Works of William Dell* (New York, 1816), 328. See also *The Building, Beauty, Teaching, and Embellishment, of the Truly Christian and Spiritual Church* (London, 1651).
[70] *Smoke in the Temple*, 14.

38

was to carry the saints "above all visible and sensible things, even as high as God himself."[71] Many could enumerate a whole series of dispensations leading from the Creation to these last times, but the common pattern was to reduce them to the three major dispensations of Moses, the historical Christ, and the Spirit or the eternal and inward Christ. God had revealed that the true head of the church, Jesus Christ, was spiritual and invisible when he inaugurated the second dispensation, but he had provided visible worship and ordinances for Christ's body, the church. In the new dispensation the church itself was to become spiritual and invisible like its head.[72] The days of formal or even, some said, *any* human ministry, of concern about polity, of Scripture and sacraments, and of set liturgies were at an end.

The people who adhered to some form of this spiritual religion of the third dispensation were a varied lot and formed a whole host of small groups of worshippers, including many spiritual puritans, spiritual Seekers, Familists, and Ranters. They shared, or, in the case of some of the spiritual puritans, were feeling their way toward certain basic beliefs, despite their many differences, and I shall link them together as "spiritualists." Their main focus was on the need for a radical rebirth or awakening of individuals and, if they believed in communal expression of religion, the church. The more conservative were tolerant of the members of the "visible" churches and saw themselves as simply farther along the religious path that more would follow. Others were less sympathetic and believed that there was a great divide between them and the "outward" believers. They agreed, however, that the conversions striven for and

---

[71] Dell, "Building, Beauty," *Works*, 100.

[72] Dell, "The Way of True Peace . . ." (1649), *Works*, 175. See also Gerrard Winstanley, "The New Law of Righteousness" (1649), *The Works of Gerrard Winstanley*, ed. George Sabine (Ithaca, N.Y., 1941), 161-162; Richard Coppin, *Michael Opposing the Dragon . . .* (London, 1659), 8-9.

achieved by the spiritual brethren and the Presbyterians, Independents, and Baptists had been insufficient. From their own experiences they knew that one could come to live totally in the power of the Holy Spirit through a union with God or Christ within. The Spirit's struggle for dominance could be long or brief, but the experience eventuated in a strong sense of release and total newness. The spiritualists spoke of God or Christ within them replacing their faculties and becoming the subject of their lives. As a result of such a rebirth one was so radically changed that he could achieve great progress in sanctification or even perfection. For many this was to be done without benefit of the law, which the new man had left behind. Although there were many variants in the case of individual groups, the spiritualists were involved in a radical version of the antinomian conceptions already mentioned.

Apart from the radical nature and—for some—mystical conception of the rebirth, the really distinctive marks of the spiritualists' conception of renewal of both the individual and the church were their use of two related but distinguishable kinds of dualism. One was a belief in the radical distinction between the divine and the human—a belief that rivaled the most extreme versions of Augustinian and Calvinistic conceptions of fallen, totally helpless man set over against the all-sovereign Lord of being. In part in reaction to the covenant theologians' emphasis on human cooperation with God and in part because of their apocalyptic determinism, the spiritualists said that man was wholly passive in the regeneration process and in all his religious life and that the human had to die for the divine to be born within. God, they said, can work through secondary agents and instruments, but such agents are completely passive and wholly unnecessary. "Everyone," said John Webster, "thinks he can go to Christ, and bring others to Christ by arguments, persuasions, and the like and for this purpose are all forms of Religion set up. . . ." But all man can do is to stop striving and be "dead to all our own wit and reason,

and all our understanding," and wait on the Lord.[73] God
works in this way so that no man can be said to join or
cooperate with him, and thus the power and glory of God
are manifested, and man's absolute dependence is borne
home.[74]

This total disjunction between divine and human agency
was maintained by the spiritualists both in their language
about the individual's relations with God and in their ideas
of church life. The covenantal doctrine of preparation was
explicitly opposed by those of the spiritualists, such as John
Saltmarsh, who had grown out of the puritan order of
preachers.[75] For the spiritualists regeneration was a process
in which man had to learn not cooperation but the ability
to be still and resign himself to the death of all aspects of his
current life and outlook on the world. A similar belief in
God's free action through the Spirit without human cooperation was applied to the life of the church. Richard Coppin
accused "formal" Christians of making "your Word and
Sacraments to be the means of the spirits working, calling
and electing, that you might tye men to your forms, wayes
and worships, and so shut up the spirit from its working,
and also men from the working of the spirit and power of
God within them. . . ."[76]

The second duality divided the physical and the spiritual.
Man was unable to cooperate with God not simply because
that would detract from God's sovereign glory and lead
man to exalt himself but because man was part of the fallen
physical creation. Although some of the spiritualists produced some rather strange metaphysics, they were normally
willing to attribute all being to the all-powerful Creator

[73] *The Drawings of the Father* (Glasgow, 1884), 18 (rpt. of a sermon delivered about 1653).

[74] Coppin, *Michael*, 95 (incorrectly printed as 55); Webster, *The
Saints Guide: or, Christ the Rule* (1653; 3d edn.; London, 1699), 1-10.

[75] See his refutation of William Prynne in *Some Drops of the
Viall . . .* (London, 1646), 6-17.

[76] *Michael*, 94 (incorrectly printed as 49).

rather than using the concepts of a dualistic ontology of two eternally opposing kinds of being. At the same time, their assumption that the Fall of man had brought about ontological changes in the creation left them with ideas hardly distinguishable from those of a spiritual-corporeal dualism. As a result of the Fall, the creation had been changed into a gross and corruptible kind of being that was antithetical to spiritual being and that could not serve spiritual purposes until it was once again transformed. The adjectives "corruptible," "carnal," "earthly," "visible," "external," "outward," "withering," "changeable," "corporeal," "fleshly," and sometimes "evil" and "devlish" were applied interchangeably to the physical creation. Although the spiritualists spoke as if the "earthly" man had to be killed and replaced by a "spiritual" man—the first Adam by the second —they also implied that within the earthly man there was or could come into existence a spiritual power or soul. Since no earthly or corporeal thing could mediate the spiritual, one could not learn of God, Christ, or spiritual reality through the senses. Man, nevertheless, as a sinful and woefully weak being, is constantly drawn to take pleasure in and to seek his well-being through his senses. This, according to the spiritualists, is his greatest sin. He must turn within, listen to the voice of the Spirit, and wean himself from "earthly" preoccupations.[77]

The implications of this spiritual-earthly dualism were important for the spiritualists' attitudes toward the individual's rebirth, the church, and the Scriptures. The individual could find religious assistance nowhere in all the fallen creation—not in other men, his own knowledge and abilities, or the life of the outward churches. His only source of renewal was the unfallen Spirit or Christ within him who could make him new. Similarly, once reborn, he continued to be de-

[77] Dell, "The Doctrine of Baptisms" (n.d.), *Works*, 397-398; "A Plain and Necessary Confutation of . . . Mr. Sydrach Simpson" (1653), *Works*, 528-529; Winstanley, "New Law of Righteousness," *Works*, 156.

pendent on the Spirit within, so that all true worship and individual witness had to be a product of the direct leading of the Spirit, and the Spirit did not act through sensible means or at least was not normally tied to such means. The man who was reborn was already becoming a spiritual being. While he lingered in the "carnal" creation, the Spirit would condescend to gather human bodies together for worship and utilize human speech for his purposes, but beyond that no visible forms or ordinances were appropriated for the religion of the third dispensation. This meant a clear belittlement of Scripture. Although the spiritualists lived more fully in the Biblical world and were more saturated with its language and imagery than most Christians before or since, their position meant that the witness of the Spirit replaced Scripture as the primary means of God's contact with man.

In addition to this distinctive conception of divine-human contact and rebirth, the spiritualists also shared a tendency to demythologize and dehistoricize the whole Christian drama of redemption. "Christ within" came to replace the historical Christ as the proper focus of the spiritual Christian. The more conservative of the spiritualists continued to believe that the deeds of the incarnate Christ were the watershed of history and had eternally abiding significance as the cause of the possibility of salvation. Others moved on to the position that the soteriological conceptions traditionally associated with Christ were suitable only for the previous dispensation, so that the historical Christ and his "outward" crucifixion could now be forgotten. Whichever their position, all could agree with John Saltmarsh that in the present dispensation it was necessary to know Christ less after the flesh and to realize that the Christ at Jerusalem could not save and that a man had to have Christ the eternal one, who had been the real subject of the assumed body at Jerusalem, come within him to crucify his earthly nature.[78] In addition,

[78] Introductory letter to Lord Viscount Say and Seale and Lieutenant General Cromwell, *Smoke in the Temple*, n. pag.

there was a tendency to view the whole divine drama of redemption portrayed in Scripture as an allegory of the struggle between the first and second Adam within each man. The great story had to be demythologized. The Scriptural references to heaven and hell, Christ's resurrection, his ascension, and the last judgment were—whatever literal value they might have, and spiritualists disagreed on this— primarily symbolic statements referring to every man's transactions with the eternal Christ within.[79]

Another characteristic linking the spiritualists was a natural concomitant of their dehistoricizing of Christianity. Not content to ignore the historical Christ in favor of the eternal Savior, many of the exponents of spiritual Christianity wanted to be more explicit about the universal possibilities of salvation than Christians had been previously. Those who desired to launch their listeners into the third dispensation without denigrating the worth of the dispensation inaugurated by Christ 1600 years before held that, in a manner unknown to men, God had elected men from every nation to be saved in Christ and to form a true invisible church despite their lack of knowledge of the historical Christ.[80] Even among the more conservative, however, there was an assumption that the eternal Christ was able to communicate with all men. John Webster, utilizing what was to become the "Quaker" Scriptural passage, John 1:9, said that the light of the eternal Christ shines in all men, for "he is the true light that enlightens every one that comes into the world."[81] Such a belief, especially when it was predicated on the assumption that it would be unfair of God to give only part of the world the possibility of salvation, had apparent similarities with the developing deistic strains of what has been called the "Liberal" thought of the latter half of the seventeenth century. However, whereas the liberals were clearly Arminians and watered down the essentials of Christianity

[79] Coppin, *Michael*, 34-36.
[80] Dell, "Building, Beauty," *Works*, 97.
[81] *Drawings of the Father*, 13.

until it resembled natural religion, the spiritualists, although their belief in Christ within all men made their positions on the will complex, continued to emphasize "free grace" and divine sovereignty. They contended, in the words of Coppin, that "no man can say, that any man died without Christ preaching to him the forgiveness of sin, but that to all men dwelling in the earth his Gospel should be preached by Christ."[82]

A final common mark of the spiritualists should be mentioned even though it was shared by others with different religious views. Most of them had a similar kind of millennial hope, and many were somewhat unique in their expectations regarding social renewal. Millennial hopes accompany all revolutions, and the imagery they utilize is simply that nearest at hand—whether the New Jerusalem, liberty and equality, or the classless society. They represent "the religious aspect of the revolution: the symbols that serve to release men's energies, that wear the guise of ultimate ends, and that always remove farther into the future when one tries to approach them."[83] As such they are very difficult to pin down.

Despite this difficulty in generalizing about the millennialism of the Revolutionary period, historians have distinguished between Christ-centered, chiliastic, temporal millennialists and spiritual millennialists. The former group thought of Christ as the King who would come to set up his outward rule over men, replacing all human authorities. The spiritual millennialists thought in terms of the more or less imminent success of the Spirit as the ruler of human hearts and the accompanying spread of true religion, but they did not look for the outward return of Christ. The spiritual millennialists were almost invariably suffering saints, who believed that whatever God had in mind for the

[82] *Michael*, 130. On the relationship between the spiritualists and liberal theology see Jerald Brauer, "Puritanism, Mysticism and the Development of Liberalism," *CH*, 19 (1950), 152-170.

[83] Sabine, "Introduction," *The Works of Gerrard Winstanley*, 37.

world, men were passive agents who could do nothing but wait for him to act. Although in religious affairs God used men as passive agents to bring about renewal, one could expect a more cataclysmic intervention in social and political realms. In the meantime they were to suffer, like the saints of Revelation, at the hands of the antispiritual forces. Many of the Christ-centered or chiliastic millennialists were suffering saints also, but others believed that they could be used by Christ to prepare for the kingdom. None of the millennialists took up arms on behalf of Christ during the Interregnum, but the Fifth Monarchists believed that they could at least prepare by urging certain actions on the government and then, after the failure of the Barebones Parliament to act on their program, by denouncing the government and destroying its authority.[84]

The more activistic attitude of some of the millennialists who looked for the outward Christ's return was, in a sense, an apocalyptic version of the prophetic activism of the more conservative puritans. It is interesting that those who were drawn to the Leveller program and then to the Fifth Monarchist movement were primarily Independents and Baptists. The spiritualists, with their divine-human dualism, were spiritual millennialists and therefore quietistic or suffering saints, although those transitional figures between the major Protestant bodies and the spiritualists, such as Saltmarsh and Dell, were drawn into a more activistic attitude in the late 1640's by virtue of their association with the army.[85] But some of the advocates of spiritual religion had their distinctive vision of millennial peace, even if they were not activists. Whereas many Baptists and Independents were concerned, with John Lilburne, about individual liberties,

[84] See Leo F. Solt, "The Fifth Monarchy Men: Politics and the Millennium," *CH*, 30 (1961), 314-324; Alfred Cohen, "Two Roads to the Puritan Millennium: William Erbury and Vavasor Powell," *CH*, 32 (1963), 322-338; and John Wilson, "Comment on 'Two Roads to the Puritan Millennium,'" *CH*, 32 (1963), 339-343.

[85] See Leo F. Solt, *Saints in Arms* (Stanford, 1959), chap. 5.

fundamental law, and reformed legal codes, and others such as Hugh Peters and William Aspinwall favored absolute rule by the saints, spiritual Seekers such as Winstanley and Ranters such as Laurence Clarkson believed that they would shortly witness the return of the communism and anarchy that had prevailed among men before the Fall.[86]

THE SPIRITUALISTS included many individuals who, like Roger Williams, found themselves testing whether the Lord's promise that he would be where two or three were gathered together was also a statement of the minimal conditions for his presence. Most were able to join with at least a few others, so that an extraordinary variety of sects appeared alongside the Presbyterians, Congregationalists, and Baptists. A group of men of an Independent stance, most of whom were prominent as spiritual leaders in Cromwell's Army until about 1647, formed—in terms of their thought, if not their historical position—a transitional group standing between the more orthodox bodies and the spiritualists. Variously known as spiritual puritans, antinomians, and Happy Finders, they included Saltmarsh, Dell, Webster, Coppin, William Erbury, Joshua Sprigge, and Thomas Collier. Often linked with them are Samuel Gorton, Hugh Peters, William Sedgwick, Walter Cradock, Richard Symonds, Henry Denne, Sir Harry Vane, and Morgan Llwyd.[87] We can find in the thought of these men a movement toward the characteristics of spiritualism, but some were still close to the more orthodox sects, and they shared certain peculiarities. They did not form a sect and thus were

[86] Winstanley, "The True Levellers Standard Advanced" (1649), *Works*; Clarkson (or Claxton), "The lost sheep found . . ." (1660), in Norman Cohn, *The Pursuit of the Millennium* (1957; rpt., New York, 1961), 353. Winstanley dropped his anarchism by 1652. See Wilhelm Schenk, *The Concern for Social Justice in the Puritan Revolution* (London, 1948), 104-106.

[87] See Solt, *Saints in Arms*, 9; Nuttall, *Holy Spirit*, 13; George A. Johnson, "From Seeker to Finder: A Study in Seventeenth Century English Spiritualism Before the Quakers," *CH*, 17 (1948), 301.

less exclusive than other spiritualists and stressed their continuity with those Christians at a less advanced point on the spiritual path. Christ's incarnation and crucifixion were still viewed by some as the central point of history and historical Christianity as an essential stage on the path to the third dispensation. They were more closely in contact with puritan theological writers than were the spiritualists, and their struggle against federal theology left them with a strong emphasis on the doctrine of election and on justification by free grace without the perfectionistic extremes of some other spiritualists. Again, although they were moving toward a Spirit-led form of worship and railed against the necessity of an educated ministry, they believed strongly in preaching and retained the forms of a visible church. Also in line with their ties to the Christianity of the second dispensation was the halting nature of their development of the doctrine of the universally available inward Christ.[88]

The terms most commonly applied to the other spiritualists were "Seeker," "Familist," and "Ranter." George Sabine has reminded us that "nothing is harder than to tell what a writer like Thomas Edwards meant by words like Anabaptist, Antinomian, Familist, or Ranter, and while he probably took little enough trouble to find out what the persons that he vilified really believed, the task was not too easy."[89] Although John Jackson thought that the term "Seeker" should be reserved for those of the waiting variety, he testified that it was also applied to groups of spiritualists who believed that they had graduated beyond outward religion and were living in the third dispensation. Seeing Scripture as a "dead letter" and the Christ of Scripture as a figure or type of the inward Christ, they moved toward a more complete realization of spiritual religion than the spiritual puritans, but without giving up meeting for Spirit-led worship

[88] Illustrative treatises on these points are Dell, *Way of True Peace* and *Crucified and Quickened Christian* [1652]; Saltmarsh, *Some Drops of the Viall*, *Smoke in the Temple*, and *Sparkles of Glory*.

[89] "Introduction," *Works of Gerrard Winstanley*, 22.

and possibly even without breaking completely with "outward" congregations. There is evidence of the existence of spiritual Seekers in England as early as 1617, but they lived a subterranean existence until their flowering in the 1640's.[90] They were not members of a self-conscious sect but simply constituted themselves as small bodies of like-minded men in various parts of the country.

Gerrard Winstanley was involved in such groups at least between 1643 and 1649. His thought exemplifies a well-developed version of the spiritualist characteristics I have described. Although the vagueness of contemporary use of the term Seeker and other difficulties prevent positive identification of many individual spiritual Seekers, it may be that they were differentiated from Ranters and Familists largely because they shared Winstanley's insistence that the Spirit never contradicted the moral law and that the true religion coming into its own in this millennium was above all a matter of "walking righteously in the Creation" and achieving reconciliation among men in a communistic egalitarian society.[91] The Digger experiment started by Winstanley and John Everard, in which small groups settled on and started planting common land, was not an attempt at social reform but simply a sign to Englishmen that shortly God would restore the Creation to its first condition of egalitarian communistic anarchy.[92]

The term "Familist" was tossed about as loosely in the Interregnum as "puritan" had been earlier, but there had existed since the sixteenth century bands of English followers of Henry Nicholas' Family of Love. This sect, founded early in the sixteenth century by David Joris, embraced an extraordinary combination of Catholic hierarchical and sacramental patterns and millennial spiritualism. Although the Familists did not view the sacraments as indispensable means

[90] Rufus Jones, *Mystical Religion*, 452-461.

[91] "Truth Lifting up its Head . . ." (1649), *Works*, 137; "New Law," *Works*, 215ff.

[92] See Schenk, *Social Justice*, chap. 6.

of grace, their Catholic appendage to their spiritualism made them unique. The most important distinguishing marks of their spiritual religion, however, were its emphasis on sanctification and its peculiar apocalyptic beliefs. Nicholas believed that he was the last of a line of prophets—including Jesus—sent from God and that he was to inaugurate the final era of love and spiritual religion. The tenets of his sect were those of the spiritualists generally, but its major distinctive feature was its perfectionism. In contrast to the antinomians' emphasis on the continuing sinfulness of man despite his mystical union with the perfect Christ, the Familists said that God had been "manned" in Christ so that man could be "godded" and reach the state Adam had enjoyed before his Fall. This came about not through a gradual ethical struggle but by means of a mystical event once man ceased "running in his will" and emptied himself in preparation for the Spirit. Christopher Vittels introduced the movement into England in the 1560's, and it continued to exist on the fringes of English life until in the 1640's it began to receive its share of Englishmen seeking a spiritual religion.[93] Some of Nicholas' works began to be translated in 1646.

The term "Ranter," like "Seeker," was used in this period to refer not to a self-conscious sect but to a variety of groups and individuals who appeared to one pamphleteer of 1651 like "locusts out of the bottomlesse pit" or "the Caterpillars of Aegypt."[94] Like the other spiritualists, libertines representing the logical extreme of antinomianism had probably existed in England before this time, although the term "Ranter" first appears in 1640-1641. Robert Barclay of Reigate and Norman Cohn trace their ancestors to the Brethren of the Free Spirit of the fourteenth century and the "Spirituels" that Calvin wrote against on several occasions.[95] The

---

[93] Jones, *Mysticism and Democracy in the English Commonwealth* (Cambridge, Mass., 1932), 123-130, and *Mystical Religion*, chap. 18; Whiting, *English Puritanism*, 283-288.

[94] Cohn, *Pursuit of the Millennium*, 322-323.

[95] Barclay, *Inner Life*, 413-416; Cohn, 321.

Ranters of the Interregnum were simply spiritualists who took certain aspects of the spiritualizing tendency to extremes, although on the surface they seem strikingly different from other spiritualists. They believed that the dispensation of the Spirit had arrived and that as a result the religion of outward forms had to give way to the immediate guidance of the Spirit. Their understanding of the operations of the Spirit was expressed in terms of the divine-human and earthly-spiritual dualisms found in the other men of spiritual religion. Like them also, but with greater vengeance, the Ranters allegorized the Scriptural story of redemption. The deeds of the historical Christ, heaven, hell, and the last judgment were all merely symbols pointing to events within each man. This dehistoricizing was accompanied by the universalizing framework as well, and there was also a tendency among Ranters to believe, with Clarkson and Abiezer Coppe, that "if the creation had brought this world into [no] propriety, as Mine and Thine, there had been no such title as theft, cheat, or a lie; for the prevention hereof Everard and Gerrard Winstanley did dig up the Commons, that so all might have to live of themselves, then there had been no need of defrauding, but unity one with another. . . ."[96]

The Ranters were also distinctive in striking ways. Rather than coaxing outward Christians to move on to a more mature stage, they simply decried all meetings for worship as useless and themselves went to the extreme of foregoing all group religious expression except, for some, social and sexual gatherings. Their most distinctive mark was their pantheism, which was simply the ultimate application of the spiritualists' emphasis on the immanence of God. God is in all creatures, and his being is "no where else out of the Creatures. . . ." "My seeking thee is but thy seeking thy selfe. My delighting enjoying thee, is no other but thy de-

---

[96] "The lost sheep found," in Cohn, 353. See Coppe, *A Fiery Flying Roll: A Word from the Lord to all the Great Ones of the Earth* . . . (London, 1649).

lighting in thy selfe. . . ."[97] A logical corollary of pantheism, especially when combined with an extreme form of antinomianism, is a pure libertinism. If all that is is God, God has no reason to give laws. But the Ranters could not deny the existence of imperfection in the world. Bauthumley termed sin "the dark side of God." Clarkson viewed it as a product of the "imagination": an act is sinful only if one thinks it sinful. Like the libertines among the Gnostics of the early Christian era, Clarkson said that no man could be free from what the world called a sin until he had committed it with a pure conscience.[98] Another correlate of pantheism taken seriously is a denial of the existence of a personal God and of personal immortality, and many of the Ranters did not stop short of this.[99]

THE differences among the spiritualists were in some instances significant—so significant that we may hesitate to group them in one category. This reluctance is in part the result, however, of a tendency to think of each sect in terms of a list of somewhat distinctive beliefs. The sects were more fluid than this approach suggests, and contemporaries within the movements as well as those looking on had great diffi-

[97] Jacob Bauthumley, "The Light and Dark Sides of God . . ." (1650), in Cohn, 342. Pantheism and a spirit-flesh dualism may seem to be a strange combination, but pantheists have often employed dualistic concepts in their systems in their attempts to account for the existence of evil. Bauthumley has the same conception of the "earthly" as the other spiritualists.

[98] "The lost sheep found," in Cohn, 351-352.

[99] On the Ranters in general, see Barclay, *Inner Life*, chap. 17; Jones, *Mystical Religion*, 465-480; and Cohn, 321-378. Many other sects grew out of the spiritualizing tendency of the time, including the Muggletonians, followers of Henry Vane, Hetheringtonians, Behmenists, Paracelsians, Weigelians, Schwenckfeldians, and Philadelphians. On these and others, see Whiting, *English Puritanism*, chap. 6. The influence on Interregnum thought of some of the spiritualists of the Radical Reformation is evident in the names of some of these groups. The apparent influence of Schwenckfeld and others on the Quakers will be briefly discussed below.

culty making distinctions. The common milieu of the spiritualists is reflected in the fact that works of the spiritual puritans Saltmarsh, Dell, Collier, Erbury, Webster, and Coppin,
the Seeker Winstanley, and many Ranters, plus translations
of works of Henry Nicholas, Jacob Boehme, and Valentine
Weigel, were all published by Giles Calvert. Calvert's publishing activity, moreover, is especially significant because it
reflects his own involvement in the world of the spiritualists.
Laurence Clarkson was sent to Calvert to learn about the
Ranters and was introduced to the movement when Calvert,
himself a Ranter, was assured that Clarkson possessed the
appropriate religious experience.[100] Morgan Llwyd, the
Welsh spiritualist, stayed with Calvert when in London.[101]
In light of this it is especially interesting that Calvert published many works of one other sect, the Quakers, and even
attended at least one Quaker meeting.[102] The Friends were
a complex group, and as late as 1669 John Owen wrote that
they were just settling down in their opinions after having
"hovered up and down like a swarm of flies, with a confused
noise and humming" for a long season—but their immediate
environment was the spiritualist movement.[103]

[100] Clarkson, "The lost sheep found," in Cohn, 350-351.
[101] Nuttall, *Holy Spirit*, 148.
[102] See "Giles Calvert's Publishing Career," *Journal of the Friends
Historical Society*, 35 (1938), 45 (hereafter cited as JFHS); and
Henry R. Plomer, *A Dictionary of the Booksellers and Printers Who
Were at Work in England, Scotland and Ireland from 1641 to 1667*
(London, 1967), 42-43.
[103] "A Brief Declaration and Vindication of the Doctrine of the
Trinity" (1669), *Works*, II, 399.

THE SPIRITUAL RELIGION OF THE
EARLIEST QUAKERS

QUAKER ORIGINS

GEORGE Fox is no longer considered the Moses of Quakerism who brought the new message down from the mountain,
but he was, with the possible exception of James Nayler, the
most eminent and influential of the early Quaker leaders.
His accounts of the period before 1652 provide what little
information we have about the immediate prehistory of
Quakerism. Fox's parents, although they stayed within the
English church, were of the puritan persuasion, and Fox in
his later years remembered himself as having been more
religious than his peers in his youth. Having left home as a
seeker in 1643, he was by 1644 meeting with groups of presumably waiting Seekers, and in that year "Truth sprang up
first (to us, as to be a people of the Lord)" in Leicestershire.[1]
Fox writes in several places of the progress of the work in
other counties from 1645 through 1648, and one reference
reminds us of John Jackson's description of the waiting
Seekers: "We did meet concerning the poor and to see that
all walked according to the Truth, before we were called
Quakers, about the middle of the nation in Nottinghamshire and Derbyshire and Leicestershire."[2] In his attempts to
narrate his progress in this period, however, Fox made clear

[1] *The Works of George Fox* (8 vols.; Philadelphia, 1831), Epistle
33 (1653), VII, 40.
[2] *Annual Catalogue of George Fox's Papers*, ed. Henry J. Cadbury
(Philadelphia, 1939), 9, 17G. See also W. S. Hudson, "A Suppressed
Chapter in Quaker History," *Journal of Religion*, 24 (1944), 108-118;
Henry J. Cadbury, "An Obscure Chapter of Quaker History," *ibid.*,
201-213.

his great misery, guilt, and bondage, and his sense of being
a lone seeker despite his meetings with other Seekers, Baptists, and others he called "tender people" or "friendly people" or even "Friends."[3] In these years Fox was telling those
he met that "there was an anointing within each man to
teach him, and that the Lord would teach his people himself," but he started "declaring Truth" more regularly and
publicly in 1647, and then in 1648 he received his commission to go abroad in the world to proclaim "the day of the
Lord."[4]

The message Fox was commanded to preach was centered
on his insight that God "did not dwell in temples made with
hands" but was within men through "that inward light,
spirit, and grace, by which all might know their salvation,
and their way to God...." Christ had died for all men rather
than for the elect, and as a result of his death "the manifestation of the Spirit of God was given to every man to profit
withal," so that they needed no man nor any sense knowledge to learn of true religion.[5] Fox preached his message as
"the everlasting gospel, which had been preached before
unto Abraham, and in the apostles' days, which was to go
over all nations, and to be preached to every creature."[6]
This was a renewed offering of the true religion of all ages
that had been lost for 1600 years rather than a new word
for men. At the same time, Fox believed that "the Day of
the Lord" was at hand—that God was pouring forth his
Spirit now and teaching his people from within with greater
power than ever before. The Seekers who had been waiting
for a new dispensation need wait no longer. Indeed, they
were in danger if they did continue waiting, for the last
times were at hand. Fox went about like John the Baptist

[3] *Journal*, 9, 12, 26-27.

[4] *Journal*, 8, 33-34. See Cadbury, "Obscure Chapter," 213 and Braithwaite, *Beginnings*, chap. 2 for a summary of Fox's progress during
this period.

[5] *Journal*, 8, 35, 34.

[6] *Journal of George Fox*, ed. Thomas Ellwood (bicentenary edn.,
2 vols.; London, 1891), I, 338.

preaching repentance in the knowledge that the day of the Lord was coming both as a vindication for the saints and as a judgment on "all deceitful merchandize and ways."[7]

Having been sent on his path of proclamation by revelations and visions from God, Fox demanded of his listeners a complete break with the "religions of the world," the gathering together of bands of spiritual worshippers, and an assault on the ways of the world. Men were to "come off" from "their churches, which men had made and gathered," with their human teachers, so that they might learn from, be empowered by, and come into union with the inner light lying like an unfertilized seed within them. This meant not simply a more vital communication with the immanent God but a turning from "all the world's worships"—"the world's fellowships, and prayings, and singings, which stood in forms without power, that their fellowships might be in the Holy Ghost, and in the Eternal Spirit of God. . . ." All true worship was a product of the direct leading of the Spirit as men sat silent and utterly dependent on the light and life of God. It required neither ministers trained in colleges and universities nor "beggarly rudiments" such as "sprinkling of infants" and other ordinances.[8] Fox also called on his listeners to move beyond "men's inventions and windy doctrines, by which they blowed the people about this way and the other way, from sect to sect. . . ." True religion interjected the products of human heads no more in doctrine than in conversion and worship; it demanded no man-made creedal tests, and judged the leadings of the Spirit only by the teachings of God as seen in the testimony of the Apostles in the New Testament.

The message Fox had been sent to proclaim, moreover, was not limited to religious concerns narrowly conceived. It included a testimony against all forms of pride, looseness, and injustice embedded in the social institutions and mores

[7] *The Short Journal and the Itinerary Journals of George Fox*, ed. Norman Penney (Cambridge, 1925), 21-22.
[8] *Journal*, 35-36.

of England. Because of the false pride engendered by social customs, Fox testified that "he forbade me to put off my hat to any, high or low; and I was required to 'thee' and 'thou' all men and women, without any respect to rich or poor, great or small. And as I travelled up and down I was not to bid people 'good morrow,' or 'good evening,' neither might I bow or scrape with my leg to any one; and this made the sects and professions to rage."[9] Fox was also moved to denounce injustice in the courts of law and the market-place and to take up in an extreme form the puritanical cry against the looseness and frivolity of public houses, wakes, feasts, sports, plays, and shows. Teachers and parents were admonished to set patterns of virtue and sobriety so that those under their care could escape lightness, vanity, and wantonness.[10]

Because of the nature of the documents available for this period of Quakerism and the later view of Fox as the great founder of the movement, historians have sometimes portrayed it as a product of a widespread response to Fox's itinerant preaching of a unique message. In fact, it appears that from 1649 to 1652-53 most of those who joined in fellowship with him had already been meeting together in groups of spiritual worshippers under the leadership of men and women who had arrived independently at Fox's religious position.

Although it is impossible to fill out the details of their preaching, it is evident that the leaders who became associated with Fox in the period 1650-53, including Richard Farnsworth, Thomas and Mary Aldam, John and Thomas Killam and their wives, James Nayler, Thomas Goodaire, William Dewsbury, Richard Hubberthorne, John Audland, Francis Howgill, Edward Burrough, and John Camm, had been through a period of seeking similar to that of Fox. They had become convinced that the Lord alone was the teacher of his children through the inner word directly available to all men and that all the forms of "will-worship"

9 *Ibid.*, 36.   10 *Ibid.*, 37-38.

in the world were at an end and either had been or shortly would be replaced by a new dispensation of the Spirit.[11] Like Fox, these men and women perceived themselves as having been from childhood more serious about religion than their acquaintances and as having gone through a life-long search for satisfying religion, a prolonged experience of doubt and despair, and a progression through "professors'" sects to the Seeker position. Like those who were to follow them into the ranks of the "valiant sixty" or First Publishers of Truth, these earliest leaders were not the "mechanick preachers" so often mentioned in connection with Quakerism but substantial yeomen, wholesale traders, schoolmasters, and even gentlemen. The leaders of early Quakerism were drawn from the same classes that had been attracted to the spiritual brotherhood, and most went through one or more puritan sects in the 1640's before joining with Fox.[12] The early Friends drew their ideas from many sources, some of them foreign, but nothing shows so clearly the extent to which the movement was a natural product of religious developments in England surrounding the splintering of puritanism as does the existence of this prepared group of purified Seekers.

Fox spent his years of seeking and witnessing before 1650 in the Midland counties, but the groups in contact with him at Leicestershire, Warwickshire, Derbyshire, and especially Nottinghamshire, where he first began to attract widespread notice in 1648-49, fell away during his imprisonment under the Blasphemy Act of 1650. From the time of his release in 1651 through 1654, the first great campaign in the Northern rural counties of Yorkshire, Westmoreland, Durham, Cumberland, and North Lancashire produced many settled local meetings and some regional associations, a solid core of more than sixty travelling preachers and missionaries supported by a central fund, and a body of controversial writings to ex-

[11] See Braithwaite, *Beginnings*, chaps. 2 to 4.
[12] On the social and economic standing of early Quaker leaders, see Vann, *Social Development*, 55-60.

plain and defend the latest outbreak of spiritual religion.[13] The work in the North was followed by campains in London and the southeastern and southwestern counties in 1654-55, and by the end of the Interregnum the day of the Lord had been proclaimed successfully throughout England and in Wales, Scotland, Ireland, the West Indies, the American colonies, Holland, Germany, and even beyond. Braithwaite's rough estimate of 30,000 to 40,000 men, women, and children Friends by 1660 has not been revised significantly by later scholars. The local meetings and regional monthly meetings had been supplemented by 1660 by the division of regional meetings into general meetings for religious communion and business gatherings attended primarily by informally elected elders who had supervised worship, discipline, and relief of the poor and suffering in local meetings, and now performed the same functions on a broader scale. The financial needs of the rapidly expanding movement brought about the first nationwide collection in 1657, and by 1660 there had been added to the county monthly meetings and irregular larger groupings multi-county meetings two or three times a year as well as separate national yearly meetings for religious and business purposes.

The members of this nationwide network not only shared a separate worship life but were also distinguished by their refusal of hat-honor, their plain language, including use of the second person singular pronouns "thee" and "thou" to high-born and low-born alike, their refusal to use pagan names for days and months, refusal of oaths, and simple dress. Despite the appearance given by these peculiar customs, many of which they shared with some Independents, Baptists, and spiritualists, and by their developing religious organization, the Friends did not view themselves as a separate sect and called themselves simply "Children of the Light," "Friends in the Truth," or "Friends."[14] The

---

[13] *The Journal of George Fox*, ed. Norman Penney (Cambridge, 1911), I, 141; Braithwaite, *Beginnings*, 132-136.

[14] The term "Quaker" was applied to them by Justice Gervase Ben-

"Friends" could not see themselves as one more addition to the hordes of sects because they were the re-establishment of the true primitive church that would press on with its expanding revival until it reached the ends of the earth. They were living in the last age of history in which God would establish his reign through the efforts of Children of the Light among all men. In the words of Isaac Penington, "The Lord of life is arisen out of his holy habitation to assault the Dragon, to discover and strip the Whore, to recover a possession for his life in the Earth, to make room in the World for his Church, which he is bringing out of the Wilderness."[15]

ALTHOUGH some of the Friends' writers spoke of their movement as the culmination of the Reformation in England and of their tenderness toward the gathered churches, the sense of the newness of their dispensation made them place the weight of their testimony on the denunciation of the apostasy of "all Churches (so called) and Professions, and Gatherings of people," who were "in a Form, and in Forms of Righteousness, without the Power, and in Immitations [sic], without Life and perfect Knowledge, so that all the Practices of Religion we beheld without Power and Life. . . ."[16] This judgment was extended to Ranters and Seekers as well as to Independents, Presbyterians, Anglicans, and Baptists. It is significant, however, that even Burrough, who was harsher on contemporaries than anyone but Fox, admitted that the "free-willers" or General Baptists had correct doctrine, that the Seekers had simplicity and a calm spirit and

nett in 1650 when Fox appeared before him charged with blasphemy. It was a reference to the shaking produced by the state of Spirit-possession. See Braithwaite, *Beginnings*, 57, 131-132.

[15] "The Axe laid to the Root of the Old Corrupt Tree" (1659), *The Works of the Long-Mournful and Sorely Distressed Isaac Penington* (2 vols.; London, 1681), I, 130.

[16] Burrough, "Epistle to the Reader," *Works*, n. pag.

had gone beyond outward forms, and that the Ranters alone had transcended self-righteousness, although they could not stand in God's judgment to the end and had fallen farther than the rest.[17] In general the Quaker writers of the Interregnum period found more reason to value General Baptists and the spiritualists than they did the complete formalists to the right of them, and in their controversies they used more tender language toward the Ranters and some Seekers than toward any others.[18] Thus, although it is extraordinarily difficult to generalize about the earlier religious lives of the 10,000 to 15,000 adults who became Friends by 1660, it is not surprising that many General Baptists, Ranters, and Seekers joined the movement.

A careful study of the various versions of Fox's *Journal*, his letters, and other material relating to the origins of Quakerism makes it clear that a great many of those who became converts early in the movement were Seekers, although the term is used more loosely in these documents than I have been employing it in references to waiting and spiritual Seekers. In view of the prominence of Seekers in the 1640's in Fox's work in the Midland counties, the conversion of the Preston Patrick group in 1652, and other indications of Seeker groups converting in the North and around London, it is probably not much of an exaggeration to say with Rufus Jones that a "very large proportion" of Seekers became Quakers between 1652 and 1655 and formed "the central nucleus of the movement."[19] Fox's message, his assertion that he and other leaders were sent with authority and power equal to that of the Apostles, and the miracles he performed were apparently enough to convince them that a new dispensation had begun. The evidence also indicates that the Baptists, especially the General Baptists, pro-

[17] "A Trumpet of the Lord . . . ," *Works*, 106-109.
[18] Geoffrey Nuttall, *Studies in Christian Enthusiasm* (Wallingford, Pa., 1948), 82-83.
[19] *Mysticism and Democracy*, 100.

vided many of the Quakers' converts. Fox's contacts with
Baptists in the Midland counties, especially the "shattered"
Baptists at Mansfield, were continued in the north, but it
was especially in the south that Friends sought out and convinced large numbers of General Baptists. Although the
numbers of Ranters were not large, they are a third group
about which we can say with some confidence that a large
proportion became Quakers. In 1652 Justice Hotham told
Fox that if God had not raised up the Quakers, the nation
would have been overrun with Ranters. Many of them
found in Quakerism the sense of total surrender to the Spirit
that they had found in Ranterism but without the libertinism and loss of community that had marked the Ranter
movement.[20] There are also reports of Familist and Independent individual and group conversions, but these were
probably not as prominent.[21]

[20] See Cohn, *Pursuit of the Millennium*, 324.

[21] Several historians have studied the socio-economic standing of
those who became Quakers in an attempt to determine their relationship to the classes that were open to the puritan message. Others have
tried to determine where Quaker converts stood in relation to the
puritan movement by carefully analyzing geographical correlations.
Such studies could provide indirect evidence of Quakers' previous
religious predilections, but unfortunately neither approach has yielded
conclusive results. Alan Cole has tried to establish that Quakers were
largely from the "petty bourgeois" classes, especially husbandmen,
artisans, and small traders, whereas Richard Vann, although basing
his conclusions on only two counties, has found many more whole-
sale traders, substantial yeomen, and even lesser gentry. Cole, "The
Social Origins of Early Friends," *JFHS*, 48 (1957), 99-118, and
"Quakerism and the Social Structure in the Interregnum," *Past and
Present*, no. 44 (1969), 71-91; Vann, *Social Development*, chap. 2.
Some objections to Vann's conclusions are found in Judith Jones
Hurwich, "The Social Origins of the Early Quakers," *Past and
Present*, no. 48 (1970), 156-162. And whereas Hugh Barbour locates
Quakerism around the edges of puritanism, finding the movement
especially weak in the strongest puritan counties, Vann disputes his
statistics and sees a stronger correlation. Barbour, *Quakers*, 42, 83-90;
Vann, *Social Development*, 15-16, n. 22.

THE QUAKER CONCEPTION OF REGENERATION

In the light of the spiritualist milieu of early Quakerism, we can best analyze the religious thought of the movement in terms of the categories of spiritualist thought.[22] The major expressions of Christianity in England had become, in the Quaker view, "notional" religions, bogged down in doctrine unfertilized by practice and in tradition or authority unillumined by personal insight and willing acceptance. According to Edward Burrough, the Friends differed from both the "notionalists" and the other spiritualists by virtue of their waiting to be led immediately by the Spirit in all they did and by virtue of the extraordinary power this gave their religion.[23] The distinctive feature of their spiritual religion—which made their emphasis on the Spirit a more powerful remedy for "notionalists" than that of other spiritualists—was their doctrine of the inner light. "Spirit," "Light," and "Christ within" were used interchangeably by Quaker writers to refer to the divine power that dwelt in all men. This divine power was not simply available to men in the form of gracious assistance from God in heaven; a

[22] I shall illustrate primarily from the works of Fox, Edward Burrough, James Nayler, and Isaac Penington—Fox for obvious reasons, Burrough because he was considered their best controversialist in the Interregnum, Nayler because he was the clearest exponent of early Quakerism, and Penington because of his theological training and skill as a writer. See Braithwaite, *Beginnings*, 285-288. Penington is sometimes linked with later writers such as Barclay and Penn, but his Quaker works began in 1658, and, with the possible exception of those on Christology, his writings are closer to the earliest treatises of Friends because of their unsystematic and occasional nature and their topics. Samuel Fisher has been called by Braithwaite the major theological writer of the Interregnum period because of his *Rusticus ad Academicos*, 1660, but his attempt to relate Quaker thought to the traditional categories of Christian theology places him closer to later writers, and I shall utilize his thought more fully to discuss Restoration Quakerism.

[23] "Epistle to the Reader," *Works*, n. pag.

"Measure" of God or the eternal Christ dwelt within each man and could become a powerful presence involving the whole of his being in a new relationship and even the operative power or subject of his faculties. A body of men and women in whom the inner light was active in this way could form a church in which Christ was the only head and actor.

Friends insisted that one manifestation of the Holy Spirit or Christ within that was necessary for everyone who wanted to reach salvation was a powerful personal rebirth involving a complete break with one's old life. Presbyterians, Independents, and Baptists also demanded a conversion experience, but according to Burrough they too often accepted "a bare confession and profession of the Name of Christ in words . . . without any real change from darkness to Light."[24] By way of contrast Friends expected "to be taken out of all created things." When Fox was reborn he came up "through the flaming sword into the paradise of God" and "knew nothing but pureness, and innocency, and righteousness, being renewed up into the image of God by Jesus Christ, so that I say I was come up to the state of Adam which he was in before he fell."[25] It was not uncommon for Children of the Light to express their conviction about the total disjunction between their old and their new lives by taking on new names for their lives as saints.[26] This aspect of Quaker religion gave them a strong resemblance to the Familists and set them clearly apart from spiritual puritans such as Dell and Saltmarsh, who believed that there were limits to the transformation one could undergo in the mortal state. The Quakers combined this radical approach to conversion with a doctrine of perfectionism. The saints on earth "may be perfectly freed from the Body of sin and death, and in Christ may be perfect and without it, and may even have Victory over all Temptations by Faith in

[24] "The True State of Christianity" (1658), *Works*, 422.
[25] *Journal*, 27.
[26] Barbour, *Quakers*, 148.

Christ Jesus."[27] When Fox was first arrested on the charge of blasphemy, he answered the judge's question about his sinfulness with the statement that he had no sin because Christ, who dwelt within him, had taken it away: in Christ there is no sin.[28]

At times the Friends' descriptions of their conversions and their extravagant perfectionistic claims made it appear that they accepted the Familist belief that through a mystical experience one could suddenly be transported beyond the fallen state of man. In fact, Quaker writers were so aware of the staying power of human sin and so wary of mystical experiences that they developed an understanding of conversion and the path toward perfection that set them apart from Familists and was one of their most distinctive marks. It is possible to predate the development of a paradigm for the Quaker conversion, and probably in the earliest days there was a wide variety of experience, but most Quakers stressed the peculiar intensity and length of the experience of God's wrath that they had undergone and compared it with the "easy" faith of other sects. Indeed, the major charge against even the spiritualists, who were granted a more advanced understanding of conversion than the more "notional" bodies, was that they had been unable to stand in the full glare of the wrathful God long enough to have the old self totally withered.[29] The Presbyterians, Independents, and Baptists, according to Quakers, did not even attempt to stand in the glare but had their pastors shield them and protect the old self. Friends believed that the orthodox doctrine of imputed righteousness and the puritan pastors' great ability to provide words of comfort and assurance to

---

[27] "A Declaration to all the World . . ." (1658), *Works*, 441. See also Nayler, "Love to the Lost" (1656), *A Collection of Sundry Books, Epistles and Papers Written by James Nayler* (London, 1716), 292-296.

[28] *Cambridge Journal*, I, 2.

[29] "Trumpet," *Works*, 108.

balance the sense of judgment and to prevent despair were certain to produce hypocrites rather than saints. Samuel Fisher wrote disdainfully of the Presbyterian Thomas Danson that "he is never without his Cordialls and Pills, to purge the head and heart from all sense of judgment, that the evil day may be put far off, and the saints be past feeling of wrath, when they sin. . . ."[30] Moreover, this long period of despair and misery, which could last anywhere from several months to several years, did not often end in a datable terminal experience that placed one safely within the ranks of the saints. Richard Vann has correctly observed that the Quakers "rejected the Baptist or Independent claim to find assurance of salvation in a single influx of grace which could be precisely dated and described for the edification and discernment of other Christians."[31] Most of the men who became Quakers had already known at least one intermission in their prolonged misery and guilt and, thinking themselves cured, had joined one of the puritan groups. It was precisely because such experiences, which had propelled many of them through the ranks of the Protestant bodies, had turned out to be deceptive and had brought only short-lived peace that they were wary of "objective" experiences.

Those who became Friends did eventually achieve a true and lasting peace, but its coming was gradual and intermittent at first, and the spiritual physicians among Friends came to distinguish two stages in the conversion process. At the beginning of the actual conversion, when a person began attending Friends' meetings regularly and was associated with them, he was said to be "convinced." Precisely because empirical experiences could be misleading, as well as because the Quakers were certain that conversion produced a healthy dose of sanctification, neither the one undergoing conversion nor the body of Friends was to pronounce judg-

[30] *Rusticus ad Academicos in Exercitationibus Expostulatoris Apologeticis Quatuor* (1660; rpt., [London], 1677), 173.
[31] Vann, *Social Development*, 32-33.

ment on a man's state at this point. The "convinced" one had to move on toward the state of justification at the same time that he satisfied Friends and himself about his condition by attending meeting, observing Quaker testimonies, and living a saintly life for a period of at least several months. John Banks warned Friends: "Because you are Convinced of the Truth, and because you know the Truth and Way of God, what it is, and so make a Profession thereof; think not that this Knowledge will serve your turn to justifie you in the sight of God, short of Obedience," for the obedient "come to know not only a Convinced Estate, but a Conversion in their Hearts and Souls."[32] By the time the Quakers had developed a high degree of organization, a distinction was observed between the "convinced" and the "converted" that allowed the full privileges of membership to be enjoyed only by the latter.[33]

Contrary to the impression given by some of their statements, most of the early Quakers also believed that perfection is a relative state and can be achieved only after a prolonged struggle. It is only because a man is in union with Christ within him and because Christ has become the active power in his life that he can be called perfect. Perfection is possible not by means of imitation and seeking to become righteous, but by surrendering to the power of God; it is "a free gift from above." It is Christ "who worketh the Will and the Deed of his own good Pleasure, who alone is well-pleased with his own Work. . . ."[34] Conceived as a personality characteristic, perfection was seen as a gradual development attained by receiving and joining to that which is perfect within one. Although one could reach a state in

[32] *An Epistle to Friends Shewing the great Difference Between a Convinced and a Converted Estate* (1692), 3-5, cited by Vann, *Social Development*, 40.

[33] On Quaker conversion, see Vann, 32-46, and Barbour, *Quakers*, chap. 4.

[34] Nayler, "Love to the Lost," *Works*, 292-296.

which he was free from conscious sin, he had to remain wary of temptation.[35]

Some of the spiritualists were concerned primarily with the power of the Spirit in individual lives; they left to the Lord the problems involved in bringing into being a spiritual church. Others were more oriented toward communal rebirth but either were of the conviction that the time was not ripe or lacked the necessary organizational abilities. The Children of the Light placed the rebirth of the true church at the center of their lives, and from the beginning they displayed an extraordinary missionary fervor and the organizational genius to make the fervor effective. Both were directed toward the rebirth and spread of vital religion in which all was dependent on the immediate leading and power of the Spirit. Some Friends, such as Isaac Penington, referred to this as the religion of the third dispensation and assumed that the history of salvation was progressive.[36] Others, with Burrough, believed that Quakerism was a rebirth of the true religion that had disappeared from the face of the earth with the deaths of the Apostles.[37] Whichever view they had, Friends believed that all churches, from the Roman Catholic to the Baptist and Familist, were involved in a form of religious life that lacked power because it was not sufficiently dependent on the Spirit. All the world was steeped in "will-worship," or a religion based on the traditions and precepts of men rather than on the direct guidance of the Spirit.

WHATEVER the peculiarities of their approach to conversion, the Quakers spoke of the radical spiritual rebirth of individuals and the church in terms of the divine-human and spiritual-corporeal dualities found in the other spiritualists. Promi-

[35] On the perfectionism of the early Quakers, see T. Canby Jones, "George Fox's Teaching on Redemption and Salvation" (unpubl. Ph.D. diss., Yale Univ., 1955), 143-146.

[36] "The Ancient Principle of Truth . . ." (1672), *Works*, II, 143.

[37] "A Measure of the Times . . ." (1657), 188-189.

nent in the works of the early Quaker writers was an emphasis on the great depravity of fallen man and his total passivity in regeneration that rivals the similar concerns of the strictest Calvinist orthodoxy. Because of the Fall, according to Nayler, man has sunk into utter death, darkness, and blindness concerning the things of God. "He is covered with thick Darkness, so that the Mind of God he knows not, nor his own woeful State he sees not, the God of this World having blinded the Eye which should shew him his Misery, and the Ear being stopt, which should hear the Voice of the Shepherd . . . so that the Voice of the Spirit he knows not."[38] Penington was equally clear about the total depravity of man, who is in "captivity" and "bondage," and complete darkness and deception so that he cannot trust any voice within him until his old self is obliterated. "He is so poisoned by Sin and Corruption, that he is to be wholly broken down and brought to nothing, even in the very Naturals, that he may be new made and built up in the newness of the Spirit."[39] Both writers, moreover, made it clear that their references to man's "bondage" were not metaphorical but stemmed from the conviction that man has no free will in his fallen state. Indeed, Penington explicitly accused both Protestants and Catholics of emphasizing free will and covenants too much and falling into a religion of "will" and "works," and he countered this theology by asserting a classical quietism in which the will of man is portrayed as always passive. It is always a servant either of God or the Devil; there is no middle ground. If it is a servant of God, it is free to do good but not evil, and vice versa. "The will is not of itself, but stands in another, and is servant to that in whom it stands, and there its freedom is bound and comprehended. . . ."[40] Friends thus understood the process

[38] "Love to the Lost," *Works*, 259.

[39] "Some Questions and Answers for the Direction, Comfort, Help, and Furtherance of God's Spiritual Israel . . ." (n.d.), *Works*, I, 363.

[40] "The Way of Life and Death Made Manifest . . ." (1658), I, 30-31; Nayler, "Love to the Lost," *Works*, 354-356.

of conversion in a dualistic manner. As the quotations from Nayler and Penington indicate, regeneration demands a total annihilation of the old self and a coming into being of a new man directly under the power of Christ within. Writers like Fox, Burrough, Nayler, and Penington seem at times to have shared the spiritualists' aversion to the language of cooperation or synergism and to images of renewal and transformation. In their view the human had to be replaced by the divine. God wills to be served by himself alone and "not with anything in Man, which is come in since the Fall. . . ."[41]

This divine-human dualism, however, is only one side of Quaker thought on the relation between God and man in conversion, for all the Quaker writers shared Fox's rejection of the Calvinist doctrines of election and original sin and, in a more halting and less explicit way, modified Calvin's position on grace and free will. The fact that many spiritualists were reacting against the modification of Calvinism they saw in covenant theology and that the Quakers obviously shared this concern makes it tempting to surmise that men such as Burrough and Nayler, who had arrived at a spiritualist message independently of Fox, were strongly influenced by him on this point and would not have rejected Calvin's position on the will had it not been for Fox's influence. At the same time, although we cannot be certain why the Friends rejected Calvinism and moved toward Arminianism, it may be that this is attributable to the peculiar hold on them of another spiritualist characteristic, namely, universalism.[42]

[41] Nayler, "Love to the Lost," *Works*, 276. Barbour has noted that in the Quaker understanding of rebirth "the power of God displaced the human will and personality, permanently, so that a man saw himself as possessed by the Spirit of God almost as a demoniac is possessed by an evil spirit." *Quakers*, 143.

[42] Throughout this study the term "universalism" will be used to refer to the belief that all men have roughly equal access to true knowledge and the grace of God through a spiritual principle within them and thus have an equal opportunity for salvation. The justification for co-opting a word that has come to refer to the Universalist

The mere existence of a concern for the possibility of salvation beyond the fold of "experienced" Christians was not in itself at odds with Reformed thought, and conservative spiritualists such as Saltmarsh and Dell, like Zwingli in his later works, used the doctrine of election to explain how men could be saved from all nations despite the fact—increasingly evident to Europeans in the sixteenth and seventeenth centuries—that many or even most men have lived and died in total ignorance of the historical Jesus Christ. But the spiritualists believed above all in experiential religion, and this use of the doctrine of election to provide for the salvation of the most benighted heathen in spite of themselves did not for long appear to be an adequate solution. Nor was it a necessary one given the epistemological implications of the spiritual-corporeal dualism they shared. Thus there arose the doctrine of the eternal and inward Christ, who was conceived as an epistemological principle that could provide all men with the knowledge and power to enable them to achieve the immortal destiny for which they had been created, without making them dependent on the vagaries of sense experience and other men. This involved not only the Arminian belief that Christ died for all men but also the Arminian tendency to use images and metaphors of cooperation and degrees of growth to discuss God's interaction with man—a tendency that was at odds with the divine-human dualism.

Whether the Quakers arrived at their position on the will because of these spiritualist concerns and were therefore "Arminians of the head" or whether their missionary impulse was more responsible, making them "Arminians of the heart," they seemed even more concerned to assert the universal availability of salvation through a principle of knowledge and grace than other spiritualists.[43] This led them to an

position that all men *will* be saved—which is clearly not part of Quaker belief—is that no other simple term is available.

[43] The terms are those of Nuttall, *Puritan Spirit*, 76-80.

anti-Calvinist position and to a modification of the divine-human dualism. The very writers most emphatic in places about the absolute sovereignty of God, the total bondage of man, and the lack of real causal agency in human beings denied that God had decided on the salvation of some men and the condemnation of others before the world began. In the same treatises in which the absolute blindness and bondage of man was stressed, it was made clear that God leaves no man without assistance, so that "a measure of it from the Father is made manifest to all mankind upon the face of the Earth, and convinceth of the evil, of Murder and Adultry, and such like; and condemneth the works which are evil, in every particular man, whether Heathen, or Christians (so called) and unto all People."[44] This "measure" will search a man's heart, try his reins, let him see his thoughts, and make manifest to him what is the state and condition of man and who is his maker, who his enemy. If he will only "stand still" and stop transgressing against the light, he will see it and experience the ability to profit by it. For "there is a creating, a quickning Power in the light, which begets a little life, and that can answer the voice of the living Power."[45] On the basis of this belief Burrough could ask both the heathen and those enemies sunk deepest in formal Christianity to turn to the truth by appealing "to that of God in all their Consciences." "I leave it to your Consciences to be the Judge; . . ." "To the Witness of God in you I do appeal. . . ."[46]

The Quaker writers left their readers in no doubt that the power within them was supernatural and not part of their own faculties, but their position nevertheless involved a modification of the Calvinistic understanding of the condi-

[44] Burrough, "A Description of the State and Condition of All Mankind . . ." (1656), *Works*, 119.

[45] Penington, "The Scattered Sheep sought after" (1659), *Works*, I, 57.

[46] "Description," *Works*, 119-120; "Epistle to the Reader," *Works*, n. pag.

tion of fallen man. Moreover, as the Quaker understanding of conversion as a long gradual process and the experiential thrust of their thought almost necessitated, they employed the kind of synergistic language found in the covenant theologians that stands in stark contrast to the divine-human dualism of most spiritualists. Friends spoke of the beginnings of rebirth in terms of the doctrine of the "Seed" within each man. The new man grows from the "Seed of God" within him that "Bruises the seed of the serpent" (Genesis 3). This seed is divine and not part of the old self, which must be destroyed. The light within activates the seed in men who are "tender," and under these circumstances the hard heart of fallen man is "threshed" and "ploughed up" and the seed begins to grow, becoming "an expanding Pearl, a heavenly treasure."[47] The distinction between the seed and the light within enabled Friends to assert that even the contact-point within man for the light was divine and not human, but the very susceptibility of the seed metaphor to the language of growth and gradual change made it impossible to maintain a divine-human dualism. Friends portrayed the conversion process in the same manner as the covenant theologians and even made the concept of the seed part of a doctrine of preparation. They described man as being made desirous of salvation so that he could turn to God and cooperate with him. Grace "secretly moves upon you, and calls to you to return to it, to be led and guided by it. . . ." It reaches the heart, "looseneth the bands of the enemy, and begetteth not only a freedom of mind towards good, but an inclination, desires and breathings after it. Thus the Father draws; and thus the soul (feeling the drawing) answers in some measure: and the soul, thus coming, is welcomed by Christ and accepted of the Father."[48] This emphasis on voluntaristic language in descriptions of the gradual growth of commun-

[47] Penington, "The Flesh and Blood of Christ . . ." (1675), *Works*, II, 188-189. See also Barbour, *Quakers*, 107-110.

[48] Burrough, "Description," *Works*, 119; Penington, "Of the Church in its First and Pure State" (1668), *Works*, II, 78.

73

ion between God and man led to the position that the process of regeneration can proceed only to the extent that a man joins the light and cooperates. He must "stand still" in the light, "own" it in obedience and subjection, "mind" the light in his dark heart and "take heed to follow it," and "abide" in the light. Can one do anything toward his salvation? Penington replied: "Of thy self thou canst not: but in the power of him that worketh both to will and to do thou mayst do a little at first: and as that power grows in thee, thou wilt be able to will more, and to do more, even until nothing become too hard for thee."[49]

Because the light was available to all men as an inward principle not dependent on the senses, the Friends seemed to be denying prevenient grace as well as introducing a synergism into their thought. However much they might emphasize the divinity of the seed and the light, their assertion that a man could take the initiative in his fallen state because of the grace available to him through a principle he was born with was no more acceptable to the orthodox of the seventeenth century than was the preparationists' belief that man could take the initiative because of his baptismal grace. Both were seen as forms of Pelagianism. To avoid this further break in the Calvinist dam, Quakers often said that the light was not constant. Much of the time fallen man was in helpless bondage until the light within him stirred and came to "life," providing the grace to respond and start the cooperative process. God provides at times "a fresh Visitation of the Life, which giveth all men a day of Visitation by the shining of its Light. . . ."[50] Listeners were warned not to ignore their times of visitation lest they be left without remedy forever, having "sinned away" their right to a divine visitation. At other times Quaker writers did little to counteract the impression that they were denying prevenient grace as it was understood by the orthodox.

[49] "Short Catechism," *Works*, I, 56; Nayler, "Love to the Lost," *Works*, 259, 267, 306, 355.
[50] Penington, "Some Questions and Answers," *Works*, I, 363.

74

The attempt to combine the divine-human dualism with this understanding of conversion as a cooperative process dependent on human initiative left Quaker writers with some strange tensions in their thought. Their theological discourse was an attempt to describe the various aspects of their religious lives rather than to set forth a logically consistent system of thought. Most Quaker writers managed to present both the dualistic and the synergistic ideas without concerning themselves with the contradictions involved, but a discerning reader will find some writers, such as Nayler and Penington, leaning more often toward the emphasis on human passivity and fallenness, while others, such as Burrough and Fisher, came down harder and more often on the need for human striving and initiative. By the 1670's the two sides of Quaker thought were even more difficult to hold together, and individual Quaker writers found themselves moving in different directions.

The Quakers and "Inward" Religion

The second spiritualist dualism, that between the physical and the spiritual, was also found in Quaker thought, and here the doctrine of the inner light produced an intensification rather than a modification of the dualism. The Friends believed that the light brought them a special immediate knowledge of God and spiritual realities through a "spiritual eye" that gave them the kind of direct knowledge or vision of God that man's faculties, operating with the phantasms arising from sense experience, could not provide. Quaker writers equated the "visible" and the "carnal" and set it over against the "spiritual." They argued that in the spiritual dispensation God communicated with man directly rather than through the senses, so that it is "the Spiritual Ministration that gives the Knowledge of God, and his Glory and Power, and not the Literal; for he that is born after the Flesh, hath his Way in the Visibles, but he that is born after the Spirit, hath his Food the World knows not of, and therefore becomes his Enemy."[51] God is a Spirit and is to be worshipped spiritually, "not with Mens Hands, nor with Bodily Exercise, farther than by the Eternal Spirit the Body is exercised; nor doth it stand in Meat and Drinks, nor divers Washings, nor Carnal Ordinances. . . ."[52] The Quakers, however, as this quotation indicates, were not extremists about their epistemological dualism. They recognized that God could communicate with men through the senses, and even saw the necessity of approaching them in this way if they were "abroad among the senses" or still at the childhood stage of religious development. The problem was not primarily that men used outward ordinances, since God himself had appointed some of those. It was that men had instituted many more of their own. Fox admitted that God could use "visible" agency, as in the case of human preaching, and that he could provide "immediate" or "invisible" knowledge of himself through such means if the agent was immediately dependent on the Spirit.[53] Similarly, Nayler wrote that "we do not despise any Ordinance of God, which he hath called any of his People to in any Generation. . . ."[54] More common, however, was the warning that the time for dependence on the "outward" and "visible" was past and that reliance on such means of grace rather than the inward testimony of the Spirit tricked men into seeking their well-being in that which could never provide it.

This dualism played an important—if uneven and unpredictable—part in Quaker thought. Moreover, contrary to the beliefs of some recent Quaker scholars, it was present in the movement from the beginning and was not a product of the second generation of Quaker thinkers.[55] It is signifi-

[51] Nayler, "Love to the Lost," *Works*, 324.

[52] *Ibid.*, 272-273.

[53] See "The Great Mistery of the Great Whore Unfolded" (1659), *Works*, III, 275.

[54] "Love to the Lost," *Works*, 323.

[55] See Creasey, "Early Quaker Christology," 195-214; *"Inward" and "Outward": a Study in Early Quaker Language* (London, 1962), *passim*; "The Quaker Interpretation of Religion," *Quaker Religious*

cant that George Keith, who, after leaving the Quakers, viewed them as victims primarily of false philosophical principles, made no distinctions between the First Publishers of Truth and the more philosophical writers Barclay and Penn. Although he said that he was opposing only the more "deistic" members, he made it clear that he regarded these men as victims of errors that had been present in the movement from the beginning and that were at least implied in Fox's thought. The dualistic implications of Quaker doctrines may have been presented more openly by such men as Barclay, Whitehead, and Penn, but the Quakers' doctrinal innovations, which had been more baldly stated by the first generation, were the result of the same philosophy.[56] Keith undoubtedly had Fox in mind when he wrote that "in these extraordinary times" there were many men who claimed no knowledge of philosophy whose thought as a whole was profoundly influenced by unexamined "philosophic" assumptions.[57]

Thought (hereafter cited as *QRT*), Vol. I, No. 2 (1959), 6; Chris Downing, "Quakerism and the Historical Interpretation of Religion," *QRT*, Vol. 3, No. 2 (1961).

[56] For Keith's views on Quakerism after leaving the movement, see *The Deism of William Penn and His Brethren, Destructive to the Christian Religion* (London, 1699); *Gross Error and Hypocrisie Detected, in George Whitehead and Some of His Brethren* (London, 1695); *An Exact Narrative of the Proceedings at Turners-Hall . . .* (London, 1696); *Second Narrative . . .* (London, 1697); *Some of the Many Fallacies of William Penn Detected* (London, 1699); *The Standard of the Quakers Examined, or an Answer to the Apology of Robert Barclay* (London, 1702).

[57] *The Arraignment of Worldly Philosophy* (London, 1694), 9. Admittedly, Fox did not move in the same circles as Penn, Barclay, and Keith before his conversion. When the four men travelled to the Continent together, it was Penn and Barclay who became intimate friends of Princess Elizabeth of the Palatine, the famous pupil of Descartes. And it was Barclay and Keith and, to a lesser extent, Penn who became friends of the members of the philosophical Ragway Circle, which included Anne, Viscountess of Conway, and Henry More. Nevertheless, the affinities between Quakerism and

Fox's dualistic position was strongly influenced by certain Scriptural phrases and was not a simple spiritual-corporeal duality. His epistemological position was based on the belief that there are two radically distinct kinds of being: that which is God and "of" or "from" God, which he described as "Unchanging," "Eternal," and "Incorruptible"; and a lower kind of being that is "of the earth," changing, and corruptible.[58] Because of his use of the second chapter of Genesis, the account of creation that attributes man's being to "earth" and his life-principle to God's breath, Fox seemed to posit two eternally distinct principles in man: his essential self or soul, which is "of God"; and a body that is "of the earth."[59] In fact, however, he did not want to contrast the "visible" and "invisible" so much as "spiritual" and "sinful" beings. "Visible" being did not become radically distinct and even harmful to spiritual being until Adam (who possessed harmoniously both "outward" and "inward" being) sinned and thereby introduced "corruption" into the world. Nevertheless, although Fox said that the seat of sin is the will, his constant equation of "visible" and "corruptible" led to unmistakably dualistic positions. Although "visible" being had been created by God and became antithetical to him only after the will's sin, it was now forever "corruptible" and part of a realm foreign to God, and it was dangerous to try to employ "sensible" means in his service.[60] When the Quakers were accused of denying all external means of

mystical Platonism were not introduced into Quakerism by Barclay, Keith, and Penn; they were present from the beginning. See the many references to Friends in Marjorie Hope Nicolson, ed., *Conway Letters: The Correspondence of Anne, Viscountess Conway, Henry More, and Their Friends, 1642-1684* (New Haven, 1930).

[58] "Mystery," *Works*, III, 327; Epistle 76 (1654), *Works*, VII, 86.

[59] "Mystery," *Works*, III, 134, 181; "Beliefs and Principles of the Priests of Scotland Contrary to the Doctrine of Christ and the Apostles" (n.d.), *Works*, III, 528.

[60] "Concerning Such Who Ignorantly Do Say that Christ Reconcileth the Serpent, Satan, Devil and Enmity . . ." (n.d.), *Works*, VI, 429.

salvation, Fox quoted Paul in justification: "We look not at things which are seen, but at things which are not seen. For the things that are seen are temporal, but the things that are not seen are eternal."[61] The position toward which he continually moved was stated succinctly on occasion: "That which is spiritual cannot feed upon that which is torn or dies of itself, but upon that which is living, and holy and heavenly and spiritual in the new covenant, for that which dieth of itself, or is torn, is not spiritual, but carnal, and the royal clean priests in the new covenant cannot feed thereon."[62]

Historians who want to stress the puritan origins of Quakerism and who argue that by "inward" and "outward" the early Quakers meant only "vital, existential" and "dead, notional" fail to perceive an important strand in the movement.[63] The words did have those connotations, but they almost invariably had dualistic connotations as well. Indeed, for the early Quakers the two were deeply intertwined. Fox usually assumed that if a practice was "outward" in the physical sense, it could not be "inner" or "vital" in the religious sense. The eating of bread and drinking of wine in the Lord's Supper cannot be an "inward" act because it employs physical elements, "for the elements of bread and wine which they [i.e., the Disciples] took in remembrance of Christ's death before he was crucified, risen, and ascended, that was without them, an outward thing...." "Bread and wine are but bread and wine, temporal things, things seen, and may turn to ashes; but the body and blood of Christ, will not do so. And bread is not spiritual, and wine is not spiritual, but are things seen and visible."[64] This con-

---

[61] "Mystery," *Works*, III, 104.

[62] "A Clear Distinction between the Old Covenant or Old Testament and the New Covenant or New Testament" (1680), *Works*, VI, 63-65.

[63] See, e.g., Creasey, *"Inward" and "Outward,"* *passim*, and Downing, "Quakerism."

[64] "A Word of Admonition to Such as Wander From the Anointing . . ." (1684), *Works*, VI, 251; "Mystery," *Works*, III, 272.

trasting of "visible" and "spiritual" runs throughout Fox's works, for it was his tendency to assume that one cannot approach God through reliance upon "any visible thing without you." Whatever is corruptible or perishes with the using can never be a true "means" to knowledge of God.[65]

In light of this tendency, it is not surprising to find Fox and Quakers in general describing the means of grace appropriate to the Christian dispensation as inward or non-physical. As a result of the Fall, man was forced to rely on signs, types, figures, and shadows for his knowledge of spiritual things. He lost his direct knowledge of God and was "driven into the earth" and made dependent on earthly things such as the "earthly" or "changing" priesthood. The significance of the new covenant that came with Christ was that in it man received a more direct knowledge of that which the physical means signified; he received "within" that to which the old signs pointed. Citing Jeremiah 31, Fox argued that in the new covenant the law is written on man's inward parts or in his heart. It was no longer necessary for men to teach other men, since all could know Christ directly through "the ingrafted word" or "the hidden man of the heart."[66] In the new dispensation of the inner light, the Spirit "draws off and weans you from all things, that are created and external, (which fade and pass away) up to God, the fountain of life. . . ."[67] The old physical elements might be useful to some as a lingering means of approach to God, but one should use them as sparingly as possible, "for the devil will lurk in a shadow or a type, or a sign, or figure, and creeps into those things, after the substance is come. . . ."[68]

---

[65] Epistle 16 (1652), *Works*, VII, 24. For the use of "outward" in the physical sense, see also Epistle 379 (Nov. 22, 1682), *Works*, VIII, 218; Epistle 222 (Jan. 12, 1662), *Works*, VII, 234; "A Word from the Lord to All the World" (1654), *Works*, IV, 34-36.

[66] "The Second Covenant" (1652), *Works*, IV, 145-146, 149-150, 155; "The Pearl Found in England" (1658), *Works*, IV, 164.

[67] Epistle 56 (1653), *Works*, VII, 71.

[68] "Mystery," *Works*, III, 326.

This attitude toward means inevitably meant a deposition of Scripture from its place as the primary means to the knowledge of God. Scripture was an "outward" thing and therefore inappropriate to the "inward" dispensation, and the inner light was conceived as able to impart all necessary knowledge to man. The Quakers, to be sure, were steeped in Scripture, so much so that some of their distinctive doctrines, including the spiritual-corporeal dualism, were at least in part the result of their literalistic reliance on individual passages of Scripture. Moreover, the Bible remained for them the final authority as a record of Christ's redemptive activities on earth, a criterion of controversy, and a guide to conduct. At the same time, since the Spirit that had given forth the Scriptures was equally active in every Quaker, the written record was in theory superfluous.[69]

Because of the strength of the spiritual-corporeal dualism in their thought, it is not surprising that Friends shared the spiritualists' tendency to demythologize and dehistoricize the gospel of Jesus Christ. It was difficult in the first years of the movement to be certain how Friends regarded the historical Christ. Quaker writers differed a good deal on this point, but in general they so emphasized the necessity of having the eternal Christ within them that they ignored the Christ of the cross. Burrough's early treatises contained no clear references to the historical Christ. His *Description*

---

[69] *Journal*, 34. Related to this spiritual-corporeal dualism and stemming from it were two aspects of Fox's thought that indicate unmistakably that he had come at least indirectly under the influence of Continental spiritualists, especially Melchior Hofmann and Caspar Schwenckfeld. Fox held that Christ's body was not "human" and fitfully expressed elements of a doctrine of Christ's heavenly flesh. In the wake of this he implied that regeneration meant not simply the rebirth of the soul but a transformation of the body in the direction of incorruptibility through the impartation of a spiritual substance, namely, Christ's heavenly flesh. Fox mixed metaphorical language with seemingly ontological claims when he wrote about these matters, but his concepts provided a basis for Barclay's view of the light as a spiritual substance and will be discussed in later chapters.

of the State and Condition of all Mankind upon the face of the whole Earth described man's fallen state and then the remedy without referring to the incarnation. *A Standard lifted up, and an Ensign held forth to all Nations* was a brief orderly statement of essential Quaker beliefs, and it too failed to mention the historical Christ. The section on "Restauration, Redemption and Salvation" attributed man's rebirth simply, if ambiguously, to Christ the eternal Son of God.[70] When pressed by opponents about his failure to mention the historical Christ, Burrough admitted that the Christ he had been referring to was the same as the one who had died at Jerusalem and risen again, making plain the fact that he took the gospel accounts literally, but his admission avoided the implication that anything done by the historical Christ had changed anyone's chances of salvation.[71]

The emphasis implied in this statement on the continuity between the various states of the eternal Christ's existence was common among early Quakers, for whom Christ was "the same yesterday, today, and tomorrow." In the words of Creasey, "In every age and in relation to every man, Christ, [Quakers] felt, had exercised these same functions: the only difference lay in the mode of their exercise, whether in Christ's pre-incarnate, incarnate, or risen and glorified state."[72] According to Josiah Coale, whether one spoke of the Word that was in the beginning with God, the Rock that followed Israel in the Wilderness, the Word that became flesh, or the quickening Spirit that dwells in man, he was talking simply about Christ the savior. Christ was equally a savior in all his states, the diversity of names not adding to his ability but merely expressing the variety of operations and states of his being. The way of salvation was the same for all men, namely, through Christ, the savior of

[70] *Works*, 117-120, 243-253.

[71] "A Declaration to all the World of our Faith; And what we believe who are called Quakers" (1658), *Works*, 440.

[72] "Early Quaker Christology with Special Reference to the Teaching and Significance of Isaac Penington, 1616-1679" (unpubl. Ph.D. diss., Univ. of Leeds, 1956), 54.

82

all nations equally "without respect of Persons or People."[73] Another way of speaking about Christ that reduced the significance of the incarnation and crucifixion as the watershed of history was to refer to the dispensation of the historical Christ as past, in accordance with Paul's statement that one need know Christ no more after the flesh.[74] Those who wished to allow for the continuing importance of Christ's deeds in the flesh stressed their influence on men rather than their atoning effect on God and referred to them as a powerful example for all mankind.[75]

These examples of the early Quakers' denigration of the atoning significance of the historical Christ were, as later Quaker history indicates, not so much part of an advanced spiritualist assault on historic Christianity as they were indications that many Quakers were convinced of the need to insist on the experience of the inward Christ in opposition to those notionalists who rested on the laurels won for them at Calvary. The Friends were still simply uncertain how to combine the traditional views of Christ's atonement with their new insights. When pressed, Fox could indicate quite unmistakably his conviction that there is no salvation under any name but that of Jesus Christ of Nazareth, who "suffered in the flesh and died, and was crucified . . . who bore the sins and iniquities of all mankind, and was an offering for the sins of the whole world, who through death tasted death for every man; all being in death in Adam."[76] Similar-

[73] "A Vindication of the Light Within" (n.d.), *The Books and Divers Epistles of the Faithful Servant of the Lord Josiah Coale* ([London], 1671), 327-329. See also Burrough, "Description," *Works*, 121-123.

[74] Penington, "The Holy Truth and People Defended" (1672), *Works*, II, 107.

[75] See, e.g., Nayler, "Love to the Lost," *Works*, 350.

[76] Epistle 388 (Apr. 10, 1683), *Works*, VIII, 236. See also "Mystery," *Works*, III, 268. Other early Quakers who emphasized the historical Christ strongly include George Fox the Younger, "A Message of Tender Love" (1660) and "His Faith Touching Four Particulars, Demonstrated" (n.d.), in *A Collection of the Several Books, and*

ly, although he believed that the most important product of the atonement had been the renewal of the inner light in all mankind according to the promise of Jeremiah 31, Fox did not neglect the traditional views of the atonement and in fact mentioned all the historic theories. Christ bore the curse and wrath of God and ransomed man by shedding his blood; destroyed Satan, death, and the power of sin; and reconciled God and man by justifying man before God.[77] Such admissions were less prominent during the early days of the Children of the Light than later, and Fox clearly had more regard for the historical Christ than many other leading early Quakers, but we must be wary of oversimplifying the thought of the early Friends.

Friends also joined the spiritualists in referring to all the developments in the soteriological path of Christ as symbols of the struggle between the first and second Adam in each man, even to the point of implying that Christ's resurrection and heaven and hell were merely events and states within man. Here too, however, when pressed, they affirmed their belief in Christ's existence in heaven with the Father, an "outward" second coming, a resurrection of every individual soul as well as body (but one should not be too curious, they said, about the kind of body he would have) and a future judgment.[78]

THE QUAKERS AND THE KINGDOM

Spiritual millennialism, the final characteristic of the spiritualists, was also found in early Quakerism, but in this aspect

---

Writings, Given Forth by . . . George Fox, the Younger (London, 1662); John Crook, "Truth's Principles" (1662), in *The Design of Christianity, with Other Books, Epistles, and Manuscripts, of . . . John Crook* (London, 1791).

[77] "The Second Covenant" (1657), *Works*, IV, 149-150; "The Pearl Found in England" (1658), *Works*, IV, 164; "Mystery," *Works*, III, 268.

[78] See, e.g., Nayler, "Love to the Lost," *Works*, 360.

of their thought, as in others, they were more complex than most exponents of spiritual religion. Like the spiritual millennialists, the Quakers were not chiliasts and did not focus on the imminent "outward" return of Christ. Their concern was with the revival of true spiritual religion, when "the Church comes again out of the Wilderness, when the Spirit and Power of God builds up again the Gospel-Church in its Primitive Glory, when the Everlasting Gospel is Preached again to all Nations. . . ."[79] This led to a spiritualizing of the eschatological events, so that Friends often spoke of the Last Judgment as past and the kingdom of God as fully present in their lives. The Last Judgment was internalized and identified with the period of misery and guilt preceding conversion, and eternal life and the New Jerusalem were said to be enjoyed already by the believer.[80] Friends, unlike many of the spiritualists, also believed that the kingdom would come and advance in the world, but unlike the chiliasts they had no interest in scouring Scripture to match predicted developments with contemporary events, did not speculate on the form and manner of the kingdom's coming, and tended toward the spiritualists' quietistic attitude toward these future events. Burrough knew that the kingdom "shall be set up and advanced in the earth, but not by the might of man, or arm of flesh, nor the multitude of an host, neither by policy or craft, nor by revenge, but by the arm of the Lord alone, through the suffering and patience of his people, doing his Will in all things . . . , and by patient suffering under the unjustice and oppression of men, and of their unjust government and Laws, till they be overturned and confounded. . . ."[81]

This quietistic attitude, as well as the spiritualist tendency

[79] Penington, "Concerning Times and Seasons . . ." (1679), *Works*, II, 494.

[80] See Barbour, *Quakers*, 186-187. In this respect Quakers resembled many of the spiritual puritans. See Theodor Sippell, *Werdendes Quäkertum* (Stuttgart, 1937), 106-108.

[81] "A Standard Lifted up . . ." (1657), *Works*, 247.

to distinguish between the spiritual and the temporal and to assume that saints could not use the "carnal" ways of the latter, appeared also in the Quaker attitude toward contemporary governments. The Friends were dependent on Scripture here and said that government, which was ordained of God, was to be obeyed "for conscience sake" when it acted in accordance with the precepts of the witness of God in all men. Unjust governments were not to be obeyed by saints in their unjust actions, but neither was a Quaker to rebel or seek defense from them, "so that what we cannot obey for Conscience sake, for Conscience sake we resist not, but suffer under that (the punishment of it) patiently, and herein are we subject to every ordinance of man, for conscience sake. . . ."[82] For the most part the Quakers stressed their recognition of the authority of God and avoided a posture or rhetoric destructive of governmental authority even when they were forced to "obey" by passively accepting the penalty following their unwillingness to abide by unjust laws.

At times, however, the Friends' acquiescence before government seems to have been based not on recognition of the divinely ordained government's authority but on their own spiritualist belief that they were not to use the "carnal" or "outward" methods and weapons necessary to oppose illegitimate governments successfully. For as often as they tried to impress on governmental authorities the tameness of their radicalism, the Quaker writers asserted two positions that were destructive of governmental authority despite Quaker passivity. One was their insistence that saints were free from all human authorities, which were all corrupt, and could submit only to the witness of God within them.[83] The other was their belief that all governments, as well as all churches, were fallen and that there was in the world of human governments none of that righteousness that is the only legitimate basis of governmental authority. According to Nayler,

[82] *Ibid.*; Nayler, "Love to the Lost," *Works*, 299.
[83] Burrough, "Epistle to the Reader," *Works*, n. pag.

Paul's injunction, "Let every Soul be subject to the Higher Power," applied especially to rulers, so that "he that will rule for God, must first see that his own Soul be subject to the Higher Power, and must know one higher than he. . . ."[84] Quakers in general, like Nayler in this instance, coupled their remarks with a warning that just laws of unregenerate men were to be obeyed, but the negative implications for governmental authority of certain central Quaker tenets, which were to become evident in Penn's holy experiment, were not lost on the conservatives.

The appeal of the spiritualistic millennial views of the Quakers in the early 1650's may well have been as great as it was largely because of the widespread disillusionment that men of a prophetic or chiliastic bent experienced after the failure of the Leveller program, and in 1653 when it became evident that Cromwell was not the great instrument of the Lord he had once seemed to be.[85] The conclusion of many, especially after the failure of the Barebones Parliament, was that, since the kingdom could not come through the instrumentality of men, one could work for it only by cultivating the right spiritual attitude. In 1653 Nayler appealed to these disappointed chiliasts: "Oh England! How is thy expectation failed now after all thy travails! The people to whom Oppression and Unrighteousness hath been a Burden, have long waited for Deliverance . . . but none comes, from one sort of men to another. . . ." "The choicest of thy Worthies" are now in power, but they are as weak as other men. Expressing his disappointment with the presumed saints who ruled, he urged his readers to "arise up out of all your earthly Expectations, and stand up to meet the Lord our Righteousness, who is risen to deliver his People. . . . And now look no more to the Arm of the Flesh for Freedom, for

---

[84] "Love to the Lost," *Works*, 297. See also Braithwaite, *Beginnings*, 466-467.

[85] Sippell has called Quakerism a "vergeistigter Chiliasmus" with this in mind. *William Dells Programm einer 'lutherischen' Gemeinschaftsbewegung*, 10, cited by Nuttall, *Holy Spirit*, 111.

therein hath been your Woe; but wait for the Deliverer out of Sion. . . ."[86] Apparently many followed Nayler's advice and joined the Children of the Light.

There was another side to the Friends' millennialist hopes—one that modified their spiritualist outlook. Many spiritual millennialists who saw themselves as suffering saints found most natural the Anabaptist view of salvation-history, according to which the church appears throughout history and especially at the end-times as the beleaguered company of saints who will suffer most cruelly as the demonic powers that control the world enter their final struggle against the heavenly hosts. The Quakers shared the Anabaptist understanding of church history up to a point, since they placed the fall of the church as early as the apostolic age and implied that Christendom had remained in its fallen state until the seventeenth century. But at the same time they accepted the Calvinistic transformationism of many puritans and saw their age as the culmination of the long pattern of English reform beginning in the sixteenth century. Their expectation was that God would transform the state as well as the church and that shortly God would raise up saints to rule noncoercively in a redeemed society.[87] Friends were fairly unconcerned about how this would happen or even about the form of government by which the saints would rule. They were not necessarily in favor of kings or parliaments or protectors, nor of "names, nor men, nor titles of Government," but favored submission to the Spirit of God who could rule through any forms.[88]

So convinced were Friends that the state would be reformed, that God would rule through his saints, and that they, in fact, were his saints, that throughout the 1650's

[86] "A Lamentation (By One of England's Prophets) over the Ruins of this Oppressed Nation," *Works*, 107. See Eduard Bernstein, *Cromwell and Communism: Socialism and Democracy in the Great English Revolution*, trans. H. J. Stenning (London, 1930), 238.

[87] See, e.g., Barbour, *Quakers*, 190-191, 196-197.

[88] Burrough, *Works*, 598-606.

they were unable to dissociate themselves from governmental affairs as one would expect of spiritual millennialists. One manifestation of this situation was their constant barrage of prophetic denunciations of governmental injustices and their demands for specific political and economic reforms. These public statements should be seen as in some respects similar to John the Baptist's eschatological denunciations and calls for repentance, but they also indicate a Quaker consensus about the kinds of political reforms most appropriate for the coming consensual Christian society as well as the Friends' temptation to assume political responsibility. They had difficulty retaining any official responsibilities they held under Cromwell, but in 1656 the Balby Meeting advised Friends called to office under Cromwell to serve faithfully and set an example for others.[89] The most illuminating period for understanding the Quakers' temptation to go beyond their spiritual millennialism, however, is 1659. James Maclear has fully discussed the Quakers' willingness to join the government of first the Rump Parliament and then the Army's Committee of Safety as members of a government of saints. Convinced that England stood on the threshold of "the Day of the Lord," Fox published his *59 Particulars Laid Down for the Regulating of Things*, responded to the invitation to Quakers to join the government by helping provide lists of eligible Friends, and reveled in visions of the English army of saints sweeping toward Rome in victory. It was only after much inner turmoil that Fox became disillusioned with the chiliastic parties and advised Friends to withdraw from such "carnal" developments and to maintain strict neutrality between the contending parties.[90]

[89] Braithwaite, *Beginnings*, 313.

[90] "Quakerism and the End of the Interregnum: A Chapter in the Domestication of Radical Puritanism," *CH*, 19 (1950), 240-270. See below, chaps. 7 and 8, for further discussion of the Quaker attitude toward government and society and its significance for Penn's political activity.

THAT the Friends do not fit neatly into the spiritualist categories can be readily granted. Although all Quakers tried to combine a spiritualist belief in the passivity of man in regeneration with a kind of "Arminian" voluntaristic theology, and although all tried also to combine a tendency to allegorize scripture and de-emphasize the historical Christ with a belief in his continuing centrality, some seemed happier with the General Baptist position on Christ and sin, grace, and the will than with the kind of spiritualism found in men like Webster and Coppin. Beyond that, the General Baptist influence in theology, church organization, and sectarian customs gave the Quakers a clear Anabaptist streak lacking in the major spiritualists. Moreover, the Friends were even further from the spiritualists in their initial outlook on the state and the world. Unlike the withdrawn spiritual millennialists, but in line with the pre-Revolutionary puritan brotherhood, the First Publishers of Truth set out to conquer not only their nation but the world. Their tasks, to be sure, were for the most part limited to preaching, witnessing, and exhorting, and they expected God to break in as the main reformer, but they were confident that their message would take England by storm and sweep on to the ends of the earth and that even the state could be reformed so that social relations would reflect the will of the sovereign Lord of history. This transformationist perspective is part of the puritan mold.

Nevertheless, taking all aspects of their thought into consideration, we must conclude that the Friends fit into the spiritualist category better than any other, and that their doctrine of the inner light was clearly part of the spiritualists' search for a more direct experience of God than the puritans could allow. In the original outburst of the movement from 1652 to 1660 the characteristics of English spiritualism were especially prominent in their writings. It is true that even then the Quakers were among the more sober of the spiritualists, but their silent Spirit-led worship, their disregard for all outward forms, their belittlement of the current significance of the historical Christ and the Scriptures, and their belief that the inner light was in all men made them deadly enemies of the Anglicans, Presbyterians, Congregationalists, and Particular Baptists. Nor was it simply their obvious similarities to Happy Finders, Seekers, Familists, and Ranters that made Henry More refer to them as a product of "that smutt of Familisme." We can trace, in addition, clear evidence of at least the indirect influence of Continental spiritualists such as Sebastian Franck, Valentine Weigel, and Caspar Schwenckfeld.

Rufus Jones, in part because of his own nineteenth-century optimistic idealism, no doubt overemphasized the chasm between puritanism and Quakerism, distorting the immediate background of the movement, as well as stressing unduly the affinities between Quakerism, on the one hand, and certain kinds of spiritualists, mystics, and rationalists of the seventeenth century on the other. The affinities, however, were surely there, for the Quakers' spiritualist attempt to see God face to face was similar in ways to the mystics' and rationalists' confidence that they had unobstructed access to the divine mind. In the words of Basil Willey, "The 'inner light' of the Quakers ranks with the 'reason' of the Cambridge Platonists, the 'clear and distinct ideas' of Descartes, or the 'common notions' of Lord Herbert of Cherbury, as another of the inward certitudes by means of which the century was testing the legacies of antiquity and declaring its spiritual independence."[91] The Quakers were carrying out a spiritualist tendency that had its English origins in the puritan movement, but the doctrine of the inner light that developed out of this tendency, with its emphasis on the immediacy and universality of true knowledge of God, made them a peculiar link between the puritans, on the one hand, and spiritualists and "liberal"

[91] *The Seventeenth-Century Background* (1934; rpt., New York, 1953), 78-79.

thinkers on the other. The Friends were, in a sense, at the crossroads of seventeenth-century English religious thought. Many routes were open to them, and many different ones were taken. One of the most interesting of their intellectual journeys was taken by William Penn.

THREE

WILLIAM PENN THE QUAKER

The Path to Conversion

ENGLISHMEN may have had little difficulty recognizing
George Fox as an ill-bred fanatic thrust forward by the
turmoil of the Revolution, but some of the friends he gathered around him in the quieter times of the Restoration
were more difficult to diagnose. William Penn, in particular, dressed, spoke, and acted with greater decorum. He
normally addressed not another preacher's audiences but
men and women who had gathered expressly to hear him.
A mixed and potentially dangerous crowd they might be,
but Penn at least dressed like a responsible leader, and his
phrases were appropriate for a preacher and much less grat-
ing than those of the weaver's son. If one paused long
enough to catch the drift of the message, however, the
apparent differences quickly paled. Penn's world, like Fox's,
was made up of two kingdoms, the realms of light and
darkness. Men were either children of light or children of
darkness, inhabitants of the kingdom of God or "subjects
of the God of this world."[1] Penn called on his listeners to
come up out of the worldly kingdom with its proud ways
and vain fashions. "Come then out of it more and more, out
of the Nature, out of the Spirit, out of the Fruits, and out
of the Fashions of the World! They are all for the Fire."[2]
The call for regeneration, although annoying to Restoration sensibilities, had been uttered in England by puritans

[1] Letter, "To Dr. Hasbert, Physician at the City of Embden" (Nov.
1672), in *A Collection of the Works of William Penn. To Which is
Prefixed a Journal of His Life, with Many Original Letters and Papers*
(2 vols.; London, 1726), I, 155 (hereafter cited as *Works*).

[2] "Tender Counsel and Advice to All That Are Sensible of the Day
of Visitation . . ." (1677), *Works*, I, 199.

93

for well over a century and could be abided. Penn, however, like the spiritualists, was saying that "to be Born again, another Spirit and Principle must prevail, leaven, season and govern us, than either the Spirit of the World, or our own depraved Spirits; and this can be no other Spirit than that which dwelt in Christ; for unless that dwell in us, we can be none of his, Romans 8:9."[3] In the light of such statements, a listener was not surprised to find that Penn, like the apocalyptic fanatics of the recent dark times, was also dangling before his crowd utopian visions of transformed worlds and coming kingdoms. Even in Restoration England the fanatical sectarian attitude was still very much in evidence, and now it was cropping up in very unlikely places.

Penn began writing and speaking when his own trek from one kingdom to the other was still fresh in his mind. His conversion to Quakerism at the age of twenty-three was the result of a gradual development in religious intensity that began in his childhood. Penn was born in London in 1644 into an Anglican family that was something less than a cradle of piety. After his conversion he reported that he had been called "out of my Fathers House, and from amongst my kindred, and Acquaintance, Yea from the Glorys, Treasures and Pleasures of that Egypt and Sodom, wherein Jesus lay crucified. . . ."[4] Of his mother little of religious significance is known. She was probably of Dutch Reformed descent and was a widow when she married Penn's father. Although Margaret Penn appears to have been a faithful wife and a conscientious mother to her three children, there is little evidence that she influenced Penn's religious beliefs, although this fact did not diminish her affection for him.[5]

[3] "Primitive Christianity Revived" (1696), *Works*, II, 869.

[4] Letter to G. W., A. S., *et al.* (1668), PWP (contemp. copy in HSP).

[5] For a summary of the conflicting evidence concerning the ancestry of Penn's mother, see Hull, *William Penn*, 25-31. Regarding her attitude toward Penn's religion, see John Gay to Penn (July 23, 1670), PWP (A.L.S. in Her Majesty's State Paper Office).

Much more is known of Penn's father, who was England's naval hero in the battles against the Dutch under Cromwell and Charles II. Sir William gained wealth, fame, and social position because of his exploits, and there is much evidence indicating that his primary concern in life was to attain success and enjoyment in this world. He also expected his son to be a leader in the worldly kingdom. At the same time, despite his strong opposition to his son's religious pursuits, the Admiral was, although inconstantly, a deeply religious man. Just before his death he finally gave his blessing to his Quaker son. The younger William was deeply impressed by his father's obvious talents, his strength of character, and his occasional religious zeal.[6]

Looking back as an adult on his early years, Penn referred to himself as "having from my Childhood been both a Seeker after the Lord, and a great Sufferer for that Cause, from Parents, Relations, Companions, and the Magistrates of this World." Like so many puritans and Quakers, he tells of distinctly remembered religious experiences occurring early in his youth. The first he could recall took place during his stay at the Chigwell School when he was eleven. Penn does not describe the event, but his friend John Aubrey, who was not above embellishment, reports that once when alone in his chamber at Chigwell, Penn "was so suddenly surprized with an inward comfort and (as he thought) an externall glory in the roome that he has many times sayd that from thence he had the sense of divinity and immortality. . . ."[7] Thomas Harvey's account of Penn's

[6] Hull, *William Penn*, 17-25. John Oldmixon, writing during the younger William's lifetime, wrote that the elder Penn "was a strong Independent, and so continued till the Restoration; when finding Religion and Liberty at the Mercy of their Enemies, he very quickly made his Peace with King Charles, and his Brother the Duke of York; . . . ." *British Empire in America* (2 vols., 2d edn., rev.; London, 1741), I, 296-297.

[7] Letter, "To the Countess of Falckensteyn and Bruch, at Mulheim" (Sept. 7, 1677), *Works*, I, 80; *Brief Lives*, ed. Andrew Clark, Vol. II (Oxford, 1898), 132.

"convincement" dated his religious development from the occasion on which his father invited the Quaker Thomas Loe to preach to the Penn household at the family's Irish estate. This was an unusual deed for the elder Penn, but Loe's words brought a tearful response from the master of the household and one of the family Negroes, and the affair left a lasting impression on the future Quaker.[8] Penn variously reported that he was twelve or thirteen when his religious development began. The experience gave him a "Living Witness" to the true knowledge of God, which was renewed in him many times between the ages of twelve and fifteen. He became "a sedulous Pursuer after Religion, and of a retired Temper" and was preserved from such youthful "corruptions" as drunkenness, swearing, and cursing.[9]

At the age of sixteen Penn entered Christ Church, Oxford. Before long he found himself associating with other serious young men who objected to the "hellish Darkness and Debauchery" of Restoration Oxford. Together they longed for the return of the puritan spirit that Dr. John Owen had imprinted on Christ Church before 1660. Referring to his years at Oxford Penn later wrote:

From sixteen I have been a great Sufferer for it [i.e., religion]: at the University, by that Inward Work alone, I withstood many: I never addicted my self to School-Learning to understand Religion by, but always, even to their Faces, rejected and disputed against it: I had never any other Religion than what I felt, excepting a Little Profession that came with Education: I had no Relations that inclined to so Solitary and Spiritual a Way: I was as a Child alone; yet by the Heavenly Opening of the Scrip-

[8] "An Account of ye Convincement of William Pen Deliver'd by Himself to Thomas Harvey. . . ," *JFHS*, 32 (1935), 22-26 (hereafter cited as "Convincement").
[9] Letter, "To Mary Pennyman" (Nov. 22, 1673), *Works*, I, 159-160; "The People's Ancient and Just Liberties. . . , Postscript" (1670), *Works*, I, 39; "An Account of My Travels in Holland and Germany" (1677), *Works*, I, 92.

tures to my Understanding, and more immediate Inspirations, was I confirm'd, and abundantly comforted. I was a Secret Mourner by the Waters of Babylon, and underwent heavy Stripes from my Relations (afterwards repented of), and that frequently.[10]

Penn's difficulties with his family developed when his associations at Oxford induced him to consider himself a puritan dissenter. Among dissenters he found "something more Serious and Tender" as they gathered themselves out of the "National Pollution."[11] He began to attend the outside lectures of John Owen, the deposed Dean of Christ Church, and to participate in unauthorized worship services rather than those of the college chapel. Penn was first fined, and then in March 1662 he was suspended. The cause was obviously his religious activity, but the precise nature of his final offense is not known with certainty. John Oldmixon, who professed to have received some of his information from Penn himself for his 1708 edition, reports that Penn was expelled for joining Lord Spencer, future Earl of Sunderland, and some other young gentlemen in a riotous attempt to pull the hated surplices of fellow-students over their heads. The Harvey account, also supposedly based on personal knowledge, says that Penn was sent down for writing "a book ye Priests did not like," although this is unlikely, since there is no evidence of such a book, and Penn would probably not have failed to mention it in his many references to his Oxford sojourn.[12]

[10] Letter, "To Mary Pennyman" (Nov. 22, 1673), *Works*, I, 159-160. Elsewhere Penn reported that his sufferings began at the age of fourteen. "Quakerism a New Nickname for Old Christianity, Being an Answer to a Book Entitled 'Quakerism No Christianity,' Subscribed by J. Faldo" (1673), *Works*, II, 309.

[11] "Quakerism a New Nickname" (1673), *Works*, II, 309.

[12] Oldmixon, *British Empire*, I, 296; "Convincement," 22. R. W. Blencowe, *Diary of the Times of Charles the Second* (London, 1843), also mentions the surplice riot and indicates as well that Penn attended religious meetings of Thomas Loe while at Oxford, a credible report

After leaving Oxford Penn remained in contact with Owen. Samuel Pepys wrote in his diary that Penn was "much perverted in his opinion" by Owen, although the correspondence referred to by Pepys does not appear to have survived. Whatever Owen's influence may have been, it certainly was not in the direction of Quakerism, since Owen had already scolded the Friends in print on several occasions. Nor is it likely that Owen advised him to go to Saumur to study under Moïse Amyraut, since he had expressed in print his firm opposition to Amyraut's attempts to modify Calvinism, although he had also praised his doctrine of the church.[13] Despite the relations with Owen, Penn's ties to the puritan form of dissent were apparently broken. Penn later wrote to John Faldo that in his view the dissenters "drew dry again shortly after the Restoration," and his soul began to wander as he sought the rest he was eventually to find in Quakerism.[14] Although Penn later thought of himself as having become "a Seeker" at about this period, it is difficult to trace with accuracy his development from 1662 until his "convincement" in 1666-67. Nor is it clear precisely what he meant by the term "Seeker." He had obviously entered the early stages of the lengthy period of judgment and searching that normally preceded the Quaker's conversion, but his religious struggles alternated with periods of worldly preferences, and he proceeded on the path laid out for him by his father.

in the light of the inconvenience to which Penn put himself to hear Loe later in Ireland before his "convincement," xxxviii-xxxix.

[13] *The Diary and Correspondence of Samuel Pepys*, ed. Richard Lord Braybrooke, 4 vols.; I (Phila., 1889), 275 (entry for April 28, 1662). Owen's comments on the Quakers are in "Vindiciae Evangelicae . . ." (1655), *Works*, XII, 12, and "Of the Divine Original, Self-Evidencing Light, and Power of the Scriptures" (1659), *Works*, XVI, 292. His remarks about Amyraut are in "Vindiciae Evangelicae," *Works*, XII, 49; "Salus Electorum" (1647), *Works*, X, 222; and "Of Schism" (1657), *Works*, XIII, 138, 195.

[14] "Quakerism a New Nickname" (1673), *Works*, II, 309.

Penn's father was very distraught to find his son expelled from Oxford for religious activities. In an attempt to change the dissenter's ways, he sent him across the Channel, where he studied at the French Protestant academy at Saumur and then toured the Continent. Penn told William Sewel, the Quaker, that he lived with Moïse Amyraut, the principal and major professor at the University, while at Saumur, and a casual acquaintance reported several years after Penn's death that Penn had attributed his major theological training to his stay of almost two years among the French Protestants at Saumur.[15] Several of Penn's biographers have suggested that Amyraut's influence prepared Penn for certain Quaker beliefs and determined the liberal nature of his later religious thought, but Penn never emphasized strongly the influence of Amyraut on his thought. He occasionally listed Amyraut as an authority on a particular doctrine, but such lists usually included several Continental and English thinkers whom he had never met and whose influence was apparently small. Nor do Penn's works prove conclusively by their content or phraseology any obvious influence of Amyraut. It is unlikely, however, that Penn was not strongly affected by the reaction against Protestant scholasticism in which Amyraut was involved. Penn was also later to reflect Amyraut's emphasis on the reasonableness of the Christian faith, although on this Amyraut vacillated in several works. More specific doctrinal similarities between the Frenchman and the mature Penn include their belief that God's revelation to man came in three distinct dispensations; their position on salvation among those who had not heard of Christ (although Amyraut merely dabbled with this as a theoretical possibility); and their conscience-based doctrine of faith, so similar to the approach of John Hales, William Chillingworth, and Jeremy Taylor, all of whom also influenced Penn. At the same time, it is important to remember that Amyraut's differences from Calvin were more in method

[15] *History of the Quakers* (London, 1795), II, 239; story by E. Q., *Gentleman's Magazine*, Aug. 1737.

and presentation than in content. He considered himself a firm Calvinist, denying none of the Calvinist doctrines, and a close analysis of his works supports his claim. Despite his attempts to rescue Calvin from Protestant orthodoxy, his treatises against Arminius and his doctrines of imputed righteousness and the atonement, as well as his failure to develop his hints about salvation beyond the Christian fold, place Amyraut firmly in the Calvinist Protestant camp. He was not the mediator between Owen's form of dissent and Fox's Quakerism that he has sometimes been considered.[16]

Whatever the long-term effect was to be, Penn's study at Saumur did not prevent him from becoming infatuated with the ways of a gentleman when he left Saumur and made the Grand Tour. When he returned to London in 1664 the gossipy Pepys found him possessed of "a great deal if not too much, of the vanity of the French garb, and affected manner of speech and gait."[17] No doubt it was this period to which Penn later referred when he wrote that his search for true religion had "never suffered but one Intermission to pleas my Relations, and that was no farther then Finery, and Gayty."[18] Early in 1665 Penn, still headed for a career in public affairs, began legal studies at Lincoln's Inn. He left briefly a few months later to join his father as the latter commanded a squadron of ships in the second war against the Dutch. He returned to school but soon terminated his studies when the Inn was forced to close because

[16] See especially *A Treatise concerning Religions, in Refutation of the Opinion which accounts all Indifferent* (London, 1660). This is Amyraut's earliest and most rationalistic treatise (first published in 1631). See especially Part III, chaps. 6 and 7. Beyond this treatise, my judgments about Amyraut are drawn from the excellent study of Brian G. Armstrong, *Calvinism and the Amyraut Heresy* (Madison, Milwaukee, 1969). See also the remarks of Herbert G. Wood on Penn and Amyraut in "William Penn's 'Christian Quaker,'" in H. H. Brinton, ed., *The Children of Light* (New York, 1938).

[17] Cited by Catherine Owens Peare, *William Penn: A Biography* (Ann Arbor, 1966), 43.

[18] Letter to W. B. [William Burroughs] [1674], PWP (contemp. copy in HSP).

of the invasion of London by the plague. In January of 1666 Penn was sent by his father to Ireland to tend to affairs of law and governance relating to lands recently acquired by the elder Penn. He spent much of his time there in the company of dukes and earls. On the occasion of a mutiny by the garrison near one of the estates, Penn displayed such skill in the gentlemanly art of warfare and as a leader of men that the Duke of Ormonde, Lord Lieutenant of Ireland, wanted to make him captain of a foot company. Penn was eager to assume these responsibilities, but his father would not let him, so the future spiritual warrior returned to the more mundane duties of managing his father's estates.[19]

IN THE LIGHT of the "worldly" nature of the major events in Penn's life between 1662 and 1666, it is surprising to learn that the next important development was his decision to become a Quaker in late 1666 or more probably in early 1667. Despite the apparent continuity in his external life, it is clear from the scanty evidence available that from the time of his stay at Oxford Penn started on the path that led to this confrontation with "Christ within" and that his internal life from 1660 to 1667 included many periods of doubt and crisis like those of his Oxford sojourn. As he later recalled, in his younger years Christ had often visited his soul, reproved him, and brought godly sorrow upon him, "making me often to weep in Solitary Places, and say within my Soul, O that I knew the Lord as I ought. . . . Yea, often was there a great Concern upon my Spirit about mine Eternal State, mournfully desiring that the Lord would give my Soul Rest in the great Day of Trouble."[20] Penn's appearance and mannerisms in 1664 may have been too smooth for Pepys, but that same year Penn composed a poem that indicates that within his breast there was none

[19] See Peare, *William Penn*, chaps. 3, 4.
[20] Letter, "To the Countess of Falckensteyn and Bruch, at Mulheim" (Sept. 7, 1677), *Works*, I, 80-81.

of the stylish self-possession Pepys observed on the surface. The deadly struggle against sin that all puritans and Quakers underwent had begun.

> Ay Tyrant Lust could I thy Power stay
> And rout thy Force yt wou'd my Soul betray
> To the infernal Find, and thus resigne
> my Peace, my Joy, yea all I can call mine,
> I do soon offer up a Sacrifice
> To him whose Laws thou'st made me to despise:
> I say to his just wrath, for how alas could I
> show him my love and not pluck out mine eye!
> All dallelahs be gone, I you conjure
> No more your witchcrafts can my Soul endure
> And all Polluted ones, and blacker with Sin
> Then Leopards spotts, or th'Ethiopians Skin;
> Your In, makes their Outsides abasht to see
> What's fair without, within should blackest be.
> And let me silently converse with those
> That in a faithfull God their Trust repose:
> That covenante and that commune with him,
> whose motto's holiness, and knows no Sin
> So will my weareid Soul find sollid rest,
> not from without, but in an armed breast,
> That's proof, where Fiery darts nere can prevail
> while Heavens power is ye Souls Coate of male,
> And feed midst Xts Dr [Christ's Dear] sheep on
>   mountains high,
> above the world and all its vanity,
> There will she leap, there will she Dance, and Sing
> sweet Halleluyahs unto Christ her King;
> where Pastures neer grow barr'n nor Fountains dry
> But overflow with joy eternally.[21]

In 1677 Penn looked back on his development and said that the series of events including his expulsion from Ox-

[21] PWP (contemp. copy in HSP).

ford, his father's treatment of him as a result of that, and "the Lord's Dealings with me in France, and in the Time of the Great Plague in London" gave him a deep sense "of the Vanity of this World; of the Irreligiousness of the Religions of it." He reached the point at which he called on God in "brokenness of Spirit" and made "mournful and bitter Cries to Him, that He would show me His own Way of Life and Salvation. . . ." He resolved to follow God regardless of the sufferings and reproaches this course might bring upon him.[22] It is most likely that this took place in late 1664, when the poem was written, or 1665, when Penn was in London watching as the plague decimated the population, bringing hideous suffering and mass hysteria. For there is undoubtedly a reference to his Irish adventures of 1666 in his report that after this period of despair and renewal "the Glory of the World overtook me, and I was even ready to give my self unto it, seeing as yet no such Thing as the Primitive Spirit and Church on the Earth."[23]

When Penn abruptly turned from "the glory of the world" in late 1666 or early 1667, he was plunged into the final spiritual experience, lasting more than a year, in which he crossed from "the world" to the spiritual realm of the saints. While in Cork for business, he stopped at a Quaker merchant's and learned that Thomas Loe, the preacher who had greatly impressed him earlier, would be preaching in the city the next day. Penn stayed in the city to hear Loe preach about "a faith that overcometh the world." Overcome by Loe's words, he rose and gave a silent tearful testimony. He met with Loe afterward and began to attend Quaker meetings regularly, having "a certain Sound and Testimony of His Eternal Word" through the "Principle of Life and Righteousness" that he had known less directly and forcefully in his earlier religious experiences.[24]

[22] "Travels in Germany and Holland" (1677), *Works*, I, 92.
[23] *Ibid.*
[24] "Convincement," 22-23; "Travels in Germany and Holland" (1677), *Works*, I, 92; "Quakerism a New Nickname" (1673), *Works*,

Because Penn left only brief and scattered references to his early religious experiences, and because we know virtually nothing about a long period following the experience in Cork beyond the fact that he worshipped regularly with Quakers, it has often been assumed that he somehow escaped the harrowing bouts with despair that most puritans and Quakers underwent. Loe simply "led him gently to the final stage and made him a Quaker."[25] The evidence suggests, however, that the experiences in Cork marked the beginning of the final crisis that most Quakers suffered. The meeting in Cork led to what Friends called the "convincement," which, as I have indicated earlier, was only the first step toward full conversion and was likely to be followed by harrowing inner turmoil as well as the outer testing produced by the assumption of the Quaker testimonies against the world. The most revealing description of what was happening is found in a letter to the Countess of Falckensteyn written in 1677.

And in this Seeking-state I was directed to the Testimony of Jesus in mine own Conscience, as the true shining Light, giving me to discern the Thoughts and Intents of

---

II, 309. Scholars have never taken very seriously the account of Penn's conversion contained in the scurrilous pamphlet *Ulmorum Acherons, or the History of William Penn's Conversion from a Gentleman to a Quaker* (1682). In the pamphlet it was implied that Penn had turned Quaker in a fit of melancholy after being jilted by "his Mistress, a delicate young Lady, that then lived in Dublin etc. or as others say, because he refused to fight a Duel." The connection between Penn's romantic life and his conversion is hardly provable, but it is interesting that Penn's father wrote him in April 1667 trying to snap him out of his lover's doldrums. Requesting his speedy return to England "not withstanding any expectation ye might have fro flattering women," the elder Penn continued, "Mrs Norton formerly Sr John Lowsons daughter, was I thinke maried yesterday to Sr John Chictchley I am sure if it be not past tis concluded upon by all persons concerned and wil be spedily pformd but I thinke it was don as I sayd yesterdy; pray consider these things prudently with the understanding of a man and let me spedely heire from yo if yr ters Pattens be past. . . ." (April 9, 1667), PWP (A.L.S. in HSP).

[25] C. E. Vulliamy, *William Penn* (New York, 1934), 52.

mine own Heart. And no sooner was I turned unto it, but I found it to be that which from my Childhood had visited me, though I distinctly knew it not: And when I received it in the Love of it, it shewed me all that ever I had done, and reproved all the unfruitful Works of Darkness; judging me as a Man in the Flesh, and laying Judgment to the Line, and Righteousness to the Plummet in me. And as by the Brightness of his Coming into my Soul, he discovered the Man of Sin there, upon his Throne, so by the Breath of his Mouth, which is the two-edged Sword of his Spirit, He destroyeth his Power and Kingdom. And so having made me a Witness of the Death of the Cross, he hath also made me a Witness of his Resurrection.[26]

Although Penn probably experienced the mercy as well as the judgment of God during the ensuing months, the full sense of "Resurrection" no doubt followed a period during which judgment prevailed. Penn wrote later of "the gloomy and dark days of my early and deep Exercises" when he had had the "sweet fellowship" of Josiah Coale, with whom he spent much time in 1667 and early 1668.[27] It was primarily in this period that he gained the right to speak "as one knowing the Terrors of the Lord" and to state categorically that if one had never had his heart broken and been weary and heavy laden with the great burden of sin and cried out in agony of spirit, he was still a stranger to the Lord.[28]

Although Penn was closely associated with the Quakers in 1667, he only gradually adopted Quaker mannerisms

[26] Letter, "To the Countess of Falckensteyn and Bruch, at Mulheim" (Sept. 7, 1677), Works, I, 81.

[27] "A Short Testimony of the Life, Death and Ministry of That Faithful Servant of the Lord, Josiah Coale" (1671), ACMC, VI, 78. This essay was published as the Preface to The Books and Divers Epistles of the Faithful Servant of the Lord Josiah Coale.

[28] "A Summons or Call to Christendom" (1677), Works, I, 190; "No Cross, No Crown: A Discourse Shewing the Nature and Discipline of the Holy Cross of Christ" (1682), Works, I, 273 (first published in shorter version in 1669).

during this period of inner trial. He would be welcomed as a fellow saint only after his outward witness proved that his conversion was complete and valid. The earliest development we know about after Penn's convincement is his first arrest late in 1667. At this time Penn was still dressed and armed as a gentleman, and his instincts differed from those of Friends who witnessed to their faith by suffering passively. In fact it was Penn's attempt to eject forcibly a soldier who had come to inspect a meeting for worship that led to the arrest of everyone present. Nevertheless, when the mayor of Cork decided to release Penn, who did not appear to him to be a Quaker, Penn insisted that he was one and that he should be treated as the others were. He was granted his wish, and as he entered prison he decided to embrace the Quaker principle of pacifism. From that point on Penn's tongue became his sword.

Penn was clearly beyond most of his inner turmoil when he returned to London in December 1667 to inform his family of his new state. But he knew that the terrors and trials of the Lord in the period of judgment involved "outward Tribulations" as well as inner struggles.[29] His final severe testing came because of his family's response to his Quakerism. His father at first merely tried to dissuade him from continuing in his course, but his response became more severe when Penn for the first time became a public Friend. After a period of residence at home, he set out to visit meetings and to evangelize for the cause. He was arrested at a meeting for worship, and when his father was informed of the "turmoil" his son was creating in his new role, he expelled him from home and disinherited him.[30] Although Penn was soon reconciled with his father, he would later refer to this incident as the culmination of his process of separation from the world—the incident that caused him to suffer most acutely for his faith.

[29] Letter, "To Dr. Hasbert" (Nov. 1672), *Works*, I, 155.
[30] Peare, *William Penn*, 64-65.

He now considered himself a Friend. He had lost his natural family and home and was now "to surrender himself utterly to the movement, to be welcomed by the open and loving arms of his new companions . . . 'transported with fiery zeal' at so early an opportunity to be a martyr."[31] But the Quaker conception of the journey to sainthood envisioned a total weaning process culminating in an elevated state that Fox called "the Paradise of God," a condition of "pureness, innocency and righteousness." Penn was well on his way to such a state. His first two publications, *Truth Exalted . . .* and *The Guide Mistaken and Temporizing Rebuked*, appeared shortly after his expulsion from home in 1668. They were spirited defenses, by a thoroughly convinced writer, of Quakerism as the only true religion in England. But Penn had still to undergo the trial that imprinted indelibly on his life and character the seal of sainthood. This came when he published in November 1668 a tract called *The Sandy Foundation Shaken*, in which he reviewed a debate that he and other Quakers had had with the Presbyterian Thomas Vincent and went on to refute orthodox Protestant interpretations of the Trinity, Christ's atonement, and the doctrine of justification. The treatise produced an immediate uproar, largely because Penn's discussion of the Trinity gave the impression that his conception of the unity of God deprived Christ of true divinity. When the printer was arrested for printing the book without a license, Penn offered himself as the rightful bearer of any punishment, and within a month of publication he was in the Tower of London, charged with blasphemy.

Penn was separated from the world in a tiny room in the Tower for almost nine months, and his writings during this period indicate that his journey to spiritual separation was now completed. His letters and two published works stemming from the imprisonment, the first edition of *No Cross, No Crown . . .* and *A Relation and Description of the*

[31] *Ibid.,* 65.

Nature and Fruits of the Two Kingdoms of Darkness and Light, reveal an elevated state of mind and a sense of absolute certainty of participation in the eternal kingdom. Penn wrote the *Two Kingdoms* tract for his father, and in it he said that the Spirit had made him "daily desirous of dying to all the Sin, Pomp, and vain Fashions of this World that I might be in a Continual beholding of the Lord's Glory . . . until there be a perfect changing into his Image and Likeness from Glory to Glory; Even so come Lord Jesus."[32] To fellow Friends he wrote that he had been replenished by the love of God. "And my cup at this time overflows in true Love to the Holy Brethren, and praises overall to him, that hath thus visited me; For he has turned my Wilderness into a standing Water, and my dry ground into Water Springs, and there makes my hungry Soul to dwell, that it may prepare for a place of Habitation." Referring to the "fresh sense, I have at this time of ye presence of the Almighty, and the measure of his life that is wth me," Penn wrote, "Now have I known him indeed (whatever others say of him) to be Jesus Christ the Son of ye Living God, another then which there is not by whom Light and Salvation can be obtained."[33] Although it is unclear from the context whether he was contrasting his "worldly" days with his state since his convincement of 1666-67 or his elevated condition in prison, it is evident that he now experienced the peculiar marks of Quaker sainthood: a state of religious ecstasy combined with a calm acceptance of suffering.

As a result of this experience, Penn emerged from the tunnel of judgment a fully tempered saint and a preeminent leader among the spiritual warriors of the Lord. The "men in high places" that Penn was soon seeking to convert did not let him suffer in isolation during his imprisonment.

[32] PWP (contemp. copy in HSP). The tract was probably published *ca.* 1669.
[33] Letter to G. W., I. P. *et al.* (1668), ACMC, II, 52-54 (contemp. copy in Friends Library, London, hereafter cited as FLL).

Recognizing that one of their number was in danger of ruining his career and damaging his family, friends of the Penn family sent several ministers, including Edward Stillingfleet, to talk to him, convince him of his errors, and get him to recant. This mission was at least sufficiently successful to induce Penn to write *Innocency with Her Open Face*, in which he explained more clearly his position on the disputed points, and in his remarks on justification and atonement reflected the strong influence of Stillingfleet. Penn's affinity for certain doctrines of the latitudinarians was not incompatible with his Quakerism, however, and it is evident that the Anglicans had no success whatsoever in their attempts to interrupt Penn's spiritual journey. As he wrote shortly after emerging from prison, "I own myself one of ye heavenly Camp and Host of God who has fill'd my Quiuir with Arrows and a strong Bow hath he put into my hands, and my arm is fresh, and my heart is bold to arch agt spiritual wickedness, and yt in ye High Places first; And whether I live or dye, I leave it to ye Lord, but it's the alone thing I desire, yt if I dye, it may be for him, and if I live, it may be to him." In this mood he joined the Quaker crusade and proclaimed his controversy with the nation without fear of mortal men, "having beheld the glorious Majesty of him that is invisible."[34]

THE OUTLOOK OF THE SAINT: SEPARATION AND TRANSFORMATION

Penn's conversion provided him with a wholly new orientation in his outlook on himself and the world. An acquaint-

[34] Penn's comments on an eyewitness account of his hearing and sentencing before Sir John Robinson in 1670, called "Injustice Detected or a Brief Relation of ye Illegall Committment of William Penn by Him Called Sr. John Robinson, Lt of ye Tower, from an Eye and Ear Witness," PWP (contemp. copy in HSP); "God's Controversy Proclaimed to the Nation" (1670), PWP (contemp. copy in HSP). I have found no evidence that the latter essay was ever published.

ance with his saintly point of view, especially from 1669 to 1685, is essential for understanding his active religious and political life as a Quaker. "In this State of the New Man all is new: Behold new Heavens, and a new Earth! Old Things come to be done away; the old Man with his Deeds put off." The new man received new thoughts, new desires, new affections, new friendship, new society, new kindred, and new hope.[35] The best way to summarize the difference between the unregenerate and the regenerate was to say that the former's egocentrism has been replaced in the reborn by a theocentric outlook. In the Calvinistic tradition mediated by the puritans, Penn saw the new man as a steward living for the greater glory of God. "Our Time is not our own, nor are we our own: God hath bought us with a Price, not to serve our selves, but to glorifie him, both in Body, Soul and Spirit. . . ."[36] On occasion Penn said that it was man's ability to worship God, rather than the general use of his rational faculty, that was his defining characteristic and his peculiar duty. Such worship, defined so as to include "a Life corresponding with that Being which made him," as well as specific acts of praise and thanksgiving, was the supreme act of a man's life.[37]

According to Penn, a life redounding to the greater glory of God was above all a life of rigorous self-discipline looking toward ever greater sanctification. A saint must set a watch or sentinel in his heart, and every thought and desire must pass before it and be judged.[38] And if he is to retain the guidance of the light and to be able to act in accord with it, a Christian must lead a life of self-denial. He should be willing to deny himself both what is lawful, such as

[35] Letter, "To the Countess of Falckensteyn and Bruch, at Mulheim" (Sept. 13, 1677), *Works*, I, 81.

[36] Letter, "To the Friends of God in Bristol" (Feb. 24, 1682), *Works*, I, 230.

[37] "Christian Quaker" (1673), *Works*, I, 585; "No Cross" (1682), *Works*, I, 304.

[38] "Christian Quaker" (1673), *Works*, I, 588; "Primitive Christianity" (1696), *Works*, II, 856.

family joys, contentment, and ease, and what is unlawful. God will not normally require that he give up lawful pleasures, but he must be willing to forego them in order to keep his weapons ready for future spiritual combat.[39] Moreover, self-discipline demands that a Christian avoid the dangers of this world by developing a sober and grave manner. He should beware of lightness and jesting and be "Grave, Weighty, and Temperate."[40] With this ideal before him, Penn denounced in prophetic puritanical tones the luxuriousness and frivolity of Restoration England. "Plays, Parks, Balls, Treats, Romances, Musicks, Love-Sonnets, and the like, will be a very invalid Plea for any other Purpose than their Condemnation, who are taken, and delighted with them. . . . O my Friends! these were never invented, but by that Mind which had first lost the Joy and ravishing Delights of God's holy Presence."[41]

The use of these vanities Penn regarded as both a sign that men and women were ignorant of their true rest and pleasure and an obstruction hindering retirement of mind and self-examination. Although such activities were based on social injustices, Penn often seemed more concerned to accent the personal disorganization and waste of time that an active life of society affairs entailed.[42] Of all the sins of omission and commission through which a man denied God's sovereignty and ignored his stewardship, the failure to discipline oneself in the use of time was most odious. Penn advised his children to order their lives properly by dividing their days into time-segments devoted to worship and meditation, business, and periods for study, walking, and visits. The best way to do this was to keep a journal, as every puritan knew. "In this be [firm], and let your Friends

[39] "No Cross" (1682), *Works*, I, 289; Letter, "To Friend" (July 10, 1668), *Works*, I, 6.
[40] "A Letter of Love to the Young Convinced" (1669), *Works*, I, 442.
[41] "No Cross" (1682), *Works*, I, 356.
[42] *Ibid.*, 357, 364-366.

know it, and you will cut off many Impertinencies and Interruptions, and save a Treasure of Time to your selves, which People most unaccountably lavish away."[43]

A disciplined life of self-denial and gravity was possible only if one separated himself from the activities, fashions, and customs of men and developed the perspective of a stranger in the world. Penn emphasized this especially in his first decade as a Friend and then again in his later years when his prominent public life was past. A regenerate man has been called out of the world—out of its nature, its spirit, its fruits, and its fashions, which are all destined for the fire. "I write not to you as to the World; for you are called out of the World, by Him that hath overcome the World; that as he is not of this World, so you may not be of this World," Penn wrote to fellow-Friends.[44] A regenerate Christian is to be perfectly disentangled from the cares of the world, standing loose from and unencumbered by the visible and temporal. He is to live in the world as a stranger, with his eyes on the better world: the eternal home toward which he is traveling.[45]

Separation was required not simply because of the vain forms of gaiety that prevailed but because these were only the manifestations of more deep-seated ills. The reign of Satan had been fastened on the world in the Restoration period as never before. For Penn, separation and aloofness were above all necessary in this most degenerate of times, when marriage was viewed as a dull necessity for producing offspring, levity had replaced sobriety, lust was called love, and wantonness, good humor. "O what Tremendous Oaths and Lies! What Revenge and Murders, with Drunkenness and Gluttony! What Pride and Luxury! Chamberings and Wantonness! What Fornications, Rapes, and Adulteries! What Masks and Revels! What Lustful Ornaments

[43] "Advice to His Children" (1699), *Works*, I, 899.
[44] "Tender Counsel" (1677), *Works*, I, 199.
[45] *To the Churches of Jesus Throughout the World* (London, 1677), 8; "Travels in Holland and Germany" (1677), *Works*, I, 51.

and Enchanting Attires! What Proud Customs and Vain Complements! What Sports and Pleasures! Again, What Falseness and Treachery! What Avarice and Oppression! What Flattery and Hypocrisy! What Malice and Slander! What Contention and Law Suits! What Wars and Bloodshed! What Plunders and Desolations!"[46] For Penn, as for many puritans, the stage was a symbol of the worst vices of the times—no doubt in part because the wits of the era were so adept at ridiculing those who desired individual and social "purity." Penn wrote as one himself stung when he referred to "the infamous plays of those comical wits, Sylvester, Shakespeare, Johnson, etc. with too many of our own days, wherein the preciseness and singularity of Puritans and others are abusively represented, and exposed to the life, for the entertainment of vain and irreligious persons."[47]

It was not only the vice and immorality of the times that a saint had to flee. Penn berated in turn each class of English society because of the social injustices perpetuated by its style of life. The rulers were scolded for ruling not for God's glory but for wealth and personal glory, for oppressing and persecuting the poor, and for letting vice and vanity go unpunished. Nobles had become too worldly; judges oppressed the needy and favored the rich; lawyers played on the ignorance of the people and were concerned only for wealth; merchants and traders had gold as their god; farmers and countrymen forgot God's providence; and pastors and priests were worst of all, combining the sins of the rest. At no time in English history had there been a greater need for the pleasant streams of thorough reformation for a dry and parched country.[48]

[46] "Summons or Call" (1677), *Works*, I, 195. See also "Truth Exalted" (1668), *Works*, I, 243-244.

[47] *The Christian Quaker* . . . (London, 1674), 122-123. This is the first edition of the full treatise, including George Whitehead's part. Penn's part was published separately under the same title in 1673.

[48] "Summons or Call" (1677), *Works*, I, 193-195; Letter, "To Wil-

In his early years as a Quaker, Penn was so strongly aware of the need for separation from the world that he warned that any kind of success in the world, even that of the honest and thrifty Protestant merchant, was a sign of membership in the Devil's kingdom. Suffering and defeat at the hands of the world were the true signs of godliness. In this spirit Penn upbraided the Dutch nation of industrious merchants in 1671 for having become too rich, too high, too proud—in a word, for being moderately successful in a world in which the righteous should be only outcasts. Surely Penn's English nationalism and his father's tales of the navy's chief enemy were reflected in Penn's public letter, but it was in keeping with the young Quaker's religious views as well. The Dutch were warned that they should awaken from their state of earthly security and hope for a withering of all visible empire, trade, and treasure. And when this came about, they were to view it as a gift of the gracious hand of God, who wished for their own good to wean them from their covetous pursuits.[49] A Christian's kingdom was not of this world; a regenerate man would meet great trials and suffering here below. He was not to "consult flesh and blood" in an attempt to turn aside such suffering; he was to recognize it as preparation for the kingdom of God—a sign of membership among the heavenly saints.[50]

The need for separation from a sinful age was Penn's primary justification for the peculiar customs that were to become the trademarks of Quakerism. Unlike the majority of early Quakers, Penn had been reared in a social world

---

liam Popple" (Oct. 24, 1688), *Works*, I, 138; "Truth Rescued from Imposture" [1671], *Works*, I, 521.

[49] Letter to Quakers and people of the United Netherlands (1672), PWP (contemp. copy in HSP). Published in London, 1672.

[50] Letter, "To All Suffering Friends in Holland, or Germany . . ." (Sept. 1, 1673), *Works*, I, 161; Letter, "To the Friends of God in Bristol" (Feb. 24, 1682), *Works*, I, 230.

in which the use of titles and other means of showing respect and reverence were marks of common courtesy and
civility as much as they were reflections of hierarchical
societal relationships. Moreover, most of the people he had
to deal with were men accustomed to respect and even
deference. The Quakers' use of the second-person singular
pronoun to men of all ranks, their refusal to bow, use titles,
or doff their hats, and their refusal to take oaths caused him
considerable embarrassment. He was acutely aware that to
those who did not share the Quaker views such customs
smacked of barbarism and a perverse desire for singularity
for its own sake. He was at first reluctant to grant that
adoption of these customs was necessary for participation
in the Quaker movement. He preferred to keep the "Custom and Friendship of this World." Such customs, he said,
were certainly not the best or most important marks of
Quakerism, for salvation from sin and justification through
the power of Christ, not quaint habits, make true
Christians.[51] The customs were meaningless apart from
more central forms of self-denial, and concentration on
them could detract from the major issues. For that reason
the Apostles did not rebuke those who addressed them as
"Master" when imploring their aid for salvation.[52]

Penn, nevertheless, understood that the social habits that
these customs testified against were marks of Satan's kingdom, and he came to see the clear need for regenerate
Christians to separate themselves from such manifestations
of pride as titles, hat-respect, and similar mannerisms. The
Quakers had perceived that the world was in a state of
apostasy, and, in seeking to determine the marks of that
apostasy, they had brought every word and deed to the

[51] "No Cross" (1682), *Works*, I, 330-331; "Serious Apology" (1671),
Works, II, 62-64. Penn collaborated with George Whitehead on this
treatise.
[52] "The Spirit of Truth Vindicated, Against That of Error and
Envy . . ." (1672), *Works*, II, 132-133.

judgment of the light within. The light had indicated that the customs that they came to deny were most conducive to the world's evils. All had to do with pride, and "what Impiety is there in the World that may not in some Sense be resolv'd into that of Pride or Covetousness after Honour, as its proper Center?"[53] If one were to separate himself from the evils of the world, he could not ignore the more subtle manifestations.

"MY DEAR FRIENDS, let us be careful not to mingle with the Crowd, lest their Spirit enter us, instead of our Spirit entring them. . . ." Thus Penn warned "the Children of Light in this Generation."[54] As the statement intimates, separation for purification was only one part of the rhythm of the saint's life. Withdrawal and self-discipline provided an opportunity to tend to the wounds of spiritual battle, to regroup with fellow-warriors, and to prepare for a renewed assault on the demonic forces. In his life and writings Penn expressed clearly his understanding of the distinction between temporary withdrawal from the world and monastic self-denial and withdrawal. He believed that the regenerate Christian's life was not to be that of a recluse, for his aim should be victory over the world, not avoidance of it. "The Christian Convent and Monastery are within, where the Soul is encloistered from Sin. And this Religious House the True Followers of Christ carry about with them, who exempt not themselves from the Conversation of the World, though they keep themselves from the Evil of the World in their Conversation." Monastic or sectarian separation he called a lazy, rusty, unprofitable form of self-denial. The cross or self-denial of Christ and Christians is one directed toward mending the world. "True Godliness don't turn Men out of the World, but enables them to live better in it, and excites their Endeavors to mend it: Not hide their

53 *Ibid.*
54 "To the Children of Light in This Generation" (1678), *Works,* I, 225.

Candle under a Bushel, but set it upon a Table, in a Candlestick."[55]

Penn believed that the Quakers should serve in this world as vicarious sufferers and interceders. The desire for purification was not to make the saints either insensitive to the world's infirmities or free from its sufferings and misery. "We must make their Case as our own, and travail alike in Spirit for them as for ourselves." Friends were not only to suffer with the world as kindred spirits; they were to alleviate suffering by interceding with God. Penn often testified that he had a great fear that "the overflowing Scourge of God's Wrath and Indignation" was about to break out upon apostate England. The weight of this fear caused him to cry out, asking who there was to save and deliver the land. "Are there none to stay the Stroke? To blunt the Edge? To stop the Fury and interceed for the People, and mediate for this poor Land. . . ?" At such dark times Penn called on the Children of the Light, "his despised, but chosen Generation for whose sake He would yet have Mercy." The outcast Quakers had to stand in the gap and pray for the putting away of God's wrath, so that the land would not become an utter desolation. "The Lord is ready to hear you for this people when you are ready to interceed."[56]

Christians were also to assume responsibility for the world by serving as models and goads to unregenerate men in both an individual and a social sense. Although Penn's exclusivistic spirit waned late in his life, he never completely lost his conviction that the Quakers were the primary models for mankind. God had laid upon Friends the care both of this age and of ages to come by providing them as leaders and examples. "Yea, the Lord God hath chosen you to place his Name in you; the Lord hath entrusted you with his Glory, that you might hold it forth to all Nations; and

[55] "No Cross" (1682), *Works*, I, 295-296.
[56] "Children of Light" (1678), *Works*, I, 224-225.

that the Generations unborn may call you blessed."[57] How was it possible for men to find the true path of obedience to God and of brotherhood once again and to recover their ancient confidence in each other if some did not lead the way, holding forth a principle and conversation for the rest of men?

It was in the light of this need that Penn accepted the Quaker testimony concerning oaths and war. Like all Quakers, he found many reasons for refusing to take oaths, including the Scriptural testimony against them. But the major reason he gave was that the use of oaths gratified men's distrust of each other and accustomed them to a world in which speaking the truth was so exceptional that it required God as a witness. The practice implied fatalistic acceptance of a situation radically antithetical to the ideals of the kingdom of God, which the Quakers, relying on the grace of God, hoped to produce in the near future.[58] In a similar fashion the Quakers' pacifistic principles were seen by Penn as a model for the heavenly kingdom. In Scripture a holy, lamblike, and peaceable state had been prophesied for the "Happiness of the latter Times," so the Quakers were introducing this glorious way into a distracted world. Others were to follow their example and embrace the peaceful principle.[59]

Quakerism was born in a revolutionary era. Although for some Quakers the visionary hopes and apocalyptic expectations had faded by the time Penn joined the movement, Quaker leaders still hoped to overturn the world, and Penn was more hopeful than most. In his view the Christian had a responsibility to be the pilot of the ship of the world. He

---

[57] *To the Churches of Jesus* (1677), 6.

[58] "A Treatise of Oaths: Containing Several Weighty Reasons Why the People Called Quakers Refuse to Swear" (1675), *Works*, I, 615-616.

[59] "Key Opening the Way" (1692), *Works*, II, 788. An earlier version of this treatise was published in 1673 as an appendix to *Christianity a New Nickname*.

was to seek the helm despite his separation from the world and to guide the vessel to its eternal port rather than stealing out at the stern and leaving it without a pilot, to be driven by the fury of evil times.[60] It was primarily as preachers of the Word that the Quakers hoped to overturn the world. Having caught the puritan vision of Christian history, the Quakers intensified the eschatological hopes and understood themselves as the chosen band that would preach and convert to the ends of the earth, thereby bringing in a new era. In the early part of his career, Penn was caught up in the millenarian excitement of the times. "This," he wrote in 1671, "is the Day of the Revelation of the Mysteries of God's Kingdom; for the Spirit is pour'd forth, and the Anointing is come, and the Days of Refreshment from the Presence of the Lord are known. . . ."[61] The present age was the high point of Christian history. The Quakers were taking the helm at precisely the point at which the wave of reform that had begun in the sixteenth century had reached its crest. They had merely to guide the ship as it rode home on this wave.

Penn's understanding of Christian history was closer to most puritans' than to the Quakers' Anabaptist outlook. In his view the decline in the church had begun right after the Apostles' deaths, but the intermittent persecution of the church in the second century had arrested the decline, and it was not until Constantine and then the era of the Great Whore of Revelation 17, who mounted the papal chair about 600, that the decline reached its nadir.[62] Penn had little good to say about "that tedious winter Night of dark Apostacy" known as the Middle Ages, but he dated the ascent of the church not from the classical Reformation but from the time of the late Medieval sectarian movements. The major significance of the Reformation had been the

[60] "No Cross" (1682), *Works*, I, 295-296.

[61] "Serious Apology" (1671), *Works*, II, 84.

[62] *Ibid.*, 52-53. Presumably Penn was referring to Gregory the Great.

Reformers' appeal to the testimony of God in each man's conscience, and in this matter the way had been impressively prepared by the Waldenses, Albigenses, Lollards, Hussites, and, in minor ways, the Henricians, Lyonists, and Fraticelli. Nevertheless, when Penn presented the Quakers as riding the crest of the final wave of history, he thought of the wave as representing Protestantism and the Quakers as completing the movement that had been begun by the sixteenth-century Reformers. The early sectarian ripples were significant primarily because they led to Worms in 1521, when Luther "first of all arraigned the Christian World at the Bar of private Judgment."[63]

The Reformers had made only a solid beginning of reform. Many additional movements had been necessary to move the church from the Reformation plateau to the level of the Quakers. The Reformers had made improvements in doctrine, worship, and practice, but more in the first area than in the latter two. They had spoken of the Spirit and its operations in worship and sanctification, "but Where and How to find it and wait in it to perform our Duty to God, was yet as a Mystery to be declared by this farther Degree of Reformation." Moreover, the initial insights were lost in some places, especially where the new churches took up worldly ways and became part of the old establishment, as in Denmark, Sweden, parts of Germany, and England.[64] Although Anglicanism represented a compromise by the reformers in England with the passing old order, England had also been the scene of progress beyond the Reformers in the form of the puritan movement. Beginning with the grand martyrs of the Marian period, God had been pleased to move "from vessel to vessel" with increasing spiritual power as the world progressed toward the end-times. In many places Penn cited the Presbyterians, "Puritans," Independents, Baptists, and finally the Seekers as representing

---

[63] "Innocency" (1668), *Works*, I, 270; "No Cross" (1682), *Works*, I, 412-413; "Reason Against Railing" (1673), *Works*, II, 516.
[64] "Rise and Progress" (1694), *Works*, I, 874, 862-863.

progressive steps toward the truly spiritual era, although he also termed all members of this group "Puritans."[65]

Although, more than most Quaker writers, Penn emphasized the preparatory work done by other reformers and found allies among Anglicans as well as dissenters, he affirmed in unmistakable terms the uniqueness and superiority of Quakerism.[66] The earlier groups had failed to carry through on their promising beginnings and had fallen back into apostasy, and in any case they had lacked the clear understanding of spiritual religion that had become available in this final dispensation. The Quakers possessed a more glorious and direct vision of the truth and a more efficacious knowledge of the Spirit than had been known since the time of the Apostles. "Since those centuries, in which the Apostasy eclipsed the Beauty of the Primitive Light, there has not been so glorious a Discovery of Spiritual, Pure, and Evangelical worship, Life and Doctrine, as God hath in his Loving-kindness raised the so much despised Quakers, to own, practise and declare among the Nations. . . ."[67] Through this poor despised people, it had pleased God to visit England and all of the nations with a more direct, clear, and immediate "Sight, Sense and Knowledge" of him than men had previously been granted.[68] Penn believed that the Quakers had received a measure of the same kind of

[65] See, e.g., letter to Viscountess Conway (Oct. 20, 1675), PWP (A.L.S. in Brit. Mus.). Among the "Puritan" leaders Penn commends are John Tindal, Peter Martyr, Richard Greenham, William Perkins, Joseph Canne, William Ames, T. Collier, Joshua Sprigg, Christopher Goad, Walter Cradock, William Dell, John Saltmarsh, John Owen, J. Caryl, William Erbury, and John Everard.

[66] Penn cited the works of many Anglicans, including John Hales, Jeremy Taylor, William Chillingsworth, Henry Hammond, Ralph Cudworth, Henry More, John Smith, Gilbert Burnet, Edward Stillingfleet, John Tillotson, Robert Sanderson, William Sherlock, and Simon Patrick.

[67] For accounts of the decline of forerunning puritan groups, see "Rise of Progress" (1694), Works, I, 862-864; "Guide Mistaken" (1668), Works, II, 21.

[68] "Urim and Thummim" (1674), Works, II, 619.

anointing that the Apostles had received. Never before had a group of Christians carried with them so visibly the very marks of the true primitive church. As a traveling ministry, without pay, constantly in want and danger, and suffering great tribulations, the Quakers were moving into all the world, preaching the gospel and proclaiming the Day of the Lord.[69]

The eschatological tone of many of Penn's early works was more than a doffing of his literary hat in the direction of the traditional Biblical imagery of revival movements. Penn believed that when Christ said, "He that believes in me shall have Eternal Life, and I will raise him up at the last Day," he was referring to the seventeenth century, "our Day," "for another Day shall never dawn yn yt wch hath sprung from on high to visit. . . ."[70] This was not a constant mood for Penn, nor even a very prominent one, except intermittently, during the latter part of his life. In addition, Penn, like other Quaker leaders, had no interest in discovering the precise "joynt" of history by reading the signs of the times. His eschatological excitement rose and fell with the changes in the general tenor of the times and of his own experiences, and there were periods even early in his career as a Quaker when he was uncertain where he stood in the dispensational scheme of history.[71] Moreover, some of Penn's concern with the lateness of the historical day was attributable to his attempt to impress upon his readers their

[69] "Serious Apology" (1671), *Works*, II, 36; "Guide Mistaken" (1668), *Works*, II, 18.

[70] Letter to the Quakers (Jan. 10, 1675), PWP (contemp. copy in HSP).

[71] For example, in a work written in 1672, Penn refuted the belief that the soul sleeps with the body until the general resurrection by observing that Paul, who undoubtedly knew the course of future history, had written in Philippians 1:21: "To die is gain." Paul could not have written that if he had known that the soul was to sleep in its grave for 1600 years, and, said Penn, for all he knew, 1600 years more before the resurrection. "The New Witnesses Proved Old Hereticks: or Information to the Ignorant, . . ." (1672), *Works*, II, 160.

absolute dependence on God and their inability to control the future any more than they could manipulate their past.[72]

Nevertheless, we cannot understand Penn's attitude toward his writings and activities during at least the first half of his career without recognizing that the eschatological, apocalyptic outlook was very prominent at that time. It is true that after 1660 the original Publishers of Truth who were still alive were unable to muster the kind of apocalyptic excitement that the reign of the puritan saints had thrust upon them. But hopes were still high during the Restoration, and to Penn the temper of the times was an unmistakable indication that the Devil had sallied forth in battle array for the final cosmic assault.

Although the Commonwealth had stirred Quaker hopes, Penn saw it as the time of the Devil's preparatory activity for his Restoration assault. Not only had the saints turned persecutors, but the movement toward a Spirit-centered religion had turned into a riot of fanaticism and antinomianism. According to Penn, just before God broke forth among the Quakers several men had arisen who were attended with mighty visions and inward revelations and who were transported beyond measure. But they did not "stay low"; the spirit got out of hand; and sheer mad ranterism was the result. Some began to teach that since all that God makes is good, and all who act do so only by the power of what God creates, there is no such thing as sin. One is free to do as he desires. Others taught that what matters is not what one does but the spirit in which he does it. One can kill, lie, steal, and above all indulge in sexual relations of any sort so long as he does not do so lustfully. Such ranterism, according to Penn, as represented by the teaching of Lodowick Muggleton and John DeLabadie, was still a menace in the 1660's and 1670's, but it had crested in the 1650's and was the clearest sign of the beginnings of the Devil's eschatological uprising.[73] In fact, it was in response to this

---

[72] "Tender Counsel" (1677), *Works*, I, 205.

[73] Letter, "To Lodowick Muggleton" (Dec. 15, 1672), *Works*, I, 45.

delusion of the Devil that God had raised the Quakers. "And this, Friends, I would that you should further understand, at that very Time, when that delusive Spirit was making Havock of thousands, who placed Freedom in Sinning innocently (as they counted it) I mean to sin freely, and not to be free from Sin, did the Lord God of Purity on whose Vesture, and in whose Habitation is Holiness for ever, raise up his ancient horn of Salvation among us."[74]

This fanaticism among "thousands" was simply the prelude to the war the Devil was to wage against true godliness during the Restoration. If one was looking for the signs of the Devil's last fling and spoiling to cry "Repent! The Kingdom is at Hand," he could not miss the evidence provided by the debauchery of the Restoration. What made this era stand out from other times of massive sinfulness, in Penn's mind, was the fact that the English lived their debauched lives while professing to be a kingdom of obedient Christians. By combining their vanities, pleasures, and lusts with a continuing profession of religion, the English had become guilty of the blasphemy of all blasphemies, "the grand Destructive Atheism of the World." Heathen living plus Christian profession was much worse than heathenism pure and simple. Combining confession of God in words with such horrid denial in works made the English people the great beast that had risen out of the filthy sea, a beast with many heads and ten horns, and "Blasphemy!" written on every head.[75] "O Christendom! How art thou, and thy Children, degenerated from God, and fallen from the Doctrine of Christ, whose Holy Name thou professest! Thou art become a City full of Uncleanness, committing Whoredom under every Green Tree; following other Lovers than Jesus, whose Spouse thou professest to be. O Thou Rebel-

---

[74] "Plain Dealing; or Good Advice to John DeLabadie and His Followers, at Herford, Westphalia" (Nov. 24, 1672), PWP (contemp. copy in HSP).

[75] Letter, "To the Princess and Countess at Herford, in Germany" (1676), *Works*, I, 181-182.

lious City, thou Cage of unclean Birds, thou and thy children have filled the Earth with the Stink of your Abominations."[76] No puritan or dissenter was more scathing or scatological in his denunciations of the nation.

But it was not God's judgment and condemnation that constituted the major element in Penn's eschatological message. Judgment and sorrow, yes, but even more, victory and power for the forces of right were to be the marks of the age. This was to be the great and notable day of the coming of God's power in all the nations. The "Sun-Rising of the eternal Day" had already appeared and was spreading over the nations of the world. There were great revolutions at hand that would culminate in the setting up of the glorious kingdom of Christ in the world.[77] The world, which was raging with the fury of the Devil, would soon come to judgment and be transformed. Since the Quakers were the vanguard of the forces of change, their duties were clear and their prospects bright. Penn assured his fellow-Quakers in 1670 that the impetuous storms that had been raised lately against them were "but the certain presage of a suddain and succeeding Calm, and that our Sufferings and misadventures from ye World do but forrum the happy approaches of Truths greater Glory and prosperity."[78] "Let the winds of imagination blow, the storms of persecution beat, and the sea of raging malice foam. . . ." He was convinced that the Quakers would conquer the world, exalt God's name, and bring truth and salvation to all men.[79]

Penn often referred to the Quakers as a suffering and bedraggled lot, the Lord's remnant, pilgrims estranged from the life and spirit of this world and embarked for a more

[76] "Summons or Call" (1677), *Works*, I, 195-196.

[77] "Travels in Holland and Germany" (1677), *Works*, I, 60, 108-109; "A Tender Visitation in the Love of God . . . to All the People in the High and Low Dutch Nations" (1677), *Works*, I, 221.

[78] "A Prefatory Observation upon 'the Quakers Spiritual Court Proclaimed'" (1670), PWP (contemp. copy in HSP).

[79] "Truth Exalted" (1668), *Works*, I, 247; "Children of Light" (1678), *Works*, I, 224-225.

durable country in heaven.[80] But the sectarian tones of this picture were balanced in the 1670's and early 1680's in Penn's mind by his assurance that God's people would be outcasts in the world only a little while longer. God had heard the solitary cries, the deep and mournful supplications of the Quakers when they were as a little silly dove without its mate or the lonely pelican in the wilderness.[81] It becomes the bride of the King of Kings to be a glorious queen, "therefore hath he ordained that she shall no more sit as one desolate and forsaken, clothed in Sackcloth, which is the Garment of Heaviness: But shall be crowned with the Stars, clothed with the Sun, and the Moon shall be under her Feet; that is, the changeable World, with all its Temporary Glory shall be her Foot-stool."[82] Therefore Friends were to take heart, to look forward and lift up their eyes and continue their work of preaching. The fields were white unto harvest all up and down the nations. "For this I have to tell you in the vision of the Almighty, that the Day of the breaking-up of the Nations about you, and of the sounding of the Gospel-Trumpet unto the inhabitants of the Earth, is just at the door."[83]

THE PUBLICK FRIEND

Penn's eschatological hopes for converting and transforming England and the world were translated immediately after his conversion into effective service as a leader of the Quakers on a variety of fronts. He quickly assumed a position as one of the foremost men in the informal Quaker hierarchy of public Friends as a preacher, missionary, writer, controversialist, proponent of toleration, and organizer and

[80] Letter, "To the Little Flock and Family of God . . . in the United Provinces" (1673), *Works*, I, 162.

[81] *To the Churches of Jesus* (1677), 2.

[82] Letter, "To the Princess and Countess at Herford in Germany" (1676), *Works*, I, 180.

[83] *To the Churches of Jesus* (1677), 8.

arbitrator within the body. Penn's witness was, however, a rather distinctive one, or at least he was the most prominent of several young men who entered the movement when he did and brought about changes. At a time when the Friends were consolidating their organization for a long and tough haul before the end of history, de-emphasizing their apocalyptic hopes and stressing a kind of quietistic separation from the world and its ways—in short, changing from what Richard Vann has called a "movement" into a "sect"— Penn helped to introduce a more optimistic and activistic strain.[84]

Penn often sounded like the Interregnum Quakers because of his eschatological perspective and his apocalyptic language about the coming of the Lord with power to overturn the structures of history. But Penn's was not a quietistic or sectarian apocalypticism. Indeed, his apocalyptic imagery seems at times to be a rhetorical device for stirring the kind of hopes and fervor that would lead to action directed toward the transformation of the world. Moreover, the kind of activism that Penn called for was, at least for the Quakers or any other radical sectaries, a decidedly practical, well-planned, highly organized, and even respectable variety. Penn's view was really that of the prophetic activist—the view that had motivated those puritans of the 1640's who had summoned England to repent and take practical steps to reform the nation and that had surfaced in Quakerism when they drew up reform proposals and thought about assuming positions of political power. It was Penn's hope that England could be goaded by the Quakers into becoming the vanguard of the coming kingdom of God, and this led him into some activities that seemed strange to older Friends who had accommodated to the Restoration. His activism, however, had firm roots in the early Quaker movement and was in ways more in accord with Quaker thought than sectarian quietism.

[84] Vann, *Social Development*, 200.

Penn's career as a preacher and missionary began in the summer of 1668 while he was still living at home, and it was the embarrassment that this caused the elder Penn that made Penn briefly an outcast from his home and that thrust him fully into the arms of the Quakers. This was the beginning of a long and effective, if increasingly sporadic, period of service as proclaimer of the Word. Penn spent much of the next few years travelling and preaching in southern England and then set out in 1671 with Thomas Rudyard, who was to become the Friends' foremost legal expert, on a missionary trip through Holland and Germany. Penn's marriage in 1672 to Guli Springett, Isaac Penington's stepdaughter-in-law, seemed likely to have no effect on his itinerancy when he took his bride on a three week preaching honeymoon. Married life, increasing controversial and expository writing, and activities on behalf of toleration began to take more of Penn's time, however, and from 1672 on, although he was a prominent speaker wherever he happened to be, he went on major preaching and missionary tours only occasionally. He returned to Holland and Germany in the company of Fox, Barclay, and Keith in 1677 and went again in 1686. Notable journeys through several counties for mass meetings as well as counselling among Friends took place in 1677, 1681, 1687, 1694-95, 1705, and 1709. By the 1687 trip Penn's fame among Englishmen of all sorts, as well as his position of esteem among Friends, was so great that his meetings and activities took on the character of the later Methodist revivals. His confidence in the continuing spread of Truth was invariably revived on such trips, and his eschatological sense was also quickened. They had an especially therapeutic effect on him during his later years of frustrations and doubts. The effect on others was apparently at least as helpful. Penn never claimed to be a great preacher, and the ponderous prose of many of his works and the serene visage of his portraits do not conjure up the image of a George Whitefield, but the testimony of his listeners was that he was a highly effective evangelist.

Lord Acton has written that "the art of understanding adversaries is an innovation of the present century, characteristic of the historic age. Formerly a man was exhausted by the effort of making out his own meaning, with the help of his friends."[85] John Owen's indication that the Quakers seemed to be having more trouble than most making out their meaning expressed a sentiment shared by many contemporaries, and as a result the art of understanding adversaries had made no progress in the debate between Friends and their enemies by the time Penn joined the movement. Penn was certain that England could still be reformed by print, however, and shortly after his conversion he published his first book, *Truth Exalted, A short but Sure Testimony against all those Religions, Faiths, and Worships, that have been formed and followed in the Darkness of Apostacy . . . Presented to Princes, Priests and People that they may Repent, Believe, and Obey.* Shortly thereafter he held his first public debate with the Presbyterian minister Thomas Vincent, published his position against Vincent in *The Sandy Foundation Shaken,* and won his nine-month stay in the Tower.

Undaunted, Penn published forty more pamphlets and books in his first six years as a Quaker, and in the thirty-five years of active mental life remaining to him after that he entered the lists with well over a hundred more. Many of these were tracts on toleration, and a few were hard-to-classify political or ethical treatises, but most were controversial works, expositions of Quakerism, or appeals to conversion. Quakers had believed from the beginning that they had to explain their principles to the world in print and answer every charge made against them. Penn occasionally said about his controversies that "weakness occasions these things; and they are to go off with it," but judging from his publishing activity, which he himself had to finance until he had become famous, he viewed it as a very important

[85] *Renaissance to Revolution: The Rise of the Free State* (1906; rpt., New York, 1961), 202.

part of his witness.[86] The heart had to be drawn to true religion, but in addition "the Understanding must be Convinced . . . and feel the Truth of a Principle; such Labours have been, are and will be useful to distinguish Truth from Falsehood. . . ."[87] In addition, it was necessary to set the record straight against the lies, slanders, reproaches, and accusations of those who always attack "new and heavenly discoveries." The controversies among Catholics, Anglicans, Presbyterians, Independents, and Baptists had produced a whole phalanx of sharpened tongues and pens ready to combine against the pure Word uttered by the Friends. Penn knew that he was better trained than most Quakers for defending the Truth, and he also felt called upon to defend himself against the host of controversialists who hoped to further their causes and win fame by attacking what to them was the new Goliath of the Quakers.[88]

Henry More, the Cambridge Platonist, who had been directed toward Penn's works by George Keith, inspected two written by Penn against the Presbyterian John Faldo and "mett wth severall excellent passages in them that are very expressive of a vigorous resentment and esperience of what appartaines to life and Holinesse, and that I exceedingly rejoice, that the Quakers have emerged above yt low beginning of an heartlesse and hopelesse Familisme. . . ."[89] The Friends were even more pleased to have a talented writer in their midst eager for controversy with "men in high places." As early as 1672 Penn was appointed by the Morning Meeting of ministers, the central organ of executive leadership at that time, to a committee formed to gather anti-Quaker literature and answer it and to read and edit the works of fellow-Quakers to make certain that they re-

[86] Letter to Margaret Fox (Mar. 16, 1674), ACMC, XII, 35-36 (copy).

[87] "Testimony Concerning Samuel Fisher," The Testimony of Truth Exalted (London, 1679).

[88] "Serious Apology" (1673), Works, II, 74; Penn to John Faldo (Oct. 3, 1674), PWP (contemp. copy in HSP).

[89] Henry More to Penn (May 22, 1675), PWP (L.S. in HSP).

flected the beliefs of the society. He was a very active member of the committee as author, editor, and advisor, and on one occasion he even "fitt" a book by Fox for the press.[90] Penn's works for members of the society included exhortatory letters, such as *A Letter of Love to the Young Convinced* (1669), ethical treatises such as *No Cross, No Crown*, sermons, refutations of schismatics such as John Perrot, John Wilkinson, and John Story, historical accounts of the movement, such as his Preface to Fox's *Journal*, entitled *A Brief Account of the Rise and Progress of the People Called Quakers*, and systematic expositions of Quaker thought.

These works, which were sometimes written "with the help of his friends"—to advert to Acton's description—and were inspected by the Morning Meeting committee, were well received by Friends during Penn's lifetime, and afterward became a necessary part of Friends' personal libraries. Equally well-received by a broader public were Penn's many important tracts on toleration, including *The Great Case of Liberty of Conscience* (1670), *A Treatise of Oaths* (1675), *England's Present Interest Discovered with Honor to the Prince, and Safety to the People* (1675), *An Address to Protestants of All Persuasions* (1679), and *A Persuasive to Moderation to Dissenting Christians* (1685). These tracts stirred up much controversy and made Penn suspect in the eyes of many, but those Englishmen seeking for a way to unify the English populace found no more effective spokesman than Penn. As he wrote to Thomas Lloyd and James Harrison in regard to his *Persuasive to Moderation*, "My *Persuasive* works much among all sorts, and is divers spoak of," and had won him many friends as well as enemies.[91]

Considerably less fruitful were Penn's many public de-

[90] Sept. 15, 1673, Dec. 27, 1675, Jan. 29, 1676, FLL, The Morning Meeting Book of Records, cited by Mary Maples Dunn, *William Penn: Politics and Conscience* (Princeton, 1967), 11, nn. 14, 15.

[91] Letter to James Harrison (Apr. 24, 1686), PWP (A.L.S. in HSP). See also Penn to Thomas Lloyd (Apr. 21, 1686), PWP (A.L.S. in HSP).

131

bates and controversial works against Catholics and Protestants. In this case his confidence, somewhat shared by More, that his knowledge of theology and his understanding of the English Protestant spectrum would enable him to deal with opponents on their own terms and to express the Quaker message in the manner most likely to communicate with other Protestants, was shown to be ill-founded. He did distill the visions and experiences of Fox and the First Publishers of Truth into the theological language of the times as effectively as any Quaker writer in some treatises, such as *A Serious Apology for the Principles and Practices of the People Called Quakers* (1671; written with George Whitehead), *The Christian Quaker and His Divine Testimony* (1673; published with a second part by Whitehead in 1674), and *A Key Opening a Way to Every Common Understanding, How to Discern the Difference Betwixt the Religion Professed by the People Called Quakers and the Perversions, Misrepresentations and Calumnies of Their Several Adversaries* (1692; a different version of this appeared as part of an appendix to *Quakerism a New Nickname for Old Christianity*, 1673). There is no evidence, however, that these treatises induced Catholics and Protestants to repent.

Even less successful were the many public debates Penn had with Anglicans, Presbyterians, Independents, and Baptists or the many works he wrote in refutation of particular treatises written against Friends or himself. Penn was a very eager controversialist in the late 1660's and the 1670's, and he took on Catholics, all varieties of Protestants, and "sectaries" such as Lodowick Muggleton and John Reeves with equal readiness. These controversies sometimes degenerated into interminable debates involving *ad hominem* rhetorical feats and line-by-line exegesis and refutation stretching over four or five treatises on each side.[92] Penn himself sensed the

[92] For a good example, see William Hull's description of the debate in print between the Presbyterian John Faldo and Penn, *William Penn*, 146.

futility of these battles after 1675 and only occasionally entered the lists thereafter. In 1698 he admitted in a rejoinder to a refutation of his *A Key Opening a Way*, "I submit to Controversies as my Drudgery, not my Pleasure, otherwise than as it is my Duty. . . . It is not in my Nature to remember Injuries Twenty Years Ago, tho' this Man commits them unprovoked; Nor had I any Temptation to it, since I had all the Satisfaction I could desire but their Conversion" (in reference to Faldo and the Baptist Thomas Hicks).[93]

Penn was equally prominent as a leader and organizer within the Society of Friends. His activity in the Morning Meeting and then, after 1675, in the more important Meeting for Sufferings, is indicative of his pre-eminent position as a public Friend. At the time that Penn joined the Quakers, Fox and the other leaders were in the process of instituting in a more formal way the national—and in some respects international—organization that had grown up in sporadic fashion by the end of the Interregnum and that had fallen into disarray under the more consistent persecution of the Restoration, with its deleterious effects on the labors of travelling Friends. Although at that time he did not fully share Fox's desire to organize Friends for their self-preservation and for effective witness simply as a missionary sect, Penn's view of Quakerism as a model for and goad toward the transformation of England entailed an equally strong emphasis on organization and central leadership. Penn quickly became involved in the attempt to unify Friends by utilizing his own weighty testimony and counsel freely as a traveling Friend in local meetings and by building up quarterly, monthly, and yearly meetings. He was prominent in similar activity in Holland and Germany in 1677 during his missionary journey with Fox, Barclay, and Keith, and he also exercised such responsibilities in Pennsylvania, New Jersey, and Delaware.

[93] "A Reply to a Pretended Answer . . ." (1698), *Works*, ii, 807, 809.

Penn's activity in the three main controversies of seventeenth-century Quakerism—that started by John Perrot's insistence on wearing his hat in worship, the related struggle over individual and communal authority instigated by John Wilkinson and John Story, and the battle over George Keith's attempt to make the Friends more orthodox in theology and polity—was as great as that of any public Friend, although he was deferential to Fox's authority in the first two. In the Perrot controversy Penn published *The Spirit of Alexander the Coppersmith Justly Rebuked, or, An Answer to a Late Pamphlet, Entitled, The Spirit of the Hat* (1673), and *Judas and the Jews* (1673). His correspondence with Fox also indicates that he undertook to mediate between Fox and disgruntled Quakers during the controversy. Penn's indirect censure of Fox is evident in his statement, "George, much blame is laid upon ye procedure, hereasay yt has towards ym; and many untoward objections are started agst ye Inequitableness and hast of ye Judgment. . . ."[94] More common than advice to Fox, however, were Penn's severe diatribes against the schismatics, for he fully shared the views of Fox and other public Friends about the need for rule by an inner circle of saints within the saints. His contributions to the Wilkinson-Story controversy were *A Brief Examination and State of Liberty Spiritual* (1681) and *Just Measures in an Epistle of Peace and Love . . .* (1692). Keith made Penn and Whitehead the leading villains in his struggle against the society, and his book entitled *The Deism of William Penn* called forth Penn's *More Work for George Keith* (1696), as well as many unpublished letters and debates.

Despite the evidence of Penn's leadership in the movement, scholars have often insisted that the Quakers' esteem

[94] Fox's reply is friendly and deferential regarding Penn's knowledge of legal procedures such as those informally instituted against the schismatics. Letter to George Fox (Sept. 9, 1675), PWP (fragment of A.L.S. in J. Pierpont Morgan Library, New York); Fox to Penn (Sept. 30, 1675), PWP (A.L.S. in HSP).

for and dependence on Penn was not translated into intimate personal relations, especially with Fox, and that Penn, as a son of nobility and a worldly-wise courtier, was something of a man apart among Quaker leaders to the end of his life. Presumably many Friends, especially those of low birth, felt themselves in the presence of a man from another world when with Penn, and after Fox's death his two stepsons-in-law, William Meade and Thomas Lower, with Margaret Fox's apparent approval, led a group of Friends expressing concern about the purity of Penn's witness as a result of his rank, wealth, position at court, fame, and his way of insisting on organization and good order among Quakers. But the uniqueness of Penn's birth has been stressed too much by those who overemphasize the "proletarian" origins of Friends. As Richard Vann has recently stated, public Friends especially were, for the most part, men of wealth and standing, and neither Penn's money and his education nor even, in some cases, his friends were likely to impress Quaker leaders.[95] The cloud that hovered over Penn in the society in the 1690's had more to do with the Quakers' desire to appear acceptable and respectable to the government now that toleration was a possibility and Penn suspected of treason, and with the Fox family's concern about the possible eclipse of the departed leader, than with any insufficiencies in Penn's witness or sincere doubts about his life-style.

Penn's acceptance in the movement and his intimacy with its leaders is illustrated by what is known of his relationships with Fox, Barclay, and others. Related to Isaac Penington by marriage as well as beliefs, Penn in his earliest years as a Quaker was most intimate with Josiah Coale, Thomas Loe, George Whitehead, George Keith, and Benjamin Furly and gives evidence of a high regard for Samuel Fisher. Penn and Fox probably first met in 1671, when Penn accompanied the leader to Landsend prior to the lat-

---

[95] Vann, *Social Development*, chaps. 2 and 3.

ter's departure for America. Penn met Fox on his return to England and spent much time in the next few months with Fox and his wife Margaret. The correspondence still extant indicates that from then on there was a close religious and personal relationship between Penn and both Foxes. Penn was on several occasions helpful to Fox because of his legal knowledge, and Fox often wrote Penn asking for a speedy reply to Quaker enemies or advising him on several aspects of religious activities, but the correspondence indicates as well mutual concern for and knowledge of family happenings and other signs of intimacy. It was Penn who informed Margaret Fox of her husband's death and who was selected to write the preface to Fox's journal, about which the society took such pains.[96]

Penn's correspondence with Barclay also indicates close official and personal relations. Although there is some discussion of matters relating to theology, as when Barclay asked Penn to reply to an attack on him in his absence, and much on personal matters, Barclay appears mainly as a business agent of Penn in this correspondence. The Apologist tried to win favors from the Duke of York for Penn and worked to influence Scotsmen, and especially wealthy Scotsmen, to invest in and migrate to Penn's colony in the New World. Judging from Penn's part of the correspondence as it is evident in Barclay's letters, we would have to

[96] Copies or photos of the following letters in the PWP files are illustrative: Fox to Penn (Nov. 20-21, 1674); Fox to Penn (Nov. 25, 1674); Fox to Penn (Jan. 11, 1675); Marg. Fox to Penn (June 26, 1675); Penn to Fox (Sept. 9, 1675); Marg. Fox to Penn (Sept. 13, 1675); Fox to Penn (Sept. 30, 1675); Marg. Fox. to Penn (Dec. 11, 1677); Penn to Marg. Fox (Jan. 11, 1678); Fox to Penn (Jan. 5, 1690). In the undated letters file of PWP, see Fox to Penn (May 28) on Penn's physical "weekness"; Fox to Penn (May 24) about Penn's literary answer to Thomas Jenner; and Fox to Penn (Jan. 13) about Penn's controversial writings and including a greeting to Penn's father and mother (all A.L.S. in HSP).

rank Barclay higher as a theologian than as mediator and entrepreneur.[97]

PENN was clearly a major Quaker preacher, missionary, writer, counselor, and organizer, seeking to make Friends of all men, but his transformationist hopes were most evident in the most distinctive area of his witness, his political activities on behalf of toleration and his attempt to set up and lead a society based on Quaker principles in Pennsylvania. His belief that his religious witness required attempts to change English society through political means was evident from the time of his conversion. During his first imprisonment, Penn fired off a letter to an acquaintance, the Earl of Orrery, asking his assistance in the Friends' attempt to gain their freedom. In 1668 he went to Court with Loe, Whitehead, and Coale to appeal for relief for imprisoned Quakers, and throughout the 1670's he used his standing with Parliament and his friendship with the powerful to appeal in person and in writing to Parliament, the King and his officials, and the general public. As Cragg has pointed out, in seventeenth-century England influential friends could be especially helpful to those imprisoned because of the large variation in local political conditions and the susceptibility of local officials and jailers to political pressure.[98] What was most significant, however, about Penn's response to persecution was not his use of personal influence with friends but the fact that he regarded persecution from the point of view of a lawyer who wanted injustices corrected through legal review rather than as a saint who saw his suffering as a passive witness to the truth.

[97] See the following letters in the PWP file: Barclay to Penn (Mar. 6, 1674); Barclay to Penn (July 20, 1676); Barclay to Penn (Jan. 31, 1680); Barclay to Penn (Mar. 25, 1682); Barclay to Penn (Apr. 15, 1681); Barclay to Penn (Apr. 26, 1681); Barclay to Penn (Sept. 23, 1681); Barclay to Penn (Oct. 19, 1681) (all A.L.S. in HSP).
[98] *Puritanism in the Period of the Great Persecution*, 124.

As I have indicated, although the Quakers came into conflict with many more laws than other dissenters and were in the habit of denouncing their tormentors, they were largely passive toward governmental authority and rarely questioned the legality of either the laws under which they were imprisoned or their treatment while in prison. Penn accepted the Quakers' attitude toward governmental authority in general, but from the beginning of his bouts with the law, he was unable simply to suffer passively. Applying his belief that "true Godliness don't turn Man out of the World, but enables them to live better in it, and excites their Endeavors to mend it," Penn said that withdrawal was a dereliction of duty. Especially in those countries—like England—where God had brought a people far enough in the direction of the kingdom of heaven to give them a constitutional government and some sense of the voluntary relations of a social contract, true Christians had a religious duty to exercise and preserve their political rights and to make the fundamental law of the land operative.[99]

Beginning with the famous Penn-Meade trial of 1670, which established precedents concerning a jury's right to freedom from punishment for a verdict and its right to decide law as well as fact, he tried to prove in court that the laws being applied to Quakers were either unconstitutional or inapplicable. In this case and in later ones Penn assumed that his acts of civil disobedience were more than simply unavoidable accompaniments of religious obedience. They were a stratagem in the war to transform society. Disobedience led to legal confrontations in which his theory of fundamental rights could be employed to rid Quakers and even England herself of unjust and unconstitutional laws. To the chagrin of many of the older Quaker leaders, Penn helped to introduce this idea into the Quaker movement. In 1675 he, Thomas Ellwood, and William Meade were instrumental in organizing the Meeting for Sufferings

[99] "No Cross" (1682), *Works*, I, 296; "England's Great Interest" (1679), *Works*, II, 678-682.

as a committee for legal defense for indicted Quakers.[100]
Those who agreed with Penn decided that Friends were to
be told when they were suffering beyond the limits required
by law and were to be allowed to decide whether to suffer
quietly or sue for their rights. The Meeting for Sufferings
began to meet the last Thursday before each law term and
in executive committee weekly during court sessions. A
permanent office was secured, Thomas Rudyard was appointed solicitor, and Thomas Corbett was made standing
counsel. Penn used the legal knowledge he had acquired at
Lincoln's Inn to contest his own cases, to provide advice
for fellow-Quakers on many occasions, and to manage
Quaker relations with Parliament in the attempt to get laws
passed that were suitable to Friends.[101]

Penn led the Meeting for Sufferings into another kind of
political activity when the Meeting agreed in 1675 to urge
Friends to help elect suitable men to Parliament and to seek
to get agreements from them to work for relief from persecution. Penn himself was most active as a campaigner in the
elections of 1679-80. His 1679 tract, *England's Great Interest in the Choice of this New Parliament*, argued for the
support of candidates who espoused the political program
of the Whig party. The same year he campaigned for
Algernon Sydney for two elections in 1679 and also supported Sir Charles Worseley in the second one.[102] Although
he made common cause with the Whigs, Penn did not accept the whole of their program. His anti-Catholicism was
not as rigorous as that of true Whigs; he was neither anti-
monarchical nor for the exclusion of the Duke of York;
and he could not condone rebellion as a legitimate means
to achieve political ends. Nevertheless, his activities and
those of other Quakers associated them with the political

---

[100] See FLL, Minutes of the London Yearly Meeting, I, 25, cited by
Lloyd, *Quaker Social History: 1669-1738* (London, 1950), 84.

[101] Lloyd, *Quaker Social History*, 84-90. See also Dunn, *William
Penn*, 12, 19-20.

[102] See Dunn, 25, 32-40.

frenzy of 1680, when the Whigs and the Court party seemed to be moving rapidly toward a violent showdown. In light of this turbulent situation, the Quaker elders' disapproval of political activities flared into strong opposition. Gaining control of the Meeting for Sufferings, the elders insisted that Penn and others stop their political activities and cease using "those reflecting, disgusting terms of distinction of Whig and Tory; or any such nick-names tending to provoke one neighbor against another."[103]

With events apparently heading toward violence, Penn himself doubted the wisdom of his continuing participation in English politics. In December 1679 he told Robert Southwell "that he saw plainly so much extremity intended on this syde, as well as on that of [obliterated] that he resolved to withdraw himself from all manner of meddling, since things to him appeared violent and irreconcilable."[104] Although in 1678 he had believed that the world was on the threshold of "the great and notable day of the Lord, and the breakings-in of his eternal power upon all nations," his bursting faith in the saints' ability to move the mountains of English society was shaken in 1679-80. His candidates for Parliament were kept from their seats by fraud; Rome threatened to engulf England by means of the Popish Plot; and the ship of state was floundering on the rocks of violence.

In this dire situation Penn turned in a direction taken by earlier groups of transformationists who had found themselves hemmed in by events in England. Like the puritans of Massachusetts Bay, Penn decided that if the forces of the old order were proving intractable in England, he could turn to virgin territory and try to construct a model Christian society as close as possible to the consensual ideal of the kingdom. Penn had been active in Quaker activities in East and West Jersey since 1676, but now he began to spend

---

[103] FLL, Book of Cases, I, 98, cited by Lloyd, *Quaker Social History*, 92.

[104] *Historical Manuscripts Commission, Ormonde*, 6th Report, Appendix, 736-737, cited by Dunn, *William Penn*, 74.

all his time procuring a colony west of the Jerseys. Gaining the charter, constructing a constitution for the colonial experiment, securing settlers and wealthy estate owners, getting the new government under way, and then defending it against Lord Baltimore in a boundary dispute enlisted virtually all Penn's energies in the period from 1680 to 1685. To some Friends these appeared as rather worldly activities to be absorbing all the time of a leading public Friend, but Penn was certain that in no outward activity had he been more inwardly resigned to feel the Lord's hand as in the Pennsylvania venture. To Penn it was simply a continuation of his attempts to transform the world into a truly Christian society.[105] In his words, "God will plan[t] Americha and it shall have its day: ye 5th kingdom or Glorious day of Christ in us Reserved to ye last dayes, may have ye last pte of ye world, ye setting of ye Son or western world to shine in."[106] Since England could not be transformed through direct action, it seemed appropriate to provide her with a model. Possibly it had been too much to expect that the ecclesiastical model of the Quakers would provide an adequate goal toward the remaking of English religious, political, and social structures. A more effective form of action was to set up "a Society compleat in him throughout, as well in body as in Soul and Spirit."[107] And so Penn set his sights on America, that, in his famous words, "an example may be set up to the nations: there may be room there, though not here, for such an holy experiment."[108]

THE LATER PENN: TRANSFORMATIONIST TRANSFORMED

Penn accomplished most of his work as preacher, counselor, and writer for the Quaker movement between 1668 and 1685. These were also the years during which he

[105] Letter to Thomas Janney (Aug. 21, 1681), PWP (copy in HSP).
[106] Ibid.
[107] Letter from Penn and others in New World to Quakers in England (Mar. 17, 1684), PWP (copy in FLL).
[108] Letter to Robert Turner (Mar. 5, 1681), PWP (copy in HSP).

worked out the political and social implications of his thought and applied them in his activities in England and the New World. Beginning about 1685, the first year of the reign of James II, there appeared a change in the tenor of Penn's life and in many of his basic attitudes. Most of the new emphases were related to his growing realization that the world was more intractable than those who would turn it into the kingdom of God had expected. Moreover, it is probably fair to conclude that the pull of "the world" was stronger within Penn's own breast than he had anticipated. As other Quakers had feared, involvement in the world as courtier and proprietor took its eventual toll.

By the late 1680's he had lost most of his hope of transforming the world as God's warrior. The Pennsylvania venture had provided a means of forgetting for several years the depressing political experiences of 1679-81, but by the late 1680's it was obvious to him that the ungrateful and cantankerous Pennsylvanians no more constituted a consensual kingdom of God than any other society of sinners. Events in England appeared more manageable upon the coronation of James II, whom Penn was convinced would crown his own lifelong efforts by granting toleration for Quakers. Toleration came, but under circumstances that found Penn accused of treason because of his fawning devotion to James and the favors he thereby enjoyed. This cloud passed, but in its wake came a sojourn in debtor's prison, the temporary loss of Pennsylvania and the constant threat of permanent loss, and a relationship to his colony that was financially disastrous and personally frustrating. Moreover, within the society of Friends, where Penn remained a respected leader in the eyes of many, he had become the subject of bitter contention. It is not difficult to understand how, under these circumstances, Penn became convinced that the "old order" was to be his abode this side of the grave. Resigned to this prospect, he alternately sought respect and money from his colonists and a peaceful rural solitude away from the cares of the world. The transformationist had himself been in ways transformed.

Penn did not completely lose his vision of a new earth and a new heaven. In 1692 he could still write that the opportunity for an extraordinary harvest of souls was still before the Quakers, since "a short, but great Work will God do in the Earth; and great Judgments, of divers kinds, will begin it, and they are at the Door." The judge was at hand and the midnight cry coming as a thief in the night. "Prepare, prepare, or you are excluded forever."[109] Moreover, in 1694 he wrote his stirring theology of history, *The Rise and Progress of the People of God Called Quakers*, in which he traced history from Adam's Fall to the eschatological surge of the Quakers. "And to Thee, O England! Were they, and are they, lifted up as a Standard, and as a City set upon a Hill, and to the Nations round about thee, that in their Light thou may'st come to see Light, even in Christ Jesus the Light of the World. . . ." In his successful preaching tours of 1694 and 1695, he exhorted young Friends to take up the public ministry, for the fields were ready for the harvest in England and the surrounding nations.[110]

Penn wrote several other theological treatises in the 1690's, and he preached many sermons that were later published. Although his religious fervor and even his eschatological hopes found occasional utterance, there was a changed tone in most of his theological works. Missing were the eager, cutting responses to anti-Quaker tracts and the readiness for controversy and polemics with "men in high places." In a reply to an anti-Quaker tract by the clergy of West Dereham in Norfolk in 1698, Penn noted that he was responding only because the authorities, who could grant or withhold toleration, expected a reply. The work had no polemical intent, because Quakers, Penn noted, thought it their duty to use in a peaceable and inoffensive manner the

109 "Key Opening the Way" (1692), *Works*, II, 791.
110 *Works*, I, 873, 888.

liberty they had been granted.[111] In the excitement of delivering a sermon or tracing the course of the world's history, Penn might dwell on the evanescence of the forms of the world and anticipate God's intervention, but he no longer believed this to be imminent. The Quaker saints had already suffered to a far greater extent than any other group of dissenters, and Penn believed that it was now necessary to make a respectable accommodation with the old order.

Since the world could not be brought up to their level, Quakers would have to meet it halfway. When some Friends found odious the affirmation of loyalty they had to make in place of the forbidden oath, Penn advised them to "let things rest as they Lye quietly and friends use their freedom as occasion requires, till more can be Got."[112] When, after having lost Pennsylvania in 1692, he regained control of the colony in 1694 under terms that disturbed some Friends there, Penn advised them to accept this much goodness of God and to wait for the rest. "We must creep where we cannot go, and it is as necessary for us in the things of this life to be wise as to be innocent."[113] Impatient Friends had to learn that true religion was to bring not troubles and controversy but "a quiet and easy mind, wch as it is inwardly enjoyed, will show itself no less in all exteriour things."[114] One manifestation of the desire to avoid confrontations with other men was a new emphasis on separation from the world. The earlier rhythm of withdrawal-purification-transformation gave way to a separatism that dropped the third beat. As early as 1688 Penn preached a funeral sermon in which he encouraged Quakers to keep

[111] "Observations on the Norfolk Clergymen's Books" (1699), *Works*, I, 145.

[112] Port. 41, MS 35 (1696), FLL, cited by Dunn, *William Penn*, 162.

[113] Letter, "From William Penn to Friends in Pennsylvania" (Oct. 9, 1694), *Memoirs of the Historical Society of Pennsylvania*, III, Pt. 1, 288.

[114] Letter, "To Robert Asheton" (Nov. 1, 1700), *Pa. Archives*, 1st Ser., I, 134-135.

together as a "peculiar People" called out of the darkness of the world.[115] By 1699 the man who had once said that God's people had been called to transform the world was advising Friends to retire and carefully cultivate their souls. Saints were still warriors, but now the only enemy they should risk attacking was "the Enemy of our Souls." Penn had learned better than to try to take on the enemy that was "the World." "But then, Friends, we must keep to our Tents, we must be a Retired and a Peculiar People, and dwell alone. We must keep above the World, and clear of the Spirit of it, and those many Trifles, Cares, Troubles that abound in it, with which but too many have visibly wounded and pierced their own Souls."[116]

One such care of the world that Penn now felt Quakers should avoid was concern for government. As early as 1673 he had written that it was not the Quakers' business to meddle with government.[117] In light of his own later political activities, we must consider that a fleeting judgment. But his advice to his children in his later years was to avoid either meddling with or speaking of government. Indeed, a quiet, retiring life that avoided not only government but involvement with the affairs of others was most to be desired. A wise man would keep in mind the proverb: "He lives happily, that lives hiddenly or privately." "It is a Treasure to them that have it: Study it, get it, keep it; too many miss it that might have it: The World knows not the Value of it. It doubles Man's Life by giving him twice the Time to himself that a large Acquaintance or much Business will allow him."[118]

Penn did not himself retire to private life, but he was

---

[115] Sermon on the death of Rebecca Travers (June 19, 1688), *The Concurrence and Unanimity of the People Called Quakers . . . Sermons or Declarations . . .* (London, 1711).

[116] "An Epistle of Farewell to the People of God Called Quakers . . ." (1699), *Works*, I, 237.

[117] "Wisdom Justified" (1673), *Works*, II, 487.

[118] "Advice to His Children" (1699), *Works*, I, 900, 907.

often tempted to sell Pennsylvania and do so, and in any case he had difficulty retaining his vision of the colony as even potentially a model Christian social order. But even in his few optimistic moments regarding the colony in his later years, Penn knew that "the eyes of many" were upon them not as a religious experiment but as "a Land of ease and Quiet."[119] He had himself accepted the colony's largely secular image of itself and sought primarily to preserve his political and financial rights as proprietor.

THE discrepancy between some of Penn's early political and social thought and his later emphases suggests that some of the inconsistencies we find in his religious thought were also possibly attributable to changes in his outlook. Penn, although for the most part an exponent of Quaker insights, was at times closer to Enlightenment assumptions about man than most of his fellow-Quakers. Given the fact that these assumptions made rapid progress in England during his lifetime and that Penn was less exclusively associated with the Quaker movement and more involved in "the world" in his later life, it has seemed natural to some scholars to assume that changes in his religious emphases in later life accompanied the changes in his political and social thought.

An analysis of Penn's later sermons and theological writings, however, reveals that there was little development in his religious thought. There was possibly some movement away from his theology of regeneration during the decade of his greatest worldly prominence and success from 1678 to 1688. But Penn's public religious activity and his writing on theological matters virtually came to a halt during those years, so that it is difficult to make even that judgment, except as it can be inferred from his rationalistic treatment of conscience in his many treatises on toleration in that decade. In any case, the evidence of his last period of religious activity during the 1690's indicates that the sober

[119] Letter, "To My Ould Friends" [Pa. Assembly] (June 29, 1710), PWP (L.S. in HSP).

thoughts and the pessimism of that time yielded a renewed appreciation of the need for inner renewal. In the message of man's Fall and need for regeneration Penn no doubt found an explanation for the world's intractability as well as solace for himself. It is true that parts of *Primitive Christianity Revived* (1696) displayed more prominently than any other of Penn's writings his understanding of man as a replica in small of the divine mind and his tendency to associate the inner light with reason. Moreover, *Fruits of Solitude* (1693) and its sequel in 1699 were made up of the kind of aphorisms we associate with certain thinkers of the Age of Reason. But the general tenor of the writings of the 1690's leaves a far different impression.

Even if Penn had wished to modify his theology of salvation by regeneration through grace and to de-emphasize some of the irrational parts of Christian doctrine, he would have been reluctant to do so in print. One of the manifestations of the Quaker desire to avoid persecution after 1688 was their increased emphasis on the orthodoxy of their beliefs. To ensure their acceptability under the terms of the toleration act, Quaker theologians stated their beliefs in creedal form on many occasions and tried to express those doctrines that the Anglicans considered unorthodox as inoffensively as possible. Penn was prominent in this activity. He joined in many creedal statements and stressed his orthodox Protestant beliefs in such treatises as *A Key Opening the Way* (1692), *A Reply to a Pretended Answer to a Key* (1695), and *A Testimony to the Truth of God* (1698). In these works such doctrines as the Trinity, the manhood of Christ, the relation of the supernatural light to man's natural abilities, the atoning work of Christ, and other controverted beliefs were stated more carefully than they had been in the 1650's and even later. Moreover, it was not uncommon in the 1690's for Quakers to edit previously published works and print them with deletions of offensive sections and with changed wording where that was desirable. For example, Penn's *The Christian Quaker*, which had been printed in 1673, was reprinted in 1699 with several changes and omissions. A Preface was added tracing the history of Protestantism in England in a manner that made clear the place of Quakerism within the movement. Moreover, the first three chapters of the first edition, which had discussed Penn's bitter controversy with Thomas Hicks, were omitted, and all later references to Hicks were changed to "Opponent."[120] Similarly motivated changes can be seen in the second edition of *A Testimony to the Truth of God*, which also appeared in 1699.

Penn's religious thought in his later life would not have reflected the liberals' optimistic assumptions about man and the world even if the exigencies of the toleration act had not been present. What he had actually learned about man and the world in the course of his life was not likely to provide him with an easy optimism. It was precisely because evil had proved such a formidable adversary in human affairs that Penn lost his belief in the imminence of the kingdom and in his role in bringing it into the world. Far from underestimating the power of evil in the world, Penn counselled withdrawal in his later years precisely because the battle for the world had proven too difficult and dangerous. One finds in the treatises of the 1690's a renewed emphasis on the fact that the Quakers had the lowest view of man among Christians, on the need for judgment and rebirth in radical dependence on God, and on the distinction between the light or Spirit and the natural faculties. Penn's concern in *Rise and Progress* with the problem of declension in the Quaker ranks was typical. The sons and daughters of the early Quaker saints were failing to experience rebirth as they approached adulthood. Penn urged on them the necessity of the kind of experience he had undergone.[121] As he preached to the Grace Street Meeting in 1694, *all* men

[120] Joseph Smith, *A Descriptive Catalogue of Friends' Books . . .* (London, 1867), inaccurately lists the 1699 edition as simply a reprint with, in some copies, a new postscript.

[121] (1694), *Works*, I, 889-890.

transgress against God and fall into a state of misery. With their minds clouded by sin and a barrier between them and the life and power of God, they can hope solely "in Christ." Christ alone can bring man out of his impotent and miserable state through a regeneration of repentance, judgment, and power. Only Jesus, "the Great Mediator of the New Covenant, the Author and Finisher of our Faith," stands between every born sinner and condemnation. Whatever part of the image of God might remain in a fallen man apart from regeneration—whether an offspring of a Quaker saint or a benighted Indian warrior—he must be reborn in the power of Christ, and his life will be largely a matter of struggle with sin.[122]

There is reflected in Penn's body of writings an extraordinary number of the intellectual and religious developments that occurred in England between the days of the Puritan Commonwealth and the reign of Queen Anne. Penn's thought is more a window on the times than that of other Quaker writers both because of the breadth of his concerns, activities, and acquaintances, and because he was more often in sympathy with the liberal thought of the times than other Quakers were. Moreover, his mind absorbed and made occasional use of ideas that did not harmonize with his central convictions. As the emphases of his later works reveal, however, those convictions were religious convictions stemming from his experience of regeneration in Christ. Although the last years of his life, from 1712 to 1718, were spent in serene contentment, that is attributable not to an optimistic faith in man but to the fact that the battle-scarred and weary warrior of the Lord finally went out of his mind.[123]

[122] Sermon, "Salvation from Sin by Christ Alone" (Aug. 12, 1694), *Sermons or Declarations, Made by Some of the Ancient Preachers amongst the People Called Quakers* . . . (Phila., 1768), 58-71.

[123] Penn suffered two strokes in 1712 at the age of 68; a third early in 1713 left him with a defective memory and only the occasional ability to converse intelligibly.

FOUR

THE DEVELOPED RELIGION
OF THE SPIRIT

THE INNER LIGHT: AGENT OF REGENERATION

THE term "light" has been used in many ways in theological discourse, but it is primarily associated with the function of revelation. As light enables the eye to see what it cannot perceive in darkness, the light of revelation gives man knowledge that the darkened state of his mind prevented him from possessing. Although the Quakers' inner light did bring the ability to "see" divine truths, the Friends were as concerned about religious power as they were about knowledge. Not all Quakers would agree with Isaac Penington that there were no doctrinal differences between Quakers and other Christians, but they would agree that the Friends came forward bearing a new sense of God's power to regenerate individuals and the world.[1] The inner light was the agent that performed all the functions connected with the process of regeneration and was thus much more than a noetic principle. Apart from the clear understanding that the light was a supernatural power, the earliest Quakers understood little about the operation of the light within the human mind. Like many of the spiritualists, they talked and wrote much about a spiritual "sense," but this was simply a manner of speaking that enabled them to express the idea of the immediacy and the certainty of the confrontation with the divine presence. Both the revelatory and the gracious functions of the light were expressed by the idea that the inner light brought one into what in the twentieth century is called an "existential confrontation" with the divine

---

[1] See Creasey, "Early Quaker Christology," 249-251.

person Jesus Christ. The earliest Friends were not mystics, and they referred to the light as an impersonal principle, but they also called it "Christ within" or said that it led one to Christ within or even to God. In Fox's thought the primary function of the light was to bring a strong sense of the presence of Christ.[2] The light was a metaphor for this encounter between the divine and the human.

Quaker writers of the Restoration, who had had time to reflect on the inner light and were well aware of their contemporaries' reaction against the "enthusiasm" of the Interregnum, wrote about it more systematically than Fox, Burrough, Nayler, and their cohorts had done. The fact that the light was a source of knowledge as well as power, was found in all men, and provided a more direct access to divine truths than the route from the senses to the faculties (and could express itself primarily in terms of the moral law) gave it obvious similarities of function and form to the noetic principles of those philosophers and theologians for whom "what is most true" came increasingly to mean "what can be clearly and distinctly conceived; what is innate or inscribed upon the minds of all men in common; what is inwardly approved by the moral sense; what is consonant with nature and reason."[3] Robert Barclay's thought best represents this tendency to focus on the noetic or epistemological function of the inner light and to use philosophical concepts to express the spiritual-corporeal dualism present in Quakerism. When he referred to the light as a spiritual sense, he was not loosely drawing on an analogy but saying that the inner light was a new divine faculty within the human psyche. To avoid confusion between Quaker and "enthusiastic" claims, it was necessary for him to say that not "the proper essence and nature of God" but "a spiritual, heavenly, and invisible principle" was within man. The light or principle was a *"vehiculum Dei"* or "spiritual substance"

[2] See T. Canby Jones, "George Fox," 56-58, 153-180.
[3] Willey, *Seventeenth-Century Background*, 78.

that gave man as clear and certain a grasp of divine truths as he had of any natural knowledge. There are echoes of John Smith, the Cambridge Platonist, in Barclay's statement that "this divine revelation and inward illumination, is that which is evident and clear of itself, forcing, by its own evidence and clearness, the well-disposed understanding to assent, irresistibly moving the same thereunto, even as the common principles of natural truths do move and incline the mind to a natural assent; as, that the whole is greater than its part; that two contradictories can neither be both true, nor both false."[4]

It will be essential to follow the intellectual paths pursued by the Quaker theologians of the Restoration as they tried to work with the spiritual-corporeal dualism bequeathed to them, but it is equally important to recognize that the more systematic Quaker thinkers continued to write about the light primarily as an agent of regeneration and a mediator of the confrontation with the divine within man. For Samuel Fisher the light brought the power and the grace of God "by a supernatural, and spiritual, inward immediate Revelation . . . by God himself . . ." or by leading one to Christ. God through the light not only provides knowledge but does all he can to save man without forcing him to respond. The difference between "outward" or subject-object knowing and having the light is like that between reading a book and having an inner tutor working powerfully and effectually.[5] For Barclay as for the earliest Quakers, the difference between Protestants and Catholics, on the one hand, and Quakers on the other, was that the former insist on exerting their own wills rather than relying wholly on the power of the Spirit working through the inner light. Salvation lies not in literal but in "experimental" knowledge of Christ. God through the light "invites, calls, exhorts, and strives" with man, "draws, invites, and inclines" to God,

---

[4] *Apology*, 28-29, 69, 136, 138.
[5] *Rusticus*, 32, 37, 601, 602, 627, 685.

and "moves, blows, and stirs" the soul by confronting man in a new and powerful way and raising and quickening him.[6] Quakerism continued to distinguish itself from its rivals by virtue of its reliance on the power of the Holy Spirit because it remained convinced that man's blindness could be cured only as his radical sinfulness was eradicated.

WILLIAM PENN accepted Barclay's idea of a "spiritual substance," but the concept was not prominent in this thought, and we may suspect that the higher reaches of the philosophical speculations of Barclay and Keith escaped his intellectual grasp. Penn was, however, at least as interested as Barclay in relating the inner light to some of the universal epistemological principles or faculties being expounded in the latter half of the seventeenth century by men who found the Catholics' ecclesiastical authority, the Protestants' Scripture, and the enthusiasts' "Spirit" inadequate foundations for religious knowledge. The inner light, which provided an "infallible Demonstration" of divine truth, was at times indistinguishable in his mind from the Platonic and Stoic principles of a divine Reason permeating the cosmos and linking human minds to God.[7] Like Barclay he made certain that the Quakers' loose talk of God or Christ within them could not be construed as a claim to be "godded," so that all their thoughts and impulses were those of God. Penn distinguished between God himself or the "Fulness of God" and the "Measure" or "Degree" of divine being that was in man in the form of the light. He was unwilling to dispense with the idea that the light within is God because of its Scriptural foundation, but he held that it is more proper to speak of the light as "of" or "from" God and to emphasize that God "measures himself forth, in his inward Dis-

---

[6] *Apology*, 278, 323, 131, 132, 144, 178.

[7] "Sandy Foundation" (1668), *Works*, I, 248. See especially *A Defence of the Duke of Buckingham's Book of Religion and Worship, from the Exceptions of a Nameless Author* (1685).

coveries, according to man's Capacity."[8] It is no more proper to "locate" the omnipotent God in a man in whom the divine light shines than it is to say that the sun is in a house in which it is shining.[9]

Despite this caution Penn understood the inner light primarily as the Holy Spirit's means of bringing man into an encounter with the divine presence and power. The power of the light was the means of overcoming the twin evils of the age: the placid profession of a lifeless, legalistic, formal Christianity and the crisis of authority caused by the proliferation of sects ostensibly based on Scriptural principles. It was first of all the means to the kind of religious experience that "the Carnal, Fleshly, and Historical Christian of the Outward Courts, and Suburbs of Religion" lacked. According to Penn's diagnosis, dissenters as well as Anglicans had begun to settle for formal creedal profession combined with abstention from immoralities as an adequate expression of the regenerate life. "O, how many profess God and Christ, according to the Historical Knowledge of both, but never come to the Mystical and Experimental Knowledge of them."[10]

The second problem of the age, according to Penn, was that the Protestant solution to the problem of religious authority had led to an impasse. As Catholics had predicted, the attempt to base both beliefs and actions solely on Scripture without the formal guidance of the church had led to a myriad of conflicting assertions about the major doctrines of the faith and about church polity. Scripture, according to Penn, had yielded so many contradictory answers to important questions that exegetes had been able to find there whatever they wished to discover. They seemed to devote

[8] "Key" (1692), Works, ii, 780; "Brief Answer" (1678), Works, ii, 672; "Christianity a New Nickname" (1672), Works, ii, 294-297; "Counterfeit Christian" (1674), Works, ii, 580.

[9] "Key" (1692), Works, ii, 780.

[10] Letter, "To Dr. Hasbert" (Nov. 1672), Works, i, 156, 155.

most of their time to writing tracts to prove that Scripture contained only the answers which they had found.[11]

> That the Scriptures are Unintelligible without it [i.e., the inner light] is easily prov'd from the Variety of Judgments that are in the World about most of the Fundamental Doctrines contained therein; as about God's Essence and Similitude, Christ and the Spirit, their Divinity, Predestination, Original Sin, Free-Will, Redemption, Satisfaction, Justification, Faith and Works. In short, the whole End of Christ's coming, Living, Dying, are strongly controverted. Now were the Scriptures so clearly capable to determine in these Matters, the Differences would quickly end; but since the utmost Ability they of themselves can give, is not enough to render those Things obvious, that are now doubtful and disputable; There is a Necessity of Man's Recourse to some other Thing, which is able to discover the Mind and Intention of the Holy Pen-Men.[12]

The solution to both problems lay in gaining a renewed internal or experiential acquaintance with spiritual realities—a knowledge that would quicken one's perceptions and give certainty and power. Such knowledge came "by the Light and Spirit by an Inward Revelation and Operation."[13] In Penn's view a renewed belief in and dependence on the Holy Spirit was the greatest religious need of the day. Whether God's "Holy and Unerring Spirit" was to be recognized as both the proper guide for the Christian life and the proper rule of faith and judge of controversy was "the main Hinge on which all turns." It deserved man's most serious consideration much more than all other subjects in

---

[11] "General Rule" (1673), *Works*, I, 595-596, 605.

[12] "Reason Against Railing" (1673), *Works*, II, 508. See also "Invalidity" (1673), *Works*, II, 337-338.

[13] Letter, "To Dr. Hasbert" (Nov. 1672), *Works*, I, 155.

dispute among religious men.[14] The Spirit could take the legalistic, "notional" Christian and prod beneath his surface piety and lead him to a deeper self-examination, thereby bringing the fresh and living touches of faith and saintly living. For the "sectary" who was scanning the Scriptures to find the will of God or some clue to right doctrine and polity, the Spirit was a true guide, bringing the sure and certain experience of truth known in the depths of one's being. What is spoken by the immediate life and power of the Spirit is of more authority, force, and efficacy than the bare reading of Scripture, "as a Letter cannot give that Impression which we might justly suppose the Lively Presence, Mind and Voice of the Person that writ it might."[15]

The significance of the Spirit or light was that it led to a personal confrontation with Christ. The more than noetic, or existential, dimension was less consistently present in Penn's understanding of the light than it was in Fox's thought, but it was, nevertheless, prominent. The remedy for a powerless "historical" faith and for the uncertainties of the Seeker was a recovery of the sense of the presence of Christ as a living power in one's life. Widespread unwillingness to open oneself to a personal confrontation with "Christ within" was responsible for the presumption and legalism, on the one hand, and the despair and uncertainty, on the other, that were so prevalent.[16] Penn believed the fundamental tenet of Quakerism that the light brought Christ to all men, but he also believed that only those who had been confronted by Christ in a special way, and who had responded favorably, had a "divine and kindred Membership" in Christ or had come into "Union" with him.[17] Such men knew that the ultimate authority in religion was

[14] "Spirit of Truth" (1672), *Works*, II, 96.

[15] "A Brief Answer to a False and Foolish Libel, Called 'The Quakers Opinions'" (1678), *Works*, II, 674.

[16] "Travels in Holland and Germany" (1677), *Works*, I, 103-104.

[17] "A Reply to a Pretended Answer, by a Nameless Author, to William Penn's 'Key' . . ." (1695), *Works*, II, 823-824.

not Scripture but Christ himself. They knew that the only power that can shake a man out of his self-righteous "profession" and drive home to him the truths of God was the living, personal power of Christ, not "mere words," which are in themselves lifeless.[18] Christ, the immediate speaker to his church, must be known in one's heart. Without that immediate presence of Christ as the light, guide, king, lawgiver, bishop, and heavenly shepherd, one can neither know nor do anything of spiritual significance.[19] As God is in Christ, according to the gospel of John, so Christ is in men by his Spirit and light, dwelling in the hearts of the regenerate to comfort and console them, and in the wicked to reprove, condemn, enlighten, and instruct them.[20]

The inner light, then, was the agent of the whole process of regeneration—a loosely used metaphor to cover the many operations of the grace of God. In Penn's writings the term "light" could refer to any aspect of God's relationship with man and all of God's revelations and actions in regenerating man. The light gives one knowledge of God, self, and duty, sorrow for one's sins, the power to forsake sins, perseverance, and the justified state of forgiveness.[21]

At other times Penn used the light to refer more specifically to certain parts of the regeneration process. "We never limited all Divine Inspirations and Operations to the Light, meerly as it is Light. . . . We ever meant a Principle in Man, that is not of Man, that is variously denominated by its various Operations: Light, from Discerning and Distinction: Spirit, from Life and Power: Word, as it speaks forth God's Mind to Man: Truth, in the Inward Parts, as it deals truly with Man, and would redeem him from lying

---

[18] "Spirit of Truth" (1672), *Works*, II, 146; "Christianity a New Nickname" (1672), *Works*, II, 238.

[19] "To All Those Professors" (1677), *Works*, I, 214-215.

[20] "Tender Visitation" (1677), *Works*, I, 219-220; "Christianity a New Nickname" (1672), *Works*, II, 282.

[21] "Rise and Progress" (1694), *Works*, I, 892; "Christian Quaker" (1673), *Works*, I, 524-529.

Vanities: And Grace, as it is God's Gift and not Man's Understanding, or Man's Merit."[22] In this typical quotation the light is associated with "Discerning and Distinction" and is explicitly separated from the principle that provides the knowledge or facts of revelation. The "Light" brings the ability to discern—presumably by an intuitive process giving a feeling of inward certitude—the voice of God in one's thoughts and readings and the hand of God in his experiences. The light conceived in this way is, then, the perfect aid for the man who is confused by various competing interpretations of Scripture and for the lifeless legalistic Christian.

To express this function of the light, Penn, with most Quaker theologians, likened the light to a spiritual sense or a set of spiritual senses. Answering an opponent who had said that man knows by "reasoning" but not by "sense or conscience," Penn wrote, "And very sorry I am for this Opposer, that he allows Man no Spiritual Senses, or that which answers to our Outward Senses; and if he does, surely they are to See, Hear, Smell, Taste and Feel something else than himself."[23] Penn spoke of a spiritual sense much less commonly than most early Quaker thinkers. He believed, with Richard Baxter and many Restoration nonconformists and Anglicans, that the Spirit operated on man's rational faculty in regeneration. Penn's conception of man's reason was broad and vague. It did not necessarily preclude the connotation of immediacy attached to the idea of a spiritual sense, but Penn feared the label "enthusiast" and intended the reason to be the control-point of the experience. Nevertheless, he did speak of a spiritual sense commonly enough. It was "a kind of sagacity" or instinct by which one could discern whether what another said was true or "of the Spirit" or whether one's own exegesis and actions were truly Spirit-directed.[24] Elsewhere "sense" re-

[22] "Reply to a Pretended Answer" (1695), *Works*, ii, 819.
[23] *Ibid.*, 819.
[24] "General Rule" (1673), *Works*, i, 605.

ferred to a realization of the true state of one's sinful soul. "The Divine Sense in the Soul is begotten by the Lord: 'Tis his Life and Spirit, his holy Breath and Power, that quickneth the Soul, and maketh it sensible of its own State. . . ." Or the "blessed Sense" or "Holy Sense" brought "the inexpressible delights and ravishments of Soul" that come from communion with Christ or the gracious powers arising from this relationship: the ability to resist temptations, and urges to humility, obedience, love, and patience.[25]

What unites these varying uses of the idea of a spiritual sense is their function in describing a relationship between knower and known that transcends the objective, noetic frame of reference. By using the word "sense" to refer to the revelatory process, Penn stressed the immediacy, the certainty, and the affective nature of the experience and contrasted it with the kind of objective knowing that involves a split between subject and object. He was saying that the light is more than an epistemological principle that brings knowledge not provided elsewhere; it is the conveyor of an experience of existential confrontation.

THE DIVINE AND THE HUMAN IN QUAKERISM

The Quakers' understanding of conversion as a long process involving a period of unmitigated judgment and then a gradual growth of sanctification leading to perfection was developed in the Restoration period by the addition of a distinctive doctrine of justification and by refinements in the Friends' ambiguous position on grace and free will. Both these developments made more evident their divergence from the spiritualists' divine-human dualism. At the same time, the dualistic or quietistic approach to the relations between man and God continued to influence the thought of most Quakers. One manifestation of this was their con-

---

[25] "Tender Counsel" (1677), *Works*, I, 200, 198; Letter to Ancient Friends F. S. *et al.* [1669], ACMC, II, 128-129. Printed in Preface to 1669 edition of *No Cross*.

tinued emphasis on the radical depravity of man and the need for the utter annihilation of the human so that it might be replaced with the divine. The Quakers thought that they differed from all other Christians because they "more fully disclaim their own [Righteousness,] as Dung and filthy Rags, and establish Christ's Righteousness alone. . . ." and ascribe every man's salvation solely "to God alone, and his meer Mercy and free Grace. . . ."[26] Barclay said that fallen man can know or do nothing right and is wholly helpless and doomed to continued fallenness unless rescued by divine power. Any good tendencies in man come from the divine seed within him, not from anything human.[27] Socinians, Pelagians, Semi-Pelagians, Papists, and most Protestants were all portrayed as having an insufficiently pessimistic understanding of fallen man's plight. Similarly, when referring to the regenerated man, the Quaker theologians said that the cause of man's salvation was not any works of his own nor even the works of Christ done at Jerusalem, but the deeds done by Christ within, who assumed control of the human personality at conversion.[28]

At the same time, the Quakers' understanding of conversion as a long process involving a confrontation between the divine and human beings, their tendency to use the language of voluntarism and "willing adherence" rather than constraint, and their denial of Calvinism led to a significant modification of this dualism. First, the tendency of the earliest Quaker writers to combine their dualistic language with synergistic metaphors and an emphasis on Biblical passages stressing human initiative led to a more clear-cut synergism in all of the Restoration writers, and, on the issue of prevenient grace, to a divergence among them seen most clearly in a comparison of Fisher and Barclay. Both men clearly denied the Calvinist position on original sin, election, limited atonement, and grace as an irresistible coactive power, but Fisher placed his emphasis on human

[26] Fisher, *Rusticus*, 32, 36. [27] *Apology*, 15, 101.
[28] *Rusticus*, 138; *Apology*, 213-214.

ability to cooperate through man's initiative with God's ever-present grace, whereas Barclay clearly affirmed prevenient grace and put the Quaker position as close to Calvinism as possible without denying human cooperation after the initial grace. Fisher made fleeting reference to the Quaker position that the light becomes an active "life" during special periods of visitation when it provides the power to respond that is normally absent, but more common was his insistence that God's grace is universally and more or less constantly available to men. Citing the many Scriptural passages advising men to choose life and all the Scriptural "compellations, complaints, consolations, wishings, adjurations, condemnations, threatenings, and entreaties," he took the position that such language must mean that God through his grace has set two ways before men and invited them to stir themselves and work out their own salvation.[29] God says, in effect, to man: "Wherefore why, will ye die, turn, turn your selves and live, and work out your own salvation with fear and trembling, for I have done my part, a friends part, towards you, I have wrought in you both to will and to do, of my free grace, of my good pleasure, it wants but your putting that into act, which I of my free grace have put into your power, and your willing and doing accordingly, and your getting up, and trading with your Talent. . . ."[30]

Fisher's clearest analogy for the situation of fallen man was that of starving men who have been given enough help to set themselves up and feed themselves. Some men help themselves to the food made available; others do not.[31] To the charge that this was a Pelagian, Arminian, Socinian, and Papist position, Fisher could only reply that it was Scriptural doctrine and was the only belief that preserved God from injustice and hypocrisy. To Richard Baxter's accusation that this was an insufficient account of God's grace, Fisher said that Baxter wanted to be compelled to be good,

[29] *Rusticus*, 625-632, 685-686.   [30] *Ibid.*, 632.
[31] *Ibid.*, 659.

and "he may fret himself till he fry in the Fire of his own peevish Spirit, before he shall find such a Grace from God to his Salvation, while himself lives in the neglect of that he has. . . ."[32] To the orthodox objection that his doctrine gave the glory of salvation to man's will rather than to God, Fisher replied that he gave the main glory to the universal grace of God, "and though secondarily and immediately the case be left by the Lord to depend on mans choice, as it was in the first Adam (though I know such as are perfectly restored by the second, stand a little surer than he did, I say, when perfected in his Life) yet if man chuse Life and live, when Life and Death are set before him (as they are) God is no more robb'd of the Glory of his goodness, then he would have been by Adams standing, if he had stood, when God set him *in aequilibrio*, to stand or fall. . . ."[33] Fisher's position left the initiative with man both in the beginning and throughout the regeneration process.

Markedly different on this point was the doctrine of Barclay, who presented the Quaker position as one mediating between the Calvinist's ignorance of the seed in the heart and their view of grace as an irresistible power, on the one hand, and the Catholic, Arminian, Socinian, Pelagian, and Semi-Pelagian flattery of man on the other. According to Barclay, Augustinians, Lutherans, and Calvinists reacted too strongly to Pelagianism and Semi-Pelagianism and made God the author of sin, made him delight in sin, rendered the grace of Christ ineffectual, and made the preaching of the gospel a mockery and illusion. The Semi-Pelagian position recently revived by the Remonstrants, which was that men will be saved if they begin by doing what they can (*facienti quod in se est*), relied too much on human will.[34] The proper position was that Christ tasted death for every man and gives to him a time of visitation in which he has a measure of grace or the Spirit, through which God invites, calls, exhorts, and strives with him, and, if he does not resist,

---

[32] *Ibid.*, 695.   [33] *Ibid.*, 658-659.
[34] *Apology*, 113-129, 178.

works his salvation. The doctrine, "wholly excludes the natural man from having any place or portion in his own salvation, by any acting, moving, or working of his own, until he be first quickened, raised up, and activated by God's Spirit."[35]

Barclay emphasized that man is dependent on the powerful grace given at the times of visitation and that he cannot move or stir the light whenever he pleases, and he tended to emphasize the initiative of God's grace in the cooperative interaction between God and man that follows the initial visitation. "He that resists its striving, is the cause of his own condemnation; he that resists it not, it becomes his salvation; so that in him that is saved, the working is of the grace, and not of the man; and it is a passiveness rather than an act; though afterwards, as man is wrought upon, there is a will raised in him, by which he comes to be a co-worker with the grace. . . ."[36] The Quaker position as portrayed by Barclay, and its relation to that of other Christians, came through most clearly in the illustration in which he referred to fallen man as in a dark pit with stupefied senses, hardly aware of his plight. Semi-Pelagians and Socinians said that the man in the pit finds someone outside and engages him to rescue him. Arminians and "Jesuits" said that a deliverer comes on his own, puts down a ladder, and waits for the man to climb it. Quakers said that a deliverer comes at certain times and informs the man in the pit of his misery and hazard, "forces [him] to a certain sense of [his] misery," and gives him a pull to lift him out. If he does not resist, he will be saved.[37]

[35] Ibid., 132.   [36] Ibid., 146.

[37] Ibid., 147. Barclay also allowed that special individuals, such as Mary and Paul, were given a special kind of irresistible grace (148). On Barclay's general position, it is interesting that one S. P. (possibly Simon Patrick), in A Brief Account of the New Sect of Latitude-Men . . . (1662), described their position on this doctrine in a way that made them very similar to Barclay: they are between Calvinists and the Remonstrants, allow that some men are absolutely and irresistibly elected, but say that most have free will and are lost only if

Fisher and Barclay presented developed versions of the dichotomous tendency seen from the beginning of Quakerism because of its strange attempt to combine the spiritualists' dualism of the divine and human and an "Arminian" reaction to Calvinism. Possibly Quakers coming from the General Baptist tradition, as Fisher himself had, found his stance congenial, whereas those more imbued with the spiritualist position or Calvinist orthodoxy preferred Barclay's position. Because of the Quaker leaders' regard for Barclay's *Apology*, his position should possibly be considered the more normative of the two. The differences between them should not be overstressed, however, since both represented clear modifications of the orthodox Protestant position presented in the Synod of Dort and the Westminster Confession.

Although the covenant theologians of the puritan tradition before 1640 and then those who agreed with Richard Baxter's approach to regeneration did not oppose Calvinism as represented by Dort and Westminster, this should not blind students of the period to the obvious similarity between the Quakers' approach to the human-divine interaction and that of the preparationists and the Baxterites. Both wished to view regeneration as a long process involving God's attempt to coax and persuade man into a willing acceptance of the offer of grace. The Quaker emphasis on a period of unmitigated judgment did not significantly modify their "voluntaristic" and "personalistic" or anthropomorphic description of regeneration. It is noteworthy that this aspect of their thought placed them closer to Baxter than to the antinomians he so forcefully opposed and who represented the spiritualist tradition. And the fact that the Quakers' synergistic position was part of an open attack on Calvinism made them obvious allies on this point of the

---

they willfully refuse to cooperate with grace. See John Tulloch, *Rational Theology and Christian Philosophy in England in the Seventeenth Century* (2 vols., Edinburgh, 1872), II, 34-35.

many Anglicans of the Restoration who were so emphatic about their opposition to the theology of Dort and Westminster.

Another prominent aspect of the Friends' understanding of regeneration gave them affinities to the Baxterites as well as to certain schools of thought within Anglicanism and to the General Baptists, all of whom bore the imprint of "Arminianism" and "Socinianism." These two labels were applied rather loosely in the latter part of the seventeenth century, but in general they referred to, among other things, a reaction against Calvinist orthodox theology, a dependence on strictly Scriptural language in doctrine, confidence in the rationality of Christian doctrines, a distinction between essential and nonessential doctrines, and an attempt to unite Christians through a minimalist approach to doctrine.[38] One of the doctrines of Calvinist orthodoxy that was modified in the thought of the Falkland Circle, the Cambridge Platonists, the latitudinarians, some of the General Baptists, and the Unitarians John Biddle, Henry Hedworth, and Thomas Firmin, as well as Baxterites, was the doctrine of justification or "imputed righteousness." Despite their differences, these groups all tended to equate justification and sanctification because of their agreement with the conception of Christianity expressed in the title of Edward Fowler's work, *The Design of Christianity, or, a plain demonstration and improvement of this proposition, That the enduing men with inward, real righteousness, or true holiness, was the ultimate end of our Saviour's coming into the world, and is the great intendment of the blessed Gospel* (1671). From the beginning of their movement, Friends

[38] For excellent descriptions of Arminianism and Socinianism, respectively, as they were known in England, see Tulloch, *Rational Theology*, I, chap. I, and Herbert J. McLachlan, *Socinianism in Seventeenth Century England* (London, 1951), 9-24. "Arminianism" was also used in England before 1640 to refer to the high Anglican or ceremonialist school of Laud, and in this use it had connotations somewhat different from those I have given it.

had tended to argue that men "can be no further justified then in such measure as [they] are sanctified before God. . . ." but the doctrine was not well developed. After 1660 some rather involved theology centered on this issue.

As in the case of the Quaker position on free will and grace, so here too Barclay placed the Quakers between Calvinism and Catholicism. The papist position, said Barclay, is that when one participates in the church's ceremonies, the church and the pope reward one's human initiative by applying the merits of Christ that are controlled by them. The Protestants rightly rejected this doctrine, but their substitution of the doctrine of justification by faith alone, without regard for continuing wickedness, was no better. The error of both was that they failed to make the inner renewal by grace the essence of justification.[39] Barclay was stating a truth recognizable in all Quaker works, namely, that the Christ with whom one comes into union at regeneration performs within man the good works that justify him before God.[40] Coupled with this was usually the assertion that men are not justified before God because of the works done by Christ as a man at Jerusalem. But whereas the earliest Quaker writers were uncertain how to relate the historical Christ to the inward Christ who justified them, and thus tended to speak of him as simply fulfilling the law and types of the Old Testament and providing an example, Barclay developed what he called a doctrine of twofold justification.[41] Christ's death on the cross qualified the wrath of God and made possible the forgiveness of past sins, and Christ's presence and activity within makes man currently acceptable before God. "This last follows the first in order, and is a consequence of it, proceeding from it, as an effect from its cause: so as none could have enjoyed the last, without the first had been, such being the will of God; so also can none now partake of the first, but as he witnesseth the

[39] *Apology*, 190-195.   [40] See Fisher, *Rusticus*, 155.
[41] On the earlier position, see Fisher, *Rusticus*, 154.

last. Wherefore as to us, they are both causes of our justification: the first the procuring efficient, the other the formal cause."[42] Barclay made clear the priority of the "formal" cause, which he termed "the immediate, nearest"
reason for God's acceptance of man.[43]

Barclay claimed the support of Richard Baxter's *Aphorisms of Justification* for the position that the sanctification
of man by Christ within is the cause of justification.[44] He
cited Baxter as a supporter of the rest of his doctrine of
justification as well. Because the Quakers approached conversion as a long process, and because of their fear of producing hypocrites, they agreed with Baxter in his battle
against the antinomians over the existence of conditions for
justification. "Faith and repentance, and the other conditions called for throughout the gospel" are "a qualification
on our part necessary to be performed" before one can be
reconciled to God. "And if we are already perfectly reconciled and justified before these conditions are performed,
(which conditions are of that nature that they cannot be
performed at one time, but are to be done all one's lifetime)
then can they not be said to be absolutely needful. . . ."[45]
Whereas Barclay quoted Baxter in support of his position,
the fact that on this point both men were also in accord
with a wider circle is seen in the fact that George Whitehead cited the latitudinarian Edward Stillingfleet in support
of precisely the same conditional approach to justification.[46]
Fisher tended toward the view that the conditions or

[42] *Apology*, 196.   [43] *Ibid.*, 213.

[44] *Ibid.*, 218. We can also find the basic elements of the doctrine
of a twofold justification in Baxter. See Frederick J. Powicke, *A Life
of the Reverend Richard Baxter: 1615-1691* (London, 1924), 240;
Orme, *Baxter*, II, 46-49.

[45] Barclay, *Apology*, 200-201.

[46] "Some Passages out of Edward Stillingfleet's 'Discourse of the
Sufferings of Christ'; which are evidently Contradictory to John
Owen, and Tho. Danson," in *The Divinity of Christ, and Unity of the
Three that bear Record in Heaven* (London, 1669), 86-87.

"works" within men that are necessary for justification, although they are done by Christ, are in a certain sense "ours" or "our own" because we do them with the power he gives us.[47] Barclay, always more wary of flattery, said that they were "works of grace" rather than works of the law since they were done by Christ as the immediate author and worker of them and that they were a *sine qua non* rather than a cause, in the proper sense, of justification. Nevertheless, like Baxter, he insisted that they were a necessary part of justification and were even, in a qualified sense, meritorious, because God "cannot but accept and reward them." Elsewhere Barclay said that the works have "this merit of congruity or reward."[48]

In the light of these developments in the direction of liberal Anglican and modified puritan positions on justification, it is not surprising to find that the Friends also continued to speak of perfection, but in somewhat more modulated tones than previously. Fisher based his perfectionistic statements strictly on Scriptural grounds and said that perfection was capable of addition.[49] Barclay referred to perfection as a state that admits of daily growth and from which one may fall if he drops his guard. He also wrote of a more advanced state but refused to elaborate on it because he had not attained it himself.[50] Whitehead equated the Quaker position with the latitudinarian insistence that it is possible for man in this world to live soberly, righteously, and godly, do as he would be done by, and maintain kindness and good will toward all men.[51]

THE DIVINE AND THE HUMAN IN PENN'S THOUGHT

In the course of a long debate with Penn, Baxter pinpointed the self-contradictory nature of the Quakers' attempt to combine the idea of man's total passivity in regeneration

[47] *Rusticus*, 137-138.
[49] *Rusticus*, 143-145.
[51] *Divinity of Christ*, 91-92.

[48] *Apology*, 199, 227.
[50] *Apology*, 230-231.

with a belief in the universal availability of the light to all who would use it:

> W. Pen told me yt they hold yt there is not ground of our Justification but our being passive under Gods opera-tion. And yet they hold yt we all yt have ye Spirit and sufficient Light, as bad as they desaine us (and oft cry out Take thy condemnation with thee for not obeying yt Light and Spirit) But if passivity be all yts necessary in us on our pt to ye Justification, no Act of will, thought or deed was necessary, and so ye want of none was no sin, and Passivity is not voluntary or at our choice but unavoidable and thenn all ye difference cometh only from God who operatith on some and not on others. These things I thinke canot be reconciled.[52]

The account of the debate preserved in Dr. Williams' Library, London, is in Baxter's handwriting, and it is there-fore not surprising that it includes no adequate reply by Penn to this charge. But it is not likely that even an account in the hand of Penn would provide a satisfactory explana-tion, since we find in Penn's published works a strong emphasis both on man's helpless fallenness and bondage and on the constant availability of the light to those who will exert themselves to make use of it. The Quakers' doctrine of the inner light and their belief that there is "that of God in every man" have caused both friends and opponents from the seventeenth century until today to argue that the Quakers rescued man from the ignominious position as-signed him by the puritans and that their optimism about man was especially evident in the thought of the enlight-ened Founding Father. The evidence leaves us with a more ambiguous picture than this view implies.

Strikingly prominent in Penn's thought was the belief

[52] Penn-Baxter Debate (Oct. 5, 1675), ACMC, xv, 9 (holograph in Dr. Williams' Library, London).

that there is a great chasm between the infinite Lord of being and the "poor Worms" who are his creatures. Penn's attitude toward man is evident in his advice to his children:

> Be Humble: It becomes a Creature, a depending and borrowed Being, that lives not of it self, but breaths in another's air, with another's Breath, and is accountable for every Moment of Time, and can call nothing its own, but is absolutely a Tenant at Will of the great Lord of Heaven and Earth. And of this excellent Quality you cannot be wanting, if you dwell in the Holy Fear of the Omnipresent and All-seeing God; For that will shew you your Vileness and his Excellency; your Meanness, and his Majesty; and withal, the Sense of his Love to such poor Worms. . . .[53]

When opponents accused Quakers of exalting or revering man because of their doctrine of the inner light, Penn hotly countered that no people or testimony since the world began had had a lower view of man.[54] Anglicans and dissenters believed that man had been created with a rational faculty that enabled him both to induce truths about God and the world from observation and to possess innate knowledge of the natural moral law. Penn, with all Quakers, believed that neither natural nor fallen man could have any knowledge of spiritual realities without a special influx of divine light. Man had been endowed with a reasonable soul, faculties of intelligence, and a body fitted with sense organs. "But still the Light, with which this Soul is lighted, in reference to God and Things appertaining to its Eternal Well-being, belongs not to Man, as Man."[55] "Blessed be God,"

[53] "The Advice of William Penn to his Children" (1699), *Works*, I, 902.
[54] "The New Athenians No Noble Bereans: Being an Answer to the Athenian Mercury of the 7th Instant, in Behalf of the People Called Quakers" (1692), *Works*, II, 804.
[55] "The Christian Quaker" (1673), *Works*, I, 582.

said Penn referring to this belief, "that hath made us sensible of our own Weakness, Emptiness, and Poverty."[56]

Penn believed that fallen man is not simply without spiritual knowledge; he is in radical and continual opposition to God. The natural or unregenerate man hates God and his light and is so far from having even one good thought that he is unwilling and unable to reprove evil ones.[57] Man's will is God's enemy; it must be eradicated and replaced by a divine will.[58] Penn's emphasis on the control of man's faculties by sin was so strong that he commonly held that the natural man had to be eradicated and replaced by a wholly new man rather than simply freed from sin's control. What was needed was not renewal or transformation but the complete death of the old or fallen self. A man had to die to his own will, inclinations, imaginations, and conceits. His own worship and righteousness and even contrition had to become as odious to him as his sin and unrighteousness.[59]

This belief in the necessity of an utter rupture between the old life and the new led Penn to an appreciation of the peculiarly intense Quaker stress on unmitigated periods of judgment and condemnation. The Quakers, Penn believed, were unique in arguing that man had to be brought to complete passivity rather than simply "purified" as other Protestants urged. In his view the puritans wanted to cleanse man's heart, appeal to the remaining image of God in him, and bring him to a condition in which his beliefs and worship were purified and his strivings for sanctification strong. For

[56] Sermon, "Salvation Through Christ Alone" (1695), in *Sermons or Declarations*, 61-62.

[57] "Urim and Thummin: or the Apostolical Doctrines of Light and Perfection Maintained, Against the Opposite Plea of Samuel Grevill . . ." (1674), *Works*, II, 621.

[58] "Tender Counsel and Advice" (1677), *Works*, I, 203-204.

[59] "To All Those Professors of Christianity, That Are Externally Separated From the Visible Sects and Fellowships in the Christian World . . ." (1677), *Works*, I, 210-213.

this reason they balanced their judgments and condemnations with reminders of God's mercy toward sinful man. Penn was convinced that the puritan form of spiritual guidance was unjustifiably flattering to man and could not lead to the thorough self-condemnation required. In fact, those who gave such guidance were agents of the Devil. It was Satan who tried to keep man's will alive by convincing him that there was some good in it and that his reason had at least the bare outlines of truth, so that a new fire could arise from the old embers. But in fact "the Worship of God standeth in the Will of God; and is not brought forth of the Will of the Flesh, or of the Will of Man."[60] This was, Penn admitted, a harsh indictment of man, "a bitter Cup to the Creature; few will drink it! They are hard to be perswaded to sit still, and patiently to wait for the Salvation of God, to let him work all their Works in them and for them." They will not have the "Mouth in the Dust" and all flesh silent.[61]

Because he viewed man's situation in this manner, Penn taught that the first step in regeneration was a prolonged and unrelieved experience of judgment and condemnation. One came to know God's inner light as a sword, a hammer, an axe, a consuming fire, an everlasting burning against sin. Christ was the refiner and purifier.[62] In a reply to a work that accused the Quakers of being misanthropes and hypochondriacs who dwelt too much on the wrath of God and seemed always sad and dejected during their conversions, Penn argued that one who lacked this sense of utter judgment and who did not bear a daily cross had not truly been reborn. Those who styled themselves Christians while strangers to the terrors of the Lord and his fiery trials of purgation—both inward and outward—were still of the

[60] "Tender Counsel and Advice" (1677), *Works*, I, 203-204.

[61] "Summons or Call" (1677), *Works*, I, 197.

[62] "Wisdom Justified of Her Children, From the Ignorance and Calumny of H. Hallywell . . ." (1673), *Works*, II, 491; "No Cross, No Crown" (1682), *Works*, I, 273.

synagogue of Satan, still subjects of the God of this world.[63]

Despite Penn's adherence to the divine-human dualism and his emphasis on fallen man's helplessness, his discussions of the relationship between divine and human agency in regeneration vary widely in different works and manifest in an acute form the contradiction in Quaker thought. On the one hand, to emphasize God's initiative and the necessity of divine grace, Penn distinguished between the passive periods of the inner light and the "times of visitation" in which the revelatory light became a confronting, exhorting, condemning light and a source of gracious power. There are times in every man's life when the "Enlightenings" grow into "Enlivenings and Quickenings." The light at such times actively strives with sinful man: grace appears and urges man's condemnation and repentance. "They have a Day of Grace; God calls; his Spirit strives; his Long-Suffering waiteth, as in the Days of Noah, for their Repentance. And this is that which will give the greatest Weight in the Scale against the Rebellious, at the great Judgment, that they had a Talent; a Seed was sown, Grace did appear; and all had Light, but such lov'd Darkness rather than Light; because their Deeds were evil." If one repeatedly failed to respond to the gracious initiative of God at such times of visitation, when the "Light" became "Life," he could be afflicted with spiritual blindness. In him the light would be pressed down, crucified, and quenched, so that no possibility of regeneration remained.[64] The deadening effect of tradition or custom or the effects of poor education could also weaken the light, but in fairness to the victims of such ill fortune, God had devices—such as Christ's incarnation—for renewing the

---

[63] "Wisdom Justified" (1673), *Works*, ii, 491; Letter, "To Dr. Hasbert" (Nov. 1672), *Works*, i, 155.

[64] "Reply to a Pretended Answer" (1695), *Works*, ii, 825; "Counterfeit Christian" (1674), *Works*, ii, 586; "Plain-Dealing With a Traducing Anabaptist; or Three Letters Writ Upon Occasion of Some Slanderous Reflections, Given and Promoted Against William Penn by One John Morse" (1672), *Works*, ii, 182.

light. Blindness resulting from repeated unwillingness to respond to the occasional forceful confrontations with the light, however, was a cause of deserved damnation.[65]

At the same time, Penn was not so consistently pessimistic about man and his plight as the earliest Quakers or Barclay had been. In some of his works he seems to have been strongly influenced by Stoic and neo-Platonic approaches to man, according to which man's soul is a glorious divine jewel among the corruptible things of the earth because it is a replica in small of the divine mind itself. At times, Penn leaves the distinct impression that man's main problem is his soul's partial bondage in an alien and seductive world rather than his willful disobedience of his Creator.[66] Moreover, Penn was more determined than most Quakers to avoid the charges of cruelty, aloofness, hypocrisy, and partiality levelled against the Calvinistic conception of God, and he was equally concerned to lay upon man's own shoulders the responsibility for his continuing sinfulness. As a result he tended to refer to the inner light as a principle of knowledge constantly available to men, and, with Fisher, to urge men to take the initiative and turn to God. Those who act on the light or knowledge available to them will find that God then turns the light into "life" and helps those who help themselves by giving assistance in the form of power. First comes the light, showing one what is evil in general and in the individual in particular, and reproving him. If he is obedient to it, the light becomes life, the blood of cleansing, and fellowship with God and man. Penn's mode of speaking and writing often left the initiative with man at all stages of the process of rebirth.[67] His empha-

[65] "Christian Quaker" (1673), *Works*, I, 525-526; "The Invalidity of John Faldo's Vindication of His Book, Called, 'Quakerism No Christianity'" (1673), *Works*, II, 351.

[66] See esp. "Primitive Christianity" (1696), *Works*, II, 857-866; "Defence of the Duke" (1685), *Works*, II, 716. See below, chap. 5.

[67] See, e.g., "Primitive Christianity" (1696), *Works*, II, 857, 864; "Rise and Progress" (1694), *Works*, I, 891-892.

sis on the light as a form of constant knowledge led him on occasion to call it "innate" knowledge and to equate it with the "natural" knowledge of God and the moral law known in the hearts and consciences of all men.[68]

THE divine-human dualism was also modified in Penn's discussion of conversion in terms of the doctrine of justification. Since the stage of judgment did not end until the man of sin had been eradicated, the divine mercy and acceptance did not begin until the convert was already in an advanced state of sanctification. Especially in his early writings, Penn said that after a man was judged and condemned, God inclined him to purity and then finally redeemed him if he continued on the path to complete righteousness. Following the judgment the Spirit brought power to forsake sins. To those who truly repented and became obedient, he applied the mercies of Christ for forgiveness and brought justification. Penn was, in fact, arguing that justification "is subsequential to the mortification of lusts, and sanctification of the soul, through the spirit's operation."[69]

This reversal of the steps on the Reformed path to regeneration is found primarily in Penn's early polemical attempts to combat the tendency among conservative Christians to separate justification from sanctification. To refute the "notional" Christians who held that view, Penn argued that "we are no further saved by the historic Work of Redemption than we are renewed and transformed by the contemporary Indwelling Presence of Christ."[70] As death came into the world through actual sinning, so life or justification comes by actual righteousness, not imputed status.[71] Ac-

[68] "Defence of a Paper" (1698), *Works*, II, 898; "Primitive Christianity" (1696), *Works*, II, 857.

[69] "Sandy Foundation" (1668), *Works*, I, 261; "Invalidity" (1673), *Works*, II, 407-408, 414; "Reason Against Railing" (1673), *Works*, II, 522-523.

[70] "Urim and Thummim" (1674), *Works*, II, 628.

[71] "Reason Against Railing" (1673), *Works*, II, 522, 531-532; "Serious Apology" (1671), *Works*, II, 66.

cording to Penn the "professors'" reliance on the external transactions of Christ was against both Scripture and reason. They argued that the New Covenant had the virtue of bringing leniency and mercy, but in fact it demanded a high righteousness, since Christ added to the law and demanded that disciples take up their crosses and follow him.[72] Right reason, moreover, made utter nonsense of the orthodox doctrine. From Penn's point of view, the doctrine made God guilty of justifying the wicked and, to the obfuscation of all meaningful discourse, rendered a man justified and condemned, dead and alive, redeemed and not redeemed at the same time.[73]

To oppose the "professors'" understanding of justification in this manner was to imply that a man did not in fact come into a renewed relationship with God and receive God's mercy until he had begun living the elevated life of a nearly perfect servant of God. His youthful polemics notwithstanding, that was not Penn's understanding of the process of conversion as it appears in most of his works. He believed more strongly than many early Quaker writers that there were sound reasons for distinguishing between justification and sanctification and that what was needed was not a refutation of orthodox doctrine but a modification of it. "So that thus far we can approach the honester sort of Professors of Religion . . . viz., That Men may be reconciled, and in a Sense justified, while Sin may not be totally destroyed: That is, God upon their repenting of past Sins, tho not then clearly purged from the Ground of Evil, may and we believe, doth remit, pardon, or forgive former Offences, and is thus far reconciled; that is, he ceaseth to be angry or at a Distance from them, as when they went on in a State of Disobedience to the Light."[74] Penn wanted to

[72] "Urim and Thummim" (1674), *Works*, II, 628. See also "Sandy Foundation" (1668), *Works*, I, 257-264.
[73] "Sandy Foundation" (1668), *Works*, I, 263; "Reason Against Railing" (1673), *Works*, II, 522.
[74] "Christian Quaker" (1673), *Works*, I, 580.

emphasize that the period of judgment was succeeded by acceptance by the God of mercy only in the context of a shattering and unmistakable experience of repentance. One was not to rely on the promises of Scripture and the spiritual guidance of learned exegetes who said that God accepted sinners who could affirm the creed, attend worship regularly, and abide by the basic precepts of the moral law at least most of the time. If one had not experienced deep despair and overwhelming guilt and then gained a strong sense of repentance, he could know with assurance that he was not a converted man, no matter what the "external" authorities said. Conversely, if a man had received such an experience, he could glory in his sainthood regardless of the number of learned authorities calling him a deluded enthusiast or a fanatic.

Penn believed that a suitable understanding of justification was one somewhere between the Calvinist error of "faith without works" and the Papist error of "works without faith." He appears to have been close to Barclay in his approach to justification. He understood the Catholic position to be that a man is justified because of the merits he gains through grace and through his own cooperative efforts, so that there must be a "proportion" or "equality" between man's actual state and his status before God. To guard against this demand, which seemed to place man in a situation in which he could demand justification as his "wages," Penn replaced the idea of "merit" with that of "rewardableness." What happens within a man when he moves from judgment to acceptance does have "an inducing, procuring and obtaining Power and Virtue" in relation to God's favor. But since regeneration is a gradual process, and one must be accepted while still in certain respects a sinner, renewal does not "earn" acceptance. "Merit is a Work proportioned to the Wages: Rewardableness is a Work without which God will not bestow his Favour, and yet not the Meritorious Cause." Thus "the creature obeys the commands of God, and does not merit, but obtains only, and God rewards the creature, and yet so as that he gives too."[75]

In order to oppose the "Calvinist" doctrine of free grace based on imputation, Penn also used the idea of a twofold justification. He found justification employed in two distinct but connected ways in Scripture. In certain passages it means remission, imputation, pardon; in others it must mean "to be made inherently just, righteous or holy." It refers to the process by which the very ground of sin is destroyed.[76] Rather than believing that Scripture contains two different views of justification, Penn decided that justification must be defined broadly enough to include two steps:

Justification may be taken in a two-fold Sense; Compleatly, and Incompleatly; or rather thus, compleat Justification hath two Parts; the first is, not imputing past Sins, or accounting a true Penitent, as Righteous, (or clear from the Guilt of past sin) as if he had never sinned, through the Remission which God declared and sealed to all such in the Blood of his Son; and thus far Righteousness as imputed goes, and is the first Part, or Justification begun. The Compleat, or last Part of Compleat Justification, is the Cleansing of the Conscience, and regenerating the Mind from the Nature, Power and Indwelling of Sin, by the effectual working of the heavenly Power of Christ. . . .[77]

By dividing justification and including under the term "Compleat Justification" an experience of repentance and partial sanctification, Penn assured himself that justification would be understood as a proleptic process and that justi-

[75] "A Seasonable Caveat Against Popery" (1670), *Works*, I, 472; "Serious Apology" (1671), *Works*, II, 68.
[76] "Christian Quaker" (1673), *Works*, I, 580; "Reason Against Railing" (1673), *Works*, II, 523-524; "Quakerism a New Nickname" (1673), *Works*, II, 281.
[77] "Invalidity" (1673), *Works*, II, 411.

fication and sanctification could not be separated. He specifically stated that without the second or "Compleat" justification the general pardon for past sins that came through Christ's death was not "brought home" and applied to the individual soul.[78] The first part of justification was attributed to the "historic Christ" and the second and more significant part to the "eternal Christ" or "Christ within." Although Christ's death on the cross was necessary to release man from the burden of past sins, the cause of acceptance or justification by God was the active presence "within" man of the eternal Christ through the activity of the Spirit. According to Penn, the decline in rebirth among puritans was largely attributable to their belief that the whole of justification is an effect of Christ's suffering and death. To insist that one was justified only when Christ was "within" man, covering for his present state, was to make justification necessarily an "experience" and to make the knowledge of one's interior state more authoritative than any kind of external authority.[79]

The righteousness with which "Christ within" clothes us is indeed his, according to Penn, but we have it as a possession, "for it is ours not by Nature, but by Faith and Adoption; it is the Gift of God. But still, though not ours, as of or from our selves . . . yet it is ours and must be ours, in Possession, Efficacy and Enjoyment, to do us any Good; or Christ's Righteousness will profit us nothing."[80] It is this righteousness that is in man through the indwelling of the eternal Spirit of Christ, and the works of righteousness that this Spirit enables a man to do are the cause of his acceptance by God. Although it is to Christ's power that he ascribes his regeneration, the rejoicing must be in himself. "'Tis not the Oyl in another's Lamp, but in our own only, which will serve our Turns; I mean the Rejoycing must be in ourselves, and not in another: Yet to Christ's holy

[78] Ibid., 412.
[79] Ibid., 410; "Reason Against Railing" (1673), Works, II, 524.
[80] "Rise and Progress" (1694), Works, I, 891.

Power alone do we ascribe it, who works all our Works in us."[81] Penn's doctrine shifted the focus from Christ the interceder to Christ within, who is known in experience and through his effects. It is a man's present state of sanctification, "his being found acting and working in the Living Faith," that causes his acceptance with God.[82]

With this understanding of the requirements for justification, Penn said that one moved from the state of judgment to that of acceptance when he had reached "a Foundation of true Repentance." When one finally knows oneself to be "exceeding sinful," and sin has become "a Burden to the Soul," he begins to feel the active presence of Christ within and feels certain of acceptance. "For though Sin may not be mortified, yet if there be a Foundation of true Repentance laid, the Guilt of former Iniquities . . . is not imputed."[83] Penn could describe this decisive, climactic stage of regeneration, in which the foundation of repentance is laid, as the period of "faith." But when he did, he was careful to define the term inclusively. On the one hand, faith is primarily trust and assurance and provides one with confidence that God has accepted him. It is "entirely believing and trusting in God, confiding in his goodness," and relying upon his conduct and mercies with full assurance of the remission of sins.[84] On the other hand, faith is "more than a meer Assent of the Understanding to a verbal, though a true Proposition." From it inevitably flow works of holiness; indeed, no man can be said to believe who does not obey, "for that is believing in God, to do as he says." Those who truly believe receive an inward force and ability to mortify lusts, control affections, resist evil motions, deny themselves, and overcome the world.[85]

[81] "Serious Apology" (1671), *Works*, II, 66; "Reason Against Railing" (1673), *Works*, II, 523.

[82] "Invalidity" (1673), *Works*, II, 409.

[83] "Reason Against Railing" (1673), *Works*, II, 529.

[84] "Address to Protestants" (1679), *Works*, I, 752.

[85] "A Discourse of the General Rule of Faith and Practice. And Judge of Controversie" (1673), *Works*, I, 608; "Address to Protes-

Penn shared the Quakers' tendency to speak and write as if they believed that a truly regenerated man was once again an innocent child of God, living "above" the life of sin. He spoke of the state of life following conversion and justification as one of "Perseverance unto a perfect Man, and the Assurance of Blessedness."[86] Salvation is "being saved from Sin here, and the Wages of it," not being saved from it hereafter, as he believed puritans and Anglicans held.[87] Penn based his belief in perfection on Scripture, "wherein not only a Perfection from Sin, but the going forward to a perfect Man in Christ, is exhorted to, and prayed for; therefore not unobtainable."[88]

These remarks were more significant, however, as rebukes to puritan forms of self-satisfaction than as indications of Penn's style of sainthood, for the courtier and proprietor lived more fully "in the world" than most Quakers. Friends, according to Penn, were fully aware of the human frailties that attend all men in this life; even to the saints they attributed only partial abilities.[89] The perfection attainable in this life is a relative perfection; it is not the perfection "in Fulness of Wisdom and Glory" reserved for another world.[90] Indeed, perfection in the proper sense can be applied to man only "when taken for the Author of it." Christ is perfect, and Christ is active within the regenerate, so that, once a man's own spirit has been effectively subdued, one can call him "perfect" because of Christ within— if he is careful not to refer the perfection to man himself.[91]

---

tants" (1679), *Works*, I, 752; "No Cross, No Crown" (1682), *Works*, I, 280.

[86] "Primitive Christianity Revived" (1696), *Works*, II, 856.

[87] "Christian Quaker" (1673), *Works*, I, 523.

[88] "Wisdom Justified" (1673), *Works*, II, 492.

[89] "A Testimony to the Truth of God" (1698), *Works*, II, 880.

[90] "The Counterfeit Christian Detected and the Real Quaker Justified . . ." (1674), *Works*, II, 570; "A Key Opening a Way to Every Common Understanding . . ." (1692), *Works*, II, 781.

[91] "Reason Against Railing" (1673), *Works*, II, 532-533.

In addition, Penn emphasized that Quakers did not believe that man was ever secure from temptation. Perfection does not come, even in a relative or partial sense, when regeneration occurs but only after a lifetime of struggle against sin. Following conversion the saint begins a great campaign. He has a long wilderness to travel through with many difficulties to surmount and many enemies to subdue, not only in the world but within his own breast.[92] Penn warned his friends, "Redeeme ye Time and Double your diligence to make your call and your Election sure, for many are not sure, nor past danger, and will certainly fall if they watch not wherefore as you are encompassed about with pretious promises be you encompassed about alsoe wth feare and Reverence towards God. . . ."[93]

Penn's doctrine of perfection, then, amounted to little more than an exaggerated form of the puritan confidence that Christ was stronger than the Devil. It was not based on a belief in man's unqualified perfectibility or primarily on a failure to understand the extent of sin's inroads on human nature. Rather, it stemmed from the Quaker experience of God's converting and translating power and a desire to rebuke faltering saints and to glorify the all-sovereign God. "I know my weakness," said Penn, "but I also know His strength, and he is able to glorify himself, and turn his poor people by me."[94]

THE "OUTWARD" AND THE "INWARD" IN QUAKERISM

Geoffrey Nuttall has suggested that the Friends' belief that the Spirit dwelt in them as it had in the earliest Christians was what set them apart from the more orthodox Christians of their time. This "enthusiasm," based on the

[92] "Wisdom Justified" (1673), *Works*, II, 493.
[93] Letter to Friends (March 3, 1695), PWP (contemp. copy in FLL).
[94] Letter to John Blakling, Thomas Camm *et al.* (Apr. 16, 1683), PWP (copy in FLL).

182

assumption that "the more independent of normal earthly conditions they could be, the better . . . : at least as evidence for the presence of God's Spirit with them, and for the authenticity of their inspiration," manifested itself in various forms in the first generation, including the moral, didactic, emotional, and spiritual.[95] The form of enthusiasm that came to the fore in the second generation of Quaker writers might be called an intellectual enthusiasm, or the belief that knowledge of spiritual realities is not dependent upon "so fallacious a foundation as man's outward and fallible senses" but comes by means of "inward supernatural senses" in the form of self-evident or luminously clear and distinct propositions.[96] Whereas English Protestants, whether satisfied Anglican or puritan, believed that man in this world was limited to observing what Luther called the "backside" of God, Friends were confident that they could, by means of the inner light, observe the Word as it came from the very "mouth" of God. Fox's insistence that man could be confronted by God and partake of his power only if he bypassed the "visible" world and experienced God more directly was a source of much reflection on the part of Keith, Barclay, Whitehead, Penington, Penn, and others acquainted with the Platonic and neo-Platonic thought present in the spiritualist milieu and the "new" or "Cartesian" philosophy that became so influential in England from 1640 to 1700. As a result the fledgling and fitful metaphysical, anthropological, and epistemological principles stemming from the spirit-body dualism in Fox's thought came to be expressed at times much more systematically.

None of the Quaker writers was a philosopher, and few could be classified as systematic theologians, but the philosophical position that they more or less consciously drew

[95] *Christian Enthusiasm*, 47 *et passim*.
[96] Barclay, *Apology*, 44; "The Possibility and Necessity of the Inward and Immediate Revelation of the Spirit of God" (1676), in *Truth Triumphant through the Spiritual Warfare, Christian Labours and Writings of . . . Robert Barclay* (London, 1692), III, 571.

upon constituted a form of dualism with developed meta-physical, anthropological, and epistemological positions. The metaphysical position was the belief that there are two kinds of reality, denominated spirit and body, or thought and extension. Spirit or thought was considered to be the higher form of being, and the two are very different—although not necessarily antithetical—and can interact only in an unnatural manner. Spirit is immutable, eternal, and sentient—an active intelligence. Body is corruptible, temporal, and insentient—a passive instrument of spirit. Since all mental activity is a function of spirit, it follows that man, although superficially a compound of spirit and body, is essentially a spirit in the sense that his soul is self-moving and self-sufficient. It is not dependent on body for life or fulfilment.

The developed form of the epistemological doctrine that accompanies this metaphysical and anthropological position assumes that all true knowledge has spiritual reality or ideas as its object. To know something is to bring to consciousness an idea that already existed in the mind. Body cannot be the cause of ideas, although sense impressions can be the occasion for the rise to consciousness of an idea in the soul. The only kind of knowing, however, that truly deserves the name is that which takes place without the intervention of sense impressions. The religious assumption of this epistemology is that God is completely spiritual, as are all things pertaining to him. Man's religious knowledge is gained by direct communication between his spirit and God, and religious expression or worship should be as spiritual as possible, involving primarily mental and not physical activity. Man's objective is to escape after death into an incorporeal realm where his soul can contemplate God forever.[97]

We rarely find the dualistic metaphysical position stated

---

[97] See Barclay, "Immediate Revelation," *Truth Triumphant*, III; Keith, *Immediate Revelation, or Jesus Christ the Eternall Son of God, Revealed in Man and Revealing the Knowledge of God* ... (London, 1668).

explicitly in Quaker writings. Moreover, the anthropological and epistemological implications were never carried out
completely or even substantially by any Quakers, although
they were most prominent in some of the works of Barclay,
Keith, and Penn. If they had been carried out consistently,
Quakerism would have denied the ultimate religious significance of both the contingent facts of history and sense
knowledge. It would have slighted both the incarnate Christ
and Scripture. The anthropological beliefs would have led
to a docetic Christology and a doctrine of man that envisioned historical man as an imprisoned soul and that had little
room for the resurrection of the flesh. The Restoration
Quakers travelled down all these paths, but not consistently,
and sometimes they doubled back. Most often they attributed the salvation of all men to the deeds of the incarnate
Christ and spoke of Scripture as the great witness to them.
Especially did they modify the anthropological doctrine,
since they spoke of man as in some sense an integral compound of body and soul. They clearly affirmed that man,
although essentially "spirit," was a created spirit and not a
spark of God's being whose goal was absorption in God.
Moreover, they believed, although confusedly, that man's
sin was attributable to his will and thus to his "spiritual"
part, not to the fact that the soul was encased in a body.

The philosophical dualism, nevertheless, had important
implications for the Quakers' religion, and at times it received a fairly systematic statement. Barclay, who was always apologetic about his philosophizing, kept it to a minimum in the *Apology*, but in certain other treatises he
developed clearly the epistemological foundation for the
attitude toward sense knowledge prevalent in Quakerism
and elaborated the philosophical assumptions so evident in
the thought of Penn. Especially important in this regard is
his *Possibility and Necessity of the Inward and Immediate
Revelation of the Spirit of God*. In this work Barclay was
refuting the position that the essence of the Christian religion lies in knowledge of contingent truths, namely, matters

of fact about the historical Christ, and that, since man possesses innate ideas only of necessary truths, he is dependent on the use of his outward senses to learn these essential truths about Christ through Scripture corroborated by miracles.

To this argument Barclay responded in several ways. First, even in learning about natural contingent truths we are dependent on the senses only in a minor way. For there are implanted in our minds the ideas of all things in the spiritual and corporeal realms. Sense experience may be the occasion for the rise to consciousness of a particular idea, but there is nothing in the corporeal motion stirred up in us by the "outward" sense object that can form an idea in us, since ideas are spiritual things, and the lesser or corporeal cannot produce the greater or spiritual. Moreover, even in relation to natural contingent truths, we are not strictly dependent on sense experience as the occasion of an idea's coming into the consciousness. For God through the inward senses can raise to consciousness even natural contingent truths by means of a supernatural immediate revelation that makes our perception of these contingent truths as clear and certain as our perception of any necessary truths. When God operates on us immediately to reveal a contingent truth, we through the inward senses recognize this as God's operation, and hence as a necessary truth that is revealed, although contingent in content, since God cannot lie. The proposition that every divine revelation is necessarily true is as clear and evident as that every whole is greater than its parts, so the contingent truth becomes a necessary truth. Moreover, God not only can but invariably does reveal himself and his spiritual truths to us by means of these "inward supernatural senses," since he and his truths are "spiritual" and therefore require a "spiritual" rather than a corporeal sense to discern them.

Barclay's ingenious way of making contingent truths into necessary truths may be of interest to the historian of philosophy, but more consequential for Quaker thought was the philosophy on which the argument rests and the assumption that the essential truths of Christianity must be known in the same way that self-evident innate ideas are known and must not be dependent on fallacious and deceptive sense experience. Given this understanding of man's knowledge of God, it was difficult to continue to emphasize the contingent truths of history, especially since Barclay admitted that there is saving knowledge of God among those unacquainted with the historical Jesus and on occasion wrote that men should move beyond the contingent truths to more mature beliefs.[98]

Barclay wrote in *Immediate Revelation* that the divine operation perceived by man's spiritual senses could be called a "Spiritual Body." As natural ideas are stirred up in us through perception by outward senses of outward and natural bodies, so divine ideas are aroused through perception by inward supernatural senses of a "certain principle, which is a body in naturals in relation to the spiritual world; and therefore may be called a divine body: not as if it were part of God, who is a most pure Spirit; but the organ or instrument of God, by which he worketh in us, and stirreth up in us these ideas of divine things." Barclay called this body the flesh and blood of Christ by which the saints were nourished.[99] Quakers often referred to the eating and drinking of the body and blood of Christ as a metaphor for regenerating communication with Christ within, but the idea that the saints are influenced by a spiritual body in an ontological sense had several uses in their dualistic approach to the world. Most important was the idea that Christ's spiritual body could serve as a mediating principle between the completely spiritual and therefore bodiless God and the sinful compound of lesser spirit and body that was fallen man.

Fox wrote often about the need for man to feed upon the flesh of Christ, and at times he contrasted the true eating of the heavenly flesh with the "outward" eating of the flesh

[98] *Truth Triumphant*, III, 561-585.
[99] "Immediate Revelation," *Truth Triumphant*, III, 577-578.

and beasts under the old covenant. In these passages the major contrast is between "notional" or impotent knowledge of Christ and a powerful confrontation with "Christ within," and the "eating" is taken in a metaphorical sense. Nevertheless, at times more than this metaphor is implied, for Fox linked "outward" and "inward" eating in the existential or mystical sense with "outward" and "inward" eating in the physical sense, thereby implying that there is an inward or spiritual "flesh" to correspond to the outward flesh of Christ. The tendency to view the flesh as an incorporeal substance was strengthened by Fox's belief that regeneration or "feeding on Christ's flesh" brought changes toward "incorruption" not only in the soul which was "of God" but also in the body which had through sin become "of the earth" or "corruptible." It seems reasonable to assume, especially in light of all Fox says about the "heavenly" flesh of Christ that he brought down from heaven, that there lurked in Fox's mind the idea that the regenerate, who became, with Christ, "heavenly, living and spiritual," experienced an ontological change in his body also, which became less corruptible through its contact with the heavenly flesh of Christ.[100]

[100] See "A Clear Distinction Between the Old Covenant . . . and the New Covenant . . ." (1680), *Works*, VI, 57-59; "Mystery," *Works*, III, 323; "A Word of Admonition . . ." (1684), *Works*, VI, 251; Epistle 18 (1652), *Works*, VII, 26; Epistle 222 (1662), *Works*, VII, 232-233. See also Barbour, *Quakers*, 152. This aspect of Fox's thought is one of the clearest areas of evidence of Continental spiritualist influence on him. Spiritualists such as Hans Denck and Sebastian Franck wrote much about a spiritual eating and drinking of Christ's flesh and blood in dependence on John 6, as did Caspar Schwenckfeld. The spiritualists also had soteriological schemes for deification, and deification was combined in Schwenckfeld's thought with a conception of grace as a kind of spiritual fluid that changes man toward incorruptibility. These ideas about feeding on Christ are related to the doctrine of the heavenly flesh of Christ that also, as we shall see, influenced Fox. See Williams, *Spiritual and Anabaptist Writers* (Philadelphia, 1957), 35, 163-180; Rufus Jones, *Spiritual Reformers of the Sixteenth and Seventeenth Centuries* (New York, 1914), chap. 5.

The idea of Christ as a spiritual substance or body that serves as a mediating link between wholly disparate spiritual and corporeal being was most clearly developed by George Keith, while he was still a Quaker, in *The Way Caste Up* (London, 1676). From the beginning of the world the Word or Christ, which was not a distinct substance or being from God and thus could not mediate between God and man, became such by being clothed with flesh or manhood. Christ has been a mediator throughout all time, not simply during his period of "outward" flesh, so the flesh or manhood that he took on at the beginning was a kind of spiritual body. Christ did this so that he could form a link in an ontological sense between God and man. As a pure Spirit, God cannot have direct contact with corporeality. Man, although his soul is spiritual, is flesh even in his soul in comparison with God. So the Word became a heavenly flesh, or advanced a step nearer to man, so that the heavenly flesh could be extended or grafted into man, and man could thereby become more spiritual.[101]

DESPITE THE prominence of the spiritual-corporeal dualism in Quaker thought, it was, as I have indicated, by no means thoroughly applied to all aspects of Quaker religion. Even Friends as systematic and clear as Barclay seem never finally to have decided whether by "outward," "fleshly," and "carnal"—terms that they knew referred to or described the Enemy—they meant simply "sinful" or "corporeal and sinful." As a result they used them in both ways and remained ambiguous on the question of the usefulness of "outward" means in their religious lives. Following Fox, the Restoration Friends said that the fundamental difference between the old covenant and the new is that in the old covenant men learned of God through priests and stone tablets, and expressed their religion in temple sacrifices, whereas in the new covenant "the Spirit teaches the righteous immediately,

[101] *The Way Caste Up*, 95-103. See Creasey, "Early Quaker Christology," 79-87.

objectively, and continually" without books, priests, or any other physical medium, and worship is the utterance of the Spirit within one. As is made clear especially in Jeremiah 31:33, Hebrews 8:10-11 and I John 2:27, the New Testament is superior to the Old because it is "inward" in the nonphysical sense.[102]

At the same time, the Restoration Quakers, preoccupied with questions of organization and survival in a time of persecution, were more explicit than the earliest Friends about the fact that the new covenant was a mixture of inward and outward. According to Barclay, "God hath seen meet, so long as his children are in this world, to make use of the outward senses, not only as a means to convey spiritual life, as by speaking, praying, praising, etc., which cannot be done to mutual edification, but when we hear and see one another; but also to entertain an outward, visible testimony for his name in the world. . . ."[103] Fisher denied that Quakers believed they were above all ordinances. Quaker ordinances include "to meet and wait with his Saints on the Lord, to stand in his Counsel, . . . to pray, preach, write, dispute, and do all that I am called to, in the Light, in the Movings of his Spirit, these all, and an Hundred more that might be named, are Ordinances of God, which I am under. . . ."[104]

The emphasis of the Restoration Friends in their attitude toward the outward means of grace and religious expression was that of the spiritualists Dell and Saltmarsh, who saw themselves as simply further along the spiritualist path than less fortunate Christians, rather than that of the Ranters, who decried all outward forms. Although some forms would remain as long as men were mortal, true Christians were supposed to try to wean themselves from the ordinances and means that had central prominence in their religion. The sacraments of baptism and the Lord's Supper had been allowed as transitional religious means during the time of change from the outward worship of the old covenant

[102] *Apology*, 57-59.   [103] *Ibid.*, 357.   [104] *Rusticus*, 119.

to the fully inward worship of the new. Christians should have outgrown them by now, they said, but second-generation writers were more discriminating than earlier Quakers had been in discussing the sacraments. Fisher said that Quakers did not deny their usefulness and legitimacy for those "as are not satisfied in the Lord, unless they use them. . . ." The trouble was that most people either changed them from their instituted form into something—usually superstitious—that they were not intended to be or else "dote upon and Idolize" them to the exclusion of communion with God himself. Fisher did not forbid "the due use of any, that ever was in mere outside service required and appointed of God himself, when performed in its proper place and season, from a right Principle of inward Power, to the right end. . . ."[105]

Especially indicative of the ambiguity of the Quaker approach to means of grace was their attitude toward Scripture. Because Scripture seemed to them the main object of puritan idolatry, and because of their exuberant testimony to the inner light, the Interregnum Friends were especially harsh on it. The major problem with Scripture, in addition to the fact that many Christians worshipped it, was simply the fact that it was an outward or visible means of grace more appropriate to the old dispensation than the new, which needed a spiritual means of illumination, namely, the law written on the heart of all men by the inner light. Beginning with Samuel Fisher, the Quaker critique of Scripture added to its arsenal the weapons of the textual critics who were beginning to cast doubt on the adequacy of the copies of Scripture extant in Europe.

Adding to this material and developing arguments of their own, the Catholic writers of the seventeenth century were intent on proving that Scripture was not an adequate replacement for the church as an ultimate religious authority. Fisher made use also of this *machine de guerre de nouvelle invention* formulated by the followers of Montaigne in

[105] *Rusticus,* 119-120; Barclay, *Apology,* 406.

France and employed widely by Catholics in England.[106] Admitting that he shared many Catholic views about Scripture even while he claimed for Quakers a greater regard for Scripture than Catholics had, Fisher argued that the text had been corrupted because of poor copying, the need to supply Hebrew vowels, the difficulties of translation and the stupidity and dishonesty of translators, and conscious changes for doctrinal purposes. Comparison of texts revealed that in some manuscripts whole lines and sections were missing, and references in the patristic fathers indicate the existence of complete books that are now missing. Moreover, although Fisher accepted the perfection of the original copies—because of divine inspiration—he found in Scripture itself no promise by God to guide the process of canonization, so that it was perfectly proper to prefer apocryphal books to some of those that strictly human authorities included in the Scriptures. Beyond that, the nature of the literature made it difficult to understand the meaning of many books and passages, and, since Scripture was like a shadow or lifeless picture rather than a living authority, it was easy to take passages out of context and perform other feats obscuring the real meaning and providing support for whatever one happens to want to prove.[107] Summing up his critique, Fisher warned: "Nay, Friends, Gods Word is stable and permanent, and not a tittle of that can be turned besides it self, by the tattling Tongues, and pidling Pens of men, that for Money make it their whole Lives business to Transcribe, Translate, Interpret, and give you their thoughts upon this, and that, and T'other Text, till through the throng of their Thoughts, and the mists of their meanings, and Misrepresentations, and Mis-interpretations, ye can see little of

[106] See Martin I. J. Griffin, "Latitudinarianism in the Seventeenth-Century Church of England" (unpubl. Ph.D. diss., Yale Univ., 1962), 102-108.

[107] *Rusticus*, 167, 175-178, 194-197, 229, 234-236, 270-277, 292-296, 331-332, 397, 449, 453, 459.

that they have translated for you out of their uncertain Transcripts. . . ."[108]

Joining Catholics in their polemic against English Protestantism was not the way to win Friends and influence people in seventeenth-century England. So paranoid were most Englishmen about Catholics that they looked on Quakers as papists in disguise even when they failed to note the similarity between Quakers and Romanists on justification, grace and free will, and Scripture. Restoration Quakers, and especially those writing after 1688, when the Quakers were promised toleration if they adhered to the basic Protestant doctrines, did not want to be associated with Catholicism, and many of them chose not to make use of the Catholic polemic in their attempts to explain the significance of the inner light as a replacement for Scripture. Another reason for a modification of the attack on Scripture during the Restoration was the simple recognition of the great dependence of Friends on Scripture as a source of doctrinal and ethical guidance and of knowledge about the historical Christ, who was increasingly given a central place in the Quaker message.

Some Friends had an additional reason for expressing their regard for Scripture. Penn and Whitehead, among others, saw affinities between their own thought and some of the doctrinal positions and the theological minimalism of Anglicans of the latitudinarian school. The latitudinarians were deeply involved in the polemic against Catholics on Scripture, and, in addition, they turned away from Catholic and "enthusiastic" views of church authority toward Scripture as understood by reason for a clear statement of the essential doctrines of the Christian faith, and even advocated using strictly Scriptural phrases to express controverted doctrines. Friends who were conscious of similarities with the liberal Anglicans, and who were in the habit of pointing up those similarities to justify their own differences from Cal-

[108] *Rusticus*, 331-332.

THE DEVELOPED RELIGION

vinist nonconformists on election, free will, universal salvation, justfication, and other doctrines, could not afford to ignore the great regard for Scripture of the liberals.[109]

Barclay's position on Scripture in his *Apology* represents the conservative position rather well. He made clear the priority of the light over Scripture, but he was careful to express his high regard for Scripture even in its current imperfect form and did not utilize the arguments of the biblical critics. To be dependent on Scripture without the light would put one in the unfortunate position of trusting transcribers and translators more than was comforting, but Barclay was convinced that God had preserved the Scriptures uncorrupted through the long period of the church's apostasy. Some manuscripts contained different readings from others, and some of the references by Christ and his apostles to Old Testament passages did not agree with present copies, but the Scriptures were clear in the essentials of the Christian faith, and they could serve as an excellent source of comfort and guidance and as a judge of controversies. They were "the most excellent writings in the world; to which not only no other writings are to be preferred, but even in divers respects not comparable thereto." They had to give way to the inner light as the primary rule of faith simply because the new or spiritual dispensation required a spiritual rule—a guide that confronts man "immediately" and can give him certainty about his religious state.[110]

The "Outward" and the "Inward" in Penn's Thought

Penn's spiritual-corporeal dualism was not systematically elaborated anywhere in his writings, but he was an adherent of both the "old" or Platonic and the "new" or Cartesian

[109] On the place of Scripture in liberal English religious thought of the latter seventeenth century, see Roland Stromberg, *Religious Liberalism in Eighteenth-Century England* (London, 1954), 13-24.
[110] *Apology*, 73-95.

philosophy, and he allowed the dualism to influence his thought more than most Quaker writers did. He distinguished sharply between the two kinds of being that constitute reality: "That which is intelligent, which in its pure Nature knows, comprehends, governs and orders all visible, elementary and corporeal Beings, and yet is Invisible, Spiritual, Rational and Internal (as is manifest from its Heavenly Meditations, its secret Thoughts, its serious Reflections, acute Memory, and profound Reasonings about the Causes and Effects of all Things) cannot but be of a Nature more refined, excellent, and noble, than to fall under the same Generations, Revolutions, and Corruptions, those inferior visible Beings are subject to."[111] Few dualists in the Christian tradition have held that there are two *completely* independent kinds of being, and Penn accepted the Platonic Christian assumption that matter is dependent for its existence on spirit and thus that God created all that is. Since he accepted as axiomatic the principle that all "productions" partake of the nature of their "producer," it was difficult for him to conceive of visible, corruptible being as coming from God, but he was finally able to accept this position.[112] That, however, was the only modification of the dualism he allowed, and as he developed the implications of his metaphysics, he revealed his firm adherence to the position that mind and matter are disparate and even antithetical kinds of being.

Penn assumed, first of all, that the two could not be changed into each other or be transformed so as to approach the nature of each other. This belief is evident in his discussion of the idea of a bodily resurrection. He opposed the idea that men will arise in the general resurrection with the same body, numerically or substantively speaking, that they possessed on earth. They will arise not with a transformed body but with a new body, an incorruptible or spiritual one

---

[111] "New Witnesses" (1672), *Works*, II, 161.
[112] "A Defence of the Duke" (1685), *Works*, II, 712.

without the "accidents" of grossness or corruptibility. He was unable to see "how that which is Dust should be eternal [i.e., by transformation], whilst that from which it came, is by Nature but Temporal." All such talk of changes in properties between physical and spiritual substance he labeled "Popish Transubstantiation."[113] "Grossness" was an essential part of corporeal matter, and such being can have nothing to do with spiritual being. When talking about the resurrection of men, Penn did not explicitly deny that men will have some kind of bodies, but he said that the bodies will be new and different ones, not the same ones in changed form. To demonstrate that even renewed "outward" flesh and blood have no part in heaven and in the soul's felicity, he quoted Paul concerning the inability of flesh and blood to inherit the kingdom, as well as Paul's statement that he wanted to be absent from the body and present with the Lord.[114] In some of his joint statements with other Quakers in the 1690's, when Quakers were anxious to prove their orthodoxy, Penn associated himself with a more orthodox position, but that was against his natural propensity.

By granting resurrected man some kind of "body," Penn modified his dualism. But he never said what kind of body would be suitable, and he wrote of heaven and what is fitting for spiritual realms in a way that excludes all that is normally associated with corporeal being. In Penn's view, to argue that the soul would not be complete without a body was to imply that heaven is an earthly place where one sees and walks and where the outward senses can be exercised and enjoyed. To Penn's mind this idea was more congruent with "Mahometism" and the Koran than with the Christian gospel.[115] He clearly believed that it was impious to associate God and truly spiritual being with corporeal being of

---

[113] "Quakerism a New Nickname" (1672), *Works*, II, 298; "Invalidity" (1673), *Works*, II, 438.
[114] "Reason Against Railing" (1673), *Works*, II, 533-536, 545.
[115] *Ibid.*, 545; "Defence of a Paper" (1698), *Works*, II, 896.

any sort. "He is a Spirit, to whom Words, Places and Times (strictly considered) are improper and inadequate. And tho' they be the Instruments of publick Worship, they are but Bodily and Visible, and cannot carry our Requests any further, much less recommend them to the Invisible God; by no Means: they are for the Sake of the Congregation: 'Tis the Language of the Soul God hears; nor can that Speak but by the Spirit. . . .' "[116] There is something about physical means, including even words, that renders them unsuitable for spiritual purposes. Religion and the kingdom of Christ are calculated not to our senses but to our souls, and the more "mental" or "incorporeal" one's communications with God, the more adequate to the nature of God.[117]

To expound Penn's metaphysical principles I have already indicated the nature of his anthropology. He turned to Genesis 2 to explicate the nature of man. As in the case of most Quaker writers, his discussion is unclear. Man, according to Genesis, has two origins: the breath of God and dust. It is uncertain whether Penn understood this to mean that there was a soul already existent within created body, but distinct from it, into which God breathed life; or whether he believed that God's breath really formed the soul. On the one hand, he wanted to affirm that man's soul is not an emanation from God and thus is not of the same substance as God. The distinction between soul and God was clearly maintained. Penn distinguished between the "natural soul" that has lost knowledge of God and the "Life" that must be given to the soul by the supernatural light. In his view, when the Quakers called the soul "infinite," "eternal," or "divine," they were referring to the "Life" provided by the light—the "Life" that God breathed into it originally and that gave access to God, but that had been lost through Adam's Fall and could be regained only through God's gra-

[116] "No Cross, No Crown" (1682), *Works*, I, 298.
[117] Letter to Richard Butler, Earl of Arran (Jan. 9, 1684), PWP (A.L.S. in Bodleian Library).

cious inbreathing. Only when referring to its "Primitive Perfection" could one properly refer to the soul as divine.[118]

On the other hand, he distinguished radically between soul and body. In some sense the soul is much more like God than the body, in even the most sinful of men. The soul is "unending," so that when the body dies, the soul lives on, even in the most unregenerate of men. Only the soul "came from God" and can communicate with God and be with him. Penn did not hesitate to affirm the doctrine of creationism and to refute traducianism.[119] To establish the position, he argued that souls do not resemble parents the way bodies do; that anatomists cannot find souls; and that souls do not have sex as an essential attribute. Thus the soul and the body must have separate origins, the one coming from God, the other from the dust. Despite the Fall the soul can never be portrayed as completely lacking a knowledge of divine things. Although in sinful man it lacks "Life," it retains an "Instinct of a Deity" that is ineradicable.[120]

According to Penn, man is not truly a compound of body and soul, but essentially incorporeal soul. The body is merely an "outward Garment which shall be worn while it last, shall then be put off."[121] It is only by a figure of speech that the body is included as part of a man.

> Man cannot properly be said to dye whilst his Soul lives, but he may be said to cease to be in this Visible World, or to depart out of it, and to lay down his Mortal Body; so that the Body dyes but not the Man; I know it is a

[118] "Counterfeit Christian" (1674), *Works*, II, 584; "Invalidity" (1673), *Works*, II, 433, 436.

[119] Creationism is the belief that souls are created directly by God and placed in the body that is germinated from the union of man and woman. Traducianism is the belief that the soul, like the body, is a product of the procreative act. Most Platonists in the Christian tradition have been attracted to the creationist position.

[120] "New Witnesses" (1672), *Works*, II, 158-161; "The Great Case of Liberty of Conscience" (1670), *Works*, I, 451.

[121] Sermon on the death of Rebecca Travers (June 19, 1688), ACMC, XXX, 21ff. Printed in *Concurrence and Unanimity* (1711).

common Phrase, but synedochically spoken, where that is ascribed to the whole Man, which only belongeth to the Mortal Part of Man. In short, because such Murderers, who are said to kill Men, kill only the Bodies of Men; those Jews who crucified Christ, properly crucified the Body of Christ only, though in a more Mystical Sense, they may be also said in that very Action, to have murdered the Prince of Life and Glory, I Corinthians 2.[122]

Penn's separation of the soul and body was not simply a philosophical deduction; it was an important part of his faith. When Thomas Loe, the man responsible for his conversion, died, Penn wrote to Guli Springett that Loe "left ye Body, and is ascended far above all Visible and Created Things to ye full possession of ye pure Eternal Rest and Sabbath of ye holy God. . . ." The body, which Penn always referred to as "it," was respectfully laid into the ground, having finished the work for which it had been created.[123] Citing "the best Platonists and Descartes" as his authorities, Penn argued that since the body is incapable of pleasure and pain, it need not share in the soul's rewards and punishments. Similarly, he defended the Quaker custom of not dressing in mourning clothes with the argument that the mourning should be worn by the mind or soul, since the body is not sensible of the loss or even an essential part of man.[124]

Since corporeal being is radically distinct from the being of God and of spiritual reality, and since man is essentially incorporeal spirit, Penn had to assign a low position to religious knowledge gained through the senses. As the spirit-body dualism was more or less prominent depending on Penn's mood and on the nature of the writing, so were the epistemological implications, but at times they were very

[122] "Invalidity" (1673), *Works*, II, 417-418.
[123] Letter to Guli Springett (Oct. 7, 1668), PWP (contemp. copy in HSP).
[124] "Invalidity" (1673), *Works*, II, 440; "Rise and Progress" (1694), *Works*, I, 870-871.

prominent indeed. "Man . . . is a Composition of both Worlds; his Body is of this, his Soul of the other World. The Body is as the Temple of the Soul; the Soul the Temple of the Word, and the Word the great Temple and Manifestation of God. By the Body the Soul looks into and beholds this World; and by the Word it beholds God, and the World that is without End."[125] Man, in other words, has two routes to knowledge. Knowledge of the things of this world comes through the senses and follows the normal path through the faculties. Knowledge of spiritual or eternal things comes in a more direct manner. As the light of the sun and the external eye combine to give knowledge of this world, so the inner light and man's soul combine to provide a vision of spiritual and immaterial objects.[126]

Penn did not maintain an absolute distinction between "worldly" and "religious" knowledge. He accepted—as did even the most thorough Platonists of the time—the arguments for religion and Christianity based on empirical knowledge. He did not deny the validity of the "evidence of testimony" that made the miracles of the New Testament an important argument for the truth of Christianity. He used the argument from prophecy as well. In his *Visitation to the Jews*, he asked, "How could so many Men that you have not taxed with ill Lives or Atheistical Principles, agree together to put so great an Imposture upon the World, as the Pen-men of the New Testament-writings must needs have done, if what they write were Fictions?" Miracles and the correspondences between prophecies and historical events, such as that concerning the destruction of Jerusalem, were empirically verifiable, and the fact that Jews did not step forward to refute Christian claims concerning Christ's miracles and fulfilment of prophecies was for Penn an argument for the truth of Christianity.[127]

[125] "Primitive Christianity" (1696), *Works*, II, 866.

[126] "Defence of a Paper" (1698), *Works*, II, 898.

[127] "A Visitation to the Jews" (1695), *Works*, II, 848-853; "Defence of the Duke" (1685), *Works*, II, 716-717.

Penn also used the arguments for religion that were based on the regularity and design observed in nature. When he observed nature, he saw "the Stamp and Voice of a Deity every where, and in Every thing, to the Observing." The world wears the mark of its Maker everywhere and is "a great and stately Volume of natural Things; and may be not improperly stiled the Hieroglyphicks of a better. . . ."[128] The wisdom and power of that Being who disposed the world and framed it into the glorious and regular thing we see it to be, show him to be what men call God, the "Great Workman."[129]

Such arguments, however, were wholly secondary for Penn; they do not appear prominently in his works. More often he held that arguments for religion involving the senses were satisfactory only to those primitive men who were wandering in lowly and outward ways—ignorant men unaware of the path to God to be found within their own souls. Christ, for example, had employed miracles merely because of the darkness and carnality of his times. Since men were not in every case ready for the direct influx of divine light and more direct ways of knowing, God had condescended to gain their attention by crude coercive means, but true faith and knowledge were of a more noble nature. "For had not the Lord Jesus observ'd the Darkness and Carnality of those Times, to be so great, as without reaching through the black Clouds of their Traditions and Superstitions, by the Hand of his Miracles (or visible Signs to their Understandings, or rather Senses) there was no likelihood of fastning a Conviction on them, there never had been need of an external Miracle in any such Sense. I would that Men should know, we have receiv'd and maintain'd our Faith in Christ by more noble and sublime Arguments. . . ."[130] The process by which one knows directly or "immediately" without the interposition of the senses

128 "Fruits of Solitude" (1693), *Works*, I, 821, 820.
129 "Defence of the Duke" (1685), *Works*, II, 713.
130 "Serious Apology" (1671), *Works*, II, 38-39.

is a "more solid Ground for Faith and Knowledge" than any sense knowledge can be.[131]

PENN related his spirit-body epistemology to Christianity by speaking of the relation between the old and new covenants in the manner of Fox. The relationship was that between shadow and reality, so that the time before Christ was a primitive era during which man was not capable of possessing direct knowledge of spiritual truths. At times Penn attributed this plight of man to the Fall, thereby implying that man had been created with access to God through the knowledge implanted within the mind but that the Fall had necessitated a slow and laborious tutoring process until man was once again ready for "inner" knowledge. Elsewhere Penn spoke of an evolution from primitivism without reference to the Fall. Man had developed in history until he became sufficiently sophisticated to communicate with God directly. In either case the time of the old covenant was portrayed as one in which man had been enlightened through lowly means suited to his "dull" state. During the "Childish State of the Jews, God was pleased to allure them after an Expectation of higher Things, by Types and Prophecies of that far more Excellent and Exceeding Glorious Dispensation of the Light and Love of God in after Ages."[132] Such practices as priestly instruction of the people and sacrifices and ceremonies were dim pointers to the future dispensation, as was the written law of the Jews.

The Christian dispensation was for Penn the time of fulfilment in which man was enabled to go beyond childish ways of knowing. He placed great emphasis on the promise of Jeremiah 31:33, where the prophet is promised a law written on the heart for the new age. The significance of the Christ-event was that the types and shadows of the old covenant were fulfilled and outmoded by Christ, who is now within the heart of everyone. At the same time, the

[131] "Quakerism a New Nickname" (1672), *Works*, II, 292.
[132] "Christian Quaker" (1673), *Works*, I, 570.

written law was surpassed with the coming of the "law within."[133] The new covenant brought an eternal and unchanging principle of knowledge, and thus God's word to man is no longer dependent on the corruptible and changing ways of men and matter.

This approach to the significance of the Christian dispensation had obviously negative implications for the doctrine of means. If the distinction between the old and the new covenants is that between "outward" and "inward" in the physical—as opposed to existential or mystical—sense, then, properly speaking, it is impossible to give "outward" means and forms of expression any function in the Christian dispensation. "This World is a Form; our Bodies are Form; and no visible Acts of Devotion can be without Forms. But yet the less Form in Religion the better, since God is a Spirit: for the more mental our Worship, the more adequate to the Nature of God; the more silent, the more suitable to the Language of a Spirit."[134]

Penn was at least as concerned about organizational matters and about order and regularity within the Quaker fold as the other public Friends were. Even in his most dualistic moments he argued for the continuing usefulness of—indeed necessity for—outward means and religious expression. He held, first, that men could adapt to the new "spiritual" ways only gradually, and that, in fact, as long as they were compound beings living in a corporeal world, they would profit from sense knowledge in the religious realm. Direct or "immediate" knowledge of spiritual realities was an ideal to be striven for, but because man's life in this world entails corporeal being, and because he is so constantly attracted to physical objects and lives his life "abroad among the senses," he must be appealed to on that level. "For as the Weakness of Men should not call the Ability of the Light in Question, nor their Carnality take off from the Light's Sufficiency, Spirituality, or Divinity, so neither doth the

---

[133] "Serious Apology" (1671), *Works*, II, 39-41.
[134] "Fruits of Solitude" (1693), *Works*, I, 842.

Sufficiency of the Light render all Means accommodated to Man's Weakness vain or needless. . . ." At times Penn argued that knowledge acquired through physical means could lead to the direct, unmediated knowledge that is more appropriate for the Christian dispensation. "Means in God's Power are us'd not as settled Teachers, but as Instrumental in God's Hand to testifie of and direct to that one Great Prophet and Living Teacher in the Hearts of Men, that all may come hither and be taught of him."[135] How this could be, considering the passivity of corporeal reality and its unsuitability for "spiritual" purposes, Penn did not say. But in regard to both "means" and the incarnate Christ himself, he argued that in some way "every Mediate Conviction gives an Addition of Life, and Strength to the Immediate Conviction" that is a product of the direct action of the divine light.[136]

This position enabled Penn to affirm that because of the "Imbecillity" of men, the Scriptures remain obligatory means of knowledge of God where they are known.[137] Similarly, in preaching, God can use the minds and mouths of men to approach other men. The Spirit is the only proper teacher of men, but to say this is not to deny that the Spirit can teach by employing ministers and preachers as instruments and, in a loose sense, agents. The Spirit supplies the "matter" and the divine power, but the preacher provides the words or the "Covering of Expression" by the Spirit's appointment.[138] "God was in Christ, and Christ in his Ministers reconciling the World unto himself, that he might be the Immediate Priest, Prophet and King to the Souls of People."[139] For similar reasons, according to Penn, Quakers employed assemblies, spoken prayers, prophecies and spiritual songs—all external expressions and yet all appropriate

[135] "Reason Against Railing" (1673), *Works*, ii, 506, 515.
[136] *Ibid.*, 505; "Quakerism a New Nickname" (1672), *Works*, ii, 254-255.
[137] "Counterfeit Christian" (1674), *Works*, ii, 589-590.
[138] "Invalidity" (1673), *Works*, ii, 389-390.
[139] "Reason Against Railing" (1673), *Works*, ii, 541-542.

because of the weakness of men. In fact, virtually any means may be appropriate so long as they are employed with the direct, immediate guidance of the Spirit and not used "in and from Man's mere Wit, Will, Innovation or Invitation."[140] Because of man's lowliness, external means are necessary, but they are employed validly only when the Spirit is their immediate guide and mover. One must wait on the Lord to lead; man is to be only a passive agent of the supernatural power of God.

Despite the necessity of the continued use of means, Penn's confidence in the possibility of unmediated knowledge of God placed his doctrine of means in the position of a lingering element that men should strive to overcome. God's condescension was a gracious act, and man should respond by striving to make the most of his inner knowledge and reducing his dependence on outward means as much as possible, thereby releasing God from his unseemly union with physical, corruptible elements. Penn had confidence that there could be progress from the outward to the inward during the successive ages of the Christian era, as there had been from the time of the old covenant to that of the new. Especially did he believe that the new dispensation in his own time had brought progress in that regard. For this reason he was willing to allow the use of means even while urging his readers to go beyond them.

It was in this manner that Penn dealt with the sacraments. Like all Quakers, he said that no sacraments were properly part of the new covenant. "But we, believing Christ to be the End and Substance of all Signs and Shadows under the Gospel to his People, have therefore in Reverence to the Substance, and not in disrespect to the Visible Signs, Declined the Use of them; though at the same time we do not Condemn those that Conscientiously practice them."[141] Now that Christ dwells within, there is no longer any need

---

[140] "Key Opening the Way" (1692), *Works*, II, 782-783.
[141] "The Quaker a Christian" (1698), ACMC, xxxvi, 23ff. (Printed in 1698). Written with John Everett and Thomas Story.

for the signs and shadows that point to and remind of Christ. For this reason he argued that the passages that Christians have normally viewed as instituting the sacrament of baptism were to be taken metaphorically as references to the baptism of the Spirit.[142] But because of the words concerning the eucharist, "Do this till I come. . . ," he held that in the early period of the Christian dispensation God had allowed a continuation of the old kinds of external means. The Jews had become over-ceremonious and were not easily weaned from external things, and many Gentiles had to be taught spiritual truths while still in a primitive state. Thus means could be employed until Christ came in the Spirit at Pentecost; and for the very weak and ignorant they could be used after that when necessary. Nevertheless, Penn believed that by the seventeenth century the need for them had been overcome.[143]

At times he actually envisioned the extension of this principle to all means and to all outward religious expression. George Keith, after leaving the Quakers, suggested that this was the result of the consistent application of Quaker principles, but presumably he thought of himself as applying a *reductio ad absurdum* argument, for he suggested that the Quakers should need neither words nor "any Meetings at all of Men and Women outwardly Assembled. . . ."[144] Whether or not Keith expected his former colleague to take this argument seriously, in fact he was merely describing Penn's fondest hopes for the true church. Discussing the ministry in *Primitive Christianity Revived*, Penn said that as men grow in grace, the dispensation will be less in words and more in life, "and Preaching will in great Measure be turned into Praising, and the Worship of God, more into

---

[142] "Invalidity" (1673), *Works*, II, 401-402; "Wisdom Justified" (1673), *Works*, II, 474-475.

[143] "Quakerism a New Nickname" (1672), *Works*, II, 277-279; "Serious Apology" (1671), *Works*, II, 60.

[144] *The Arguments of the Quakers . . . Against Baptism and the Supper Examined and Refuted* (London, 1698), 28-29.

walking with, than talking of, God."[145] This implied that in the ideal future there would be no need for means or physical sensuous vehicles in God's dealings with men. There would be a need only for sensuous means for man's worship of God—to express his praise and thankfulness. But Penn went on to express the hope that there would be in the future less need for regular organization and meetings for worship of any kind. In the true "Life of Conversion and Regeneration" to which all the dispensations of God have tended, "every Man's a Temple, and every Family a Church, and every Place, a Meeting-Place, and every Visit a Meeting. And yet a little while, and it shall be so yet more and more. . . ."[146] There will be a need for "Signs and Forms," "such necessary and essential ones as are coupl'd to our very being, and requisite Converse among Men," but the visible organized church in even the minimal Quaker form would disappear.[147]

THE polemic about Scripture played an especially prominent role in Penn's writings, and his attitude toward this means of grace shows especially clearly his ambiguity about "outward" means. In his early writings Penn seems to have been strongly influenced by Fisher and presented as radical a critique of Scripture as is found in any Catholic attacks. Later his affinities with liberal Anglicans and his search for a minimal set of Scriptural doctrines on which all Christians could agree made him stress the sufficiency and clarity of the Bible in direct contradiction of his earlier arguments.

Penn was firmly convinced that the Spirit or the inner light could and did operate "beside, with or above the Scriptures" as well as through the use of physical agents other than Scripture.[148] He believed that the Spirit, without the use of any created means, could bring "Instruction, Dis-

[145] "Primitive Christianity" (1696), *Works*, II, 873.
[146] *Ibid.*, 873-874.
[147] "Pretended Answer" (1695), *Works*, II, 834.
[148] "Invalidity" (1673), *Works*, II, 359.

coveries and Revelation" in the same infallible way that these had come to those very men who had written the Scripture.[149] Penn believed that God could reveal through the light any kind of particular information. The Spirit or light, which had revealed to the prophets and certain heathens many things concerning the future incarnation of Christ, and which had provided Moses with an account of the creation, could have supplied mankind in all ages with the history of Christ's visible appearance had not the story been told in Scripture. In addition, the Spirit did, in fact, regularly provide particular revelations of the same direct kind as those that had come at the birth of the church. If one professed to be religious without receiving such experiences, he was grounding his religion in other men's apprehensions and precepts.[150] Occasionally Penn wrote that Scripture was primarily a record of the impressive spiritual experiences of others rather than a normative authority. Scripture was "but the Mind and Teachings of the Divine Light in others, declared and recorded," "a Declaration of Faith and Experience; therefore not the Rule or Judge."[151] When writing in this vein, he said that the primary function of Scripture was to provide narratives of the experiences of the early church and thereby serve as a source of comfort, confirmation of our own experiences, and exemplary behavior.[152]

Penn made especially good use of the Pyrrhonist destruction of the Bible as a religious authority formulated by Catholics. Exponents of the *machine de guerre de nouvelle invention* emphasized the difficulty of proving Scripture divinely inspired, its contradictions and barbarities, the likelihood of lost books, textual corruptions, poor copying and translating, and the general unsuitability of its metaphorical

[149] "General Rule" (1673), *Works*, I, 601-602.
[150] "Counterfeit Christian" (1674), *Works*, II, 572, 591; "Truth Exalted" (1668), *Works*, I, 242, 244-245.
[151] "General Rule" (1673), *Works*, I, 597, 608.
[152] "Serious Apology" (1671), *Works*, II, 37.

and figurative material for the purposes to which Protestants put it. Penn employed all these arguments and often improved on them in ways not available to Catholics. One such argument was his attack on the form of the Scriptures. Penn pointed out that the Scriptures are not suitable as a norm of doctrine and life because they are not the product of an orderly process of codification. The books were brought into being on diverse occasions and filled immediate historical needs by providing comfort, warnings, prophecies, and other limited assistance. As a result they possess none of the marks of a "Great Rule." They lack internal consistency and contain many apparent contradictions on points of the highest importance. Nor do they possess the clarity essential to such a rule. Moreover, the language of Scripture is often inappropriate for a doctrinal norm. There is much figurative language and allegory; there is no attempt to define terms; and there is a general lack of coherence and plainness of language. Finally, the problem of translation, large enough in any circumstances, becomes virtually insuperable with this kind of language and material.[153]

According to Penn, the fact that the writings that now compose the New Testament canon were scattered and uncollected for several centuries also reduces their usefulness as a religious authority and indicates that the church could exist without a canonical Scripture.[154] Moreover, the present state of the books in the canon indicated to Penn that the centuries before collection had not been kind to the Christian records. There were about three thousand alternate readings in the Greek New Testament alone. Under the circumstances this was unavoidable, since writings kept in this fashion without a centralized control group are notoriously liable to "sophistication, mistranslation, false copies and infinity of other problems."[155]

[153] "Invalidity" (1673), *Works*, II, 376.
[154] *Ibid.*, 325-326; "New Athenians" (1692), *Works*, II, 799.
[155] Letter to Friend W. B. [1675], PWP (contemp. copy in HSP). See also "Serious Apology" (1671), *Works*, II, 43; "Invalidity" (1673), *Works*, II, 325-326.

Equally problematic in Penn's mind was the process of canonization itself. There was strong evidence that many important books had been excluded or were unavailable to the canonizers. Luke, among others, refers to many inspired writers who have written of Jesus, and his use of the word *polloi* precludes the explanation that he was referring to Matthew and Mark alone. Again, according to Penn, there is no external proof that the writings we possess were actually inspired by the Spirit. In fact, the "authority"—presumably Penn meant attributed authorship and antiquity—of several books, including Hebrews, James, II and III John, II Peter, Jude, Revelation, and even Matthew, has been legitimately questioned. Finally, the uncertainty surrounding the procedures of collection and canonization was compounded by the "disputatious" atmosphere of the fourth century. The Council of Laodicea was held not only "about the time of Julian the Apostate" but at a time of great doctrinal dissension within the church, when each party was ready to bend doctrines to suit its own beliefs. Under the circumstances, Penn concluded, one has "no more reason to believe the Truth of those great Things related in that Part of Scriptures yet remaining than any Legend of Rome."[156]

Basil Willey has written of late seventeenth-century Englishmen: "An age which discovered God effortlessly in the starry heavens above, and in the moral law within, could not but be embarrassed by having to acknowledge dependence upon the annals and legends of an unenlightened Semitic tribe."[157] Despite the occasional vehemence of his

[156] "Invalidity" (1673), *Works*, II, 339-340, 325-326. Although Penn's typically English Protestant anti-Catholic bias is evident even in these remarks, his ready employment of the *machine de guerre* may help to account for the widespread suspicion that he was secretly a papist—a suspicion that surrounded him throughout his life as a Quaker. In his writings he sometimes cited the Catholic Pietro Soane Polano as his authority for arguments against Scripture. His dependence on "Catholic" arguments at other points was surely noted by Anglicans and nonconformists for whom the polemic against Catholics over Scripture was of prime importance.

[157] *Seventeenth-Century Background*, 80.

negative remarks about Scripture, Penn's attitude was not primarily attributable to an enlightened embarrassment. He was concerned, rather, about the fact that a wrong kind of dependence on Scripture was in part responsible for the religious problems of his time. For the most part, despite his hyperbolic attack on puritan claims for Scripture, his opposition, especially in his later years, was not to Scripture as such but to the belief that Scripture was an adequate authority apart from the immediate guidance of the Spirit.

According to Penn, the Quakers were not trying to "justle" Scripture from its rightful place as an authority; they merely wanted people to "experience" what they claimed to believe and to have the witness fulfilled in themselves. The Quakers' great emphasis on the Spirit was not meant to exclude Scripture but to counteract a tendency to put the letter of Scripture in place of the Spirit. When Quakers seemed to de-emphasize Scripture, Penn said, they were to be understood as speaking comparatively. Their intention was not to denigrate Scripture but to emphasize the necessity of confronting Christ, the light and Spirit that was the source of Scripture. The points to be made regarding a proper reliance on Scripture were two. First, one should know that the mere reading of Scripture does not give the power to believe or act on it. Only if one approached Scripture with the light or Spirit already active within him could the Bible be of assistance. Too many people believed that one could buy the Spirit from a bookseller, whereas "the Mysteries of Regeneration are as puzzling to natural Wit and earthly Wisdom as before."[158] Second, one needed the guidance of the Spirit to ascertain the true meaning of Scripture because of its lack of clarity, its contradictions, and other characteristics making it unsuitable as a rule of doctrine.[159]

[158] "Urim and Thummim" (1674), *Works*, ii, 623-624; "Invalidity" (1673), *Works*, ii, 364; "General Rule" (1673), *Works*, i, 601-602.

[159] "A Defence of a Paper, Entituled Gospel-Truths, Against the Exceptions of the Bishop of Cork's Testimony" (1698), *Works*, ii, 912.

The conservative side of Penn's attitude toward Scripture is most clearly evident in his statement that his attitude toward religious authority was the essential Protestant position, which puritans had abandoned when they began idolizing Scripture. The doctrine of the Reformers, "the great Foundation of our Protestant Religion," was that Scripture and Spirit operated together as mutually dependent coordinate authorities.[160] Writing of his basic religious principles, Penn began, "1st, That the Grace of God within me, and the Scriptures without me, are the Foundation and Declaration of my Faith and Religion, and let any Man get better if he can."[161] Citing Zwingli, Luther, Melancthon, Calvin, Bucer, Erasmus, and the English reformers Rogers, Philpot, Bradford, Hooper, and Lambert, Penn discussed the Quakers as the last in the long line of Protestants who believed "that the Double and Agreeing Testimony of the Spirit of God Within, and the Scriptures of Truth Without, is the Rule and Judge of Faith, Doctrine and Practice; yea, that the Spirit is given to Believers to be the Rule and Judge by which they are to understand the True Sense and Meaning of the Scriptures."[162] The Reformers may have emphasized Scripture more than Spirit, since they wished to contrast it with popish doctors and councils, but they did not mean to elevate it to the exclusion of immediate dependence on the Spirit's instruction. They had known what the Quakers were once again called to emphasize, namely, that the Spirit and Scripture must be taken together, since they harmonize and bear reciprocal testimonies to each other.[163]

Penn's positive statements about Scripture often went well beyond the admission that the Spirit could—and commonly did—employ Scripture as its primary means of reve-

---

[160] "Address to Protestants" (1679), *Works*, I, 779; "A Just Rebuke to One and Twenty Learned Divines . . ." (1674), *Works*, II, 607-608.
[161] "Fiction Found Out" (1685), *Works*, I, 126.
[162] "Defence of a Paper" (1698), *Works*, II, 913.
[163] "Invalidity" (1673), *Works*, II, 343, 363; "New Athenians" (1692), *Works*, II, 799.

lation. We find in his writings arguments assuming that Scripture was a unique kind of authority that could be used as a criterion for judging the validity of leadings of the Spirit or for solving doctrinal and ethical disputes between "inspired" sects. Such arguments are attributable in part, especially after 1688, to Penn's desire to have the government consider the Quakers Protestants and thus grant them protection under the Toleration Act. Equally strong, however, was his fear that the Quakers would be linked with fanatics and enthusiasts who were likely to assert that the Spirit had told them to say and do strange things. Indeed, Penn himself believed firmly in social order and was frightened by libertarians who had no control mechanisms for their spiritual leadings. He often tried to make man's rational faculty such a controlling factor in his own version of spiritual Christianity, but at times he employed Scripture in this way as well.

In this vein Penn often threw back the charges of enthusiasm hurled at Quakers by those Christians wrangling over theological niceties. The cause of most theological disagreements was man's tendency to impose his own interpretations on the words of Scripture. Most of the disputes centered around man-made creeds and deductions from Scripture that amounted to the substitution of human opinions for the Word of God.[164] The real enthusiasts, said Penn, were those who wanted to make Christian communion dependent on a certain doctrine of predestination or free will or church organization that they "deduced" from Scripture, rather than those who claimed spiritual or experiential support for a Biblical idea. Defending the Quaker attitude toward swearing, Penn argued: "Now we think this will not prove us Enthusiasts, nor Silly; for we argue from a Text, and not our own Dreams and Fancies. Had we only pretended the Authority of a private Revelation for this Assertion, and that not true, then it had been Enthusiasm, and we Enthusi-

---

[164] "Invalidity" (1673), *Works*, II, 355-357, 364; "Address to Protestants" (1679), *Works*, I, 774-775.

asts in the worst Sense."[165] Contradicting his *machine de guerre* arguments concerning the ambiguity of Scripture and its unsuitability as a rule of faith, Penn explicitly argued that the great controversies of the church's history, such as those over free will at Dort, church polity in England, Arianism, and the rest, would have been avoided if men had stuck to the words of Scripture. What man, he asked, can presume to be wiser than the Spirit? The Scriptures are the expression of the mind of God and Christ and thus cannot be accused of such shortness, ambiguity, and obliquity that men need to make them more intelligible.[166]

Most of Penn's use of Scripture as a permanently valid criterion for Christians, apart from the Spirit's immediate guidance, had to do with controverted doctrines, the moral law, and certain passages of Scripture "more particularly relating to our days" that rule out specific practices and doctrines.[167] Because of the possibility that a man, through constant sinning, could have a "seared conscience" and extinguish his inner light, Penn allowed that the moral law of the Bible, the "standing and permanent truths" or "general, permanent, indispensable commands concerning faith and holy life" were permanently valid.[168] He also cited Scripture as justification for the peculiar Quaker practices in such matters as the use of hats, swearing, and nonobservance of holy days. In defense of the nonobservance of holy days, for example, Penn quoted Galatians 4:9-11, where Paul wrote that the Galatians were in bondage because of their observance of the law on such matters. This, according to Penn, "is Defence enough for us; for if the Apostle said it, the Holy Ghost said it; and we are sure, whoever require or practice any thing contrary to this Reproof, they are great Strangers to the Liberty of the Gospel. . . ."[169]

[165] "New Athenians" (1692), *Works*, II, 793.
[166] "Address to Protestants" (1679), *Works*, I, 745, 791.
[167] "General Rule" (1673), *Works*, I, 600-601.
[168] "Wisdom Justified" (1673), *Works*, II, 467; "The Skirmisher Defeated and Truth Defended" (1676), *Works*, II, 600.
[169] "Serious Apology" (1671), *Works*, II, 51.

Penn, then, emphasized at different times both the inadequacies of Scripture and its usefulness. He believed that the puritan attempt to balance freedom with order, and enthusiasm with rationalism, had veered to the right, so that faith had become assent, and order had become legalism. As a result, religious profession had taken on a formal, lifeless air, and the various Protestant sects found themselves fighting over patches of Scripture without the certain insights provided by the Spirit. The solution, which Penn shared with other Quakers on the left wing of spiritual puritanism, consisted in so preaching the Spirit as to enable men to realize that the only power capable of sanctifying and unifying them, and the final authority for a Christian, was Christ himself present with man through the Spirit. The Spirit normally would operate through the use of Scripture, and Scripture, moreover, could serve as a controlling criterion of spiritual experiences. But according to Penn, it was important to state clearly that the Spirit was the agent, Scripture the subordinate means, and that the Spirit could bring Christ to a man independently of Scripture. Only such a strong emphasis on the Spirit and the inner light could make clear the absolute necessity of having an experiential base to one's religion. Creedal affirmation could become vital faith and the Christian hope become "sure and certain" only when one had been confronted with "Christ within."

FIVE

SPIRITUAL RELIGION AND
RATIONALISM

WHEN Adolph Harnack looked into the well of Christian history and saw a Jesus clothed in nineteenth-century garb, George Tyrrell suspected that Harnack's inability to penetrate the reflection on the surface was attributable to faulty historical vision.[1] Many of those who have looked into the well of Quaker history have had a similar propensity for seeing their own reflection. Voltaire found the quintessential Quaker to be a predecessor of the *philosophes*; Ralph Waldo Emerson saw a budding Transcendentalist; the Congregationalist historian Geoffrey Nuttall spied a left-wing puritan; and neo-orthodox Quakers such as Maurice Creasey find a genuine son of the Reformation.[2] In these circumstances we do not need to possess a high regard for the historical vision of men such as Voltaire and Emerson to surmise that there may be something peculiarly difficult to visualize in its entirety at the bottom of the well. The immediate background of the Quaker movement may have been the splintering of puritanism and the rise of spiritualism, but Voltaire and Emerson were not wholly mistaken in seeing the germs of their differing kinds of rationalism there as well.

The aspect of Quakerism that has been most responsible for the widely divergent interpretations of the intellectual thrust of the movement has been the doctrine of the inner light. Most interpreters could probably concur with Nut-

[1] *Christianity at the Crossroads* (London, 1910), 44.
[2] Frederick Tolles, "1652 in History: Changing Perspectives on the Founding of Quakerism," in Anna Brinton, ed., *Then and Now: Quaker Essays Historical and Contemporary* (Phila., 1960).

tall's judgment that the message of George Fox and Quakerism constituted an "appeal to individual, personal experience" as the focal point of one's religious life. Nuttall terms this appeal "the authentic voice of the seventeenth century," since the doctrine of the inner light was a manifestation of the general perception of the age that it was no longer either desirable or possible to accept one's religious beliefs on the authority of either an infallible church or an infallible Scripture interpreted by scholarly saints. The Quakers' inner light was one of several principles developed in seventeenth-century England to provide the "inward certitude" in matters of belief and conduct that adherence to external authorities could no longer produce.[3] Agreement on this general level, however, does not take one very far toward an understanding of Quakerism or the inner light, because "the appeal to individual, personal experience" was made in the name of a wide variety of epistemological principles. These, in turn, were attached to varying understandings of man, his condition in this world, and his relation to God. For the purposes of understanding the broader intellectual milieu of Quakerism in general and the more rationalistic side of Penn's thought in particular, I shall discuss them against the background provided by several prominent seventeenth-century principles of inward rational certitude.

RELIGION AND REASON AMONG PURITANS AND ANGLICANS

As Perry Miller has written, there was an "equilibrium of forces, emotional and intellectual, within the Puritan creed."[4] I have already discussed the way in which, during the splintering process of the 1640's, the "emotional" side of the puritan movement led to a search for inner certainty

---

[3] *Holy Spirit*, 26-27. The phrase "inward certitude" is Basil Willey's, *Seventeenth-Century Background*, 127. See also G. R. Cragg, *From Puritanism to the Age of Reason* (Cambridge, 1950), 47-49.

[4] *Seventeenth-Century Background*, 77.

of salvation through the experience of the indwelling of the Holy Spirit. Unable to achieve assurance from a religion that they believed equated conversion with intellectual acceptance of doctrine and demanded of its "saints" merely an external observance of the laws of God, spiritualists began to replace Scripture with an inner authority. Since the experience of the Spirit was more affective and "immediate" than those mediated through the normal senses and faculties, which were passive in the experience, many spiritualists emphasized the uselessness of their faculties in religion. Man's reason came in for some especially severe denunciations. For the spiritualists the means to inward certitude could best be described as a spiritual "sense" that provided an overpowering experience of divine presence and communication.[5]

If the splintering of puritanism left some men with a better grasp of the emotional than the rational aspect of the movement, it did the opposite for others. Partly in response to the "enthusiasm" of the Interregnum, nonconformists such as Richard Baxter, David Clarkson, John Howe, and Stephen Charnock accentuated the idea that revealed truth was congruent with the natural truths of reason and that in the experience of regeneration one's rational perception was renewed, so that the saint began to understand—if only in part—God's ways with man. They were drawing on a moderate kind of rationalism that had always been part of the puritan movement and was well expressed by John Preston:

Faith addeth to the eye of reason, and raiseth it higher for the understanding is conversant, as about things of reason, so also about things of Faith; for they are propounded to the understanding, only they are above it and must have faith to reveale them . . . as one that hath dimme eyes, he can see better with the help of Spectacles: even so doth the eye of reason, by a supernaturall faith infused. So that all things which wee beleeve, have

[5] See Nuttall, *Holy Spirit*, 39-41.

a credibilitie and entitie in them, and they are the objects of the understanding; but we cannot finde them out, without some supernaturall help.[6]

This rational approach to regeneration was for many puritans part of a larger faith that man, although wholly dependent on God, was nevertheless the only creature in the world who possessed the *imago Dei*. This meant that he alone was destined for a personal relationship with God. Man's service to God was to be a freely given service based on his acceptance of God as his proper Lord and Master. It was to be an allegiance based on firm "conviction," and, as Preston indicated, "conviction" was in part based on a measure of "understanding."

By the latter half of the seventeenth century the "intellectual" elements in the puritan creed had placed many nonconformists in a position to respond positively to the developing intellectual climate among progressive English thinkers. They took an interest in both the "new science," which was seeking to comprehend and control God's ordered creation, and the attempt to modify dependence on "the dead weight of tradition" and "lifeless authority" in spiritual matters.[7] Unlike many fellow-"moderns," however, they saw validity in the new thought because of elements in their theological background more than because of their subjection to Baconian and Cartesian influences. In their interest in the "new science" and their belief in the rationality of religious experience, they were developing ideas that were to be found in the Reformed traditions stemming from Zwingli and Calvin.[8] From these teachers the puritans had

[6] *Life Eternall or, A Treatise of the Knowledge of the Divine Essence and Attributes* (London, 1631), 46-47.

[7] Cragg, *From Puritanism to the Age of Reason*, 8.

[8] Although historians should be grateful to Perry Miller for uncovering puritan rationality, Miller jumped too quickly to the conclusion that the puritans' covenant theology represented their attempt to join forces with the "new philosophy" of the age as it attempted, in Bacon's words, "to extend more widely the limits of the power

inherited an aversion to the "quiddities" and deductive mentality of late Medieval scholasticism and a determination to
worry less about the essence of the divine nature and to
employ their mental efforts to discover what they could
about God's creation. As Robert Merton has written, the
puritan "scheme of orientation embraced an undisguised
emphasis upon utility as well as control of self and the external world, which in turn involved a preference for the
visual, manual and concretely manageable rather than the
purely logical and verbal."[9]

As they wished to learn the laws of nature in order to
become better stewards of God's creation, so Interregnum
and Restoration puritans and nonconformists such as Richard Baxter and John Howe applied their active, inquiring,
rational spirit to the religious realm in order to understand
the sovereign God well enough to grant him heartfelt "conviction." According to Baxter, the Christian religion is "the
most rational in the world." "Reason, which is our nature,
is not destroyed, but repaired, illuminated, elevated, and
improved by the Christian faith."[10] The difference between
the rationality of earlier puritans, such as Preston, and that
of many Commonwealth and Restoration figures following
this tradition was that the reason of the latter had a larger
function in providing inward certitude. The riot of Scriptural polemics of the early Commonwealth had proved once

and greatness of man." Zwingli and Calvin, Renaissance humanists of
the first rank even before they became Reformers, had bequeathed
to the Reformed tradition attitudes toward natural theology, the liberal arts, and reason that could be developed by puritan theologians
within a Christian humanist framework and without the promethean
outlook of many of the "new philosophers." Miller has given the
impression that puritans had to be schizophrenic to be interested in
both Calvin and in reason and the new science. See especially *Errand
Into the Wilderness* (1956; rpt., New York, 1964), 92.

[9] "Science, Technology, and Society in Seventeenth Century England," *Osiris*, IV, ed. George Sarton (1938), 474.

[10] "The Reasons of the Christian Religion," in *The Practical Works
of Richard Baxter* (4 vols.; London, 1838), II, 98, 92.

and for all that the bare words of Scripture were unable to provide a sure and certain guide. The only recourse available was to look within man for a guide to Scripture. Puritans who, like Baxter, had a firm grasp of the intellectual side of the movement became convinced that certainty in religious matters was achieved by the testimony of the rational faculty to certain ideas found in Scripture and to the credibility of the Scriptures as a whole. Baxter argued for the reasonableness of Christianity on the basis of arguments from prophecy and miracles, the personal character of Christ, Christianity's suitableness to man's notions of God, its adaptation to his character and wants, and the power evident in the lives of converted men.[11] Baxter continued to believe that reason had to be illuminated by divine grace, but he expected grace to come not as a blinding insight or a sense of Spirit-possession but as a persuasive, illuminating power that enabled one to see and to understand what his mutilated faculties had previously failed to find credible.

Nonconformists (and Anglicans) who spoke of their inner assurance in terms of reason did not necessarily deny any of the central tenets of puritan thought. They remained convinced, first, that although the experience was known primarily as an appeal to reason, it was a product of God's gracious initiative. They continued to divide men into the regenerate and the unregenerate, and they believed that God determined who belonged in which camp. Second, there was nothing about the claims of men such as Baxter and Howe that necessarily conflicted with the puritan belief that God always remains "hidden" in his revelations of himself and communicates with man through indirect modes

---

[11] See especially "The Reasons of the Christian Religion" and "The Unreasonableness of Infidelity," in *Practical Works*, II. See also Clarkson, "Of Living by Faith" and "The Excellent Knowledge of Christ," *Practical Works* (3 vols.; Edinburgh, 1864-1865), I; Charnock, "Upon the Wisdom of God," *Complete Works* (5 vols.; Edinburgh, 1864-1866), II; Howe, "The Principles of the Oracles of God," *The Whole Works of the Rev'd John Howe* (7 vols.; London, 1813), VII.

of knowing—mediating agents or secondary causes. Baxter meant by "reason" a discursive faculty more often than a Platonic source of insight, and thereby continued to emphasize the inability of reason to see other than "through a glass, darkly" in this world. No man had a direct vision of God. A third way in which the conservatism of the moderate rationalists manifested itself was in their continued awareness that the transcendent, omnipotent God was not to be fathomed or understood by man except in a limited way. They wanted to assert more clearly than puritans had in the past that when God regenerated a man, he condescended to come to him and persuade him personally. Nevertheless, they knew that much about God and his ways with men would remain incomprehensible. With Baxter they realized that they had "reason to acknowledge the imbecility of [their] reason, and its incompetency to censure the wisdom of God."[12]

PURITANS who were strongly influenced by Platonism, including some who inclined to spiritualism, such as Walter Cradock and Sir Harry Vane, found little cause to distinguish between the "Spirit" and "reason." For them the appeal to an inner spiritual authority was associated primarily with a luminous awareness of eternal truths personally validated, and the reason involved in regeneration was the Platonic source of divine truth. Such men gradually found themselves less convinced of the advisability of distinguishing sharply between the regenerate and the unregenerate, of the fittingness of making sense-knowledge the path to religious truth, and of the credibility of a religion that believed in a God who remained finally incomprehensible. If such wayward puritans moved far enough in their new concerns, they found themselves close to what Jerald Brauer has called "the liberal spirit" that became dominant in English religious thought in the latter half of the seventeenth

[12] "The Unreasonableness of Infidelity," *Practical Works*, II, 393.

century.[13] This liberalism, which many historians have interpreted as the philosophical and religious counterpart of the rationalistic Cartesian assumptions of the "new science," was based on a more or less explicit rejection of the classical Protestant assumptions about man's moral and intellectual abilities. It combined its more optimistic assessment of man with an anthropomorphic conception of God, who was defined in terms of what seemed self-evidently true to the rational mind of the era. Its major philosophical and religious concern was the description of an epistemological principle that was believed to operate equally in all men to provide them with a clear vision of the central truths about God and man. This meant a search for a minimum set of self-evident theological truths that were viewed as either innate in men or obvious to all through their experience.

Toward the end of the century the new epistemological principle was conceived more and more in Aristotelian fashion, as in the thought of John Locke. More significant for our purposes in discussing Quakerism and Penn are the many Stoic or Platonic principles prominent in the second half of the century. The kinds of inward certitude that were desired by men such as John Goodwin, William Walwyn, some of the men known as the Cambridge Platonists, and liberal Anglicans such as John Tillotson and Edward Fowler were forms of direct intellectual knowledge or even intellectual-mystical vision of God. For such men the knowledge provided by the senses was too uncertain to serve as the source of essential religious truth. If the senses necessarily played the major role in gaining knowledge of this world, especially that provided by the new science, the most important knowledge of the next world came through an intellectual intuition. Although Tillotson and Fowler and their fellow-latitudinarians are normally associated with the revolt against innate ideas and with the attempt to make Christianity "probable" on the basis of reasoning about the

[13] "Puritanism, Mysticism, and the Development of Liberalism," *CH*, 19 (1950), 156.

sense-knowledge on which it rested, such arguments were relevant only to their attempts to prove the supernatural or "unessential" truths of Christianity. Their certainty about the essential truths of all religion was based on more direct modes of knowledge, and these latter truths were the more important ones to them.

Some of the Cambridge Platonists and certain members of the Royal Society segregated knowledge of this world and the next in this manner in an attempt to limit the materialistic and skeptical implications of the new science. It seemed to them that the materialism of Hobbes could become widespread unless they demonstrated the limits of mechanical explanation and provided an idealistic superstructure that validated other, more direct ways of knowing.[14] The movement to bypass means and to assert the possibility of a direct approach to God, however, was based on more than a fear of materialism. Writers such as John Smith and Edward Fowler were drawn toward Platonism and Stoicism because of their confidence that the structure of reality conformed to the laws of the human mind. What was most clearly and distinctly conceived in the mind of man was real and true. From this point of view, it was not necessary for God to condescend to speak man's language—to deal with physical beings through physical means and in indirect ways. Man was essentially spirit, and God could communicate with him by directly illuminating his highest faculty, his reason, with intuitive overpowering awareness of his truth. For the divine nature is in this view the perfection of all the higher faculties of the human soul. It is all the soul's highest thoughts realized.[15]

The process by which inward certitude of religious truth came to be largely a function of autonomous reason, or what came to be called the "light of nature," was twofold. The first step was the attempt to combine reliance on uni-

[14] See Louis Bredvold, *The Intellectual Milieu of John Dryden* (Ann Arbor, 1934), 55-56.
[15] See Tulloch, *Rational Theology*, II, 173.

versal Platonic reason with a belief in God's initiative in personally validating the truths of reason. We find in the Cambridge Platonists, in the words of Jerald Brauer, "a belief in the presence of universal truths either innate in all men or clearly evident to all who would use their faculty of reason," but at the same time an emphasis on the need for divine illumination to make these truths vividly known.[16]

At times liberals such as John Smith so emphasized the initiative of God's gracious Spirit in confronting man that the kind of inward certitude they sought appears very similar to that experienced by spiritual puritans. Smith wrote that true knowledge of God was like a personal relationship, an experience in which the reason was raised by the Spirit to a kind of "sense" or vision that words could not convey. Unlike the spiritual puritans, however, Smith did not attribute the experience to a "sense" in order to emphasize that the whole person is caught up in it, for his metaphysical assumptions precluded allowing sense-knowledge or the imagination to sully the clear light of truth. Rather, he was stressing the immediacy of the knowledge of God as an intellectual-mystical communion between the illuminated "Candle of the Lord" and the mind of God. He described it as an experience in which the "Eye of Sense" was shut and "that Brighter Eye of our Understandings, that other Eye of the Soul" had a "naked intuition" of God's essence.[17] Smith's distance from puritanism is seen in the

[16] Brauer, "Liberalism," 156-157.

[17] "A Discourse Concerning the True Way or Method of Attaining to Divine Knowledge," in *The Cambridge Platonists: Being Selections From the Writings of Benjamin Whichcote, John Smith, and Nathanael Culverwel*, ed. by E. T. Campagnac (Oxford, 1901), 92-93; "The Excellence and Nobleness of True Religion," in *Cambridge Platonists*, 180. Smith and Henry More were, among the Cambridge Platonists, somewhat distinctive in the extent to which they were influenced by the epistemology of Descartes and "Platonism" in general, but one can see similar tendencies in the thought of Benjamin Whichcote, Nathanael Culverwel, and Ralph Cudworth. See Jay G. Williams, "The Life and Thought of Benjamin Whichcote" (unpubl. Ph.D. diss., Columbia Univ., 1964), chap. 5.

fact that he understood this as the end result of a process in which one left Scripture and all sense-knowledge behind and ascended to God by a process of intellectual and moral discipline.

Smith was convinced that faith never contradicted reason, that all men had an innate knowledge of natural law, and that they would be judged leniently or harshly in accordance with the amount of light they had possessed. But he shied away from speculating about a basic minimum of necessary beliefs, from obliterating all significant distinctions between the regenerate and the unregenerate, and from making a set of innate truths in all men the ultimate authority in religion even apart from a special mystical-intellectual experience. These steps were taken, if in a halting way, by liberal clerics such as John Tillotson and Edward Fowler. Martin I. J. Griffin has written of the latitudinarians: "In an age when confidence in human reason ran high, none trusted it so much as they did."[18]

Although the latitudinarians had a highly complex understanding of reason, they are best known for their concept of "moral certainty," the term attached to their attempt to show that one could be certain that the evidence of the senses on which Scripture's origin and its accounts of miracles were based is a strong enough foundation for a secure faith. In fact, however, the surest foundation of their religious convictions was their neo-Stoicism. Tillotson and Fowler especially had a deep conviction that what they could clearly and distinctly conceive was true, and they posited an essential harmony between the mind and reality. All that exists in creation was seen as part of a static, harmonious, orderly reality governed by law—both natural

[18] "Latitudinarianism," 110. Griffin, whose study is the most comprehensive and lucid treatment of the latitudinarians I have seen, includes in the group, in addition to Tillotson and Fowler, Edward Stillingfleet, Simon Patrick, Thomas Tenison, William Lloyd, Gilbert Burnet, and Joseph Glanvill.

and moral—that reflects the inmost nature of God's being. Because man is a rational creature, his mind can be placed in congruence with the law. Although he does not possess innate ideas, properly speaking, he does have what can be called an innate faculty of thinking by innate modes of thought, answering to the inherent rationality of the exterior universe. "By this scheme, rationality was inherent in the processes of the mind as a part of the rational universe; or, to put it differently, the rationality implicit in the constitution of reality infused the structure of thought."[19]

On the basis of this epistemology, the liberal divines assumed that the "light of nature" was the ultimate authority in religion. All revelations had to be tested by the beliefs of natural religion, and in fact Christianity contained only a few articles not evident to man's rational faculty. These were not essential but were merely aids to the performance of the natural law.[20] One gained inward certitude without spiritual illumination by virtue of his clear and distinct knowledge of the universal moral law, which both defined God's being and set man's goals. All men possessed the same clear and certain ideas about right and wrong, and since the attributes of God were simply these ideas of right writ large, man could know with certainty not only how man should act, but also how God should act and even—since God always acts as he should—how he would and did act. Tillotson rejected Calvinism because "I am as certain that this doctrine cannot be of God as I am sure that God is good and just, because this grates upon the notion that mankind have of goodness and justice."[21] Whatever failed to conform to man's ideas of goodness and justice was not of God.

[19] *Ibid.*, 129.
[20] Fowler, *The Principles and Practices, of Certain Moderate Divines of the Church of England, Abusively Called Latitudinarians Truly Represented and Defended* . . . (2d edn.; London, 1671), 72-73.
[21] *Works*, ed. Ralph Barker (14 vols.; London, 1695-1704), X, 358.

QUAKERISM AND RATIONALISM

The spiritual sense of William Dell, the regenerated reason of Richard Baxter, the mystical reason of John Smith, and the light of nature of Edward Fowler—all were epistemological principles by which men gained what in the seventeenth century was called "conviction." Disagreement about the intellectual connotations of the inner light is largely the result of attempts by students of the Quaker movement to link the Friends with all these principles of "inward certitude." Voltaire and Emerson were admittedly influenced by their acquaintance with Penn's thought to associate Quakerism with the more rationalistic forms of certainty, and Penn's thought had broader intellectual affinities than that of other seventeenth-century Friends. Quakerism, as I have tried to demonstrate, was closer in spirit and purpose to, and was more directly influenced by, the spiritualist enthusiasm of men like Dell than the more rationalistic movements— even those Platonic forms of rationalism that shared its spiritual-corporeal dualism. As Nuttall has written, there is "an utter difference of spiritual climate between the rationalist Cambridge men's logos theology and the theology of the Holy Spirit which the untutored Quakers worked out in their own experience."[22]

The First Publishers of Truth were wary of man's reason and shared with many spiritualists the belief that it, like the rest of the old self, had to be silent and cease its activity in deference to the Spirit. It is the purpose of this chapter, then, to explore the rational side of Penn's thought without linking it very closely to Quaker thought in general, for here Penn was travelling alone much of the time. Nevertheless, the relationship between Quakerism and rationalism was more complex than Nuttall's statement indicates. There were in Quakerism at least signposts pointing toward some of the paths Penn followed. As Arthur Lovejoy has written, "Identical general ideas may be operative, not only in

[22] *Holy Spirit*, 18.

provinces of thought seemingly remote from one another, but even in movements which, at first sight, appear unlike in their temper and orientation."[23]

The Friends shared the puritans' interest in the "new science" and their concern to study and extend man's control of the world in which he lived. According to Penn, Fox was something of a naturalist with "the foundation of useful and commendable knowledge."[24] The educational theories of the early Quakers and their disproportionately large membership in the Royal Society beginning in the eighteenth century are indicative of that interest. Moreover, as part of the seventeenth century's reaction against blind authority in religion as well as in "naturals," the Friends insisted that men were not to believe on someone else's authority but "were to be fully persuaded in their own minds" of the religious truths they professed.[25] Fox said that the light within leads to true reason and makes man's reason a noble faculty worthy of great confidence.[26] According to Barclay, the light never contradicts reason, "that noble and excellent faculty of the Mind," and man's enlightened reason can be useful in spiritual affairs if kept subordinate to the light.[27] Samuel Fisher was even more generous—although imprecise—in his association of the light with reason. All transgression against "the Light or Law in the Heart" "is not only against the Light of God and Christ; . . . but also against Nature . . . that Divine Nature, or Similitude of God, or right Reason, in which men stood at first, till they ran out into a reasonless kind of Reason of their own, which is not after God, a Remnant of whose Nature is in man still, and his Light in the Conscience, which is right Reason itself, leads to it. . . ."[28]

---

[23] *Essays in the History of Ideas* (Baltimore, 1948), 79.

[24] "Rise and Progress" (1694), *Works*, I, 883.

[25] Fox, "To all Kings, Princes, Rulers . . ." (1685), *Works*, VI, 312.

[26] "Mystery," *Works*, III, 64. See T. Canby Jones, "George Fox," 55-56.

[27] *Apology*, 68-69, 143. [28] *Rusticus*, 670.

Nothing is more difficult, however, than to determine what seventeenth-century thinkers meant by the term "reason," and this is especially true of those in the spiritualist milieu. Most of them were sufficiently occupied with the attempt to denigrate man's "human" or "earthly" faculties and to distinguish between reason and the Spirit that they said little positive about the former. Others, including Winstanley, used "reason" and the "Spirit" synonymously but without any very rationalistic implications. Although there is a touch of a moderate rationalism in Winstanley's attempt to explain why God allowed the Fall, primarily he used reason as one of many terms for "the incomprehensible Spirit." "Reason is that living power of light that is in all things; it is the salt that savours all things; it is the fire that burns up drosse, and so restores what is corrupted; and preserves what is pure; he is the Lord of righteousenesse."[29] Other writers linked to the spiritualists, including Sir Harry Vane, Walter Cradock, and William Walwyn, despite their confusion and shifting language, seem to have assumed that there is within fallen man a principle of reason useful even apart from the Spirit, which the Spirit could not contradict.[30]

Where Friends stood on this issue is difficult to determine, and it should not be surprising to find them differing in their emphases. As on so many issues, Fisher differed in his attitude toward reason from Fox and Barclay. The weight of the evidence suggests that the main body of Friends were no more rationalistic than Winstanley when they linked the light and reason. Like the majority of spiritualists, they placed the weight of their testimony on a divine-human dualism, held the reason of fallen man totally "carnal" and

[29] "Truth Lifting up its Head," *Works*, 104. As Sabine notes, "The opposite of reason for him is 'imagination,' the false idea of separateness from God and one's fellows, that issues in covetousness and self-seeking, and fills men with fears, doubts, wars, divisions, and lust." "Introduction," *Works of Winstanley*, 41.

[30] For references, see Brauer, "Liberalism," 160-161.

useless, and had little regard for even regenerated reason. The belief of Barclay and Fox that the light can regenerate reason and make it useful in spiritual matters resembles Baxter's view, but neither elaborated on the suggestion, and both countered it with other ideas. Certainly the Friends despised the kind of sense evidence for the credibility of Scriptures that Baxter relied on, and they did not join him in his occasional suggestions that the truths of Christianity are fully in accord with certain basic ideas about God, man, and morals with which our reason supplies us.

The attitude of the Friends toward rationalistic approaches to religion is best seen in Barclay's insistence that the Spirit is set over against tradition, Scripture, and reason as the only true foundation of religion. Some of the wisest and most diligent of men have attempted to follow right reason in religion, and they have all been led only into error. Even Barclay's admission that the light does not contradict reason did not cause him to summon reason as a spokesman for true religion, since the light, wary of all "human" or "earthly" faculties even when they have been regenerated, brings its own irresistible certainty through the spiritual senses without utilizing the outward faculties.[31] The position of most Friends was that, as Barclay also made clear, reason was an excellent agent of man's knowledge and control of "natural" things, but one must distinguish between the natural and the spiritual realms. This tended to make Quakers allies of the "moderns" at least in regard to the concerns of the new science and man's control of the world, as I have indicated, but even at this point most Friends were more wary than Anglicans and most nonconformists. Fox warned the Pennsylvanians not to cultivate their outward plantations at the expense of their inward ones. Penington felt called on to warn the members of the Royal Society that "man hath but a moment in this world, and he is here no more; and then the spirit returneth to God that gave it,

[31] *Apology*, 63-64, 68-69.

to give an account of the talent which he gave it. . . ."[32]

The Friends, then, although moderately sympathetic with the revolt against otherworldly and deductive approaches to nature, are not to be associated with Baxter's predominantly Aristotelian, moderate rationalism in religious thought. Nor were they any more consciously sympathetic to the bolder Platonic and Stoic rationalism of liberal Anglicans. Nevertheless, nonconformists and orthodox Anglicans who accused them of religious liberalism and even deism were in part correct and in part understandably confused by the Quaker message. The Friends' manner of speaking of the inner light led inevitably to misunderstanding, and, in addition, their doctrine of the light came to be defended in a rather rationalistic manner.

The confusion was based on several factors. One was the circumstance that found the Quakers putting forward their universal principle of salvation precisely at the time that many religious thinkers who shared their rejection of Calvinism but who, unlike the Friends, went on to a more optimistic anthropology, were putting forward their own versions of universal religion. There was admittedly an important distinction between the Quakers' attempt to make true religion universal and the views of those men who were primarily forerunners of the Enlightenment. Liberals such as the latitudinarians took a minimal set of absolute standards of truth and goodness as their point of reference and tried to bring historic Christianity within the confines of natural religion. The Quakers took Jesus Christ as their point of reference and tried to show how all men had been confronted with the divine judgment on human sinfulness and the triumph of redeeming grace represented by the cross of Christ. Although they agreed with the liberals that the light could bring salvific knowledge without teaching the

[32] "Some Things Relating to Religion, Proposed to the Consideration of the Royal Society, so Termed" (1668), *The Works of the Long-Mournful and Sorely-Distressed Isaac Penington* (3d edn.; 4 vols.; London, 1784), III, 99.

contingent facts about the historical Christ, this did not mean that they believed also that a man could be saved simply by living in accord with the basic moral principles common to all cultures. Fox believed that the light taught the full message of Christ, namely, judgment of fallen man and redemption through grace. It showed even the simple heathen how utterly sinful he was and that he must be born anew through the grace of God.[33] The Quakers' universalism and their attitude toward the historical Christ, however, gave their position sufficient similarity to that of the liberals to confuse even the more careful polemicists.

In addition, the Quakers' method of presentation of their principle increased its apparent similarities to the Platonists' Candle of the Lord and the latitudinarians' light of nature. When the Friends described what the light revealed to non-Christians, they often listed elements of the law of God that amounted to considerably less than a message of total regeneration. This was because of their belief that in some situations the light had to be a gentle teacher, revealing ever deeper truths as one became obedient to the small light he already possessed. In the words of Barclay, "Wait then for this in the small revelation of that pure light which first reveals things more known; and as thou becomest fitted for it, thou shalt receive more and more. . . ."[34] This tendency to describe the content of the light in terms of aspects of the moral law was reinforced by the fact that the Quakers, because of their origins and the fears engendered by the events of the Interregnum, were aware of the need to distinguish themselves more clearly from dangerous fanatics and en-

---

[33] "How All Nations May See the Light, the Life in Christ, Him the Great Mountain that Fills the Whole Earth" (n.d.), *Works*, vi, 353-355; "Election or Reprobation" (1679), *Works*, v, 390; "Possession above Profession" (1675), *Works*, v, 198-200; "To the Emperor of China" (1660), *Works*, iv, 253-254.

[34] *Apology*, 72; Fox, "Mystery," *Works*, iii, 48, 97, 178, 283; "To All Kings, Princes, and Governors in the Whole World" (1676), *Works*, v, 315; Epistle 44 (1653), *Works*, vii, 54; Fisher, *Rusticus*, 605-606.

thusiasts than from rationalists. As a result they made the moral law a criterion of the light and described its content in the law's terms. They also often wrote as if the moral law and the ethical duties flowing from its application were evident without special leadings of the inner light. Consequently, it often appeared that the Quakers' principle was indistinguishable from Lord Herbert's "common notions" or the latitudinarians' light of nature.[35]

Another Quaker teaching about the light that both caused confusion and in fact diminished the distance between the inner light and more Enlightened principles emphasized its constant availability and exhorted men to take the initiative and turn to it. Despite their confidence in God's grace, as I have earlier indicated, the Quakers wanted to lay the blame for continuing sinfulness more squarely on man than most of the orthodox were able to do. They preached about "times of visitation" and spoke of "seared consciences," but they also said that God has given to every man a measure of light according to his ability. The light could grow dim, but it never ceased to accuse one, however faintly. Moreover, with the light was given the power to believe, for God was not an unrighteous master who gives commands that he does not give the power to fulfill.[36] To those who pleaded ignorance or weakness for their continued unregenerate state, Fox replied that waiting and pleading for "ability" was a sign of lack of desire and a tempting of God, for God has given all men a sight of their sins and the strength to do something about it.[37]

Finally, some Quaker writers confused their opponents by occasionally allowing that in a sense the light within them was "natural," since Paul had said in Romans 2:14 that

---

[35] See *Apology*, 376.

[36] Fox, Epistle 46 (1653), *Works*, vii, 59; "The Doctrines and Principles of the Priests of Scotland," *Works*, iii, 553; Fisher, *Rusticus*, 625-627.

[37] "To All Those Who Would Know the Way to the Kingdom" (1671), *Works*, iv, 20-21.

the Gentiles do "by nature" the things contained in the law, and certain fathers of the early church had concurred. Fisher explained that "nature" used in this sense refers to the primitive nature before the Fall, and Barclay added that nature in this sense is not that "of the common nature of man by itself, but of that nature which hath the strength of understanding divinely given it. . . ," but the inconsistency of language on this point was especially unnerving to those few outsiders sincerely trying to understand the Quaker message.[38]

It is difficult to come to a firm conclusion concerning the extent to which these difficulties were the result of only apparent similarities and the extent to which the inner light was, in fact, rather similar in ways to the more liberal epistemological principles of the time. But when we view the whole of Quaker thought, we are likely to conclude that on these points opponents misunderstood the inner light when they saw it as simply another attempt to raise proud man to God's level of comprehension. Rather than trying to make Christianity reasonable, the Friends at least thought that they were bringing the gospel to all nations. If the light made man aware of the general laws of God, that was merely a prelude to its message of condemnation and redemption. If it was important for Quakers to emphasize the light's universality, it was equally important for them to warn men of sinning away its usefulness. If the light provided all men with the possibility of salvation, that was not to deny the important distinction between the unregenerate and the regenerate or the belief that redemption comes through the grace of God. Most Quakers sounded at times like theological liberals, but in general their message was more complex.

At the same time, there was one important point at issue between the more orthodox nonconformists and Anglicans and the Quakers about which there was no misunderstanding, for the Quakers apparently accepted one of the ration-

[38] Fisher, *Rusticus*, 668, 850; Barclay, *Apology*, 161.

alists' assumptions. The orthodox could legitimately ask where the Friends had gotten their confidence that God had provided all men with an equal possibility of gaining saving knowledge. The Friends replied that the doctrine could be found in Scripture, especially John 1:9, where the Apostle wrote that Christ enlightened every man coming into the world. Opponents denied that rendering of the Greek. George Keith's attitude after leaving the Quakers reflected the common orthodox position. According to Keith, God has given Christians a dual source of religious knowledge, namely, Scripture interpreted by the Spirit. One learns in Scripture that there is no other name by which men may be saved but that of Jesus. There is no promise of salvation to anyone except through faith in the incarnate Christ who was and is the propitiation for sins. This does not mean that salvation is impossible to the rest of mankind, "seeing God can supply that defect, by ways and methods unknown to us, who worketh by his Spirit when, where and how he pleaseth. . . ." That God has not revealed to man how and if such salvation takes place is not surprising, since he limits man to knowledge essential to his own destiny in order to thwart his pride and curiosity. To Keith it was the height of arrogance for Quakers to assert that they knew not only that God provides saving knowledge to all men but the principle by which he does it. The claim appeared to him to be a proud attempt to make God conform to what appears just and reasonable to man in order to provide answers to the humbling mysteries of life.[39]

Why did the Friends take the concern for universality of salvation that was less prominently and regularly present in the spiritualist movement and make it such a central concern? Surely the explanation that they found it in Scripture is insufficient. Their spiritual-corporeal dualism could have led them in this direction, but it did not lead all spiritualists to an emphasis as strong as the Quakers' on universality. It

[39] *Some of the Many Fallacies of William Penn*, 64-65. In the treatise Keith refers to Quakers in general, not just to Penn.

seems necessary to attribute to them the unacknowledged assumption that God's ways must be essentially understandable to men because man has direct access to the divine mind through the inner light.

Ernest Troeltsch has argued that there is an affinity between mysticism and rationalism. The point in regard to Quakerism is that there is the same "unwillingness . . . to accept the normal limitations of life" (Nuttall) in the Friends' belief that the Spirit indwelt them in a way that bypassed the senses and in the rationalist's belief that his mind is a replica of the divine Mind. Presumably that is why Barclay, who was normally so clear and sober about man, could cite Plotinus and John Smith to show that God has stamped a copy of his own archetypal loveliness on the soul, so that man can look into himself and see there the glory of God or those ideas of truth that are the nature and essence of God.[40] Whether one attributes this vision to reason or to the light seems immaterial. Nevertheless, this was a most unusual statement for Barclay and conflicts with some of his and the Friends' basic ideas. The Quakers had no conscious intention of elevating man in the manner of the bolder rationalists of the century, and if an objection to Calvinism similar to that following from the liberals' belief in the similarity between the ways of God and man lies behind the doctrine of the inner light, the Quakers were surely assuming a lesser degree of similarity.

Moreover, Quakers varied in the extent to which they based their defense of the inner light on a rationalistic premise. Early Quakers like Burrough and Nayler gave very little evidence of a concern to justify the ways of God to men. In Barclay we find somewhat more of this concern. His rejection of the doctrine of original sin, for example, was based on the fact that it is contrary to "the nature as well of God's mercy as justice" in addition to the Scriptural argument. In his refutation of the Remonstrant position on

[40] See Leif Eeg-Olofsson, *The Conception of the Inner Light in Robert Barclay's Theology* (Lund, Sweden, 1954), 44-45.

universal salvation, he noted not only the Semi-Pelagianism of the position but the fact that it does not make "the equity and wonderful harmony of God's mercy and justice towards all so manifest to the understanding."[41]

This kind of rational justification was not so prominent in Barclay's works, however, as it was in Fisher's. As on his positions on grace and free will, Scripture, and the historical Jesus, Fisher was bolder in his rejection of the orthodox Protestant position and closer to Penn than to Fox and Barclay. His more ready association of the inner light and reason has already been noted, and we also find in his thought a manifest concern to justify God's ways to man. His defense of the position that God grants all men an equal opportunity to be saved is based on extended arguments dependent on his understanding of God. Otherwise God's ways would not be equal; he would be a demander of impossibilities; and he could not be truly said to be merciful and loving.[42]

That this position is based on the belief that God's and man's ways cannot be as different as the orthodox position implies is evident in his answer to the argument that God provides man with only enough light to make him responsible for his damnation: "I say, cannot such plead again, Lord, it is true thou art our Soveraign, and mayest do with thy own as a Potter with his Clay, and dash us to pieces at thy pleasure, but thou art also a God of Righteousnesse and Truth, who hast said, thou wilt do right, as the Judg of all the Earth, and thou wilt not do that thy self, which thou damnst others for doing, as thou didst Pharoah for requiring Men to make such a tale of Brick as they had not sufficiency of Straw for. . . ." There is no law in the world that brings upon transgressors judgment and condemnation but does not hold the innocent guiltless and justify them, and there can be none in heaven either.[43] What seems reasonable and fair to man is binding on God as well.

[41] *Apology*, 105-129.   [42] *Rusticus*, 658-659.
[43] *Rusticus*, 662-663.

Penn and the "New Thought"

The Quakers distinguished their divine principle of revelation from liberal principles such as Platonic reason or the light of nature by describing the inner light in such a manner as to distinguish it from the kinds of conceptual experiences provided by the rational faculty. To describe the experience of the inner light in terms of a spiritual sense was to imply that the ideas received from the light came as part of an experience that resembled an existential confrontation. All the faculties were operative in a heightened way, but the individual was primarily a passive recipient as he was grasped by God in the whole of his being. The experience was sufficiently distinctive to be self-validating. A man simply *knew* with total assurance that God had come into his life and illumined and strengthened him. As a result of experiences with the light, his faculties, including his reason, operated with renewed power, but the experience of a "visitation" of the light was easily distinguishable from the process of reasoning well.

Penn was aware of this passive, "total" aspect of the experience of the light, and he sometimes used the "sense" analogy to describe it. Moreover, he realized that the primary evidence for the experience was simply the "infallible assurance" that it had taken place. When asked to provide evidence for his claims to have true light, he replied: "If so to believe as to have the Witness in a Man's self be sufficient to render a Man a Christian, as holy Scripture imports; then a Man's being a Christian, depends not upon a distinguishing External Evidence from what an Impostor may give, but the Evidence in himself."[44] A man knows he has the light or Spirit "from an infallible Demonstration in himself" so that he is "infallibly assured."[45]

It is significant, however, that Penn more often used the

---

[44] *More Work for George Keith* (London, 1696), 19-20.
[45] "Sandy Foundation" (1668), *Works*, I, 248; "Innocency" (1668), *Works*, I, 270.

phrase "infallible demonstration" to refer to the experience than the idea of an "instinct" or "spiritual sagacity." Penn was somewhat unique among Quakers in the extent to which he linked the inner light with man's rational powers. He knew what spiritual puritans meant when they referred to their "leadings" and confrontations. At the same time, he was more wary than were most spiritual puritans and Quakers of the kind of enthusiasm that could result if one emphasized too much the freedom of the Spirit and the uniqueness and passivity of the experience of revelation. For Penn, as for Baxter, inward certitude could not be attained without a good measure of "understanding," whether the subject was natural truths or spiritual realities. "For a Man can never be certain of that, about which he has not the Liberty of Examining, Understanding, or Judging: Confident (I confess) he may be; but that's quite another Thing than being certain."[46] Because Penn found that the light most often acted in a manner that satisfied this active, inquiring, rational spirit, he had even more difficulty than most Quakers did in distinguishing his principle of revelation from the natural principles of liberal theologians. Moreover, at times he obviously did not care to do so.

Although all Quakers were participants in "the appeal to individual, personal experience," few were as concerned as Penn not only to put spiritual wind into the sails of a church becalmed but also to take it out of the sails of all those who were bastions of authority in either theological or intellectual matters. "'Tis a strange piece of Confidence, yt any should think ye greatest part of ye World was born to believe them and distrust themselves. . . ."[47] For "Inquiry is Human; Blind Obedience, Brutal. Truth never loses by the one but often suffers by the other."[48] Penn loved "inquiry,"

[46] "Address to Protestants" (1679), *Works*, I, 778.
[47] "The Arraignment and Judgment of yt Cruel Spirit of Persecution . . . in ye Isle of Ely . . ." (1671), PWP (contemp. copy in HSP).
[48] "Fruits of Solitude" (1693), *Works*, I, 828.

he said, not for its own sake, but because he cared not to trust his share in this world or the next to other men's judgments, "at Least without having a finger in ye Pye for myself."[49] Penn, along with the "moderns" of his day, was urging that men employ the powers within them to seek to understand both the world about them and their own eternal destiny. They were to take an active part in molding the world to suit their needs and in moving toward their God-given destiny. Man was no longer to be a passive participant in his own life, accepting his truths from other men who had established themselves as necessary links between "Truth" and the individual. He had to become a master in his own house. Penn said that men had to gain "some Possession of themselves again;" they were to come "nearer to [their] own Being."[50] It was a matter of man's asserting his abilities to control his life, utilize his faculties to their fullest extent, mold his environment, and become responsible for himself.

In regard to "affairs of this world," this spirit manifested itself in Penn's empirical temper and his revolt against the deductive, speculative mentality of scholasticism. Along with many nonconformists, he argued that the educational concerns of scholasticism had been largely misguided. Christian learning had always been too involved in unnecessarily otherworldly studies, nice controversies, intricate disputations, obscurity of language, "affectedness" of style, and excess of elegance. No "experimentalist" was harsher than Penn on "the vain Quiddities, idle and gross Terms, and most sophistical Ways of Syllogizing, with the rest of that useless and injurious Pedantry (to Mankind, brought into the Christian Religion by Popish School-Men and so eminently in Vogue in Oxford and Cambridge. . .)." Even children were weighted down in schools with the burden of learning words and rules, grammar and rhetoric, and a few

---

[49] Letter to John Aubrey (June 13, 1683), PWP (L.S. in Bodleian).
[50] "Address to Protestants" (1679), *Works*, I, 794; "Skirmisher Defeated" (1676), *Works*, II, 662.

useless languages. There was, in brief, too much emphasis on words and vain speculation and not enough on "things." Penn's suggestions for more practical studies included building principles, improvement of land, medicine, chirurgery, traffic, navigation, history, government, useful languages for foreign lands, arithmetic, geometry, handicrafts, and some principles of business.[51]

Many Friends shared elements of Penn's empirical temper and his practical bent, but Penn was somewhat unusual among Quakers of his time in the extent to which he stressed his belief that it was man's duty to use the method of the new science as a technique for the mastery of nature. He argued that man should study "sensibles" or the natural world and thereby develop his mechanical and physical knowledge. In this way he could increase his control over nature, unravel its secrets, and make the natural world more useful, beneficial, and pleasurable to mankind.[52]

With these ideals in mind, Penn accepted an invitation to join the Royal Society in 1681. Two years later he commented:

> I value my selfe much upon ye good opinion of those ingeneous Gentlemen I know of ye Royall Society, and their kind wishes for me and my poor Provinces: all I can say is that I and It are votarys to ye prosperity of their harmless and usefull Inquierys. It is even one step to Heaven to returne to nature, and though I love that proportion should be observed in all things, yett a naturall Knowledge, or ye Science thereon, reinstates men, and gives them some possession of themselves again; a thing they have long wanted by an ill tradition, too closely followed and ye foolish Credulity so Incident to men.[53]

[51] "Wisdom Justified" (1673), *Works*, II, 494-495; "Serious Apology" (1671), *Works*, II, 56; "Fruits of Solitude" (1693), *Works*, I, 820-821.

[52] "Fruits of Solitude" (1693), *Works*, I, 820-821.

[53] Letter to John Aubrey (June 13, 1683), PWP (L.S. in Bodleian).

The Royal Society had much interest in the knowledge to be gained in the far reaches of the world. The New World was for the intellectual explorers of the age the very symbol of excitement and of the expansion of human knowledge. If Penn's interest in America was primarily religious and economic, it was sufficiently scientific to warrant his membership in the Society. Although he was not an active member, he sent off reports of his colony to those of its members who were his friends. On one occasion he asked Thomas Lloyd to write a short natural history or at least a "phisical lettr" for Robert Boyle.[54] In many of his letters from Pennsylvania to friends he spent as much space listing observations on the land and its native inhabitants as he did on religious, economic, and personal affairs.

"Gaining possession of oneself" or "having a finger in ye Pye" in religious matters was in Penn's mind even more important than such self-assertion in the affairs of this world. Penn often acknowledged his debt to John Hales and Jeremy Taylor for his belief that the principal enemies of true religion were "Implicit Faith and blind Obedience." The true believer was one who, with Paul, desired to "prove all Things" in order to "hold fast that which is good"— "such as would see with their own Eyes, and that dare not transfer the Right of Examination of Points that so nearly concern their Immortal Souls to any mortal Man. . . ."[55] To describe the kind of religious adherence that brought a man "nearer to his own being" or that constituted the religion of individual experience, Penn used a variety of pregnant terms with little concern for precision. True religion was a religion of "experience," "conviction" or "convincement," "conscience," "free choice," "judgment," "evidence," "understanding," and "reason." True faith, according to Penn, was a kind of "knowledge," not "opinion," and a man's "knowledge" had to be based on individual "experience" of its truth. The necessity of an empirical stance held

[54] Letter to Thomas Lloyd (Feb. 1, 1687), PWP (A.L.S. in HSP).
[55] "Address to Protestants" (1679), *Works*, I, 776.

in affairs of religion as in those of the world. "Experience," however, was not necessarily limited to knowledge gained through the senses. A man had a religious "experience" when he gained a personal or individual "conviction" about something or a "due Conviction and Determination" about it.[56] Such "experience" was contrasted with the religious "notions" of those who accepted their beliefs on the authority of the church, the coercing state, or even Scripture, without any real sense of their meaning or confidence in their truth.

"Experience" and "conviction," moreover, were impossible without a measure of "understanding" and "evidence." "For if I believe what [the church] believes, only because she believes it, and not because I am convinced in my Understanding and Conscience of the Truth of what she believes, my Faith is false, though hers be true: I say, it is not true to me; I have no Evidence of it."[57] The understanding, in turn, involves "trial" and "examination," for the "Understanding can never be convinc'd, nor properly submit, but by such Arguments, as are Rational, Perswasive, and Suitable to its own Nature; something that can resolve its Doubts, answer its Objections, enervate it's Propositions. . . . ."[58] Thus if all knowledge is based on experience, experience is based on reason, "because Reason is that part of Man, which is eminently concern'd in receiving that Experience, therefore not the Giver of it, nor yet without Reason."[59]

Penn believed that true religion was above all a religion of reason. The religion of the Jews, especially in its prophetic form, had been a rational faith, "so that if God, did

[56] "Quakerism a New Nickname" (1672), *Works*, II, 256-257; "Invalidity" (1673), *Works*, II, 359; "Skirmisher Defeated" (1676), *Works*, II, 662.
[57] "Address to Protestants" (1679), *Works*, I, 778, 795.
[58] "Great Case" (1670), *Works*, I, 452; "Address to Protestants" (1679), *Works*, I, 793-794.
[59] "Invalidity" (1673), *Works*, II, 359.

both Reason with the Jews, and his Prophets were Rational Men, then we may safely conclude That Reason is Inherent, to God, and his Elect Children; and that Pure Reason is not inconsistent with, or distinct from the Nature of Love and Faith. . . ."[60] Since Christianity is the ultimate true religion, Christians above all should welcome the inquiring mind, for their religion is most reasonable of all.[61] As the highest or purest expression of Christianity, Quakerism was a most reasonable religious expression. "God is the Fountain as well of Reason as Light: And we assert our Principle not to be without Reason, but most Reasonable."[62] Since man had been created a reasonable creature, the more reasonable his religion is "the nearer to his own being he comes, and to the Wisdom and truth of his Creator. . . ." A religion without reason cannot be the religion of the God of truth and reason. "In short, either convince my Understanding by the Light of Truth and Power of Reason, or bear down my Infidelity with the Force of Miracles: For not to give me Understanding or Faith, and to press a Submission that requires both, is most unreasonable."[63]

PENN'S RELIGIOUS RATIONALISM

Many of Penn's statements linking religion and reason are open to several interpretations. The basic question to be asked in an analysis of this aspect of his thought is whether his theological rationalism linked his understanding of the inner light more closely with the regenerated reason of puritans such as Richard Baxter and the covenant theolo-

---

[60] "New Witnesses" (1672), *Works*, II, 175. For Penn, as for Quakers in general, the adjective "distinct" had a peculiar meaning. To say that reason was not "distinct from" faith and love was not to say that the terms had identical referents but that there was nothing about reason that was antithetical to faith or love.

[61] "Address to Protestants" (1679), *Works*, I, 775-777; "Great Case" (1670), *Works*, I, 448-449.

[62] "Wisdom Justified" (1673), *Works*, II, 473.

[63] "Address to Protestants" (1679), *Works*, I, 794.

gians of New England, or with the rational principles of those theological liberals who were more or less explicitly denying the puritan conception of the distance between God and man. Was he arguing that God, although remaining unaccountable to man and in many respects incomprehensible to him, regenerates man in such a way that his divine image is renewed, so that he can make a free, rational choice to serve God and thus come into the fellowship with God for which he was created? Or was Penn associating the inner light with that conception of reason according to which "the rationality implicit in the constitution of reality infused the structure of thought," so that religion was a matter of retiring within oneself to contemplate those "clear and distinct" ideas of divinity and morality that were an "image" of God in being a replica of the Divine Mind?

Puritans who emphasized the rationality of regeneration worked with both the "Aristotelian" conception of reason as "a principle of action, a power or faculty by which truth was discovered in the sensibles, an aptitude for discovering it," and the "Platonic" conception of it as "the source of truth, the container and giver of ideas through inward intuition or recollection."[64] But they remained true to their emphasis on the hiddenness and incomprehensibility of God only where the Aristotelian conception had the upper hand. Because of Penn's attachment to a dualistic epistemology, according to which the inner light brought religious knowledge in a non-sensible way, he naturally tended to think of reason in a Platonic manner. Nevertheless, here as elsewhere Penn was inconsistent, and much of his thought on the rationality of religion was influenced by the puritan theological anthropology and lacked the perspective of the liberals. Penn's insistence on linking reason and religion was partly attributable to his acceptance, with the puritans, of the prevailing faculty psychology. The rational faculty was simply part of the necessary psychological arc an idea had to travel if it was to become for the individual a matter of

[64] Miller, *Seventeenth Century*, 190-191.

"knowledge" or "conviction." God had created all men capable of making free, rational choices. The distinctive mark of man—that which placed him above the brutes—Penn variously called man's "reason," his "reason and will," or his "conscience and understanding." "To be short, a Christian implies a Man; and a Man implies Conscience and Understanding; but he that has no Conscience nor Understanding, as he has not, that has deliver'd them up to the Will of another Man, is no Man, and therefore no Christian." Since God created man with a reason and conscience, he would not demand or allow any kind of knowing that violates or bypasses the conscience, reason, and understanding.[65]

More specifically, Penn described the psychological arc of knowledge in dependence on the puritan William Perkins. For Perkins the lynch-pin of the faculties was conscience. Valid religious knowledge, according to this view, was that which was accepted by the inner authority, conscience, and not simply received on external authority. Quoting Perkins, Penn held that conscience is the internal receptacle that God has placed in man—the practical understanding by which man knows divine things, "a little God sitting in the middle of Men's Hearts, arraigning them in this Life," "a Thing placed of God in the midst between him and Man." But before conscience can constrain one to believe a particular truth, the understanding must conceive it or have the means of conceiving it, since conscience binds by virtue of known conclusions in the mind. Things that are "altogether Unknown, and unconceived of the Understanding" do not bind the conscience.[66] The process, in turn, by which the "understanding" conceives or grasps a proposed belief is described as follows: "Faith in all Acts of Religion is necessary: Now in Order to believe, we must first Will; to Will, we must Judge; to Judge any Thing we must first Understand. . . ."[67]

[65] "Address to Protestants" (1679), *Works*, I, 794.
[66] "Skirmisher Defeated" (1676), *Works*, II, 666, 663.
[67] "Great Case" (1670), *Works*, I, 451.

Often Penn's insistence that a religious belief had to pass through the "understanding" or "reason" amounted to little more than the demand that one had to be personally convinced of the truth of a proposed belief, no matter how passive his mind had been in the "experience" of "conviction." Much of Penn's discussion of the rationality of religion is found in his treatises on toleration, in which "reason" and "understanding" are virtually synonymous with "conviction." Penn tried to demonstrate the invalidity of beliefs accepted because of coercion by human authorities. He contrasted this situation with that in which one accepted a belief on the authority of conscience. But the "conception" or "understanding" that preceded the belief's entrance into the conscience could be limited simply to understanding the literal meaning of the words. The experience might be a largely passive one in which the conviction was a product of the influence of the Spirit. The Spirit could enable one to become "convinced" of the truth of the propositions in question even though it did not bring the ability to grasp with the analytical intellect the rationality of the belief or the ability to show the falseness of opposing beliefs.[68]

When understood in this way, the affirmation that religion is a product of reason or understanding was simply another mode of acknowledging what Penn called the "Protestant principle," namely, the belief that the Spirit acts on the individual in bringing him to a position of faith and fellowship and is not content simply to mediate religious knowledge to man through the church. In these contexts Penn was merely saying that the inner light regenerated one by bringing him a personal experience of conviction in which he understood certain verbal meanings and became supremely confident of their truth.[69]

AT OTHER times Penn thought of the "understanding" or "reasoning" that preceded conscientious conviction in a more delimited way. It involved active searching, inquiring,

[68] "Skirmisher Defeated" (1676), *Works*, II, 662.
[69] "Invalidity" (1673), *Works*, II, 363.

and examining. The "reason" involved in establishing conviction was here conceived more as the discursive, Aristotelian faculty. According to Penn, "our Natural Rational Faculty is our Sight, but not our Light: That, by which we discern and judge what the Divine Light shews us, viz. Good from Evil, and Error from Truth."[70] God has given man "Senses Corporal and Intellectual, to discern Things and their Differences, so as to assert or deny from Evidences and Reasons proper to each. . . ."[71] Man is not simply to avoid implicit faith and blind obedience; he is to search actively among the Scriptures for truth and examine and weigh competing claims against the many kinds of evidence available. Penn was far from explicit concerning the workings and duties of "the [discursive] rational faculty" in religious matters, and he often shifted back and forth between discussions of reason as a discursive faculty and ideas implying a Platonic conception of reason as a source of truths. Nevertheless, we can discern two distinctive ways in which he related the inner light to the discursive rational faculty.

One was the idea that the inner light operated directly as a gracious power on the faculty of reason by regenerating it so that it was restored to a state of operation more nearly corresponding to its intended condition. This happened when a man was brought into the state of regeneration, and Penn sometimes described it as the major aspect of rebirth. Religion was reasonable in this sense because the light, in regenerating man, strengthened his rational faculty so that he could discern, compare, and judge with renewed clarity and vigor. "Man has to rectify and assist his Fallible Judgment, an Unerring, Certain, Infallible Spirit, Power, or Principle; which as Man listens unto and follows, his Understanding becomes illuminated, his Reason purified, and a sound Judgment restored."[72]

One of the uses of the regenerated reason was for deter-

---

[70] "Defence of a Paper" (1698), *Works*, ii, 897-898; "Address to Protestants" (1679), *Works*, i, 792-793.
[71] "Great Case" (1670), *Works*, i, 450-451.
[72] "Spirit of Truth" (1672), *Works*, ii, 106.

mining the meaning of Scripture and its relevance to belief
and practice. Reason was most highly valued for its use in
drawing out the precise meaning of Scriptural passages and
separating the unessential aspects from the doctrinal, ecclesiastical, and ethical guides to be found in it. Penn valued his
knowledge of languages very highly in this regard, as well
as his ability to employ his grasp of logic, grammar, and
rhetoric on the sacred writings.[73] Another prominent use of
the regenerated faculty that can be discovered in Penn's
writings was for examining history to discover the nature
of God's providential rule, as well as studying the beliefs
of great men, both pagan and Christian, who clearly possessed knowledge of divine things. As I have already noted,
Penn also believed in using regenerated reason to draw
knowledge of God from nature, which gave indications of
God's providence and attributes, as well as to establish the
validity of the evidence for the reliability of the Scriptures
and of the arguments from prophecy and miracles for the
divine authority of Christ and Christianity.

The second function of the inner light in relation to reason conceived as a discursive faculty was to provide the
criteria by which it operated. The rational faculty is our
"sight," but in its fallen state it lacks "light" or a clear insight into the basic truths by which all religious claims and
expressions are to be judged. "But as the Eye of the Body
is the Sensible Faculty of seeing external Objects, through
the Discovery that an External Light (as the Sun in the
Firmament) makes to the Eye, but is not That Light it self;
so does the Rational Faculty of the Soul see Spiritual or
Immaterial Objects, through the Illumination of the Light
of Christ Within, but is by no Means, That Light it
self. . . ."[74] Penn meant that the inner light provided knowledge of certain truths that the faculty of reason was to use

[73] Penn was not explicit in this regard, but his manner of thought
is evident in many works. See, for example, "Address to Protestants"
(1679), *Works*, I, 792-795.
[74] "Defence of a Paper" (1698), *Works*, II, 898.

to weigh and judge the religious claims of individuals and groups, the import and meaning of Scriptural passages, and one's own and others' conduct.

Nothing in the uses of reason as a discursive faculty discussed so far in connection with the inner light implies either a denial of the Quakers' clear distinction between the unregenerate and the regenerate or a demand that God conform to the conceptions of goodness and justice common to well-educated men of seventeenth-century England. According to these uses, religion was reasonable primarily because God condescended to lift man out of his helpless, fallen state in a manner that enabled him to employ his mental power to comprehend—to a degree—God's ways and thereby grant him a free and willing allegiance. With Baxter, Penn perceived that if, in accord with the idea of an *analogia entis*, it makes any sense to call God a "Person," then, although there will be much about him that man does not understand, there will be some similarities between the way in which another man treats me when he wishes to gain my allegiance and have me adopt his ideals and goals and the way in which God treats alienated man. As in all intimate human personal relationships, there had to be some mutual understanding, not just blind adherence on the one side, in the relationship between God and man. God treated man in a reasonable way because he had created him in his own image—that is, as a rational being capable of a personal allegiance.[75]

PENN also spoke of the reasonableness of religion and of the relation between reason and the inner light in a way that associated the inner light with the Platonic and Stoic conceptions of reason as a body of universal truths common to all men. He believed that it was appropriate to call the inner light a principle of "Reason" or "right Reason" because of the Johannine use of the "Logos" and because it supplied all men with the essential truths about God and man. The light

[75] "Primitive Christianity" (1696), *Works*, II, 863.

is "right Reason"—"the Reason of the first Nine Verses of
the First of John; for so Tertullian, and some other Ancients
as well as Modern Cricks, gives us the Word Logos; and
the Divine Reason is One in all; that Lamp of God which
lights our Candle, and enlightens our Darkness, and is the
Measure and Test of our Knowledge."[76] Penn normally
made clear that "Reason" used in this sense was to be clearly
distinguished from man's natural rational "faculty" or "Reasonable Capacity." "Reason" in this sense was a divine influx
through the grace of God. It was not a part of man's natural
endowment, but "the Guide and Director of our Understandings in our Choice, and that which gives Rectitude
and True Judgment."[77] Nevertheless, the combination of a
propensity for a Platonic epistemology, a concern for universality, and a desire to associate the inner light with reason led Penn inevitably to a sympathy for the Stoic and
Platonic emphases on innate knowledge popular in his day.

According to Penn, although man's "natural" faculty of
reason was helpless apart from grace, in fact it was never
without an "innate" divine light. When the Bishop of Cork
asked Penn to explain how the inner light was related to
"innate notions" or the "natural conscience," Penn replied
that the light did not consist of innate ideas, but "Innate
Notions" were "the Blessed Fruit and Effect of the Light of
Christ, the Word-God in Man, which Shines in the Heart
and gives him Knowledge of God, and of his Duty to Him.
So that the Innate Notions or Inward Knowledge we have
of God, is from This True Light that lighteth every Man
coming into the World, but is not that Light it self." The
"Natural Conscience" is "a Capacity that Man has by Nature, that is, in his Creation" by virtue of the divine inner
light.[78] Elsewhere Penn wrote that the basic truths with
which men are born are not "natural" if by natural is meant
"mere Man; his Compositum or Make." But in a sense the

[76] "Address to Protestants" (1679), *Works*, I, 778.
[77] "Defence of a Paper" (1698), *Works*, II, 898.
[78] *Ibid.*

truths known by the light are "natural" to us because of their constant and immediate presence to the mind by divine power. "If by Natural is only intended, that the Light comes along with us into the World, or that we have it as sure as we are born, or have Nature; and is the Light of our Nature, of our Minds and Understandings, and is not the Result of any Revelation from without, as by Angels or Men; then we mean and intend the same Thing. For it is Natural to Man to have a Supernatural Light, and for the Creature to be lighted by an uncreated Light, as is the Life of the Creating Word."[79]

Penn's tendency to say that men had "naturally" true knowledge of God led him at times to speak of man's "instinct of a Deity." This "instinct" was such a "natural" part of man that he could no more be without it than he could be without the most essential part of himself.[80] Indeed, it was the most essential part of man in that it was his peculiar mark, the *imago Dei* that was his defining characteristic. "For it is that Notion of God which is innate in us, and, as it were, congenial to us: We bring it with us into the World. The peculiar Seal and Mark of Divinity: A kind of Counter-part of himself in Man; his Picture in little: The Attributes that are Infinite in him, being here Epitomiz'd and Resembled in Man that by It he may have a Right Knowledge of his Creator and Sense of his Duty." As authorities for this viewpoint Penn cited a "Cloud of Witnesses" among the pagans and Justin Martyr, Clement of Alexandria, and Origen among ancient Christians.[81]

The implications of this understanding of the divine image in man go a great deal farther in the direction of the Christianity of the Enlightenment than those of the conception of the *imago Dei* of rational puritans. This was not a matter of God's condescending to treat man in a manner designed to gain his heartfelt allegiance but of man's seeking

---

[79] "Primitive Christianity" (1696), *Works*, II, 857.
[80] "Great Case" (1670), *Works*, I, 451.
[81] "Defence of the Duke" (1685), *Works*, II, 716.

God within the rational soul, the nobler and better part of man, "the most glorious Jewel of the Globe." Such was the occasional issue of Penn's Platonic leanings. "And why is Man his Delight, but because Man only, of all his Works, was of his Likeness. This is the intimate Relation of Man to God: Somewhat nearer than ordinary; for of all other Beings, Man only had the Honour of being his Image; and, by his Resemblance to God, as I may say, came his Kindred with God and Knowledge of him. So that the nearest and best Way for Man to know God, and be acquainted with him, is to seek him in himself, in his Image; and, as he finds that, comes to find and know God." More specifically, man may be said to be in God's image because he alone is immortal and because he has in his soul "those Excellencies in small, and proportionable to a Creature's Capacity," that are the attributes of God. These include the ideas of wisdom, justice, mercy, and holiness among others. Man has within his soul the ideas of those eternal principles that define God's character and outline man's duty. As he turns within to them, contemplates them, and moves toward incorporating them in his life, he becomes more luminously aware of their truth and better acquainted with God. "As Man becomes Holy, Just, Merciful, Patient, etc. By the Copy he will know the Original, and by the Workmanship in himself, he will be acquainted with the Holy Workman."[82]

Penn's belief that all men have an innate divine reason or light and that the path to God was through man's divine soul placed him clearly in the liberal theological camp. Nevertheless, his thought on these issues was complex. In the first place, it was only rarely that he sang man's praises in the optimistic and even promethean manner displayed in these quotations. This mood was prominent in a few works in the 1670's and 1680's and then appeared again in his *Primitive Christianity Revived* in 1696, but for the most part it gave way to his radically pessimistic view of the "natural"

[82] "Primitive Christianity" (1696), *Works*, II, 866.

254

man.[83] Second, although Penn was, like most Quakers, continually ambiguous about prevenient grace and stressed at times the constant availability of the light, his major tendency was to speak of true knowledge of God as coming in direct encounters with God that were a product of divine initiative as well as of human struggle and self-discipline. In this respect his thought resembled the mystical rationalism of the Cambridge men, such as John Smith, rather than the natural religion of the latitudinarians.

There were some respects, however, in which Penn did move in the direction of natural religion even more firmly than the Cambridge Platonists. One was a result of his overriding concern to distinguish between the Quakers' understanding of revelatory certitude and that of Ranters and other enthusiasts. According to Penn, "By revelation we don't mean whimsical Raptures, strange and prodigious Trances. We disclaim any Share or Interest in those vain Whimsies and idle Intoxications, professing our Revelation to be solid and necessary Discovery from the Lord, of those things that do import and concern our daily Conditions; in reference to the Honour which is due to him, and Care owing to our own Souls."[84] This distinction was common to all Quakers, but few went as far as Penn did in distinguishing between "ordinary" and "extraordinary" revelatory knowledge. He could speak of the "ordinary" knowledge of the inner light's truths in a way that specifically distinguished this knowledge from spiritual "leadings" and thus from a special experience in which one was confronted by "Christ within" and even from the mystical rationality of John Smith. "Extraordinary" inspiration included foresights and divine prospects, which allow prophecy about things to come or decisions in "signal" controversies or cases

---

[83] The mood of most of Penn's works in the 1690's was so different from that of *Primitive Christianity* that one is led to suspect that he had recently read or reread a treatise of a Platonist when he wrote the work.

[84] "Serious Apology" (1671), *Works*, II, 38.

of special difficulty. Such "leadings," which come with an awareness of the Spirit's special guidance, were not to be expected by the average man. They were rare or "peculiar." "Ordinary" inspiration comes not from particular motions or commands of the Spirit but from "the Law of Nature, as many stile it, or rather, the Law God placed in Man's Nature."[85] One need not wait for special leadings or discipline himself for special experiences, "for that is according to Truth, that is not against the Mind of Truth either particularly or generally exprest."[86] Presumably "the Mind of Truth" embodied those fundamental conceptions of truth and goodness that Penn thought would appear obvious to a reasonable man of his time. The distinction between special leadings and one's knowledge of the moral law was common to some Quakers, but at times Penn seemed to be virtually consigning direct divine illumination to the past. At the least, unlike most Quaker writers, he was not always careful to point out the distinction between the human and possibly misguided conscience and rational faculty, on the one hand, and the divine light on the other. As a result he often seemed to be appealing to man's natural conscience and thereby associating the certainty given by the inner light with what the latitudinarians called the light of nature.

A second similarity between Penn's thought and that of the latitudinarians is evident in his discussion of the content of the inner light. Some of the Cambridge Platonists were moving in the direction of reducing Christianity to a minimum of universal beliefs commonly associated with natural religion, but they avoided taking the crucial step. The latitudinarians did not, and Penn sometimes joined them in reducing Christianity to natural religion. Admittedly, taking the whole of his thought into consideration, we find that his most prominent position was that even apart from knowledge of the historical Christ, the message of the light

[85] "Invalidity" (1673), *Works*, II, 351.
[86] "A Brief Examination of the State of Liberty Spiritual . . ." (1681), *Works*, II, 692.

was one of condemnation of fallen man and an invitation to regeneration by grace. Regeneration was the *sine qua non* of salvation, for, as one reads in John 3:5, "except ye be born of water and the Spirit ye cannot enter the kingdom of God."[87]

Penn, with the other Quakers, believed that the light furnished one only with such discoveries as suited his condition and that it had to be a gradual or progressive revealer to those in a backward state. The light first shows what is evil in a general sense; then it reproves; then, if one is obedient to it, the light becomes "Life" and brings the "Blood of Cleansing" and fellowship with God and man.[88] Although men may come to serve God truly without knowing of "his Coming in the Flesh," such men were not saved on a lower principle than Christians were, but were given the knowledge and benefit of regeneration—the latter through the historical Christ—without knowing of the historical Christ. Just as pardons in human affairs are often given through the influence of benefactors who remain anonymous, so in the case of Christ is this possible.[89]

Nevertheless, Penn was less consistent than Fox and most Quakers were in taking the orthodox view of man as his point of reference. It was one thing for the uneducated weaver's son, on the basis of his faith in God, to believe that God had confronted all men with the message of man's need for total regeneration. The matter was by no means that simple for Penn. With his extensive knowledge of history and especially his familiarity with the writings of Greek and Roman philosophers and moralists, he could not wholly ignore the vast differences between the Christian message and that of all pagan writers. Faced with this discrepancy, he tried to resolve it in two somewhat conflicting ways. One

---

[87] "Spirit of Truth" (1672), *Works*, II, 100; "Serious Apology" (1671), *Works*, II, 84.

[88] "Primitive Christianity" (1696), *Works*, II, 860; "Serious Apology" (1671), *Works*, II, 38.

[89] "Reply to a Pretended Answer" (1695), *Works*, II, 815.

way was to emphasize a developmental view of man's knowledge of true religion in the course of history and to argue that where men had not yet learned the truths of the highest religion, Christianity, God condescended to save them on a lesser score. "Though much Darkness hath prevailed in most Parts of the World, and still continueth, yet then, and where the Day of Ignorance remains, and where there hath been and is a Walking with Sincerity towards God, according to their Knowledge, I do believe the Lord did and doth wink, and had and hath Mercy on men, though great Strangers to that Christian Profession so much boasted of among too many in our Nation. . . ."[90]

The other recourse was to emphasize the similarity between the beliefs of Greek and Roman philosophers such as Seneca and Cicero, on the one hand, and Christians on the other, by arguing that there was in fact little of significant difference to separate them, and that Christians had added only nonessentials to the pagan beliefs. Occasionally this emphasis on the universality of true religion led to a distortion of the pagan messages, as when Penn said that the Sermon on the Mount was identical with the highest message of antiquity and would find an echo in every man's heart.[91] More often he brought the "essential" message of Christianity into line with the pagan, especially the Stoic, "gospel" in the manner of liberals extolling man's natural knowledge of God. In every era, said Penn, God has expressed himself to "serious men" in the same manner under the outward forms of the various religions of the world. Under these forms the humble, meek, merciful, just, pious, and devout souls are everywhere of one religion. When

[90] "Reason against Railing" (1673), Works, II, 507. See also "Wisdom Justified" (1673), Works, II, 464; "Good Advice to the Church of England, Roman Catholick and Protestant Dissenter" (1687), Works, II, 750.

[91] For evidence that Penn was occasionally willing to employ omissions in quotations from pagan writers to bring them closer to the Christian message, see Herbert Wood, "William Penn's 'Christian Quaker,'" in Howard Brinton, ed., Children of Light, 21.

death has removed their masks, they will know one another even though at present the "diverse Liveries" they wear make them strangers.[92] In this vein Penn associated the Quaker's inner light with Pythagoras' "Great Light and Salt of Ages," Anaxagoras' "Divine Mind," Socrates' "Good Spirit," Timaeus' "Unbegotten Principle" and "Author of all Light," Plato's "Eternal, Ineffable, and Perfect Principle of Truth," Zeno's "Maker and Father of All," Plotinus' "Root of the Soul," and similar conceptions of Epictetus, Cicero, Seneca, and Plutarch.[93]

In stating the doctrines that linked all these men of differing religions, Penn was inconsistent. He sometimes cited as a summary of the light's message Hebrews 11:6: "For he that cometh to God must believe that he is, and that he is a Diligent Rewarder of them that seek him." Another favorite was Micah 6:8: "God hath shown to thee, O man, what is good; and what doth the Lord require of thee; but to do justly, and love mercy, and to walk humbly with thy God."[94] At other times he cited the essential affirmations of ethical monotheism: that God is one, holy, infinite, and eternal; that he has imprinted knowledge of himself on man's heart; that virtue is the end of human existence; and that obedience to God brings eternal life, and disobedience, eternal death.[95] Occasionally the list of essentials was even shorter.

Having provided man with what amounted to a natural knowledge of the essential divine truths, Penn sometimes employed this knowledge to deduce the essential characteristics of the divine Being and to circumscribe divine actions, and thus resembled the liberals in a third way. Given his occasional understanding of the *imago Dei* as a replica of the divine attributes, it was inevitable that he would at times

---

[92] "Fruits of Solitude" (1693), *Works*, I, 842.
[93] "Advice to Children" (1698), *Works*, I, 911.
[94] "Address to Protestants" (1679), *Works*, I, 767.
[95] "Invalidity" (1673), *Works*, II, 351; "Christian Quaker" (1673), *Works*, I, 541-568; "Serious Apology" (1671), *Works*, II, 48.

move beyond those Christians for whom faith must include a measure of understanding to join those liberals who believed that faith must be accommodated to reason or even be transformed into it.

Most Quakers could agree with Penn that "the Light whereby we are enlightened always commands and strictly enjoyns us Duty, Obedience, Love, Peace, Gentleness, Faithfulness, Industry, Holy Living: And whatever is supposed to the contrary we disclaim it. . . ." Any impulse or message that conflicted with the moral law was *ipso facto* known to be a product of "the Spirit of this World."[96] Nonconformists and conservative Anglicans were thankful to find this measure of sanity in Penn, but they suspected that this tendency, in itself good, was part of a more sinister attempt to limit God's freedom and sovereignty and to demand that he treat all men according to present human conceptions of justice and equity. The most common Quaker reply to this charge was to insist that their belief in a universal saving light of truth was based on Scripture and revelation and not on human standards. Penn, like Fisher, was not always so circumspect. To his mind a theology that did not provide all men equally with a clear—even unmistakable—light of divine knowledge made God "more unjust than the worst of Men."[97] Given man's clear perception of the attributes of the divine character, the Quaker principle followed naturally. Whatever an omniscient and omnipotent God knew and could do for man's salvation—an omnibenevolent God who delights not in the death of one soul—has certainly been done for man. "And because God is as Omnibenevolent, as Omniscient and Omnipotent, we must conclude he has done it."[98] "All Mankind, in all Copies and Translations, *and from the Reason of the Thing*, must

[96] "Reason against Railing" (1673), *Works*, II, 541. See also "Quakerism a New Nickname" (1672), *Works*, II, 289; "Spirit of Truth" (1672), *Works*, II, 128.

[97] "Spirit of Truth" (1672), *Works*, II, 105.

[98] "Address to Protestants" (1679), *Works*, I, 792.

be confessed to be Subjects of this Illumination" (italics mine). The denial of a universal common light sufficient to salvation is "contrary to the Impressions incident to every Man."[99]

Despite his emphasis on the sinfulness and pitiable state of fallen man, Penn did not fully share the dark side of the puritan mind. His conception of God was such that it was inconceivable to him that God should not give all men the same opportunity and reward those who in their freedom used their divine knowledge and assistance to become virtuous men. "First, I say, That it is inconsistent with the Rectitude of God's Nature, to esteem that naturally Just in himself to Man, which by his Law written in the Hearts of all Men, is adjudg'd most Unreasonable, cruel and Unjust among Men; for since whatever is Holy, Good and Upright, is derived to us from God, and that we are to be Perfect as our Heavenly Father is Perfect, it is utterly impossible that He should be Just in that which is most Unjust in man. . . ."[100]

The moderate rationalist, such as Baxter, confident though he was that God would normally deal with man according to the terms of a reasonable covenant, balanced his feeling for the glorious heights of human life with a knowledge of the tragedy and incomprehensibility of the human condition. Penn could not accept the puritan belief that God's wrath was at times inexplicably blind and that ultimately he would have to admit, with Baxter, "the imbecillity of [his] reason, and its incompetency to censure the wisdom of God." If man's innate ideas constituted a replica of the divine mind, as Penn at times believed, he could be assured that God would never act in so inexplicable a manner.

[99] "Quakerism a New Nickname" (1672), *Works*, ii, 289.
[100] "Plain-Dealing" (1672), *Works*, ii, 182.

SIX

SPIRITUAL RELIGION
AND THE CHRISTIAN GOSPEL

QUAKERISM, PENN, AND CHRISTIAN ORTHODOXY

RICHARD BAXTER often accused the Quakers of magnifying trifles and manifesting a loveless and proud attitude toward other men, but the brunt of his attack on the movement fell on the "Vomitings and diseased motions" of their doctrinal errors.[1] Other opponents of the Friends reached the same conclusion as it became evident that the heterodoxy of the Children of the Light was more than simply a product of their lack of theological training or the exuberance of their reaction against notionalism. Both the spiritual-corporeal dualism and the universalism of the Friends led them to doctrinal positions that cast doubt on their willingness to adhere to a religion that based salvation on the atoning deeds of the historical figure Jesus of Nazareth. There was much confusion and a good deal of bad marksmanship in the theological polemic surrounding Quakerism in the seventeenth century, but most opponents could agree not only on the doctrinal nature of the major problems but on the source of the Friends' doctrinal errors. Three of the most prolific and well-known opponents, the Baptist John Bunyan, the Independent John Owen, and the Anglican Henry More ranged widely and differed a good deal in their critiques, but a careful reading of their anti-Quaker tracts and passages makes it clear that in their views the Quakers' main errors stemmed from their "excluding the external Christ from the business of Religion, and only admitting the inter-

[1] Penn-Baxter debate (Oct. 5, 1675), ACMC, xv (holograph by Baxter in Dr. Williams' Library, London).

nal Christ."[2] A religion as scornful of sense-knowledge and as desirous of universalizing the possibility of salvation as that of the Friends could not help having difficulty expressing an orthodox position on Jesus Christ. Since the spiritual-corporeal dualism and the universalizing tendency were at least as dominant in Penn's thought as in that of any other Friends, his problems were especially acute. But during the Restoration period and then especially after 1688 the Friends in general and Penn in particular were concerned to minimize their doctrinal aberrations. A discussion of their general attitude toward orthodoxy and their views of the person and work of Jesus Christ enables us to see how far the spiritualizing and universalizing-rationalizing tendencies were carried in the thought of Restoration Quakers and Penn and how they were hemmed in especially after 1688.

Few Quakers shared the spiritualists' progressive understanding of the history of salvation. Friends believed that the era of spiritual religion had originally been inaugurated 1600 years ago by the coming of the gospel to fulfil the types of the law. Why God should have done this by means of a Nazareth carpenter's son who went about appealing to the senses with his miracles and who ended on a cross was difficult to explain. Moreover, we may suspect that the Friends in their more discouraged moments must have been tempted to blame the virtually complete apostasy that followed the apostolic period on the awkward and "outward" manner in which the new dispensation had been introduced. However that may be, the Friends' statement that theirs was simply a renewal of the dispensation inaugurated by Christ and that their religion was precisely that of the primitive Christian church made them more insistent than other spiritualists that they were not apostates but true and wholly orthodox Christians.

Indeed, from their perspective they alone were true Christians—the first since the apostolic era. I have indicated

[2] More, *Divine Dialogues* (2d edn.; London, 1713), 565.

that many Friends shared the English religio-nationalistic myth put forward by John Foxe and saw themselves as the culmination of a chain of English reformers, but this idea had to struggle against their more exclusivistic position in the 1650's. Throughout the Restoration period, and especially after 1688, the Quakers were drawn toward seeking allies among other Protestants and emphasizing their agreement on essentials with orthodox Protestants, but the older position held the field before the Toleration Act. According to Barclay the Friends stood over against both Protestants and Catholics. The Protestants had lopped off a few branches of the Catholic tree, but they retained the same roots and differed only in certain forms and ceremonies.[3]

The Friends justified their own orthodoxy in spite of their differences with other Christians by means of an attack on the conception of orthodoxy accepted by most Anglicans and nonconformists. They said that the essence of notionalism, which held sway among the Anglicans, Presbyterians, Independents, and Baptists, was the belief that Christianity was a set of propositions and that being a Christian was a matter of intellectually accepting those propositions. As the Quaker approach to justification indicates, however, they were convinced that being a Christian was primarily a matter of living and acting in relation to God and their fellowmen rather than affirming beliefs. To become a Friend one had to show that he could "walk righteously" in all his dealings with men and deal lovingly with fellow-saints, and he had to accept the painful and costly Quaker testimonies against the world. By failing to stick to this primitive conception of Christianity as saintly living and by turning orthodoxy into a matter of intellectual propositions, both Catholics and Protestants had perverted the ministry and the whole nature of the theological enterprise. The minister had come to be seen as one who is adept at understanding Scripture and drawing from it the essential doctrinal and ethical guidelines of the faith. For this he needed logic, lan-

[3] *Apology*, 262-263.

guages, rhetoric, and training in scholastic theology. According to Barclay, this was a proud attempt to substitute human devices for the guidance of the Spirit, which can use any man regardless of his education. Language, logic, and philosophy are not helpful to the Christian leader, and they can be harmful to him, as the monstrous attempt to wed Scripture and heathen philosophy in "school divinity" had indicated.[4]

According to the Quakers, theology had become man's attempt to "improve" on the doctrines stated by God in Scripture by drawing up elaborate versions of the main Scriptural ideas and forcing Christians to assent to summaries of these man-made doctrines in the form of creeds. Though placing Scripture below the inner light as an authority in the Christian life, Quakers believed that Christians should stick to the *ipsissima verba* of Scripture in doctrinal formulations. Friends differed in their understanding of Scriptural inspiration, but even those who believed with Fisher that the form and phraseology of the Biblical books were attributable to the human agents who wrote them, rather than to God's all-controlling inspiration, felt that it was useless for man to try to improve on Scriptural versions of Christian beliefs. Scripture was clear on the essentials, and where ambiguity remained, it was simply because, in order to describe wholly different spiritual realities, theology had to make use of words whose primary referents were in the physical world. Since the words could point to spiritual things only in an imprecise and indirect way, it was foolish to insist on adherence to particular church formulations and creedal expressions.

The Friends' attitude toward theological language and Protestant orthodoxy caused them to object to certain doctrinal formulations that they felt involved too much anthropomorphizing of the divine. Their objection to the Trinitarian formula of one divine essence in three persons was a case in point, although differences between their under-

4 *Apology*, 282-292.

standing of "person" and that of their opponents also caused
difficulty on this point, for Friends took "person" to refer
not to a separate consciousness but to an "outward" or
"human" embodied being.[5]

Most of the anthropomorphizing was to be found in the
orthodox views of Christ and of heaven and hell. To Quakers the atonement was wrongly seen by the orthodox primarily as a transaction between God and Christ analogous
to the dealings of an unscrupulous ransomer with his poor
victim. Christ was too often portrayed as a kind of freakish
divine-human "person" who came down from heaven for a
period and then climbed his invisible ladder to seat himself
next to the throne of God. Such language was necessary,
Friends believed, but Anglicans and especially nonconformists tended to understand it too literally. Although the
Quakers did not customarily address themselves directly to
the issue of theological language, their controversy on this
point was in fact a precursor of the demythologizing discussion of more recent times. This is especially evident in an
exchange between the Baptist Matthew Caffen and the
Quaker William Bayly. When Caffen insisted that Christ
could not be within man because he had ascended into
heaven and was seated at the right hand of God, Bayly initiated the following exchange:

> Which Heaven dost thou mean, said I to him? I mean,
> said he, That Visible Heaven up there (pointing over his
> Head towards the Skie). What, up there, where the Sun,
> Moon and Stars are, said I? Yea, said M. C. this is my
> Faith and my principle. . . . Then said I, Did Paul speak
> Truth and honestly to the People, or did he mock them,
> and deal deceitfully with them, when he bid them, Seek
> the things that are above, where Christ sitteth at the Right
> Hand of God, etc.? Or did he meant [sic] up there,

[5] See Edward Grubb, *The Historic and the Inward Christ: A Study
in Quaker Thought* (Bishopsgate, E.C., 1914), 52-53.

where the Visible Sun, Moon and Stars are, the Visible Heaven; how was it possible? Or wherein was it any way profitable for them to seek things up there? Or what things were they there to seek? Did any of them climb up thither, and find Christ sitting there in a Visible Single Person, as M. C. said he was there so?[6]

The Friends arrived at their attitude toward orthodoxy and their dissatisfaction with particular doctrines because of concerns somewhat peculiar to them, but their position had striking similarities to that of certain other thinkers of the seventeenth century who were dissatisfied with Protestant orthodoxy. The earlier Falkland Circle of Anglicans, the Cambridge Platonists, the latitudinarians, the English Unitarians influenced by Socinianism, and some of the General Baptists differed among themselves in many things, but they all shared with the Quakers a tendency to place "life" over creed, an opposition to the abstruse and pettifogging distinctions of scholastic theology, and a belief in the adequacy of Scripture as a guide to and statement of the essential ideas of the Christian faith. Some members of these groups would have disagreed with Ralph Cudworth on aspects of his thought as profoundly as they did with some of the Calvinistic orthodox, but they could agree with him that "he is the best Christian whose heart beats with the truest pulse toward heaven; not he whose head spinneth out the finest cobwebs. He that endeavours really to mortify his lusts, and to comply with that truth in his life which his confidence is convinced of, is nearer a Christian, though he never heard of Christ, than he that believes all the vulgar articles of the Christian faith, and plainly denieth Christ in his life."[7] In addition, all but the members of the Falkland Circle shared the Quakers' opposition to the orthodox doctrines of the

[6] *Collection of the Writings of William Bayly* (Phila., 1830), 595-596.
[7] Cited by Tulloch, *Rational Theology*, II, 236.

Trinity, substitutionary atonement, and, as we have seen earlier, original sin, election, free will, and justification.[8]

It is common to attribute the anti-Calvinistic animus of the liberal Anglicans, Unitarians, and General Baptists to their rejection of the Calvinist anthropology and their pre-Enlightened optimism about man, and on this understanding they had little in common with the Quaker attitude toward orthodoxy. This kind of rationalism was coming to the fore in the latter part of the seventeenth century, but the emphasis on Biblical doctrine and on theological minimalism in all these groups was also a result of their reaction against the attempts of the orthodox to try to improve on Scripture and to treat its all too human doctrinal formulations as if they were the very words of God. John Hales spoke for all the Anglicans, Unitarians, and General Baptists influenced by Arminianism and Socinianism when he said that the main vice of theology in this as in all ages was the substitution of human opinion or "conceit" for divine truth. "When we seceded from the Church of Rome our motive was, because she added unto Scripture her glosses as canonical, to supply what the plain text of Scripture could not yield. If in place of this we set up our own glosses, thus to do were nothing else than to pull down Baal and set up an ephod; to run round and meet the Church of Rome again at the same point in which we left her."[9] Hales also spoke for the Friends who would follow him.

Many of the Anglicans of the liberal schools and some of the Unitarians were partly motivated in their opposition to Calvinist orthodoxy by an irenical desire to unify Protes-

[8] The members of the Falkland Circle, including Lord Falkland, John Hales, and William Chillingworth, did not object to particular "Calvinistic" doctrines so much as to the general spirit of orthodoxy. This is also true of Jeremy Taylor. *Ibid., passim.* On the discomfort felt by Stillingfleet, Tillotson, Fowler and other latitudinarians with the orthodox doctrines of the Trinity and the atonement, see Stromberg, *Religious Liberalism*, 46.

[9] Cited by Tulloch, *Rational Theology*, I, 256, 254.

tants and to end the theological wrangling and splintering of sects that was weakening Protestants in the face of the Catholic challenge they all feared. They said that Scripture allowed one to distinguish the essential from the inessential doctrines in Christianity and that Christians should unite in a minimal statement of beliefs in Scriptural language. Often the Apostles' Creed was suggested as an adequate statement that all should be able to agree upon, thereby bringing Christians back beyond not only the schism following the Reformation but even the struggle between Arians and Trinitarians. This pan-Protestant irenicism was foreign to the earliest Quakers, but during the Restoration period, as Quakerism lost some of its spiritual power and as it tired of persecution, the temptation to stress the orthodox Protestantism of the Friends even in doctrines made slow inroads. After 1688 it came to the fore in the Quaker attempt to convince the authorities of their right to toleration as ordinary Protestants. As the Friends put forward their own creedal "testimonies" and referred to their agreement with the Apostles' Creed and even, with a few conditions, the Athanasian Creed, their position approached that of some Anglicans, Unitarians, and General Baptists even more than it had earlier.

SOME of Penn's treatises included at least as much of what the opponents saw as heretical "Vomitings" as those of any Quaker writer, but he also believed as firmly as others that Quakerism was "Primitive Christianity Revived." He took an active part in the defense of Quaker orthodoxy by means of the attack on the over-doctrinal or intellectualistic orthodoxy of Calvinists and other mainstream Christians. No Quaker writer insisted more regularly that the true Christian was more concerned with deeds than with creeds. "We make not our Religion to stand in a Belief of so many Verbal Articles; but a Conformity of Soul to the Grace of God." "For it is not Opinion, or Speculation, or Notions of

269

what is true; or Assent to, or the Subscription of Articles, or Propositions, tho' never so soundly worded, that . . . makes a Man a True Believer, or a True Christian. But it is a Conformity of Mind and Practice to the Will of God, in all Holiness of Conversation, according to the Dictates of this Divine Principle of Light and Life in the Soul, which denotes a Person truly a Child of God."[10] At times Penn argued that creedal standards are more harmful than helpful when imposed on believers, since they lead to the false belief that doctrinal consent counts toward one's salvation and to the neglect of righteous living.[11]

Equally prominent in Penn's thought, as we have seen, was his opposition to theological learning and to the "vain Quiddities" of scholastic theology with its proud attempt to improve on Scripture and capture the essence of divine truths. According to Penn, certain doctrines have been too much fought over, including Christ's nature and personality, the extent of his intercession for men, free will and grace, faith and works, perseverance, and the nature of the church.[12] Scripture, although clear on all the essentials of the faith, was never intended to be a rule of faith for all questions that might arise in the minds of the curious. But proud men continue to seek answers. When they cannot find them in the Bible, they make tenuous deductions from Scriptural statements and raise them to the status of articles of faith or make up their own answers and concoct Biblical support for them by misuse of the Scriptures. It was precisely the habit of putting pretended deductions from Scripture in place of the Word of God that made Catholicism so odious, and now Protestants have fallen to the same level. Moreover, they, as the Romans, claim infallibility for their human opinions and debate them in heated wranglings until nothing certain can be known, the most important aspects

[10] "Just Rebuke" (1674), *Works*, II, 607; "Key" (1692), *Works*, II, 781.

[11] "Serious Apology" (1671), *Works*, II, 84.

[12] "Address to Protestants" (1679), *Works*, I, 774.

of the faith have been forgotten, and Christian unity is broken.[13]

Penn also joined the Quaker polemic against what he saw as the too literal and naive understanding of theological language held by many nonconformists and Anglicans. He believed that too many of the "orthodox" Christians had too "crude" an understanding of theological mysteries that words can merely point to in a metaphorical and symbolic manner. In his view such concepts as the "Persons" of the Trinity, Christ's presence with the Father, Christ's atoning transactions with the Father, the incarnation and ascension of Christ, and the bread and wine of the eucharist were commonly understood in too "physical" or literal a manner. For example, when the Quakers' opponents insisted that Christ was "a distinct Person outside of Man," they apparently intended to limit Christ spatially, whereas, according to Penn, "outside" and "within" had nonspatial meanings when used in theological discourse. Penn said that Christ could be and was a "distinct Being" from those he was "within," but that did not mean that he was "at a distance" from them. Quakers, said Penn, did not deny that Christ was without as well as within them, since Christ's indwelling does not make void his being elsewhere. But they refused to set limits to Christ's presence. Moreover, the word "Person" in the phrase "Christ a distinct Person without us" led the orthodox to retain "mean and dark" ideas of God and Christ and of Christ's place of residence.[14] Although Penn never said so explicitly, his point was that theology had to make use of words whose primary referent was in the physical world to describe spiritual realities.[15]

Penn's opposition to Protestant orthodoxy diverged from that of other Quakers in several respects. For one, his oppo-

---

[13] *Ibid.*, 744-752.

[14] "Counterfeit Christian" (1674), *Works*, II, 587-588; "Defence of a Paper" (1698), *Works*, II, 894.

[15] "New Witnesses" (1672), *Works*, II, 161-162; "Tender Counsel" (1677), *Works*, I, 199; "Reason Against Railing" (1673), *Works*, II, 530.

sition to the orthodox conceptions of the Trinity, atonement, and imputed righteousness was based as much on his theological rationalism as on his belief that these doctrines were not Scriptural. Although there was a similarity between Quaker and Socinian objections to these doctrines, it is significant that the Socinians Henry Hedworth and Thomas Firmin had not found in other Quaker writings as much cause for joy as they did in Penn's *Sandy Foundation*. In this treatise Penn explicitly based his doctrines on reason as well as Scripture, and his rationalistic treatment of the doctrines bears a striking resemblance to the work of the Socinian John Knowles. Firmin and Hedworth began to regard Penn as an ally and started defending him.[16] Penn rejected their overtures and expressed himself much more carefully thereafter, but his insistence that Christian doctrines be in accord with reason made his attitude toward Protestant orthodoxy somewhat closer to that of liberal Anglicans and Socinians than was that of most Friends.

Penn also differed from many other Quakers by virtue of his stress on the common beliefs held by Quakers and other Christians and his search for a minimal set of essential beliefs on which all Christians could agree, and this too gave him affinities with liberal Anglicans that other Restoration Quakers lacked. Penn's earliest works stridently pointed to the uniqueness and superiority of Quakerism over against all other "Christian" bodies, but from the 1670's he began to stress the common faith of the major Christian bodies. No doubt his unrelenting attempts to gain toleration for Friends by means of pamphlets, Parliamentary appearances, and activities at Court led him to espouse this position. Most often he emphasized that the Quakers did not differ one iota from the principles maintained by the first Protestants in Germany and England and pleaded for amity and toleration for all true Protestants.[17] Elsewhere he argued that *all*

[16] See McLachlan, *Socinianism*, 302-312.
[17] Speech to a committee of Parliament (Mar. 22, 1678), *Works*, I, 119.

the main bodies of Christians were united in essentials. "The several species of Christians, that this Genus divideth itself into are those divers Perswasions we have within this Kingdom; the Church of England, Roman Catholics, Grecians, Lutherans, Presbyterians, Independents, Anabaptists, Quakers, Socinians: These I call so many Orders of Christians, that unite in the Text, and differ only in the Comment. . . ."[18] Penn was able to take this position because he shared the tendency manifested by irenicists from the Falkland Circle to the latitudinarians to distinguish between essential and inessential doctrines. The impulse was not absent from Quakerism, but Penn developed the idea more than most. He wanted to reduce the gospel to its bare essentials without any large confessions or lists of principles or opinions, resolved upon after curious and tedious debates by councils and synods. The Christian religion had been delivered with much brevity and plainness; it was suited to the capacity of the young, the ignorant, and the poor.[19]

Penn was careful to avoid developing a formula for the essentials of Christian belief. As we have seen, at times the essentials amounted to no more than the duties enjoined in Micah 6:8, but Penn was more demanding when he was concerned to stress Quaker orthodoxy. Then he said that true Christians were united by "the Belief of Jesus of Nazareth to be the Promised Messiah, the Son and Christ of God, come and sent from God to restore and save Mankind. . . ."[20] Occasionally the Apostles' Creed or even, with qualifications, the Athanasian Creed—"setting aside school terms"— was cited as the basic Christian creed.[21] Penn developed some of the more heterodox Quaker doctrines more than most Friends, but his desire for toleration and his theological minimalism made him stress the Protestant orthodoxy of

[18] "Perswasive to Moderation" (1685), *Works*, II, 746-747.
[19] "Address to Protestants" (1679), *Works*, I, 744-752, 773-782.
[20] "Address to Protestants" (1679), *Works*, I, 754.
[21] "Testimony to the Truth" (1698), *Works*, II, 881; "Defence of a Paper" (1698), *Works*, II, 886, 914-915.

Friends well before that became customary among Quakers. How legitimate that position was is the question to which we now turn.

THE PERSON OF JESUS CHRIST

The Friends' opponents were not disposed to accept without further questioning their assertion that they were orthodox Christians whether that claim was based on a redefinition of orthodoxy or an attempt to include Quaker thought in the old definition. But when they sought to discover precisely where the Friends stood on the central doctrines of the Christian faith, especially as they related to the historical plan of redemption through Jesus Christ, they were frustrated by what was called the Quaker "talent for obfuscation." The Quakers rarely admitted—if, indeed, they were aware—that they held some positions that had been declared heretical centuries before, and they resorted to ambiguity, inconsistency, and camouflage to avoid becoming open targets for heresy-hunters. In 1669 John Owen was still unclear where they stood on central doctrines and pleaded with them to cease their "confused noise and humming" and "to speak intelligibly, and according to the usage of other men, or the pattern of Scripture. . . ."[22] As late as 1698 the Bishop of Cork, in controversy with Penn, felt called on to make the same point, although more politely: "You must not be offended if I say, you have such a Way of Writing and Speaking, that it is very hard, in many Matters of Religion, to know what you mean."[23]

One of the main sources of confusion in Quaker thought was their way of speaking about the person of Christ. No form of the Christian faith was ever more Christocentric than that of the Friends. All men, they said, must learn of

[22] "A Brief Declaration and Vindication of the Doctrine of the Trinity," *Works*, II, 399.
[23] "Defence of a Paper" (1698), *Works*, II, 886.

Christ, and remission of sins is wholly attributable to Christ and must be preached in his name. But the Quakers were referring not primarily to the son born of Mary but to "that which saves" in all ages and in all lands.[24] For Fisher, Christ "was in the being of a true Light to the World, though slain as a Lamb in men from the very Foundation thereof; and such as walk'd in the Beams of that which came from him, came up to the sight of his Day, and Glory, with Rejoycing, as Abraham and others did, Isaiah 6 and was the Christ, or Anointed One of God, to the doing of his Work, and shewing of his Will in the World, before any Letter was written of him, and before he assumed to himself that outward Appearance wherein he dyed. . . ."[25] When the Friends were accused of denying the efficacy of the historical Christ in favor of an eternal principle, they said that there were not two Christs but only one and insisted on the continuity between the pre-incarnate, incarnate, and post-incarnate states of Christ.[26]

So strong was the Quakers' stress on the eternal activity of Christ that they had difficulty affirming the traditional doctrine of the Trinity. Their reluctance to subscribe to the doctrine in its orthodox formula of one essence in three persons was in part because of their unique understanding of the term "person" and their belief in sticking to Scriptural language in stating beliefs, but apart from that consideration their emphasis on the eternal Christ left them without any reason for distributing the divine functions among Father, Son, and Spirit. In addition, they wrote of the unity of the Godhead in a way that excluded the traditional distinctions. God the Father simply faded into the background, and Christ and Spirit were used interchangeably (although it was also said that the Spirit mediated

[24] John Crook, "Truth's Principles" (1653), in *Design of Christianity*, 364-365.
[25] *Rusticus*, 619.
[26] "A Vindication of the Light of Christ Within," *Works*, 327.

Christ's presence). The Trinitarian formula was unacceptable to increasing numbers of theologically minded Englishmen in the seventeenth century, and the Friends were often
linked with the Arian and adoptionist positions attractive to
Socinians and Unitarians and some Anglicans, but this was
clearly misleading. If they are to be linked with any of the
positions on the Godhead previously labelled heretical, it is
with the Sabellian or modal monarchian, according to which
the one God manifests himself in various forms or modes at
different times.[27] Even this link is somewhat misleading,
however, since the Friends were greatly dependent in their
theology on the Scriptural books of Paul and John and
therefore were in the habit of using especially the Johannine manner of referring to the Father, Son, and Spirit in a
way that modified their tendency toward Sabellianism.

The Quaker belief in the eternal Christ placed them more
clearly in what the orthodox saw as a heretical position in
their understanding of the person of the incarnate Christ
than in their views of the Trinity. Their insistence on the
continuity of Christ in all of his states followed necessarily
from their desire to make him a savior for all men and their
spirit-body dualism. To allow that the essential being or
nature of Christ was changed or added to in any significant
way at the incarnation was to jeopardize Christ's salvific
acts apart from the incarnation, so the Friends detracted
from the importance of Christ's body and arrived at the
Eutychean position by making the historical Christ essentially the same divine savior he had been throughout history. The spirit-body dualism led to the position that
Christ's body was not truly human or corruptible (and
hence to docetism), as well as to a tendency to make the
body an accidental part of Christ's being (in effect, Nes-

---

[27] The difference between the Friends and Unitarians on this point
should not be stressed too strongly, however, for Firmin and Hedworth were converted from John Biddle's view of Christ and the Spirit
as delegated agents to the Sabellian position. See McLachlan, *Socinianism*, 296.

torianism, but for different reasons from those that motivated the Antiochene Nestorius).[28]

The idea that the incarnate Christ possessed a "heavenly" or incorruptible flesh and blood either brought from heaven with him or brought into being by a transformation of the corporeal substance he took from Mary was prominent in the Continental Radical Reformation among both Anabaptists and Spiritualists. Melchior Hofmann was the most prominent exponent of the former position, Caspar Schwenckfeld of the latter. Fox learned of the doctrine from the spiritualists, possibly through Giles Calvert's translation of Valentine Weigel's *Life of Christ* in 1648. According to Fox, since being that was "of God" and being that was "of the earth" were forever distinct (the one incorruptible, the other corruptible), and since man's body is "of the earth," Christ could not have possessed a human body. "And carnall humane is from the ground, humane earthly, the first Adam's body, and Christ was not from the ground . . . but he was from heaven, his flesh came down from above, his flesh which was the meat, his flesh came down from heaven."[29] Fox, possibly influenced by the fact that the King James translation of Scripture never translates *anthropinos* as "human," as well as his strange dualism, equated "human" and "of the earth," so that he could not allow that Christ had a "human" nature.[30] This implied that he did not believe that Christ had had a fully human nature, sin excepted, or that Christ was altogether like man except for his sinfulness. Although Fox modified the dualism by granting that the "corruptible" or "human" was a product of sin and thereby avoided simply opposing "spirit" or "incorruption" and all "external" being, he still could not allow Christ to have corruptible material being like that of fallen man. Since, in his view, a body and soul free from sin lack

---

[28] Grubb, *Historic and Inward Christ*, 34-36, incorrectly argues that Penington originated this peculiar Christology.

[29] "Mystery," *Works*, III, 322.

[30] *Ibid.*, 181. See T. Canby Jones, "George Fox," 188, n. 7.

corruption, and since Christ took on a nature free from sin, Christ had a glorious and incorruptible body not only after the resurrection but during the whole of his earthly life. And because Scripture said that the Word came from heaven, Fox held that Christ, although of the seed of Abraham, brought his incorruptible body with him from heaven. "The second man is the Lord from heaven, and his body is a glorious body, and he is a heavenly spiritual man."[31]

Fox's Christ was thus a more exalted figure than the Suffering Servant of the orthodox view. "Incorruptible" or "heavenly" for Fox connoted freedom from misery and all the ills arising from changeableness in addition to freedom from death and sin. On the other hand, Fox did at times speak of Christ as lowly, suffering, and dying, and he clearly affirmed that Christ took upon him not the nature of angels but the seed of Abraham, so that he was in all things like his brethren. "For in that he suffered and was tempted he is able to succour them that are tempted."[32] Thus it seems necessary to assume that Fox distinguished between a "heavenly" flesh of Christ and a corruptible one and that he made only the former an integral part of Christ's person, or else that he accepted Schwenckfeld's position that Christ received from Mary a "begotten" rather than "creaturely" flesh and that it was gradually deified throughout his life.[33]

[31] "A Testimony of What We Believe of Christ," *Works*, v, 152-154; "Mystery," *Works*, iii, 139-140.

[32] "A Testimony of What We Believe of Christ" (1675), *Works*, v, 114.

[33] One of the problems in interpreting Fox's understanding of Christ's body lies in the fact that, on the one hand, presumably because Paul said in I Corinthians 15 that Christ the heavenly man came down from heaven, Fox said, with Hofmann, that his flesh came down from heaven; on the other hand, since he also wanted to keep the Scriptural affirmation that Christ was of the flesh of Abraham and was like man in all respects except sinfulness, he would seem to find Schwenckfeld's position more acceptable. For although Schwenckfeld called the flesh Christ assumed "begotten" rather than "created," he made clear that it was human flesh of the line of Abraham and that

In any case, the doctrine of the "heavenly" flesh of Christ was part of Fox's thought; the phrase was not merely a metaphor.

The doctrine of the incorruptible flesh of Christ seems not to have had much, if any, influence on many Quaker writers, and it was the kind of spiritualist speculation that the sober Friends of the Restoration tended to push into the background. It was found in various forms in Restoration Quakerism, however, and in certain thinkers additional aberrations came to the fore. I have already referred briefly to Keith's "cosmic" version of the heavenly flesh of Christ. Another version of the belief was prominent in the works of Penington. He made it clear that Christ possessed a flesh and blood "of an earthly perishing Nature" as well as a spiritual flesh and blood of the Seed's nature. The latter position was evidently influenced by the Schwenckfeldian Christology, since Penington wrote that Christ took flesh and blood of our nature, but it "was not his naturally, but only as he pleased to take it upon him and make it his."

At the same time, because he wanted to stress the continuity between the pre-incarnate and the incarnate Christ and present the former as a "complete" savior, he spoke of the heavenly flesh and blood as coming with Christ from heaven since it was "the flesh and blood of him, who took, tabernacled and appeared in the Body."[34] In addition to his doctrine of the heavenly flesh of Christ, Penington emphasized more than most Quakers had the distinction between Christ and his "Body." The names "Jesus" and "Christ" belong to "that which" or him who took or tabernacled in the body, not to the body itself. The latter was simply a garment in which Christ appeared. "Now the Scriptures do expressly distinguish between Christ, and the Garment which he wore; between him that came, and the Body in

---

it gained its special characteristics only through a gradual process of deification.

[34] *Works*, II, 13, 18.

which he came; between the Substance which was vailed, and the Vail which vailed it."[35] And since the essential Christ was the incorporeal subject that was veiled in the body, the body, strictly speaking, deserves none of man's thankful regard or any credit for his salvation. It was not difficult for zealous opponents to label Penington Nestorian for separating the two natures, Docetic and Eutychian for giving Christ a more than human nature or unduly emphasizing his divinity, and Apollinarian for implying that Christ's mind and soul were divine.

Barclay's *Apology* is often referred to as the *magnum opus* or *summa theologica* of Quakerism. The terms are misleading to the extent that they imply that the work provides a clear and systematic elaboration of all aspects of Quaker thought. Although the *Apology* is clear and systematic, it is more a handbook for believers than a *summa*. In it Barclay restrained his own speculative or "philosophical" tendencies, avoided polemics except to the extent that they were part of his attempts to differentiate Quakerism from other contemporary positions, and either muted the Quaker heresies or emphasized the more orthodox doctrinal position in areas in which Quakers had moved in more than one doctrinal direction. His avoidance of a discussion of the Trinity is an example of the former. What he wrote about the person of Christ in the *Apology* is an instance of the latter. Barclay was naturally attracted to the doctrine of the heavenly flesh of Christ, and from some of his other works, his contacts with the Ragway Circle of Cartesian philosophers, and what George Keith tells us about his thought, we know that he devoted some thought to the concept. As in the case of his epistemological principles, however, only a bare minimum of material is presented in the *Apology*, and more orthodox positions that seem to conflict with it are emphasized. Barclay discussed the doctrine of the heavenly flesh not as part of his treatment of Christ but in the section on

[35] *Ibid.*, 12, 13, 19.

communion. The body and blood of Christ on which believers feed "is that heavenly seed, that divine, spiritual, celestial substance, of which we spake before in the fifth and sixth propositions." It is not the outward body born of Mary, for that on which men feed came down from heaven, which the outward body did not, and it was in being to be fed on long before the outward body was.[36] Here Barclay referred to the "spiritual" body of Christ simply in relation to the "inward supernatural senses" by which man comes to receive Christ. Barclay did not mention the speculative impulse that made the flesh a cosmic principle, and he also ignored the doctrine in his discussion of Christ despite the fact that it cried out for the kind of clarification he brought to other doctrines. At the same time, he referred to the "outward" body without any attempt to qualify its corruptible nature or to stress, like Penington, its separation from the essential Christ. Moreover, in his discussion of Christ, Barclay denied that the Friends believed the heresies of Eutyches and Apollinarius (omitting, perhaps significantly, reference to Nestorius) and wrote with evasive simplicity: "Wherefore, as we believe he was a true and real man, so we also believe that he continues so to be glorified in the heavens in soul and body, by whom God shall judge the world, in the great and general day of judgment."[37] Barclay left more questions unresolved than he answered about the Quaker view of Christ, but his brief and relatively orthodox statements, when combined with the central salvific role he gave to the incarnate Christ, was indicative of the more orthodox road Quakerism would travel as it approached the reign of William and Mary. What Barclay swept under the rug was destined to remain there.

PENN believed that "all Worship towards God must stand in the Name and Nature of JESUS, or will never pierce the

[36] *Apology*, 415-417.
[37] *Ibid.*, 137.

Heavens."[38] "Christ is the Door, and through Him all must enter; nay through him Only we can come to God; namely, by faithfully receiving him into the Heart, and embracing Him. . . ."[39] Those who pass through the door of this "most Compleat Saviour and perfect Redeemer" will die to their sins, come alive to God, and feel the constraining power and efficacy of Christ's love. They will receive power over sin, the world, and the devil.[40] "There are no Grapes to be gathered of Thorns, nor Figs of Thistles: Keep to your own Vine and Fig-Tree, Christ Jesus; sit under him, that you may eat of his Fruit, which is the Fruit of Life, 'the hidden Manna.' " Indeed, the want of looking to him, hearing and obeying him, and having true faith in him is the cause of the presumption and despair that reign in this evil day.[41]

Penn was able to retain this Christocentric emphasis in his faith without minimizing his concern for universal salvation by referring much of what he said about Christ to the "eternal Christ," "the same yesterday, today and tomorrow." Like most Quakers, he minimized the distinctions and discontinuities among the various states of Christ's existence. He believed that although some people might have experienced the Savior less directly than others, all had the same Savior and could receive eternal life through him. There are only two churches in all the world: that of Christ and that of Satan. Something of that same divine life, power, wisdom, and righteousness that was manifest in Jesus Christ incarnate has been present to men in all ages.[42] It was not

[38] Letter, "To the Princess and Countess at Herford" (1676), *Works*, I, 178.

[39] "To All Those Professors" (1677), *Works*, I, 214.

[40] Letter to Matthew Perin and Friends (Mar. 24, 1684), PWP (L.S. in FLL). Sermon, "Salvation from Sin by Christ Alone," in *Sermons or Declarations*, 63-65.

[41] "Tender Counsel" (1677), *Works*, I, 205; "Travels in Germany and Holland" (1677), *Works*, I, 103-104.

[42] Letter to Richard Butler, Earl of Arran (Jan. 9, 1684), PWP (A.L.S. in Bodleian); "Invalidity" (1673), *Works*, II, 318.

simply that God had made salvation possible in all ages but that the same Savior had been active. When Thomas Hicks objected to the Quaker belief that the universal light in men was a "saving" light on the ground that it did not tell of Christ who was born of Mary, suffered, and died, Penn replied that the historical Christ was not the whole Christ but merely one mode of the eternal Christ's existence. One can talk in glowing terms about the incarnate Christ, "yet when all this is said, and believed . . . that which gives the Life, Power, Virtue, Strength and Efficacy to all this, and to whom therefore eminently the Work, Salvation, Power and Glory are most deservedly ascribable, is the Word that was in the Beginning with God, and was God, whose Life was and is the Light of Men, who took Flesh, and was manifested therein. . . ."[43] In Penn's view, if one made "Christ the Saviour" simply the historical Christ of the "outward" appearance, he could not understand how Christ enlightened every man coming into the world, for in that appearance he reached only a small fraction of the people in the world. That manifestation reached the Jews only, "and within that Narrow Compass he could not be said to be the Light of all Mankind that had, did, and should come into the World. . . ." The Messiah is the one who enlightens all men in an inward manner as much as the man who fasted forty days, preached sermons, performed miracles, and suffered death. Christ was present as the Messiah to men in all ages.[44]

Penn's strongly Christocentric faith, and especially his propensity for attributing all divine activities and powers in all ages to Christ, left him with very little to say about God the Father and no essential reason for distinguishing Christ and the Spirit. The nature of his thought about God is evident in his discussions of the Trinity. In *Sandy Foundation* he argued that the doctrine of the Trinity had not

[43] "Reason Against Railing" (1673), *Works*, II, 506.

[44] "Primitive Christianity" (1696), *Works*, II, 857-858; "Defence of a Paper" (1698), *Works*, II, 897.

been heard of in the first three centuries of the church, especially not from its leading figures, such as Irenaeus, Justin Martyr, Tertullian, and Origen. It was a product of the "nice Distinctions and too daring Curiosity" of the Bishop of Alexandria in his dispute with the overzealous Arius. The Bishop, the stronger of the two, arbitrarily imposed his opinion on the church, and it then received the weight of the name of Athanasius—"a stiff Man, witness his Carriage towards Constantine the Emperor"—through the Athanasian Creed. The doctrine thus established was that the Godhead was one "Substance" with three "Persons" or "Subsistences." The young Penn argued that according to his understanding of the terms, every subsistence had to have its own substance, so that the orthodox doctrine amounted to tritheism. Belief in this doctrine was analogous to the belief that Paul, Peter, and John were three persons but one apostle. In *Sandy Foundation* Penn barely went beyond such games of logic to set forth his own view of the Godhead. He limited himself to Scriptural quotations to prove that God is one, and aroused suspicions by observing that the orthodox doctrine of the Trinity scandalized Turks, Jews, and infidels and thus obstructed their reception of the faith.[45]

Thereafter Penn stopped opposing the "doctrine of the Trinity" and said that he could affirm the essential beliefs involved in it. Since Scripture speaks of "Three that bear witness," he could say that in the Godhead there are three witnesses and that the three are one. Moreover, the term "Trinity" was now acceptable to him, since it was simply a derivative of the Latin word for three.[46] Penn said that he believed in both the eternity and the full divinity of Christ and denied only "Popish-School-Personality" or a "Trinity of Separate Persons in One Godhead," which still seemed to

[45] *Works*, I, 254, 251-252, 264.
[46] "New Athenians" (1692), *Works*, II, 804; "Truth Rescued from Imposture, or a Brief Reply to a Mere Rhapsody . . ." (1671), *Works*, I, 488.

him to be tritheism.[47] In addition, he affirmed the full divinity of the Spirit: "We believe in One Holy Spirit, that proceeds and breaths from the Father and the Son, as the Life and Virtue of both the Father and the Son, a Measure of which is given to all to profit with. . . ."[48] To make clear his orthodoxy on these doctrines, Penn explicitly rejected the thought of the adoptionist Paul of Samosata and of Macedonius, who denied the divinity of the Spirit.[49]

Because Penn followed other Quakers in being unwilling to apply the term "persons" to the members of the Godhead and also objected to calling them "distinct," he had difficulty clarifying his understanding of the triadic nature of the Godhead. He refused to select a noun for the three components to replace "person" and simply said that they were distinct in the sense that "Fatherhood and Sonship are certainly not the same."[50] Moreover, he placed such emphasis on the unity of the Godhead and used the terms "God," "Word," "Christ," and "Spirit" so interchangeably that it is difficult to give credence to his claim to believe in a Trinity in anything like the orthodox sense. The unity of the Godhead was conceived of as that of a concrete, individual being. Such, at least, was the implication when Penn wrote that the three are "of One Nature, as well as Will"; that they are "normally distinguished, yet essentially the same Divine Light"; that the Son did not purchase man's salvation from the Father since they are one; or that if the whole Christ had died on the cross, God would have died, and all creation would have ceased to exist.[51] This was also the implication of his tendency to call Christ "the true and living God" and "the only Lord of Glory" and of his inter-

---

[47] Letter, "To John Collenges" (Jan. 22, 1673), *Works*, I, 164-166.
[48] "Serious Apology" (1671), *Works*, II, 67.
[49] Letter, "To John Collenges" (Jan. 22, 1673), *Works*, I, 164, 166.
[50] "New Athenians" (1692), *Works*, II, 802.
[51] "Key Opening the Way" (1692), *Works*, II, 783; "Innocency" (1668), *Works*, I, 267; "Serious Apology" (1671), *Works*, II, 65; "New Witnesses" (1672), *Works*, II, 164.

changeable use of "God is Word" and "Word is God."[52] Furthermore, he occasionally said that he approved of the doctrine of the ancient heretic Sabellius and that the Son "was not Eternally a Son but in time a Son."[53] In such passages Penn appears to be a modalistic monarchian who made "Christ" the primary name for the "monarch."

On the other hand, he was not consistent in this regard. Possibly his carelessness made him appear more monarchian than he was. Writing about the pre-existence of Christ, he said that Christ was pre-existent in the form of God and in equality with God, and yet even then was distinct, since he was the express image of God the "Divine Immortal Substance." Moreover, regardless of the impression given by his theological expressions, his living faith and his dependence on Scripture led him to use language implying that at least the Father and Son were "distinct" enough to have an inter-relationship. In his exegesis of Hebrews 7 he referred to the infinite faithfulness between God and Christ. In his extensive use of the Gospel of John, Penn made no attempt to bypass the evangelist's phrases about Christ's coming forth from the Father, doing the Father's work, and leaving the world to return to him.[54]

Taken as a whole, however, and with due consideration for its characteristic emphases, Penn's thought provides no clear doctrine of God and no significant functional separation of God the Father and the Spirit from Christ. If pressed, he would probably have said that God was the creator, ruler, and judge and the Spirit the agent that makes one aware of Christ's presence within. But his emphasis on the eternal Christ, who has always been "the Blessed and

[52] "Spirit of Truth" (1672), *Works*, II, 137.

[53] Letter to J. L., S. D. *et al.* (Jan. 17, 1674), PWP (copy in HSP). Letter, "To John Colleges" (Jan. 22, 1673), *Works*, I, 166. On the other hand, in "New Athenians," which Penn wrote with several other Quakers, he said that Quakers should not be called "Sabellian." *Works*, II, 807.

[54] "Spirit of Truth" (1672), *Works*, II, 136.

alone Mediator betwixt God and Man," was so strong that the Word, "the true and living God," emerged as the one focus of faith and theological reflection.[55]

Penn's preoccupation with the possibility of salvation beyond the pale of Christendom made it even more difficult for him than for other Quakers to take a wholly orthodox approach to the doctrine of the person of Christ. Since Christ was a savior before and after his incarnation as well as during it, Penn was reluctant to allow that anything essential was added to the "eternal Christ" at the incarnation. The incarnate Christ had to be portrayed simply as a continuation of the conscious life of the eternal Christ. This meant that Penn could not believe that the bodily nature that Christ added became an integral part of his being, even for a brief period, or that its assumption constituted a "change" in the nature of the Word's being. If he allowed either, it would be impossible to say that Christ is the same Savior as the one the ancient Hebrews and heathen had experienced. "Did the Body God prepar'd for his Son to do his will in help to constitute him Christ, as much as the Apostle's Body did help to constitute him Paul? If it did, why may not we say that Paul was among the Fathers in the Wilderness so many hundred Years before he was born, as the same Apostle doth assert, Christ by Name to have been the spiritual Rock of which the Fathers drank in the Wilderness?" Similarly, since the Christ who dwells with man today is the same Christ men knew before and during the incarnation, the body was not truly a part of him, since Christ dwells in his people, and a body cannot dwell in them.[56]

The other strain in Quakerism leading in the direction of Christological difficulties, the spirit-body dualism, presented similar problems for Penn, and he made liberal use of Pen-

[55] "Testimony to the Truth" (1698), *Works*, ii, 877.
[56] "Invalidity" (1673), *Works*, ii, 415; "New Athenians" (1692), *Works*, ii, 802.

ington's ideas to resolve them. Believing that reality was made up of two disparate and even antithetical kinds of being, namely, spirit and matter or the unchanging and the changing, Penn insisted that it was impossible for the unchanging eternal Word or Christ to "become" or "change" by adding to his nature—especially by adding to his person a changing body. The infinite, immortal, eternal nature could not change into a mortal corruptible creature; God could not become a dying man. Like can only beget like, immortal being begetting immortal being.[57] Viewing the same problem from a different angle, Penn insisted not only that the Word could not change in the incarnation but that, since corporeal changing being was obviously attached in some way to the incarnate Christ, it must be possible to distinguish between what happened to the body and what happened to "Christ." Not the eternal Word but the body of flesh was subjected to all the natural passions of heat, cold, hunger, thirst, life, and death. Christ, to the extent that he was body, was not God. "To conclude, Though the Divine Word of Life and Light died not (for Christ as God over all blessed for ever, could not die) yet his Body did. . . ." To make that "which" died and rose again the entire Christ is to exclude divinity from Christ.[58] Christ's body was simply the "vail" or "garment" that he wore. Christ "took" flesh rather than being "made" flesh. The statement, "the Word took Flesh, and pitch'd his Tent or Tabernacle in us," was Penn's favorite Scriptural description of the event.[59]

Penn thus opened himself to Keith's charge that he denied "the Hypostatical or Personal Union of the two Natures." The body or "man" may be called "Christ" only by "metonymy, whereby the thing containing gets the name

[57] "New Witnesses" (1672), *Works*, II, 163.

[58] *Ibid.*, 161, 163; "Reason Against Railing" (1673), *Works*, II, 506, 518.

[59] "Invalidity" (1673), *Works*, II, 418; "Spirit of Truth" (1672), *Works*, II, 137.

of the thing contained." Sometimes Penn said that it was improper to call Christ the God-man, for the term is unscriptural and implies too close a union of the two natures. Because of the "Administration and Service" of that body of Christ, it may be appropriate to attribute to it the name "Christ," "being so nearly related," but still it is better to reserve that term for the divine nature that dwelt in the body.[60]

Penn was not always satisfied to leave the natures of Christ separated in this manner. As on most issues, he had his more and his less orthodox moments. When he was interested in stressing the Protestant roots of Quakerism, he said that he was not satisfied with this wide distinction between the two natures but had reverted to it for the sake of clarity. There were those among the orthodox, according to Penn, who "equated" the body and Christ and said that the person of Christ died on the cross. They would not admit that there was "something left over" of the divine Word that transcended the incarnate union or that the incarnate Christ was not the whole Christ. Penn sometimes said that if he could get agreement on those points, he would not scruple to allow "the Man Jesus to be the Christ of God." He had no objection to John Faldo's speaking of Christ "as consisting of a Divine and Human Nature, that is, God and Man," if Faldo admitted that the flesh and blood and the human soul did not constitute the whole Christ.[61]

Especially in his later works Penn placed a strong emphasis on the union of the two natures in Christ and at the same time made it clear that it was a full human nature—including body and soul—that he had in mind. Normally the Quakers assumed that the conscious, sentient, or active part of Christ was the divine Word and that the "flesh" was a passive agent that he took on to appear among men. With-

[60] "Invalidity" (1673), *Works*, II, 419. See Keith's discussion of Penn on this point in *Some of the Many Fallacies*, 35.

[61] "Quakerism a New Nickname" (1672), *Works*, II, 284-285; "Invalidity" (1673), *Works*, II, 416, 419.

out being consciously Apollinarian, the Friends, with their conception of man as a compound of activity-passivity or spirit-matter, divided the divine and human natures of Christ in the same way. This was to imply that Christ had an incomplete manhood, since he had no "active" human soul. Penn was no exception, but at times he went beyond this position to a more orthodox one. Although he usually said that it was the "Flesh" that Christ added at the incarnation, he could write that Christ "took on him the Nature of Man, and was made Flesh," and that Christ was "Truly and Properly Man."[62] When the emphasis on Christ's continuity became a source of controversy with puritans and Anglicans, he could deny that he was making a distinction between the eternal Christ and Jesus and thereby making "Jesus" simply a passive instrument of the eternal Christ. "Nor did we ever say, that Jesus of Nazareth is Christ's instrument to appear in, and by, for man's salvation; but, that 'the Word took flesh,' and this is the Christ, or Anointed of God: and though sometimes the term Christ is given to the Word, sometimes to the prepared body he took . . . yet 'God manifest in the flesh' and 'Immanuel,' God with us, in our nature, is that Christ of God. . . ." Jesus Christ, the same who was born of a virgin, the Son of Man in a suffering state, who died and arose, is now the Son of Man in glory.[63]

In another respect Penn's view of the person of Christ was more orthodox than the beliefs of many early Quaker writers, for he avoided speculation about the "heavenly" or "incorruptible" flesh that many Quakers attributed to Christ. Penn shared their belief that Christ could not have taken on as an integral part of his being a full human nature without taking on its corruption. But he did not try to preserve Christ from this by developing a doctrine of Christ's heavenly flesh. Because his dualism was more consistent than

[62] Sermon (Aug. 13, 1699), ACMC, PWP (copy in FLL); "Key Opening the Way" (1692), *Works*, II, 783.
[63] *More Work For George Keith* (1696), 3; "Key Opening the Way" (1692), *Works*, II, 789.

Fox's, he could emphasize Christ's incorruptibility by stressing that what Christ assumed at the incarnation remained essentially "separate" from his being. The flesh that Christ took from Mary and that suffered and died was simply an appendage; its addition did not in any way affect Christ's center of consciousness. With this idea of the separation of the two natures, he saw no need to develop a doctrine of Christ's exalted heavenly flesh. Indeed, possibly it was because his dualism was so strict that the idea of a heavenly "enfleshment" of Christ was not a workable solution. In this regard it is significant that Penn, unlike Fox, did not speak of man's soul lying in death because of sin, and he had great difficulty accepting any meaningful doctrine of the resurrection of the body.

Whatever the reason, Penn did not use the doctrine of Christ's heavenly flesh. Although he defended Fox's refusal to apply the term "human" to Christ and recited Fox's reasons for this, he seems to have been confused about what Fox, Penington, Barclay, and others meant by the heavenly flesh or "spiritual body" of Christ. On the one hand, he argued against the "New Athenians" that Fox and Barclay, when they spoke of the spiritual body of Christ, meant a "Spiritual" or "Immaterial Substance." If the "Athenians" did not understand that, they must be strangers to both "the New and Old Philosophy." On the other hand, Penn implied in his defense of Fox and Barclay that the heavenly flesh was simply a metaphor suggested by the Gospel of John's discussion of eating Christ's heavenly flesh. It was a metaphor for the regenerating communion with "Christ within."[64] Penn himself spoke of men being fashioned after death "like unto Christ's glorious body, which is spiritual, glorious and immortal," but only in reference to the resurrected Christ. Although he used the term "body" to refer to this future state, he excluded all the attributes of sentient being.[65] At any rate, when he was directed in controversy

[64] "New Athenians" (1692), *Works*, II, 801-805.
[65] "Spirit of Truth" (1672), *Works*, II, 145.

toward a consideration of Christ's human nature, he did not
object to the term "human" when applied to Christ. As long
as the body of Christ was not, except by a figure of speech,
made an integral part of his being, Penn took no pains to
describe Christ's human side as exalted or incorruptible.[66]

The Work of Jesus Christ

The early Quakers used their "talent for obfuscation" in
their discussions of the work as well as the person of Christ,
and on this matter they seem to have been as confused as
they were confusing. Two questions arose as a result of
their doctrine of the inner light and their belief in the eternal Christ. What did the incarnate Christ do to save men?
How is the historical Christ soteriologically related to those
many persons who know the eternal Christ but who have
never heard of Jesus of Nazareth? On the one hand, some
of the Friends tended toward rather novel answers to these
questions. Because of their emphasis on the unity of the
Godhead and their concerns about unduly anthropomorphic
conceptions of divinity, the traditional doctrine of the
atonement seemed to many a less than satisfactory account
of Christ's work.

More in keeping with their thought was the idea that in
some way the promise of Jeremiah had come true as a result
of the Biblical drama of Christ. But there seemed to be no
obvious causal connection between Christ's dying on a cross
and rising again, on the one hand, and having the light of
God shine more brightly and immediately within men on
the other. Nor did it seem reasonable to many Friends to
believe that this set of historical deeds could have an effect
on those who came before they took place or who never
learned of them. Moreover, as Penington had so clearly
emphasized, it was more appropriate to attribute whatever
good resulted from Christ's deeds to his active divine part

[66] "Key Opening the Way" (1692), *Works*, II, 783; *More Work for
George Keith* (1696), 3.

rather than the "body" he assumed, and since the incorruptible, unchangeable divine part could not suffer and die, what the divine incarnate Christ accomplished soteriologically could be done as easily in his pre- and post-incarnate states. As a result of these considerations many Quakers tended to ignore the question about the saving value of the historical Christ's deeds.

In answer to the second question, concerning Jesus and the heathen, they attributed the salvation of all men to the eternal Christ, who was the same divine unchangeable being who for a period inhabited the body. Jesus of Nazareth did not seem especially important to them, but when pressed some Friends would speak of the historical Christ as the one who fulfilled the law, the types, shadows, and sacrifices that went before and especially provided men with an example of sanctified living.[67] They emphasized, in other words, the manward rather than the godward direction of Christ's deeds. If they allowed the idea of atonement at all, they would insist that the idea of a "rigid satisfaction," in which Christ made full payment to God for man's sins, was incompatible with the idea of free remission and grace. Whatever value Christ's death had in the eyes of God, according to Whitehead, who summoned Edward Stillingfleet's doctrine to his support against the Presbyterian Thomas Danson and the Independent John Owen, it was not a "strict Payment" and was supplemented by God's remission and our own faith and repentance.[68]

At the same time, the Friends did not like to be portrayed as betrayers of the central doctrine of the Christian church, and some of them were shocked at the thought that they might be. When pressed they could stress not only the sameness of the eternal and historical Christ and their belief in the Scriptural accounts of Christ but the conviction that Christ's death was the center-point in the history of salva-

[67] Fisher, *Rusticus*, 154.
[68] "Some Passages out of Edward Stillingfleet's Discourse of the Sufferings of Christ . . . ," *Divinity of Christ*, 85-88.

tion. Not all the early Friends were equally loyal to Jesus of Nazareth, but figures as central as Fox and Nayler provided a basis for the Friends' later more orthodox views. As I have indicated earlier, Fox could say on one occasion that the true cross that Christians should value was not an "outward" thing of stick or stone but the power of God as it comes to man's unrighteous acts, and then at other times state in the strongest terms the necessary atoning value of Christ's death.[69]

Fox was also convinced that, in some way that he did not understand, Christ's death affected even those men who had never heard of him. At times he seemed willing even to belittle the universal light available to all men by implying that the heathen were at a disadvantage in not having Christ preached to them and that Quakers should make every effort to make converts. To the Turks he wrote that Muhammad had deceived them and that their salvation required their acceptance of the Lord Jesus Christ, the man who had died for the sins of the world at Jerusalem. Fox also wanted Friends to preach to the Indians and Negroes of the New World that God had created the world in six days, destroyed it by flood, and then sent Christ to die for the nations, "for God hath some to be brought out from amongst those heathens. . . ." The Indians were also to be told that this "time of visitation" brought by Quaker missionaries might be their last chance to be saved.[70]

Thus although early Friends generally denied or strongly modified the traditional atonement theories, they could also affirm them with a vengeance. And whereas it was common to attribute the salvation of most men to the eternal Christ without mentioning Jesus of Nazareth, Fox could emphasize missionary work in a way that made his message of universal salvation identical to that of most orthodox Christians,

[69] Epistle 222 (1662), *Works*, VII, 232-233; "Concerning daily Sacrifices and Offerings" [1688], *Works*, VI, 383.

[70] "To the Turk" (n.d.), *Works*, IV, 216-221; Epistle 292 (1672), *Works*, VIII, 41-42; Epistle 355 (1679), *Works*, VIII, 160.

who held that although the heathen hardly had a true knowledge of God, God would not damn those ignorant of him. During the Restoration period Quaker writers gradually began to settle somewhere between these extremes on both issues. Barclay's discussion of these matters in the *Apology* illustrates both trends. On the atonement he was probably readier to use the traditional language about Christ's "offering" and "sacrifice" than many Friends, who remained uncomfortable with the godward side of Christ's reconciliation between God and man, but it became customary in Quakerism to grant some modified validity to the idea. Barclay wrote of "the atonement and sacrifice of Jesus Christ," who "offers up himself a sacrifice to God for our sins." Remission of sins is by virtue of this most satisfactory sacrifice through the "merits" of Christ. In this act "God slew the enmity in himself." Nevertheless, although he avoided argumentation, Barclay did not refer to Christ's act as one of "satisfaction," and in listing the benefits of the deed he stressed man's knowledge of the love of God expressed therein and the comfort and love that it produces in man.[71]

On the question of the relationship between the death of Christ and the salvation of those who do not know him, Barclay formulated the compromise that came to prevail widely in the movement. His way of balancing universality and particularity was to affirm that the deeds of the historical Christ were the cause of the saving light's presence in all men's hearts, together with the acknowledgment that one did not have to know of the historical Christ to benefit from his deeds. Through a particular act carried out at a particular time in history, the saving light flowed into every corner of the world and backward and forward into every moment of time. But men may be partakers of the mystery of Christ's death even though they have not heard of Jesus if they allow the light within them to make of them lovers

[71] *Apology*, 132, 139, 140, 196.

and doers of good.[72] Faith in and knowledge of the historical Christ is "not such an essential part, as that without
which the Christian religion cannot consist; but an integral
part, which goes to the completing of the Christian religion:
as the hands or feet of a man are integral parts of a man,
without which nevertheless a man may exist, but not an
entire and complete man."[73] At one place in the *Apology*
Barclay suggested that knowledge of the historical Christ
was but "the rudiments which young children learn, which
after they are become better scholars, are of less use to
them, because they possess and have the very substance of
those first precepts in their minds."[74]

PENN often gave the impression that he saw nothing essential or unique in the historical life and death of Christ. "This
is Christ, as the Word-God, and Light of the world, through
every Dispensation, One in Himself, tho' to Mankind he has
variously appeared, not by different Lights, but different
Manifestations only, of One and the same Eternal Light of
life and Righteousness."[75] He, like Burrough, could omit
all reference to the historical Christ in talking about the
Christ available to all men, and he was not concerned to
preach the incarnate Christ's atoning deeds to the heathen.
This became evident in his relations with the Indians of
Pennsylvania. Penn, nevertheless, granted that in some sense
Christ was the center of history. It was "Glad Tidings"
indeed "after so black and cold a Season as had long over-
cast the Heavens, to have the 'Glorious Sun of Righteousness' appear in that Blessed Body, prepared and anointed for
that Purpose, in Manner transcendent, to all former Manifestations of Himself."[76] According to Penn, the Quakers'
emphasis on the inward Christ was simply meant to redress

[72] *Apology*, 139, 180.
[73] "Immediate Revelation," *Truth Triumphant*, III, 566.
[74] *Ibid.*, 170.
[75] "Christian Quaker" (1673), *Works*, I, 568.
[76] *Ibid.*, 567.

an imbalance. It was wrong to conclude that they intended to deny the significance of Christ's outward coming, life, death, resurrection, and the benefits thereof. They believed that Christ was the "Saviour-General of the Whole World" in that appearance.[77]

In his earliest discussions of the historical Christ, Penn was so intent on demonstrating that changes in man's state— rather than in God—were the result of Christ's deeds that he virtually ruled out the traditional theories of atonement. In *Sandy Foundation* he held up for ridicule the orthodox idea of satisfaction. After citing several Scriptural passages that he felt ruled out the idea of a necessary satisfaction to God, he argued that the doctrine had absurd consequences. It made Christ more compassionate than the Father, robbed God of the gift of his Son for redemption, transferred man's debt from God to Christ, and left men in no way obliged to God. In addition, the doctrine led logically to nonsense. If one held that Christ as God made a payment to God, then, since the Father and Spirit are also God, the Father must be said to pay the debt to God also. If God simply paid himself, nothing of significance could stem from the event. More important, however, than the absurdity of the doctrine were its consequences. Men drew from this belief in a satisfaction paid for all by Christ a false sense of security and a dangerous doctrine of freedom. Taught that God did for them what they could not do for themselves, they made no attempt to repent and to improve their lives. To these men Penn wrote "that the Condemnation or Justification of Persons, is not from the Imputation of another's Righteousness, but the actual Performance, and keeping of God's Righteous Statutes or Commandments, otherwise God should forget to be Equal." Penn seems to have been saying that satisfaction was wholly excluded, so that one's salvation depended on what he did for himself rather than on what Christ did for him. "At the Tribunal of the great

<hr />

[77] "Address to Protestants" (1679), *Works*, I, 771.

Judge, thy Plea shall prove invalid, and thou receive thy Reward without Respect to any other Thing than the Deeds done in the Body."[78]

Against the orthodox doctrine of satisfaction, Penn said in *Sandy Foundation* that the incarnate Christ was a gift and an expression of God's love for the salvation of men in four ways. Christ abolished the old "outward" covenant; he offered free and universal salvation to all who would believe and follow him; he seconded his doctrine with signs, miracles, and a self-denying life; and he ratified and confirmed all by offering up his body.[79] First, by abolishing the old covenant Christ made it unnecessary for man to indulge in ceremonies, sacrifices, "propitiatories," meats, drinks, and washings.[80]

Apart from that, however, it appears from the context and general tenor of Penn's thought at this time that the other three accomplishments of Christ amounted to little more than the provision of man with a pattern of sanctification. Christ the perfectly righteous one fulfilled the law not in the place of man but as a pattern for him.[81] Finding man "abroad among the senses," Christ entered the sensible world to confront man and to show him God's love for him. Salvation comes through Christ's blood in the sense that his crucifixion was the greatest expression of the divine love and provides a strong incentive for man to respond. The "Outward Blood" of Christ was then and is now to be believed in as a seal, ratification, and confirmation of the glad tidings of salvation that Christ held forth to those who would take up the cross and follow him. "And therefore with good Reason was Remission of Sins preached in His Blood, because it was the most Visible Eminent Act of his Life, both fittest to recommend his Great Concernment for poor Man, and confirm the Truth of that Blessed Gospel

---

[78] "Sandy Foundation" (1668), *Works*, I, 260, 259.

[79] *Ibid.*, 256-257.

[80] "Counterfeit Christian" (1674), *Works*, II, 569.

[81] "Sandy Foundation" (1668), *Works*, I, 260-261.

he preached to him in the World."[82] Just as the death of Christ differed from his other deeds simply in degree, so that symbolically it can stand for the rest, so also all his deeds while he was incarnate can be seen as winning man's salvation because they show most poignantly what he has done and does for man throughout history.

When Penn wrote in this manner, he not only tended to rule out any atoning significance to Christ's death but, in addition, was so concerned to get men to exert themselves toward regeneration that he appeared to be precluding the idea that the death provided renewed regenerating power for individuals. Christ's deeds should goad men into making use of their free will. Nevertheless, Penn was not, even in these early years, content with this theory of "moral influence." Although his major emphases seemed to preclude the idea, from the very beginning of his writings he termed the benefits of Christ "free" and implied that somehow, as a result of Christ's death, God forgave man on different terms than he had done previously. Moreover, in the bulk of his later writings dealing with this issue, Penn developed a fuller and more traditional view of Christ's work by allowing some elements of the theory of satisfaction and by writing more of the internal aspects of the grace that came through the historical Christ.

In his apology for *Sandy Foundation*, Penn explained more carefully his views on the Trinity and said that he had meant to deny only "rigid Satisfaction." By this he meant the belief that God punished Christ for man's sins as well as any other theories that could lead to false security.[83] From that point on in his writings, although he liked to emphasize "the Feeling of a Particular Benefit," Penn admitted that there was a "Farther Benefit that Accrueth by the Blood of Christ, viz., 'That Christ is a Propitiation and Redemption to such as have Faith in him.'" The body of Christ did indeed propitiate and provide a "General Bene-

---

[82] "Quakerism a New Nickname" (1672), *Works*, II, 281-282.
[83] "Innocency" (1668), *Works*, I, 268-269.

fit," "in that it was a most precious Offering in the Sight of the Lord, *and drew God's Love the more eminently unto Mankind*, at least such as should believe in his Name. . . ."[84] (italics mine). It can be said that Christ is the propitiator, mediator, and intercessor, whose body was an offering for sin, who bore the weight of the iniquity of the whole world and sealed remission in his blood to those who believe. "You know that you are bought with a Price; now you feel it, and in Measure discern the Preciousness of that Price which hath bought you, namely, 'the Life of the dear Son of God.' " What Christ did and suffered satisfied and pleased God, who had become displeased with fallen man.[85]

In some of his later works Penn also accepted the other orthodox metaphors referring to the deeds of Christ. "We say he then overcame our Common Enemy, foiled him in the open Field, and in our Nature triumphed over him that have overcome and triumphed over it in our Fore-Father Adam, and his Posterity. . . ." Here and elsewhere Penn referred to Satan and the cosmic powers and to the corporate Fall of mankind in Adam from which men must be redeemed.[86] At the same time, if we ask whether Penn meant, by his emphasis on Christ's "once for all" deed for all men, what Barclay did—namely, that this particular death of Christ provided the possibility of saving knowledge and free remission for all men everywhere whether they knew of it or not—we get an ambiguous answer. On the one hand, he wrote that through this offering of himself once for all, Christ "hath forever perfected those (in all Times) that were sanctified. . . ."[87] Presumably this meant that those in all ages who have responded to the light with-

---

[84] "Christian Quaker" (1673), *Works*, I, 577-578.

[85] "Primitive Christianity" (1696), *Works*, II, 868; "Reason Against Railing" (1673), *Works*, II, 547; "Tender Counsel" (1677), *Works*, I, 199; "Brief Answer" (1678), *Works*, II, 670.

[86] *A Testimony to the Truth of God* (London, 1698), 34; "Primitive Christianity" (1696), *Works*, II, 867; "Quakerism a New Nickname" (1674), *Works*, II, 231-233.

[87] "Primitive Christianity" (1696), *Works*, II, 867-868.

in them, no matter how faintly it shone, will be saved not only because of their faith and obedience but because the death of Christ extricated them from the masses of unredeemed men and relieved them of the guilt of their sins. For according to Penn, "It is very possible that a Man may receive Benefit by a Medicine, of whose Composition he may be ignorant."[88]

But Penn seems to have been more troubled than Barclay and Fox by the thought that a particular historical deed could have universal relevance. Properly speaking, according to Penn, we cannot attribute to the bodily and thus to the truly historical part of Christ anything but an "instrumental" effect. It cannot be the efficient cause of anything, for causality can only be attributed to an instrument "Parabolically, Hyperbolically or Metaphorically." Hence "ultimately and chiefly, not wholly and exclusively, the Divine Life in that Body was the Redeemer." We ought to attribute salvation in the proper sense to the divine "Word-God" and say that what was witnessed in the body "confirmed" the salvation wrought by God.[89] The incarnate Christ was indeed a scapegoat bearing the sins of the world, "though it is not the Work, but God's free Love that remits and blots out, of which the Death of Christ and His Sacrificing of Himself was a most certain Declaration and Confirmation."[90] Since Penn believed that the "Word-God" was the "active" or conscious part of Christ, the "person"—which did not change as a result of the incarnation but had always been saving men—God or Christ has been freely forgiving man throughout history on some basis other than foreknowledge of the historical Christ. In Penn's equivocal expression, although the deed of Christ was in some sense a cause, in the more proper sense it was a symbol. "What shall we say then, but that Justification in the first Sense, since Adam's Day to this, hath been God's free Love upon Repentance;

[88] "Reply to a Pretended Answer" (1695), *Works*, II, 815.
[89] "Christian Quaker" (1673), *Works*, I, 578-579, 575.
[90] Letter, "To John Collenges" (Jan. 22, 1673), *Works*, I, 166.

and above all that by Christ's visible Appearance and Suffering, and in his Name, was Remission, Pardon, or Forgiveness preacht, or held forth to the whole World, upon their believing therein, more eminently than ever."[91] The death of Christ can serve as a symbol to focus man's attention on Christ's ongoing love for man.

Even if in only a "secondary" or "instrumental" way, there was a causal relationship between Christ's death and remission of sins in all men. As we have seen in discussing Penn's doctrine of regeneration, he normally distinguished between the basis of remission for past sins and that for remission of present sins. The death of Christ covered only for past sins, and the inward Christ and one's resulting regeneration accounted for his present status before God. But in passages where he stated especially strongly the atoning significance of Christ's death, Penn could also say that the gifts of sanctifying power that brought present regeneration were made possible by the deeds of the historical Christ. This is so "because Christ died a Sacrifice for the Sins of the whole World, by which he put Mankind into a Capacity of Salvation, and has given every one a Talent of Grace to work it out by. . . ."[92] Christ's obedience had influence on man's salvation "in all Parts and Branches of it," because his deeds obtained gifts for men. "In short, we do Believe and Confess that the Active and Passive Obedience of Christ Jesus affects our Salvation throughout, as well from the Power and Pollution of Sin, as from the Guilt; He being a Conqueror as well as a Sacrifice, and both, through Suffering. . . ."[93]

Apart from the general gracious power that might flow from Christ's deeds, Penn spoke specifically of the renewal of true knowledge of God that came with the second covenant in fulfilment of Jeremiah 31. The new covenant dif-

[91] "Christian Quaker" (1673), *Works*, I, 580.

[92] "Key Opening the Way" (1692), *Works*, II, 784.

[93] *A Testimony to the Truth of God* (1698), 32; "Primitive Christianity" (1696), *Works*, II, 869-870.

302

fered from the old because in the new each man had an immediate daily revelation from Christ within, whereas in the old the people had had to receive the law of God from the priests' mouths. In the new covenant established by Christ's death, all come to know God "from an infallible demonstration in himself and not on the slender grounds of men's lo-here interpretations, or lo-there. . . ." No longer were men to be dependent on the words of other men's lips or books, on their senses, or on vague intimations of truth in their breasts. As God had promised to the Jews, he had in the gospel dispensation made all men "infallibly assured" of truth from their own internal knowledge, wiping out the deadening effects of sin and history.[94]

Despite his desire to be orthodox, Penn had difficulty showing how the renewed gracious power and inner knowledge could be traced to the historical Christ in the same way that remission for past sins could be traced to him through the theory of atonement. Although Penn granted Christ's bodily death only a secondary or "instrumental" effect, he at least could show a credible causal connection between the historical Christ and the drawing of God's love more eminently unto mankind. It was more difficult to demonstrate a causal relation between a renewed non-sensible knowledge and Christ's appearance in the flesh. Especially in the light of Penn's epistemology, opponents could ask why the Word should condescend to the level of man's senses if God's primary concern was to draw man out of the sense world into a realm of purer religious knowledge, since the "outward" cannot convey "inward" truths. Penn could only reply that men had become preoccupied with the sensory world, so that God had had to approach them where he could find them.[95] It is not surprising that Penn's response failed to satisfy his opponents. His position was that of one saddled with the task of incorporating into his

[94] "Serious Apology" (1671), *Works*, II, 39-41, 48; "Sandy Foundation" (1668), *Works*, I, 248-249.
[95] "Quakerism a New Nickname" (1672), *Works*, II, 231-233.

thought a complex of religious ideas that were fundamentally alien to his assumptions about man's knowledge of God. Penn tried diligently to stretch the universalizing, dualistic framework of his thought in order to accommodate the historical Jesus, but the fit remained an awkward one.

SEVEN

SPIRITUAL RELIGION
AND THE KINGDOM OF GOD

PURITANISM, QUAKERISM, AND THE KINGDOM:
COERCION AND FREEDOM

DEBATES about the existence, definition, and contours of puritanism have filled many books and journals in the last forty years. Theology and religion have been the focus of many of them, but none have been conducted with greater zeal than those concerned with the political, economic, and social implications of puritan thought. Max Weber's thesis about the relation between puritanism and capitalism has probably received the most attention, but an equally significant argument has been waged between those who emphasize the repressive aspects of puritan political and social life and those who see the movement as standing for "voluntary consent." William Haller, Geoffrey Nuttall, and Edmund Morgan, among others, have stressed that the puritans believed that "Christian faith and Christian practice are essentially voluntary things" and that the thrust of puritanism was in the direction of toleration, self-government in church and state, and economic and social freedom.[1] Other scholars have insisted that although there was what Michael Walzer calls an "essential voluntarism" at the heart of puritanism, it was subservient to the confidence of the saints that they alone had the right and the ability to rule the masses of the unregenerate and that their rule had to be repressive enough to curb the beastly instincts of fallen man.[2] It is my belief

[1] Nuttall, *Visible Saints*, chap. 3, and *Puritan Spirit*, chaps 7, 9; Haller, *Rise of Puritanism*, 162-172 and chap. 5, and *Liberty and Reformation, passim*; Morgan, *Visible Saints*, 28-29, 41.
[2] See Walzer, *Revolution of the Saints*, chaps. 1, 5, 6, 7; Leo Solt, *Saints in Arms, passim*.

that puritanism attempted to hover in the middle of a con-
tinuum connecting several related pairs of polar ideas. The
pair of ideas most significant for the ecclesiastical, political,
and social implications of puritanism were coercion and
freedom. Without attempting to assess the causal relationship between the various puritan groups and the rise of religious liberty, democracy, and modern social norms, I would
argue that the Haller-Nuttall and the Solt-Walzer approaches to puritanism represent attempts to emphasize
somewhat too exclusively some important but opposing aspects of a movement that embodied conflicting political and
social norms.[3]

The primary mark of the ideal Christian society, according to all puritans, was the effective, direct rule of the sovereign God over all human affairs. The puritan contribution to Christian thought on ecclesiastical, political, and
social matters that came to the fore among the Independents and Baptists in the Interregnum was the belief that
God's sovereignty is effectively regnant in human affairs
only when individuals and societies accept that sovereignty
freely and spontaneously without external physical coercion
or the internal coercion of implicit faith. The puritans derived from their Reformed background the belief that man,
who had been created in the image of God, was living truly
in that image only when his actions mirrored those of his
free and sovereign Creator. They believed that God was a
sovereign, independent, self-determining Being who, as
Lord of the laws of being, was free from the necessity of
adhering to independent absolutes and from the necessities
of the created order. They also believed, with Calvin, that
man is created with the capacity to reflect in himself this

---

[3] At the same time, it would be misleading to fail to point out that
I see more than problems of emphasis in the work of Walzer. Without
denying the validity of his central thesis about puritanism, I question
his implication that all puritan attempts to get men to internalize society's restraints upon them amounted to making character dependent
on a neurotic form of self-repression.

divine differentiation between voluntary determination and natural necessity.[4]

For this reason, in the words of Walzer, "God's command sought out not only pious acquiescence, but a kind of eager consent, a response registered, so to speak, not in the mind or the heart so much as in the conscience and the will. Men must make themselves 'serviceable'; God's willfulness required human willingness. The two came together, finally, in the Puritan idea of the covenant."[5] Man fulfils his destiny by accepting freely and with understanding a relationship of loving dependence on God and mutual love and service with his fellow-men. Such fulfilment is compatible with neither the internal coercion of blind faith nor the external coercion of human ecclesiastical and political authorities. It is precisely the need for such coercion that denies God immediate effective sovereignty over human history. Most puritans, to be sure, believed in the value of coercion in both ecclesiastical and social affairs, but many of them came to see in the 1640's that coercion must serve the cause of freedom by internalizing discipline and that it must give way as the kingdom approached. The stances of the Independents and Baptists on religious liberty, their consensual ecclesiastical life, their support of the Parliamentary struggle for "Liberty and Justice" and, on a much smaller scale, their participation in the Leveller movement all indicate the ascendancy of the voluntaristic principle among many of the saints.

The coercive side of puritanism was equally manifest in

---

[4] David Little, "Max Weber Revisited: The 'Protestant Ethic' and the Puritan Experience of Order," *Harvard Theological Review*, 59 (1966), 422. See also "The Logic of Order: An Examination of the Sources of Puritan-Anglican Controversy and of Their Relation to Prevailing Legal Conceptions of Corporation in the Late 16th and 17th Century in England" (unpubl. Th.D. diss., Harvard Univ., 1963). A revised version of this study has been published as *Religious Conflict, Law, and Order: a Study in Pre-Revolutionary England* (New York, 1969).

[5] *Revolution of the Saints*, 167.

the 1640's and 1650's. Faced with social insubordination and political and economic radicalism as well as with mounting sectarianism and heresy, Presbyterians matched their renewed theological stress on authority with an increasingly shrill call for repression of the human depravity manifest in the heretical and schismatic sects and for the return of the king. The Presbyterians' social position and prejudices, however, may have had as much to do with their repressive tone as their theology did. The differing socio-political perspectives of the Presbyterians, on the one hand, and many Independents and Baptists on the other, represent a clearcut separation of men of differing situations and interests into separate camps. More indicative of the continuing tension within puritan thought and more illustrative of the bipolar nature of the movement is the fact that many of the moderate and radical puritans, despite the pull of voluntarism, were drawn at various times into the ambit of the fanatical saints with their zeal for positive reform. As Woodhouse has noted, "Puritanism was not only committed in all sections [i.e., among radicals as well as conservatives] to the ideal of the 'holy community,' but, in most of them, strongly drawn to the establishment of its reign outside the body of the elect, where, since persuasion could be of no avail, reform must be by coercion."[6]

It was especially among the sectarians influenced by a Christ-centered millennialism, such as the Fifth Monarchists, that the zeal for coercively reforming the nation came to the fore, but the temptation was strong even for the spiritual millennialists, with their outlook as "suffering saints," especially if they were close to the army and stirred by its victories. Presumably this is why many of the army chap-

[6] "Introduction," *Puritanism and Liberty*, 44. Woodhouse is often linked with Haller as an advocate of the "voluntaristic" interpretation of puritanism—probably because of the familiarity of his explanation of the puritan influence on democratic developments—but his analysis is more complex than that and is based on a recognition of the tensions I have mentioned.

lains turned from their spiritual millennialism in the late 1640's to the expectation that the rule of saintly men would be a more appropriate prelude to the coming of the kingdom of God than the Levellers' rule of law.[7]

Many of the army chaplains were what I have called spiritual puritans, who formed the link between orthodox puritans and the spiritualists. Although it is impossible to generalize about the socio-political doctrines of the spiritualists both because of their individualism and because many of them had no well-formed socio-political views, it is not surprising that there were among them many strongly drawn toward the idea of the coercive rule of the saints. For the divine-human dualism of the spiritualists was in fact an extreme version of the theological basis in puritanism for the belief in the rule of the saints, namely, a combination of an extremely pessimistic Augustinian-Calvinist view of man with a tendency to divide mankind into two distinct camps, the regenerate and the unregenerate. The sense of divine determinism that is an essential part of the apocalyptic attitude made them react strongly against the covenantal theologians' attempt to soften this dichotomous view of man so that they could urge men to cooperate with God in order to become personally reborn and help to reform the nation. The renewed assertion of the radical sinfulness and helplessness of men, the belief that the old self had to be exterminated and replaced by the inward Christ as the subject of the new man, and the perfectionistic confidence in the real saintliness of the new man were a combination that made the distinction between sinners and saints as great as it could possibly be. It was natural that Thomas Collier should come to the conclusion that "those who are saved spiritually, know best what is good for the nations temporall well-being, for they seek not their own, but others good."[8] Especially the more conservative spiritualists who were called antinomians deprived the fallen man of both his natural rea-

[7] See Solt, *Saints in Arms*, chap. 5.
[8] *A Vindication of the Army Remonstrance* [London, 1648], 6.

son and any spark of light stemming from baptism and
therefore had no reason to expect him to act otherwise than
as a beast unless coerced. The saints, on the other hand,
could be identified by their experience and their behavior
and given their rightful positions of authority.

As WILLIAM BRAITHWAITE has written, the "chief political
duty" of Friends during the Restoration was "to establish,
by steadfast witness and patient suffering, the supremacy of
conscience over unjust law."[9] Because of their position as
upholders of conscience against persecution, and because of
their peace testimony, the Friends have come to be seen as
enemies of coercion and as the seventeenth century's foremost champions of consensualism. Although it is true that
voluntarism was the dominant note of their ecclesiastical
and socio-political norms, the Quakers, like the puritans and
spiritualists among whom they arose, were drawn toward
the coercive rule of the saints as well as toward the consensual ideal. Their divine-human dualism was significantly
modified in ways that affected their socio-political doctrine, but they shared the spiritualist tendency to re-assert
with a vengeance the puritans' dichotomous understanding
of mankind. The early Friends were convinced that no
religious body saw so clearly as they the radical depravity
and helplessness of the masses of men or emphasized so
strongly the need for total renewal by the indwelling Spirit.
Combined with this was a perfectionism that at least for a
few years was as radical as that of any of the spiritualists.
Having set themselves over against all other Christians as
the only truly regenerate men of their time, if not since the
Apostles, the Children of the Light were naturally drawn
to a belief in the legitimacy of their rule over the children
of darkness. This explains their continual flirtation with the
idea of rule by the saints in the 1650's.

Cromwell may have been over-defensive, but the persecu-

[9] *Second Period of Quakerism*, 94.

tion he allowed the Quakers to undergo despite his desire to befriend them indicates his recognition that the Friends were related to groups that were ripe for a revolutionary chiliastic movement. Bernstein has suggested that Nayler's Christlike procession to Bristol, which took place shortly after Cromwell's despotism had reached its height with the appointment of military deputies, may have occupied the attention of Parliament for weeks and even months afterwards because the government was looking for revolutionary designs.[10] The Friends' temptation to join a government of saints in 1659 is indicative of the same attitude. Even more significant is the Quaker attitude toward Cromwell's government of saints. The opposition to his regime expressed in later Quaker publications should not mask the fact that Friends expressed few objections at the time to the arbitrary foundations of Cromwell's rule. What was important to them in governmental matters was not the form of government nor the manner in which it came into being, but the personnel. The question of ultimate importance was: are they among the reborn? In Fox's mind the illegitimacy and, at times, authoritarian nature of the rule were acceptable so long as there was a possibility that Cromwell would lead a government of saints.

The coercive implications of Quaker theology were only fitfully expressed, however, especially after the Restoration, except in certain ecclesiastical policies. The dominant tone of their ecclesiastical and socio-political views was their voluntaristic hope for willing, loving relations between men and God and among men. As I have indicated, the Quaker confidence that all men had been given an equal opportunity for salvation implied a modification of the puritan belief in the complete freedom of God, but the Friends believed with the puritans that the sovereign Lord of all being wanted man to mirror his own freedom with a free and willing, rather than a forced, response to his offer of grace. They

[10] *Cromwell and Communism*, 244.

discussed the relations between God and man in regeneration with voluntaristic metaphors and synergistic ideas at
least as fully as did the covenant theologians. Moreover, although this was in tension with their spiritualistic divine-
human dualism, the Friends' theology provided a more
clearcut justification for this conception of divine-human
relations than did that of the preparationists, who continued
to call themselves Calvinists.

The Quaker belief that all men possess an inner light of
truth, combined with their studied ambiguity on the question of prevenient grace, provided a sure foundation for
their conviction that all men possessed and could respond to
the light of truth within them. All men have the light of
God written in their hearts and minds, so that a particular
visitation of the light "answers to something, and reaches
to something in their particulars, though the words be
spoken without them from the light." Moreover, since God
does not demand what he gives not the power to fulfill, "the
Lord that gave man the law (within), gave him power and
ability, who said his ways were equal, and righteous. . . ."[11]
It is on the basis of the doctrine of the inner light that Burrough could appeal to "the Witness of God" and "that of
God in all their Consciences" when he was trying to persuade the unregenerate to respond to the truth.[12] Since God
demands willing and loving adherence, coercion is not a
proper policy in religious affairs, and because of the inner
light it is not necessary to coerce men in religion and to
rule over them in socio-political affairs without their participation. The light of truth can be appealed to in religious
as well as governmental matters.[13]

[11] "Mystery," *Works*, III, 127; "The Doctrines and Principles of the
Priests of Scotland," *Works*, III, 553.

[12] "The Epistle to the Reader," *Works*, n. pag.

[13] Hugh Barbour's discussion of early Quaker socio-political thought
sets forth the idea of the rule of the saints exclusively and argues that
the Friends granted sinners no "right" to toleration and assumed that
they could not rule themselves and thus had no governing rights. The

The consensual ideals of the Friends were manifested in their positions on toleration, ecclesiastical polity, and socio-political doctrine. The consensual tendency gained the ascendancy over the coercive in the Restoration period because it was more in accord with the central tenets of Quakerism, but it is also true that the situation of the Friends aided in the victory and that coercive tendencies were still present. This is evident from the fact that in their politics within the society the temptation to unlimited personal rule by the apostolic leaders became increasingly evident. This was, of course, rule by some saints over other saints, but it was a manifestation of the central idea of rule-of-saints coercion, namely, that of unrestricted personal rule on the basis of direct spiritual guidance rather than rule by law and by checks and balances. The disappearance of coercive tendencies from most Quakers' positions on toleration and their socio-political views probably happened in part because in these areas the rule of the saints was so far from the realm of possibility. The history of Quakers and others in the 1650's suggests that the strength of the temptation to coercive rule was directly proportional to the possibility of assuming power or at least influencing governmental policy. With the return of the Stuarts, the Friends were far from power and influence, and it is significant, as we shall see, that when Quakers assumed power in Pennsylvania the consensual ideals had to struggle once again with coercive tendencies.

The essential characteristic of the socio-political doctrine

---

only implications of their thought for political doctrine were autocratic, coercive ones. On the basis of this understanding of the earliest Quakers, Barbour views the later Quaker position on toleration and Penn's belief in Whig principles of rule by law and self-government as attributable to other than Quaker influences and representative of a decline in the early Quaker witness. This seems to me to be a one-sided reading of the socio-political implications of Quakerism that stems from an overemphasis on the orthodoxy of Friends on the issue of prevenient grace and free will. See *Quakers*, chaps 7-9.

of Friends in the seventeenth century, however, was not their coercive tendency but their belief that the kingdom of God was breaking into history and that a truly Christian society of willing men in loving dependence on God and mutual service to each other was a distinct possibility. Against the revolutionary backdrop of the Interregnum, the success of the gospel ministry was seen as merely the prelude to the transformation of the orders of history. The Quakers returned to what Theodor Sippell has called a "vergeistigter Chiliasmus" at the Restoration and emphasized the inner existence of the kingdom in the saints, but their eschatological hopes, as those of other sects, continued to influence them. The differing reactions of the Quakers and other nonconformists to the persecution they experienced under the Stuarts illustrate the continuing Quaker hope for the transformation of society into a consensual utopia. The other nonconformists saw nothing wrong with avoiding persecution wherever it was possible to do so without openly denying their Master, but once apprehended they tried to accept their plight as a necessary, if insignificant, part of the rule of the all-sovereign God and even as a punishment for their continuing sinfulness and a means to increased sanctification. Friends, in contrast, refused to meet in secret or to take any measures to avoid arrest and harassment because of their belief that their suffering was the form of witness most likely to bring home the Spirit's judgment on their tormentors and lead them to regeneration. Consequently, although they did not seek legal redress for their plight until at least 1668, they sent off blistering denunciations to their captors and missed few opportunities for personal and epistolary appeals to the consciences of officials and informers. Even the most perverse judges and despicable spies had "the Witness of God" in them to which Quakers could appeal. Friends' hopes became increasingly sporadic as the century wore on, but the utopian gleam in their eyes never faded completely.[14]

[14] See Cragg, *Puritanism*, chap. 3; Barbour, *Quakers*, 201-212.

314

THE FRIENDS' voluntarism was manifest in their views on religious liberty. Most of those puritans who finally realized that coercion rarely had the positive effect of driving a man toward regeneration and the new order were willing to provide religious liberty only for Protestants and only under certain circumstances. By contrast, Fox and his fellow-Quakers were fully convinced that coercion could have no positive effect in producing saints and that "soul liberty" had to be given to absolutely all men. According to Fox, coercion was properly used to restrict men's religious expression only when applied to the punishment of evildoers as defined in 1 Timothy 1:9, 10; in religion, it was not helpful and most often produced effects opposite to those intended.[15]

Not only the weak in faith but those without any religion or with a false faith were to be protected. "And let him be Jew, or Papist, or Turk, or heathen, or protestant, or what sort soever, or such as worship sun or moon or stocks or stone, let them have liberty where every one may bring forth his strength, and have free liberty to speak forth his mind and judgment." Those with truth on their side had no need to fear the open encounter.[16] Milton and many others were beginning to share this confidence that truth would triumph in an open field, but none except the bolder rationalists provided so evident a basis for their confidence as the Friends did with their doctrine of the inner light.

The Quakers based their appeals for toleration on a wide variety of arguments. Most prominent was their belief that to interfere with God's lordship over conscience was to deny him his full sovereignty and to put oneself in direct conflict with him. This was not an appeal to human rights but to the rights of God, but it nevertheless made clear that Quakers stood not simply for toleration for themselves be-

[15] "To All Kings, Princes, Rulers, Governors, Bishops and Clergy, That Profess Christianity in Christendom," *Works*, VI, 312, 319.
[16] "Truth's Triumph in the Eternal Power, Over the Dark Inventions of Fallen Man" (n.d.), *Works*, IV, 279.

cause they had the Truth, but for religious liberty for all men.[17] The Friends were certain that the light would never tell them to restrict religious liberty except in the name of the moral law, just as they were certain that the light could never contradict their constant knowledge of the moral law in any particulars. The directive to observe religious liberty was, then, part of the moral law known to all men. The Quakers sometimes called it the law of nature and right reason, as when Barclay argued that it was against sound reason and the law of nature to force conscience.[18] Most significant in the present context, however, is the fact that Friends employed arguments based on their belief that true religion can be grounded only upon willing acceptance on the basis of personal understanding and adherence.[19]

The Quakers also allowed their voluntarism to affect their understanding of the communal life of the church more fully than puritans and nonconformists. They carried to its complete application the principle of the priesthood of all believers. There was no need for election or ordination to set aside special leaders, since Christ was present in the community through the leadings of the Spirit. Moreover, because of their divine-human dualism, the Friends argued

[17] Barbour distinguishes early Quakers from Penn by arguing that "their pleas for conscience never undercut their claim of absolute authority for their own leadings by the Spirit," thereby implying that they might, without contradicting themselves, resort to coercive rule of the saints in a way that restricted religious expression on religious grounds. He also argues that Penn alone related his pleas for conscience not only to reason and the law of nature but to the self-interest and expediency of his readers. See *Quakers*, 212, 218-220, 240-245. Penn did employ the argument from conscience with a more rationalistic twist, and he appealed to the interests of his readers more prominently than other Quakers, but his appeals to conscience and reasonable self-interest were by no means unique. See, e.g., Burrough, "The Case of Free Liberty of Conscience in the Exercise of Faith and Religion" (1661), *Works*, 814-820.

[18] *Apology*, 460.

[19] See Burrough, "Liberty of Conscience," *Works*, 816; Barclay, *Apology*, 460.

that the Spirit could and did work through any members. Since human agents were passive when the Spirit spoke through them, the ability to think and speak clearly and religious training were not prerequisites for leadership. And once the Spirit spoke through one or more passive agents, if a decision was called for by the body as a whole, even the limited coercion involved in majority rule was excluded. The decision was a product of the consensus of the group, since the Spirit was able to draw all men present to a recognition of the truth. The church was to be the model consensual society serving as a goad and a prod for the transformation of all society.

The Quakers' dependence on the immediate guidance of the Spirit did give them a similarity to the primitive Christian church, but equally striking was the resemblance embodied in the fact that a group of Quaker leaders came to exercise the same kind of authority that the early Apostles had possessed. This was in part a result of the Friends' intentional imitation of the early church, and it was not necessarily in conflict with the consensual and even the egalitarian ideals, since the Spirit had never promised to spread the important "leadings" equally among all Friends. The fact, however, that the travelling First Publishers of Truth, with some important exceptions, were men of higher social standing than their fellows and thus better educated and more accustomed to leadership made the Quakers' admittedly informal hierarchy appear similar to those "worldly" ones more openly based on talent and training. Moreover, when inevitably the Spirit began to speak in somewhat contradictory ways, the Children of the Light concluded not that the Spirit's message was bound to be mediated through the insights of secondary agents but that the messages coming through the leaders were divinely inspired and those conflicting with them all too human.

Fox in particular normally made the assumption that one who disagreed with him on an issue on which he felt the Spirit's guidance was acting against the light in his own con-

science. But the tendency of all the public Friends to assume
authority in local meetings and to centralize leadership was
evident by 1666, when the leaders sent out an epistle denouncing Friends who would not submit to being judged
by the church and more particularly "by the Spirit of Truth
in the elders of the same." By the time of the controversy
raised in the society in the 1670's by John Story and John
Wilkinson, the leaders made clear their belief that individual guidance by the Spirit, when in conflict with the continual witness of the society and the position of the leaders,
had to give way.[20] This hierarchical development was more
directly a product of the Quakers' organizational needs than
of their coercive tendencies. They had to organize more
highly than in the past because of their increasing size, the
need to maintain a unified witness, and the threat to their
existence posed by governmental policy. Their propensity
for the rule of the saints simply helped them decide how
to solve the problems calling for discipline and unity.

The social and political opinions of the Friends during the
Restoration were less ambiguously in accord with the voluntaristic aspect of their thought. I have already referred to
the Quakers' temptation to assume control as saints and their
lack of developed political thought in the Interregnum.
Often they seemed content to let God handle political matters, and they expressed no preference among monarchy,
aristocracy, and democracy. Nevertheless, one would have
had difficulty convincing Cromwell and his immediate successors of the political passivity of the Friends. They subjected England's rulers to a continuing stream of criticism
for the injustice of their rule and to a series of specific
demands for political and economic reforms. As I have indicated, these statements were fashioned in an atmosphere intense with eschatological expectations. The denunciations
were meant as warnings and calls to repentance in prepara-

[20] Braithwaite, *Second Period*, 247. See also chap. 8, pp. 228-250, and
chap. 11.

tion for the coming kingdom, and the reforms demanded
were seen in the manner that Winstanley viewed his Digger
experiments. They were, in the words of Isaac Penington,
"emblems of that blessed state, which the God of glory hath
promised to set up in the world."[21]

Nevertheless, it is possible to overemphasize what Alan
Cole has called the Quakers' "conspicuous lack of interest
in the contemporary fashion for Constitution-making" and
their lack of a systematic theory of the state.[22] Despite the
implications of their belief in rule by the saints, the Quakers'
reform proposals in the 1650's make it clear that even then
the political program most in tune with their religious principles was based on "Justice and Liberty"—the war cries of
the Parliamentary program of the 1640's and, in a radical
form, of the Levellers. It was out of a concern for "the
rights, liberties, and persons of the Nation" that they demanded protection from arbitrary imprisonment, the provision of lawyers for the imprisoned poor, abolition of the
death penalty for offenses other than murder, reform of
legal codes in the interest of popular comprehension, speedy
and fair trials, and public assistance for the poor, hungry,
and widows.[23] One Quaker, who signed only with his ini-
tials, E. B. (Edward Burrough or Edward Byllynge), in *A
Mite of Affection* in 1659 demanded annual parliaments,
equal constituencies, annual rotation of offices, decentraliza-
tion of legal procedure, reform of prisons and poor laws,
abolition of "all servile Tenures or Copy-holds . . . being
the badge or yoke of the (Norman) Conquest."[24]

Although the Friends developed no political theory in the

[21] *Somewhat Spoken to a Weighty Question* (London, 1661), 4.
[22] "The Quakers and Politics, 1652-1660" (unpubl. Ph.D. diss., Cambridge Univ., 1955), 127. See also Barbour, 197.
[23] Fox, "To Both Houses of Parliament" (1660), *Works*, IV, 264-266;
"To All Magistrates, in London . . ." (n.d.), *Works*, IV, 135-137; "A
Warning to All the Merchants in London . . ." (1658), *Works*, IV,
160-163.
[24] 6, 8, 9, 14, 18, 19, 27, 29.

Interregnum, these demands indicate their desire to reduce coercion in both the political and the socio-economic realms. In these areas as in religious matters, the Friends believed that every man must have what Penn called "a Finger in ye Pye for myself." A consensual society was not necessarily a completely egalitarian one, but it was one in which all men had some control over their lives and were not under the control of those with absolute political power or inordinate economic and social power. Asked Fox: "Hath not all ye earthly Lordshipp, tyranny, and oppression, sprung from this ground, by which Creatures have been exalted and sett upp one above another, trampleing under foot and despiseing ye poor?"[25] In a truly Christian society men would have different functions, but they would serve each other as they served God, namely, in a willing and loving and not a coerced manner. They would be mutually dependent. It became evident in the Restoration that in the political realm this meant a society based on self-government and fundamental law. According to Edward Burrough, good government is based on annual election of the rulers by the people, subjection of the rulers to law and examination, publication of the laws for all to know, and fair punishment. The justification for his confidence in the ability of all men to govern themselves is evident in his belief "that every Law of man ought to be grounded upon the Law of God, pure Reason, and Equity being the Foundation thereof, that God's Witness in every man may answer to it."[26] Even the mystical Isaac Penington, who had warned the Royal Society against spending too much time with the concerns of this world, demanded "Christian liberty" in the political realm. "They only are a free People who have their Governments of their own Choyce." "Freedom is of more worth than your estates, yea than your lives

---

[25] Norman Penney, ed., *Extracts from State Papers Relating to Friends 1654 to 1672* (London, 1913), 42.

[26] "A Declaration to all the World of our Faith," *Works*, 441.

and therefore deserves to be higher prized. . . . Pursue your
Freedom whatever it costs."[27] Fox, although he warned the
Pennsylvanians not to neglect their inward plantations, also
admonished them to prize their liberty, both natural and
spiritual.[28]

Friends still developed no consensus on particular political
forms, but when Penn's experiment in Pennsylvania was
taking shape many of them took the opportunity to comment on the various frames of government and to advise
and admonish Penn. All those dissatisfied with his government expressed the same complaint: Penn had not given the
people enough power and had reserved too much for himself. Penn attributed their carping to envy.[29] Whether or
not some Friends were envious, it is probably true that
many of those who did concern themselves with political
matters saw in Penn's experiment too much evidence of his
aristocratic background and too much confidence in his
saintly rule. Compared with the vast majority of his contemporaries, Penn was a liberal, and, in ways, a radical in
his political and social theories. But the Quakers concerned
with social theory wanted to apply the consensualism of the
Quaker conventicles more fully to the political and social
realms than the friend of kings and nobility could countenance. Although Thomas Rudyard, the Quakers' foremost
lawyer, was interested more in appearance than in reality in
this instance, he expressed the Friends' and others' understanding of the relationship between Quaker religious and
political principles when he warned Penn that too aristocratic a government would "reflect on us as a people who
affect Grandure beyond our pretensions, and sett up that

[27] "The Right, Safety, and Liberty of the People," cited by Rufus
Jones, *Mysticism and Democracy*, 150.

[28] Epistle 404 (1685), *Works*, VIII, 291.

[29] Letter to Stephen Crisp (Feb. 28, 1685), PWP (A.L.S. in
ACMC); Letter to Margaret Fox (Oct. 29, 1684), PWP (copy in
FLL).

in state polity which in our religious Capacity we have struck against beyond any people whatever."[30]

The Quakers also applied their consensualism in the socio-economic realm, where they hoped that the coercion involved in vast inequalities and indigence could be eradicated. Fox demanded that society begin to implement the sharing of goods and services to be found in the Quaker conventicles. The prosperous were upbraided for luxurious living while the poor suffered and starved, and magistrates were directed to provide for the poor, the hungry, and widows.[31]

PENN AND THE KINGDOM: REFORM IN RELIGION

Penn's understanding of the nature of the kingdom and its relationship to his times reflected the central ideas of Quakerism. His view of the implications of the gospel for ecclesiastical, social, and political life was much better articulated than that of most Quakers because of his education, his legal training, and his prominence as a man of affairs. Although the thrust of his thought and actions reflected the radical consensual transformationism of the First Publishers of Truth, Penn's knowledge of law and political realities, as well as his social position, made him somewhat more conservative than many Quakers on certain issues. During the first part of his career as a Quaker the impetus provided by his conversion led him to espouse social and political ideas as bold as those of any Quakers. But even during that period the marks of his social position and his confidence in the wisdom of a saintly elite were clearly evident. Moreover, as one seeking in a practical manner to influence his contemporaries to put into effect some of the Quaker ideas, Penn quickly learned to argue for his ideas in terms of worldly

[30] Penn Papers, Charters and Frames of Government, fol. 63, HSP, cited by Gary B. Nash, *Quakers and Politics: Pennsylvania, 1681-1726* (Princeton, 1968), 36-37.

[31] "To all Magistrates in London . . . ," *Works*, IV, 160-163.

interests, to set realistic goals, and to compromise. It was one
thing to behold visions and seek to implement them as Fox
did by sending off prophetic admonitions and directives to
rulers. It was quite another to try to turn the visions into
reality by means of Parliamentary election campaigning, influence at court, and colonial endeavors.

A large majority of Penn's published works discuss the
issue of religious toleration. He employed an extraordinary
variety of arguments on behalf of his cause, most of which
had been aired by his immediate predecessors and contemporaries. Penn's originality as a tolerationist consisted largely in the ingenuity with which he drew up variations of
arguments intended to convince his readers that it was to
their interest as individuals, citizens, and merchants to replace coerced uniformity with the blessings of toleration.[32]
His basic concern with toleration, however, stemmed directly from his perception that coercion by human authorities was inimical to true religion. Although his arguments
and emphases varied with the needs of the hour, his basic
contention—and the reason for his preoccupation with the
issue—was his belief that a man's religious life was authentic
only when he willingly and spontaneously granted his allegiance to God on the basis of understanding and conviction and without the base motives introduced by coercion.
As we have seen, a religious relationship based on coercion
rather than what Penn called "conviction," "experience,"
or "reason" is not a proper relationship because it is not the
one for which man was created. Indeed, a religion based on
coercion deprives a man of his humanity. "Let then the
tares grow with the wheat, errors in Judgment remain till
remov'd by the powr of light and conviction, a Religion
without it is inhuman. Since reason only makes humanity;

[32] Penn's arguments have been comprehensively analyzed in Dunn,
William Penn, and Hans Joachim Dummer, *Die Toleranzidee in William Penns Schriften* (Lengerich, Westfallen, Germany, 1940). We
are concerned only with the religious arguments and with the implications of Penn's view of toleration for the political and social realms.

should men Supercede that to be conformists that essentially
makes them better than beasts, to witt understanding; to
Conclude men by authority is coercive, to conclude by
Conviction is manly and Christian."[33]

Given man's nature and destiny, it was, said Penn, a moral
impossibility to accept religious beliefs on other men's directives without conviction. As we have seen, he believed that
Luther's Reformation had recaptured the truth that meaningful religious belief must be based on "experience," and
that although one's mental ability might not be high, he
could not be said to "experience" what did not pass through
his "Reasonable or Understanding Part." Man's "experience" and "understanding" were products of grace and
might include a high degree of mental passivity or submission to authority, but only authority that is filtered through
conscience is acceptable, and only God is the Lord of
conscience.[34] Because God had constituted man this way,
Penn argued that "to convince and persuade" were not only
the highest duty of any church but the only successful
techniques.[35]

Coercion in religion was unacceptable also because it
placed a limitation on the freedom of the sovereign Lord of
being. God has reserved to himself the right to be Lord of
man's conscience. For the state or any human authorities to
attempt to rule man in religious affairs amounted to usurpation of the throne of God. Coercion by the Anglican church
was especially odious to Penn in this regard, since Restoration Anglicans, unlike Catholics or puritans, presumed to
usurp God's position even though they did not believe that
they had been granted infallible guidance.[36] Persecution,
moreover, flouted God's authority by limiting his freedom

[33] Letter to Richard Butler, Earl of Arran (Jan. 9, 1684), PWP
(A.L.S. in Bodleian).

[34] "Invalidity" (1673), *Works*, II, 359; "Saul Smitten to the Ground
. . ." (1675), *Works*, I, 716.

[35] "Perswasive to Moderation" (1685), *Works*, II, 745.

[36] *Ibid.*, 745-746.

to introduce new religious dispensations, for it assumed that human criteria were adequate for judging the validity of religious experiences. Since God always introduced new dispensations in a manner contrary to the ways of the world, governments that attempted to regulate religious beliefs were in danger of placing themselves in the position of barring a valid operation of the Spirit. Persecution on behalf of a national religion meant that "heaven is barr'd from all further Illuminations, let God send what Light he pleaseth, it must not be received by Caesar's People, without Caesar's Licence. . . ." Nations that placed themselves in such a position were ripe for a dreadful visitation of the wrath of God.[37]

Penn wrote of religious liberty and liberty of conscience as "our undoubted Right by the law of God, of Nature, and of our own Country."[38] In most of his treatises on toleration he stood for absolute religious liberty, arguing that no man, whether private citizen or public official, had a right to interfere with a man's religion because of religious, as opposed to social, considerations. When faced with the objections of Anglicans and conservative nonconformists who believed that such freedom would lead to anarchy and that error had no rights, Penn appealed to the providence of God and the power of truth. There was, he felt, a greater likelihood of finding truth where all have liberty to seek after it than where this liberty is denied to all but a few. Surely a Christian should have at least enough confidence in the ways of the sovereign Lord of history to assume that man did not have to add his insignificant weapons to the arsenal of truth.[39]

Despite his adherence to the ideal of complete religious liberty, Penn was more conservative than most Quakers in

[37] *The Continued Cry of the Oppressed for Justice* . . . (London, 1675), 20-21.

[38] "Great Case" (1670), *Works*, I, 464.

[39] "Address to Protestants" (1679), *Works*, I, 795; "Good Advice" (1687), *Works*, II, 756.

his conception of socially acceptable religious activity. Although he implicitly made a distinction between religious belief and expression, on the one hand, and "practice" on the other, and was willing to limit only the latter, he was not wholly consistent in this regard. Moreover, although he was not unique in limiting religious activities in the interests of morality or the common welfare, he placed a higher value on social order than most Quakers.[40]

Penn spoke and wrote loosely about denying religious liberty to any group with "Exotick" ideas that detracted from society or to religious societies that were possibly inconsistent with the safety of the civil government or whose presence was detrimental to governmental authority. "I do with the last Duty and Deference a Man can bear to his King and Country, Wish and Pray for their Prosperity: I would by no Means that any Man should be indulg'd to their Detriment: I should besides my Civil Obligations, cancel those of Conscience before Almighty God, if I thought it. . . . T'were past a scruple with me that his Liberty should at all Times purchase the publick Safety."[41] Fox as well as Penn believed that governors were ordained of God and were to be given obedience for the sake of conscience, but Fox's passionate remarks about full religious liberty for heathens as well as Christians imply that he would not have advocated the restriction of religious freedom quite as freely as Penn in the interests of social order. The gentleman, courtier, and proprietor of Pennsylvania placed a higher premium on law and order than did the weaver's son.

Although most of Penn's "moral" restrictions on religious activity were directed against fanatics and strange sectaries who broke the moral law, his willingness to restrict religion in deference to civil safety and stability was also evident in his changing attitudes toward toleration for Catholics. From

[40] "Pretended Answer" (1695), *Works*, II, 810.
[41] "Defence of the Duke" (1685), *Works*, II, 719; "Address to Protestants" (1679), *Works*, I, 817; *Christian Liberty as It Was Soberly Desired in a Letter to Certain Foreign States* . . . (London, 1675), 6.

the time of his earliest writings Penn indicated his strong aversion to Catholicism on both religious and political grounds. There was much anti-Catholic polemic in his first published work, *Truth Exalted*, in 1668, and in 1670 he published a comprehensive attack on the truth of the Roman Catholic faith. Although he found many doctrines and "superstitions" with which he disagreed, his strongest opposition was to the authoritarianism of the religion and its civil implications. Catholics were "blind Men" who had foregone all individual religious experience and accepted their faith unquestioningly from the Pope. More significant for Englishmen, however, was the fact that Catholicism, in addition to being "an utter Destruction of all true and solid Religion," had very dangerous civil implications. It taught that the Pope had authority to release Catholics from allegiance to some aspects of moral law. This could have a deleterious effect on the social order, as when children were released from obedience to parents to enter a religious order, or when stealing and murder were condoned because of their service to Rome. More important, the Pope could release Catholics from oaths and obedience to rulers who were deemed heretical or from laws that conflicted with canon law. Indeed, it appeared to Penn that the whole design of the Catholic hierarchy was "but to over-ballance the Civil Power, and render themselves Masters of the Swords and Purses of Princes, and Common Wealths, to maintain them in Idleness, Plenty, and Pleasure."[42]

To a man of this viewpoint the appeal of the arguments for excluding Catholicism from England was strong, at least until the reign of James II. Nevertheless, Penn stood by his principle of religious liberty and argued on behalf of toleration for Catholics in England through most of the 1670's and then again after 1685. The anti-Catholic hysteria of the late '70's and early '80's was too much for him, however; he became a true believer in the Popish Plot. In the midst of

[42] "A Seasonable Caveat Against Popery" (1670), *Works*, I, 480, 482-484, 484.

this tempest he wrote *One Project for the Good of England*, in which he argued that, in light of the many "civil" reasons for excluding Catholics, "there seems a Discharge upon the Civil Government from any farther Care of their Protection. . . ."[43] Considering Penn's concern for civil order and the suspicion of popery that lay upon him, we must grant him courage for holding out as long as he did, but this and other shifts on the Catholic question indicate, at the least, that the combination of public pressure, fear of civil disorder, and his own prejudices could lead to a considerable diminution of his allegiance to the principle of religious liberty. Penn returned to his position in favor of Catholic rights by giving them the same rights as all other Christians in Pennsylvania. When the Crown placed the colony under Governor Fletcher, the Assembly was called on to pass a law making all office-holders take the anti-Catholic test attached to the Toleration Act of 1689. Penn allowed this to stand when he resumed control, but his Charter of 1701 returned to the more liberal position. When the Crown ordered the colony to put into effect the Test Act in 1702, Penn counselled disobedience, but his colonial agents saw the futility of obstructionism, and Penn gave way.[44]

Penn restricted religious liberty not only in the interests of civil order and general morality but also because of his belief that social existence was possible only if the society's members shared a "general religion." Unlike Fox, who was willing to abide with heathens of all sorts, Penn thought that morality was possible only if it was grounded in religious principles shared by the members of the society. Although he often argued for toleration by holding that religious beliefs had nothing to do with political and socioeconomic matters, Penn was hardly a secularizer. He did not believe that religion should henceforth be kept out of public life or that political judgments suffered when religious

[43] (1679), *Works*, II, 687.
[44] See Isaac Sharpless, *A Quaker Experiment in Government* (Phila., 1898), 124-128.

considerations influenced them. He believed, rather, that religion was the best bond of human society, and he looked forward to the time when there could be a national church once again.[45] But such uniformity had to come by consent, not constraint. "But since 'tis so hard to disabuse Men of their wrong Apprehensions of Religion, and the true Nature and Life of it, and consequently as yet too early in the Day to fix such a Religion upon which Mankind will readily agree as a common Basis for Civil Society, we must recur to some lower but true, Principle, for the Present. . . ."[46] Penn looked forward to a time when all men would agree in their religion and would freely consent to allow their religious beliefs to determine all of their social behavior.

The "lower Principle" to which men had to recur in the interim was not simply a minimal restriction on antisocial behavior nor even a general moral consensus. It was a minimal set of religious beliefs. In Pennsylvania Penn allowed as residents only those who professed a belief in one almighty and eternal God, his status as Creator, and his providential rule over the world. Possibly for political reasons, citizenship was restricted to "such as profess faith in Jesus Christ, and that are not convicted of ill fame, or unsober and dishonest conversation. . . ." In accord with the Quaker view of the state as an institution for saintly supervision of morals, offenses against God such as swearing, cursing, lying, profane talking, and obscenity were outlawed.[47] Penn believed

---

[45] "Good Advice" (1687), *Works*, II, 754.

[46] "One Project" (1679), *Works*, II, 682.

[47] "Laws Agreed Upon in England" (1682), *Pennsylvania Archives*, 8th Ser., I (Harrisburg, 1931), lxii-lxiii. See also Dunn, *William Penn*, 67-68. By way of contrast, when Penn was involved with other Quakers in setting up a colonial government, he acquiesced in the Concessions of New Jersey, which did not demand of residents a general religion but simply stated that no person was to be called in question or molested for his conscience or for worshipping according to his conscience. Instructions from William Penn *et al.* to Richard Hartshorne (Aug. 26, 1676), PWP (Printed in *N.J. Archives*). There is nothing in Penn's thought to justify the restriction of citizenship to

strongly in the value of "general religion" as a basis for social living, so that unless Fox's "Heathen" and "Turks" could accept this creed, they would have to look somewhere other than Pennsylvania for the opportunity to exercise their "natural right" to religious liberty.

In his application of the principle of consensualism to communal affairs in the ecclesiastical realm, Penn occupied the same position in relation to his fellow-Quakers as he did on the issue of religious liberty. He stood with them in their major emphases, but his aristocratic, hierarchical view of social relations and his practical experience as an ecclesiastical leader led him to appreciate the need for balancing freedom with the necessities of a humanly contrived order.

Like all Quakers, Penn was firmly convinced of the evils attendant upon the use of authoritarian ways in the church. In his view one of the great evils of his era was the fact that ministers had too much authority over both church members and public officials. The people believed implicitly on the authority of ministers, and rulers sought ministerial sanction for everything they did.[48] In this respect Protestant ministers seemed hardly distinguishable from Catholic priests. At times an uncompromising anti-cleric, Penn charged that no class of men had been so universally in all ages the bane of soul and body as that abominable tribe, the clerics. Ministers commonly made worldly comfort and honor their primary concern to an extent unmatched by rulers, judges, nobles, lawyers, and even traders and mer-

---

"outward" Christians. It would have been consistent with his somewhat ambiguous assumptions about the inner light either to have no restrictions or to limit citizenship to Quaker saints, although the former seems to follow more easily. Probably his restriction to Christians was attributable to pressure from the king's advisors or to Penn's recognition of its political wisdom. It was the position he espoused in his pleas for toleration in England, except when he was willing to exclude Catholics.

[48] "Address to Protestants" (1679), *Works*, I, 774-776.

chants. Moreover, when men sought to escape priestly control, they became victims of the weapon of excommunication. Because of their tendency to abuse their power, the clergy had taught Quakers not to allow "such personal and pastoral Dignity and prerogative Power to any Man."[49]

In addition to giving free reign to the human tendency to abuse power, a hierarchical form of church government led inevitably to a de-emphasis on the personal experience of the Spirit. In a true church each individual had to be convinced of what he believed and could not believe on someone else's authority. For this reason, Penn, although he used most of the traditional definitions of the church, most often defined it with William Tyndale as "a Company of People agreed together in the sincere Profession and Obedience of the Gospel of Christ."[50] Since the Spirit was possessed by all members, in Quaker meetings no one presided. "CHRIST only being their President, as He is pleased to appear, in Life and Wisdom, in any One or more of them, to whom, whatever be their Capacity, or Degree, the rest adhere with a Firm Unity, not of Authority, but Conviction, which is the Divine Authority and Way of Christ's Power and Spirit in his People. . . ."[51] The Spirit not only appeared and spoke through any member but taught that each was to judge according to his own lights the message of those who spoke. Moreover, it was not to be thought absurd if a very lowly person felt called to contradict a learned one. The Spirit could in a moment endow the simplest person in the world with more wisdom than one who had spent an age in study.[52]

Such extreme egalitarianism has always proved to be virtually incompatible with the demands of unity and order in a visible human community. It has normally been espoused

---

[49] "Invalidity" (1673), *Works*, II, 375; "Guide Mistaken" (1668), *Works*, II, 9; "Summons or Call" (1677), *Works*, I, 194-195.

[50] "Address to Protestants" (1679), *Works*, I, 778.

[51] "Rise and Progress" (1694), *Works*, I, 877.

[52] "Address to Protestants" (1679), *Works*, I, 784-786.

only by churchmen who were more interested in the invisible than the visible church, and it has invariably led to a continual division process where it has been tried in a particular community. It was the visible communion of the church, however, that the early Quakers were intent on reestablishing, and they therefore placed much stock in unity and order. There had to be some kind of church authority to separate the tares from the wheat and to discipline those who by their actions cast aspersion on the community. In the words of Penn, "There is either such a Thing as a Christian Society, sometimes call'd a Visible Body, or Church, or there is not: If there be; then this Church either has Power or not: If no Power, then no Church." The Church had been given the Spirit to discern truth from error. It could determine controversies and rid itself of innovators and false spirits.[53]

Penn dealt with the problem presented by the attempt to combine egalitarianism with such a conception of unity and order in two ways. In his more optimistic moments he argued that through the power of the Spirit the combination was possible. Judgment in the church had been given to all members. If in a multitude of counsellors there is safety in worldly matters, why not also in spiritual matters? Indeed, a higher unity could be expected in the church than in worldly bodies, because the latter had merely common rational structures to draw them together, whereas the saints had a kind of spiritual instinct for the truth. "Sheep know Sheep, not only by Sight, but Instinct, and Wolves; too. . . . So do the Sheep of Christ know each other by the Instinct of that Divine Nature they are mutually partakers of, and by it do they discern the Wolf within, notwithstanding the Sheep's clothing without."[54]

[53] "The Spirit of Alexander the Coppersmith Justly Rebuked . . ." (1673), *Works*, II, 192; "Judas and the Jews . . ." (1673), *Works*, II, 196-227.
[54] "Judas and the Jews" (1673), *Works*, II, 208, 200.

In principle there was no need to set up a judicial body, since the vast majority of saints would instinctively recognize those who lacked the spirit of truth and righteousness. If the Spirit somehow failed to provide instinctive guidance, there were empirically applicable criteria by which all members could judge. First, God is a God of order, so that he would not allow contrariety and discord—as opposed to diversity and variety—in his church. It could be assumed that those who introduced disunity by innovations were in error.[55] By applying this standard, local groups of Quakers could easily perceive without organizational or central guidance that the followers of John Story, for example, who wished to introduce the practice of keeping hats on during worship and who thereby introduced discord into Quakerism, were not under the guidance of the Spirit. A second way in which the wheat and the tares could be separated without departure from democratic procedures was to allow all to judge according to the inevitable outcome of an erroneous movement. "In the mean while [God] satisfies the Minds of those who are truly led by his Spirit, and Withering, Decay, Murmuring, Complaining, and finally Apostacy will follow upon the Pretenders, as is fulfilled in the present Judasses."[56]

Before long, experience had taught Penn that there would be occasions when the majority would have to acquiesce in the decisions of the leaders even when they did not fully understand them. As on the issue of religious liberty, so in this instance, Penn insisted that true liberty of conscience was not incompatible with external counsel or direction. As some members of the physical body of man have more important functions than others, so in the church, members are unequal. Some have been called to lead, others to follow and witness, so that "some are in that Sense more Honourable than others." Although the leaders should refrain from

[55] "Brief Examination" (1681), *Works*, ii, 693-695.
[56] "Judas and the Jews" (1673), *Works*, ii, 211.

meddling unnecessarily in local meetings, it was only reasonable that the "publick Travellers" and some of the more eminent among the members should serve as judges in cases of discord.[57]

Although Penn was not unique among Quakers in recognizing the need for an informal spiritual hierarchy, he placed a higher value on order within the community than even most of his fellow "publick Labourers," and he was less likely than they to be tolerant of aberrant and shocking forms of witness. Aristocrat that he was, Penn was fearful of the tendency of many of the saints to confuse the Spirit with their own misguided wills. He took an active part in the controversies among the Friends and was particularly harsh in his public and private denunciations of schismatics such as Wilkinson and Story. Against them he set the judgment of the leaders of the church, whom he tended to see as the apostles of this latest dispensation, bearing the same burdens as the Apostles of the primitive church. Indeed, they were a direct continuation of the apostolic witness. Christ had said to the Apostles, "Go ye therefore and teach all Nations . . . And lo I am with you to the End of the World," thereby indicating the need for apostles throughout history. Who could honestly say that the world was now more Christian and no longer in need of the sure guidance of apostles?[58] But if this implied that the Quaker leaders were simply the eminent guides for the seventeenth century corresponding to church leaders in all ages, more common was the view that they were the first truly inspired leaders since Christ's Apostles in the primitive church. They corresponded to those truly Spirit-possessed prophets who initiated the rare new dispensations in history. As "the first Instruments of his several Dispensations to the Sons of Men," such leaders must exercise great authority among the people

[57] "Brief Examination" (1681), *Works*, II, 695-697; "Spirit of Alexander" (1673), *Works*, II, 193; "Invalidity" (1673), *Works*, II, 374.
[58] "Serious Apology" (1671), *Works*, II, 54-55.

they have gathered and must prevent them from falling away.[59]

As in the primitive church, this leadership was a group affair, and Penn considered himself among the leaders. Although he did not refer to Fox as the "Peter" of the new dispensation, Penn clearly viewed him as the pre-eminent prophetic figure of the times. Fox was God's "Angell and Speciall messenger," "the first and chief Elder of this Age," "the blessed Instrument of, and in, this Day of God." God had visibly clothed him with a divine preference and authority: his very presence expressed a religious majesty.[60] At the same time, Penn continued to regard Fox as simply the first among equals. He believed that the group authority of the leaders was the truest guide and the ultimate court of appeal. There would be no reason to stigmatize the whole body of Quakers should it be found that Fox was deceived in his spiritual leadings. "And what Good Christian would stigmatize an entire Body for the Defects of an individual Member?" Fox simply shared authority with the other leaders, who were not "of his Party, but God's Free-Men, and True Christians."[61]

Because of this emphasis on the authority of the apostolic leadership, Penn's adherence to egalitarianism and individualism was in practice tempered. Although there were criteria by which all true saints should be able to recognize error, in actual situations of division the surest guidance was to be expected from the "Elders." Of the Story schismatics Penn rhetorically asked: "Did they separate upon a sober triall, examination and judgment of matters first had, in ye presence and wth ye help of those eminent for faithfullness,

[59] "Just Measures in an Epistle of Peace and Love . . ." (1692), *Works*, II, 777.

[60] Letter to Margaret Fox (Jan. 8, 1678), PWP (A.L.S. in HSP); "Rise and Progress" (1694), *Works*, I, 879, 883.

[61] "Spirit of Truth" (1672), *Works*, II, 92; "Judas and the Jews" (1673), *Works*, II, 211.

for integrity and wisdom among ye Brethren. . . ?"[62] If not, that in itself was reason for condemnation. The clearest test was whether or not one had unity with the elders, who were "in the holy plain, yet deep counselling power" of the Lord; and who stand over against "the Wise, Prudent, Self-contriving, head-ordering spirit" that was bound to arise among the membership.[63]

PENN AND THE KINGDOM: POLITICAL AND ECONOMIC REFORM

The major reason that Penn's support for toleration of Catholics wavered was his belief that one's attitude toward religious affairs had a strong effect on his socio-political views. "That Principle which introduces Implicit Faith and Blind Obedience in Religion will also introduce Implicit Faith and Blind Obedience in Government." Conversely, one who exercised his own authority in religion and accepted responsible selfhood in relation to God and man would demand authority and responsibility in socio-political affairs as well.[64] Penn believed that the "free and voluntary" relations existing among church members were the model for all social relations in the kingdom and the ideal toward which history was moving. Although religion was "more free and mental" and government "more corporeal and compulsive" in this world, the distinction between the two realms was not absolute and was destined to disappear as men learned to accept responsibility in their relations with their fellowmen.[65] The regenerate were to serve as the mod-

[62] "The Result of the Meeteing Betweene John Story and William Penn held at Thomas Gouldnyes in Bristoll the 12th day of 12th mo 1677," PWP (copy in HSP).

[63] Letter to William Mucklow (Oct. 11, 1672), PWP (contemp. copy in HSP).

[64] "England's Great Interest" (1679), *Works*, ii, 681; "Skirmisher Defeated" (1676), *Works*, ii, 662.

[65] Preface, First Frame of Government (1682), *Pa. Archives*, 8th Ser., i, xlvii.

els of social order, the "little City and Hill of God," and to lead mankind into the proper kind of social existence. Given the state of the world, the practices of the saints might seem disruptive of good government, but the Scriptures prophesy a holy, lamblike and peaceable state for the "latter Times," and it was the duty of Quakers to introduce the new order into the world.[66] They were to "lay a foundation for other ages to understand their liberty as men and Christians, that they may not be brought into bondage, but by their own consent. . . ."[67]

Penn joined his fellow-Quakers in placing great emphasis on the need for godly rulers, occasionally even to the point of agreeing with Fox that the man was more important than the form. He said that a society could not function well if its rulers did not provide a godly example. "I need not put you in mind, I hope, what Efficacy and Influence the Example of Authority had always had on the minds of the people, nor can you be insensible that ye Management of those that stand invested with the power of the Laws often works stronglier on the minds of those about them than the apprehensions of the Laws themselves."[68] For this reason Penn wrote in the preface to his First Frame that men are more important than the form, for the worst frame in good hands will do well enough, and the best in poor hands will be subverted. "Governments, like Clocks, go from the Motion, Men give them, and as Governments are made and moved by Men, so by them they are ruined too. Wherefore Governments rather depend upon Men, than Men upon Governments."[69]

[66] "Children of Light" (1678), *Works*, I, 224-225; "Treatise of Oaths" (1675), *Works*, I, 615-616.

[67] Instructions from William Penn *et al.* to Richard Hartshorne (Aug. 26, 1676), PWP (Printed in *N.J. Archives*).

[68] "William Penn to Justices of Newcastle, 1701," in *Pa. Archives*, First Ser., I (Philadelphia, 1852), 143.

[69] Preface, First Frame of Government (1682), *Pa. Archives*, 8th Ser., I, xlviii. Gary Nash has suggested that Penn was not wholly pleased with the First Frame, which he accepted in place of some of

More often Penn argued, on the basis of his political experience as well as his view of man, that the only safeguard against the corrupting effects of political power was a structural limitation on the power of any one man or group of men. He opposed absolute political power in any form, whether that of great monarchs who "play at ninepins with their Ministers, distroy their Creatures that they may create again;" revolutions by the saints in God's name, as in the "Oliverian Tyranny" and usurpation; or Parliament's tendency to disregard fundamental law to root out religious dissent.[70] Like the puritans of Massachusetts Bay, Penn believed that the only society worthy of the name was one based upon the common consent of the members in a social contract. "There is no Government in the World, but it must either stand upon Will and Power, or Condition and Contract: The one Rules by Men, the other by Laws." But while the Bay puritans believed that the fundamental law or constitution to which the people agreed was to be drawn primarily from Scripture, Penn said that it was a product of the common possession by the people of "Universal Reason" or the divine-natural law. The immutable law thus perceived provides the terms of the social contract and is the source and criterion of all governmental authority. This law stands above all governing agents as a limitation on their authority and power, so that all promulgations of positive law and acts

---

the more liberal earlier versions because of the wishes of the Quaker grandees he wanted to attract to the colony. On this reading Penn's remark about the greater importance of men than of forms of government was an indirect admission of the less than ideal structure of his government. Nash's suggestion makes good sense, especially in light of Penn's agreement with the more liberal Concessions of New Jersey and the greater liberalism of earlier frames, but Penn's remark also fits in with his confidence in the rule of especially prepared and talented saints.

[70] Letter to Henry Sidney (Mar. 22, 1682), PWP (A.L.S. in Brit. Mus.); "Serious Apology" (1671), *Works*, ii, 86.

of law enforcement that go against the fundamental law of the constitution are illegitimate exercises of authority and are not to be obeyed. Elected representatives are limited by fundamental law just as much as divine-right monarchs are, since there can be no "transessentiating" or "transubstantiating" of being or rights from the people to their representatives.[71]

Penn developed his theory of government by consent and by law in the context of English politics of the 1660's and 1670's. With the Whigs, he believed that Englishmen were fortunate in having precisely the kind of limited government that he envisioned as ideal. That, at least, was true in theory, and it was the duty of the Whigs to remind the government of its historical basis and to bring practice more into line with the legal basis of the society. One should not whisper unlimited power in the king's ears, because no crown rested more firmly on fundamental law than the English crown.[72] The fundamental law that was embodied in the English social contract was derived from both a theological-rational source and a historical source. The English government, like all governments, was limited by the demands of "Synteresis" or "Universal Reason" or the divine-natural law. Penn could define these as the determinations of right reason concerning moral and just living; or, more concretely, according to the Ciceronian formula: *Honeste vivere, alterum non laedere, jus suum cuiq* [sic]; *tribuere.*

---

[71] "England's Present Interest" (1675), *Works*, I, 674, 677-684; "One Project" (1679), *Works*, II, 682-683. There is also much of relevance to this topic in *The People's Ancient and Just Liberties*, an account of the Penn-Meade trial that Penn said he did not write but that he agreed with and defended. In light of the facts that it purports to quote Penn, that many of the phrases on governmental theory in the treatise show up in Penn's works, and that the 1726 version of his works uses it as the official account of the trial, we can use it for evidence of Penn's own ideas, although it was probably written by Thomas Rudyard.

[72] "Wisdom Justified" (1673), *Works*, II, 487.

He also cited the Golden Rule.[73] In *The People's Ancient and Just Liberties* the fundamental law was defined as "such Laws as enjoin Men to be Just, Honest Vertuous; to do no Wrong, to Kill, Rob, Deceive, Prejudice none; but to do as one would be done unto; to Cherish Good, and to Terrify Wicked Men; in short, Universal Reason. . . ."[74]

The other limitation on government was the historical growth of the three fundamental rights of Englishmen: the rights to property, to a voice in law-making, and to a voice in the application of the laws. Although Penn spoke of these English rights as a separate source of limitation, more properly—since the natural law covers all areas and is a final authority—these rights were simply the special emphases within natural law that had developed in the course of English history as the basic guidelines for governmental form and power. Accepting the "Saxon myth," Penn argued that these rights had prevailed in Saxon and then Norman England and were simply reinforced and explicitly stated in the *Magna Carta* and the Petition of Right.[75]

The first fundamental right, that to property, was interpreted as including title and security of estate and life and liberty of person for all except those who violated a fundamental right of another. This meant, among other things, that one could not be imprisoned or fined simply because of a dissenting religious belief or for religious expression that did not break the moral law. The free government of England predated Christian times, so that the foundation of government was originally civil and could include no religious considerations.[76] Moreover, when later, in the Saxon contract, the king was bound "to maintain the holy Christian

[73] "England's Present Interest" (1675), *Works*, I, 675; "The People's Ancient and Just Liberties" (1670), *Works*, I, 22, 29; "Serious Apology" (1671), *Works*, II, 72.

[74] (1670), *Works*, I, 22.

[75] "England's Present Interest" (1675), *Works*, I, 674-692.

[76] *Ibid.*, 688, 675-677.

faith," this provided no justification for excluding any particular kinds of Christians. Since the form of Christianity established in the realm had changed several times without change in the fundamental contract, it was evident that laws outlawing all but Anglicans were "superficial" or "temporary" laws. They could be changed when it was expedient to do so—if one were disposed to grant them any legality at all in light of their conflict with the first fundamental English right.[77]

The second fundamental right that Penn traced back to ancient times was the right to a voice in the legislative process, which meant in England of the seventeenth century the right of property-owners to vote for Members of Parliament. The third fundamental right involved the citizen's participation in the enforcement of the law: primarily the right to participate in juries so that citizens would be tried by their peers.[78] Penn also noted several additional necessities regarding law enforcement that came under the third fundamental right. These included publication of the law in a simple form intelligible to all, due haste in the process of trial and detention, equality of treatment before the law, equitable punishments, the use of imprisonment only as a last resort, and decent prison conditions.[79] These provisions had been prominent in Quaker lists of political reforms since the 1650's.

Legislative and executive power sought to implement the fundamental law by developing and enforcing "superficial" or "temporary" laws. Such were laws passed to deal with present occurrences and emergencies. They had authority only so long as they served their intended limited purpose and at the same time did not become inequitable because of changing circumstances. Such laws had continually to be

[77] For a more detailed discussion of Penn's contractual theory, see Dunn, *William Penn*, 58-63.
[78] "England's Present Interest" (1675), *Works*, I, 677-679.
[79] "Serious Apology" (1671), *Works*, II, 72-73.

reviewed, and at times Penn seemed to assume the individual's right to decide when a temporary law was inequitable or no longer needed and could be disobeyed.[80]

In her study of Penn as a political theorist, Mary Maples Dunn has argued that Penn's adherence to the theory of social contract and fundamental rights was largely attributable to his belief that the success of the Whig cause provided the best prospect for liberty of conscience for Quakers and other dissenters. When in the 1680's Penn believed that toleration could best be achieved through support of the Stuart understanding of government, he dropped his Whig theory.[81] There is much support in Penn's writings and his life for the position that much of his political thought was directed toward the attainment of liberty of conscience for dissenters and that acceptance of this principle was his primary immediate political goal. Moreover, from the mid-1680's there was an escalating conservatism in Penn's political views, and we find only sporadic use of Whig theory from then on. Nevertheless, an understanding of Quaker religious thought makes it clear that Penn's alliance with the Whigs was far more than a marriage of convenience. The same religious concerns that made liberty of conscience so important for him were responsible for his emphasis on individual rights and consensualism in the political sphere.

When Penn spoke of religious liberty, he had in mind the preservation of freedom for both God and man, but his emphasis was on enabling man to "come into his own" as a free and voluntary agent in religious affairs and on ridding him of unnecessary human authorities. This free man, however, was a social being who could fulfill himself only in relations with his fellow-men. The thrust of Quakerism was not toward the development of solitary individuals autonomously "tuned in" to God but, rather, toward a transformed social existence in which righteous men "came into

[80] "Great Case" (1670), *Works*, I, 453-455; "England's Present Interest" (1675), *Works*, I, 675.
[81] *William Penn*, chaps. 4 and 5.

their own" as free men living in willing subjection to God and mutual loving dependence on each other. Penn's advocacy of social contracts and fundamental rights stemmed directly from his essentially puritan belief that, in the words of John Winthrop, a reformed society should include "a due forme of Government both civill and ecclesiastical," and that this form was determined by the fact that those who had been liberated from bondage had been made free to undertake responsibilities and obligations in socio-political as well as in ecclesiastical affairs.

For the puritans of Massachusetts Bay, this "due forme" was predicated on a sharp distinction between the regenerate and the unregenerate. It called for liberty solely for the regenerate, since only those who had been favored with God's mysterious election decree would be able to employ it well. Although the Quakers attempted to preserve the distinction between the camp of the Lord and the hosts of Satan, their doctrine of the inner light and their opposition to "harsch Calvinism" led to a minimizing of that distinction. They believed that at least at some time in their lives all men could exercise their initiative and respond to the divine law written on their hearts. By denying the predestination decree and hedging on prevenient grace, the Quakers placed the responsibility for one's destiny at least partly on his own shoulders. They framed their message as an appeal to respond to the light within and to accept the responsibility of a renewed relationship with God and men. Although most Quakers withdrew from political speculation after the Restoration, those who did not, such as Penn, could be expected to see that the belief in an inner light in all men was also a basis for appealing to all men to accept responsibility in socio-political affairs. In light of the Quakers' hopes that the unregenerate could become the regenerate by responding to the inner light, possibly one should see Penn's advocacy of the social contract, individual rights to life and liberty, and the right to participation in legislative and executive affairs, as analogous to the New World puritan's use of "converting ordinances." The use of consensual procedures in political affairs was not a privilege one gained with regeneration but a means to social regeneration. At the very least Penn's adherence to the social contract and participatory government were products of his Quaker hopes that the consensualism which the Puritans expected to become a reality in the eschatological kingdom could be realized here and now.

IF the possibility of man's "coming into his own" in the political realm depended on increased political rights and privileges for the lowly individual, a similar objective in the social orders other than the political demanded a similar leveling process. A Christian society could not arise where the rich squandered their wealth on personal luxuries while the vast numbers of poor suffered in abject dependence on occasional alms.

> But that the Sweat and tedious Labour of the Husband-Men . . . should be converted into the Pleasure, Ease and Pastime of a small Number of Men; that the Cart, the Plough, the Thresh, should be in that continual Severity laid upon Nineteen Parts of the Land, to feed the inordinate Lusts and delicious Appetites of the Twentieth, is so far from the Appointment of the Great Governor of the World, and God of the Spirits of all Flesh, that to imagine such horrible Injustice as the Effects of his Determinations, and not the Intemperance of Men, were Wretched and Blasphemous.

Accepting responsibility to live a godly life and to serve God in one's domestic, economic, and social life was an impossibility for those unable to support their family, find and maintain a suitable job, and engage in normal social intercourse. Widows, orphans, the aged and ill, and the hopelessly poverty-stricken lacked the opportunity to accept responsibility for themselves. Instead of relationships of mutual loving dependence they experienced a one-sided and complete dependence on the unconcerned rich.[82]

As in the political realm, so in the socio-economic, absolute power in the form of social control by the few had to be eliminated; power had to be redistributed. But whereas the dispersion of political power necessitated an emphasis on personal privileges for the many, distribution of power in economic and social affairs demanded—at least temporarily—increased coercive powers for the government over the wealthy few. In good puritan fashion, but with the Quaker's more egalitarian point of view, Penn demanded that government impose limits on personal luxuries and forcibly redistribute wealth. But he understood this coercion as a dynamic factor not only because it would increase the the freedom of the many but because it would prevent the rich from coming into complete bondage to their evil lusts and perhaps drive them in the direction of regeneration. Just as government punished acts of vice and immorality not only in the interests of general morality but also to prevent those who acted immorally from falling into an abject dependence on the Devil, so also the rich misers were to be coerced so that they might escape bondage to their pride and other evil lusts.[83] The saints were to coerce the sinners to be free.

When emphasizing the need for consensualism in the political realm, Penn spoke of government as limited by the demands of synteresis or right reason, which he equated with the Golden Rule or the general demands of morality and equity. When addressing himself to the need for reducing the extremes of wealth and poverty in the interests of consensualism, he tended to conceive the fundamental law in terms not of Ciceronian conceptions of equity but of the Biblical prophetic understanding of morality and social justice. In this context the duties belonging to Caesar included:

[82] "No Cross, No Crown" (1682), *Works*, I, 372-373.
[83] *Ibid.*, 346-347; "Address to Protestants" (1679), *Works*, I, 733.

"To love justice, do Judgment, relieve the Oppressed, right the Fatherless, be a Terror unto Evildoers; and a Praise to them that do well."[84] Whereas fundamental law conceived in Whig terms was most likely to keep government from harassing the propertied middle class, fundamental law conceived in Biblical terms brought judgment on luxurious livers both for their inherent immorality and their social isolationism. According to Penn, "There can be no pretence of conscience to be drunk, to whore, to be voluptuous, to game, swear, curse, blaspheme, and profane; no such matter. These are sins against nature, and against government, as well as against the written laws of God." Not only was such activity patently immoral; in addition, it prevented men from acting on their natural duties as other men's keepers. Governments should not endure great excesses of drinking, for example, while the backs of the poor are almost naked and their bellies pinched with hunger.[85] Luxuries and excess in apparel, feasting, and furniture were to be regarded as sacrifices of the poor to lusts. Government should prevent such sins by reviving the old sumptuary laws and making new ones to prevent pride and prodigality. Penn considered himself to be offering a practical plan for England when he suggested that if the unnecessary expenses of most social ranks could be brought into one public purse, there would be more than enough money to maintain the poor and the dependent.

> I therefore humbly offer an Address to the Serious Consideration of the Civil Magistrate, That if the Money which is expended in every Parish in such vain Fashions, as wearing of Laces, Jewels, Embroideries, Unnecessary Ribbons, Trimming, Costly Furniture and Attendance, together with what is commonly consumed in Taverns, Feasts, Gaming, etc. could be collected into a Public

[84] *The Continued Cry of the Oppressed* (1677), 17; "Address to Protestants" (1679), *Works*, I, 797.
[85] "Address to Protestants" (1679), *Works*, I, 733, 723.

Stock, for something in Lieu of this extravagant and fruit-less Expense, there might be Reparation to the broken Tenants, Work-Houses for the Able, and Almshouses for the Aged and Impotent.

Such a public bank would please the just and merciful God and provide a noble example of gravity and temperance to foreign states. With this program the poor would regain power over their lives and begin to prepare for the respon-sible selfhood that all would exercise in the kingdom of God.[86]

[86] "No Cross, No Crown" (1682), *Works*, I, 373. See also "Address to Protestants" (1679), *Works*, I, 725-729.

EIGHT

THE KINGDOM COME: PENNSYLVANIA

THE HOLY EXPERIMENT

ALTHOUGH the king's debt to Penn's father was one factor, it seems impossible to draw from the available evidence precise conclusions regarding the factors motivating Charles to grant Penn extensive land in the New World. Penn's motives in asking for the grant are less heavily shrouded in secrecy, but as in most of his major decisions, many motives seemed to coalesce. As Nash indicates, "Pennsylvania . . . offered the rare opportunity to serve at once God, personal fortune, and fellow-Quakers."[1] In Penn's own mind, however, the primary motivation for the Pennsylvania undertaking was religious. Indeed, that was the only motive he admitted possessing, although he often granted that it would be only fair for God to give him some external reward for his efforts. In none of his "outward" undertakings had he felt so strongly guided and inwardly resigned to the Lord's will as he did in the decision to seek Pennsylvania. For that reason he was confident that the hand of the Lord was upon the colony and that, for his part, a renewed dedication to the service of God was required. "Well, sure I am God had not cast my Lott here but for a service to his truth, and I know his hand was and is in it, It is no such common and uncleane thinge, as some in their rashnesse have said of it. But a singular and precious providence for god hath made it matter of Religious Exercize to my soule in getting and setling this Land. And it is the Lord and to his service do I dedicate my dayes in the helpe of his people here. . . ."[2]

[1] *Quakers and Politics*, 10.
[2] Letter to John Alloway (Nov. 29, 1683), PWP (copy in FLL);

348

Penn was no less certain about the nature of the religious goal to be achieved by his efforts. It was "that an example and standard may be set up to the nations" of an ideal Christian society. "And ye dominion under this part of ye whole heavens is a giving to ye Saints of ye most hight, and our part of ye kingdoms of this end of ye world, growing to ye kingdoms of ye Lord and his Christ, whose authority is getting up wthin and so wthout . . . so will ye Creation be delivered, and ye earth obtain her Sabbaths again."[3] The wrath of God would hang over the nations until the governments not simply of ecclesiastical bodies but of whole nations began to rebuke and punish vice and to cherish virtue.

In most of Penn's early correspondence with the colonists, one finds evidence of his belief that Pennsylvania was center-stage in history. The eyes of remote countries as well as neighboring regions were believed to be fixed on the young colony. There would be a heavy burden upon any saints in such a position, but Penn felt that it was especially important that the Quakers of Pennsylvania play their roles perfectly. The Quakers alone among England's dissenters had been accused of disowning good government as well as true religion. The "holy experiment" in Pennsylvania was their opportunity to show that a society founded and operated along the lines of Quaker ideals not only could work but was the answer to mankind's ills.[4] Penn knew that he

---

Letter to Thomas Janney (Aug. 21, 1681), PWP (A.L.S. in HSP). Several of Penn's fellow-Quakers believed that his motives were largely economic, since it seemed to them that one could perform no real service to the gospel in the wilderness. Penn was accused of pursuing worldly goals and of enticing Friends to desert their suffering brethren in England. See Letter, "To my Old Friend" (July 12, 1682), *Works*, I, 124; Letter from William Penn *et al.* to Settlers in West Jersey [Sept. 1676], PWP (printed in *N.J. Archives*).

[3] Letter to Robert Turner (Aug. 25, 1681), PWP (copy in HSP). Letter from Penn and others in New World to Quakers in England (Mar. 17, 1684), PWP (copy in FLL).

[4] Letter to Robert Turner (Mar. 5, 1681), PWP (copy in HSP). "An Epistle to the People of God, Called Quakers, in the Province of

would have many colonists who were not Friends, but the Quaker stamp on the new society was seen in the legal provisions for marriage, the requirement that pagan names for the days and months be avoided in government, provision for arbitrators or peacemakers to be attached to the courts, the provision for affirmations and attests in place of oaths, and the failure to provide a militia.[5]

Penn's concern to demonstrate that the unique Quaker brand of sainthood was compatible with good government points to the aspect of the Pennsylvania venture that most clearly distinguishes it from the similar undertakings in New England. Although Penn's political theorizing and his activism made him somewhat unusual among the Quakers, his vision of Pennsylvania and his early hopes for the colony reveal the influence of the Quakers' distinctive radicalism and optimism. He expected to achieve a much fuller realization of the consensualism inherent in the puritan conception of social existence than most puritans themselves dared hope for in this world. Pennsylvania was to be largely noncoercive. At the same time, Penn retained his aristocratic view of human affairs and his confidence in the personal rule of saints. His society, although largely noncoercive, was to combine its consensualism with hierarchical social and even political patterns. As in the case of church disputes, so in Pennsylvania, he expected that unanimity would be achieved through the leadership of a responsible elite. Beyond that, Penn reserved great power for himself. The colony was to be governed by a combination of democracy,

---

Pennsylvania . . ." (1684), *Works*, II, 707-708; Letter to Thomas Lloyd *et al.* (Aug. 12, 1684), PWP (copy in HSP). In the words of Edwin Bronner, "William Penn and his friends were primarily interested in planting a utopian community, based on the beliefs of the Society of Friends." *William Penn's Holy Experiment: The Founding of Pennsylvania 1681-1701* (New York, 1962), 14. See also Nash, *Quakers and Politics*, 164, 338-339.

[5] See Bronner, *Holy Experiment*, 55.

aristocracy, and monarchy precisely as England was ruled.

Penn incorporated in the Frame of Government of 1682 and in his "Laws Agreed Upon in England" the theory of fundamental rights that he had espoused in England. The Frame and the "Laws" were to serve as a contract, and those who qualified as freemen could participate in both lawmaking and law enforcement. Freemen voted for representatives to the Provincial Council and the Assembly, the upper and lower elective bodies. For the Council they were to elect "Persons of most Note for their Wisdom, Virtue, and Ability." Any freeman could be chosen for the Assembly.[6]

Participation in the execution of laws took two forms. First, the Council was to present yearly to the governor a double list of nominees for judges, treasurers, and masters of the roll, and the Assembly was to present a similar list for the offices of sheriff, justice of the peace, and coroners. The governor chose his officers from these lists.[7] Second, freemen could serve on, and all would be judged by, juries of peers, since all trials were to be by free jury. In addition, in accord with his principle of equal and humane treatment before the law, Penn produced a penal code that was an attempt to incorporate the demands the Quakers had made upon Cromwell and Charles II. In accord with Penn's voluntaristic ideal, the code raised even poor and ignorant defendants and criminals above the level of abject helplessness to which they were often reduced in England. All were given a copy of the charges against them at least ten days before the trial and were allowed to plead their own causes in court. Legal fees were to be moderate; offenses were bailable except in cases of murder and treason, the only capital crimes; and imprisonment for debts was discouraged. Moreover, in accord with Penn's unwillingness to allow men to be placed in situations of utter dependence, lands and goods of a debtor were liable for payments of debts, but where

---

[6] First Frame of Government (1682), *Pa. Archives*, 8th Ser., I, l-liv.
[7] *Ibid.*, liv-lv.

there was legal issue, two-thirds of the land could be reserved for heirs.[8]

In regard to the fundamental right to life, liberty, and property, Penn promised his colonists that they would be deprived of liberty or property only for breaking the laws passed by their representatives and that, within certain necessary limits, such laws would not infringe on their right to religious liberty. "That all Persons living in this Province who confess and acknowledge the One Almighty and Eternal GOD, to be the Creator, Upholder and Ruler of the World, and that hold themselves obliged in Conscience to live peaceably and justly in civil Society, shall in no ways be molested or prejudiced for their religious Persuasion or Practice in Matters of Faith and Worship, nor shall they be compelled at any Time to frequent or maintain any religious Worship, Place or Ministry whatever."[9] The exclusion of atheists and heathens reflected Penn's belief that religion is the best bond of human society, as did his stipulation that electors and elected and appointed officials were to be Christians, although, as I have noted, this stipulation may also have stemmed from Penn's concern to please the king's government. One important restriction on the rights of citizens was the stipulation that the governorship was not subject to popular will and was, moreover, hereditary. However, although the governor was given three votes in the Council, he had, at first, no explicit veto on legislation, although it later became evident that Penn interpreted the Charter as including a proprietary right of veto. Penn felt that this was limitation enough for a proprietor: "For the matters of liberty and privilege, I propose that which is extraordinary and to leave myself and successors no power of doing mischief, that the will of one man may not hinder the good of the whole country."[10] From time to time throughout his

[8] "Laws Agreed Upon in England" (1682), *Pa. Archives*, 8th Ser., I, lviii-lix.

[9] *Ibid.*, lxii-lxiii.

[10] Letter to Gov. Markham (Apr. 10, 1681), PWP (L.S. in Mass. St. Archives, State House, Boston).

colonial period Penn asked the colonial legislators to suggest changes in the constitution under which they were
operating.[11]

Whatever the restrictions, Penn felt in 1681 that he was
ready to grant "whatever sober and free men can reasonably
desire for the security and improvement of their own
happiness."[12] Several years after the birth of the colony,
Penn, desirous that all Pennsylvanians should understand
their "inestimable inheritance" as freeborn Englishmen, had
printed in Pennsylvania the first forty pages of *English Liberties: or, The Freeborn Subject's Inheritance* together with
Penn's Patent and the Second Frame of Government. *English Liberties* was a 1682 publication designed to acquaint
dissenters with their rights by the printing of the *Magna
Carta*, the Petition of Right, and other documents, together
with commentary and sections on parliamentary powers,
laws against dissent, and court procedures. In his preface to
his abbreviated re-publication, Penn said that his aim was
"that it may raise up noble resolutions in all Freeholders . . .
not to give away anything of Liberty and Property that at
present they do (or of right as loyal English subjects ought
to) enjoy, but take up the good example of our ancestors,
and understand that it is easy to part with or give away great
privileges, but hard to be gained if once lost."[13]

[11] See, for example, "Concerning Certain Deficiencies in the Form
and Substance of the Government and Some Other Matters" (Mar.
30, 1700), *Pa. Archives*, 4th Ser., 1 (Harrisburg, 1900), 110.

[12] "William Penn's Letter to the Inhabitants of Pennsylvania, Previous to His Departure from England for This Country" (April 8,
1681), *Memoirs of the Historical Society of Pennsylvania*, III (Philadelphia, 1834, 1836), Pt. II, 205-206.

[13] "Excellent Privilege of Liberty and Property Being the Birth-
Right of the Free-born Subjects of England" (1687), cited by Fred-
erick B. Tolles, *Meeting House and Counting House* (1948; rpt., New
York, 1963), 12-13. Winthrop Hudson has recently provided sound
reasons for attributing *English Liberties* to Penn rather than to Henry
Care, the author listed in the 1700 edition. See "William Penn's
English Liberties: Tract for Several Times," *William and Mary Quar-
terly*, 3d Ser., 26 (1969), 578-585.

Penn's visionary hopes for Pennsylvania embraced an even more radical kind of consensualism than was built into its legal foundations. In addition to his demands for consensual reforms, Fox called on governments to try to implement the will of God by appealing to "that of God" in every man rather than by threats and punishments. It was his hope that all government could be transformed into a spiritual rather than a coercive activity.[14] Although his hopes were to be quickly destroyed, Penn carried this vision of peaceful social relations to Pennsylvania with him. In his preface to the First Frame of Government he said that government and religion were an emanation of the same divine power, so that in reality government could be said to be "a part of religion itself, a thing sacred in its institution and end." Religion is "more free and mental" and government "more corporeal and compulsive" in its operations, but only in the case of evildoers, "government itself being otherwise as capable of kindness, goodness and charity, as a more private society." "They weakly err, that think there is no other Use of Government than Correction, which is the coarsest Part of it: Daily Experience tells us, that the Care and Regulation of many other Affairs, more soft and daily necessary, make up much the greatest Part of Government; and which must have followed the Peopling of the World, had Adam never fell, and will continue among Men on Earth under the highest Attainments they may arrive at, by the Coming of the blessed Second Adam, the LORD from Heaven."[15]

Government could operate in this peaceful manner so long as God had full dominion over the spirits of the people—at least to the extent that those who were not subject to the truth in themselves for love's sake submitted willingly to the authority of their leaders.[16] Because of his assump-

[14] "Saul's Errand to Damascus," *Works*, III, 589.

[15] Preface, First Frame of Government, *Pa. Archives*, 8th Ser., I, xlvii.

[16] Letter from Penn and others in New World to Quakers in England (Mar. 17, 1684), PWP (copy in FLL).

tions about the inner light, Penn believed that social harmony was possible. In 1684 he expressed to his colonists the hope that they would be obedient to God, retain a natural affection for one another, and refrain from taking their problems to the courts, "that so I may never have an Occasion to exercise any other Power than that of Love and Brotherly Kindness."[17] During his first sojourn in the colony he wrote to his Quaker friends in England of the wonderful way in which the Spirit guided the affairs of the governmental assemblies. Decisions were reached harmoniously in the power of the Spirit precisely as in Quaker meetings. The Lord's presence "is in a wonderfull manner ecstended dayly to us in our assemblies, so that whatever Men may say our wilderness flourishes as a Garden, and our desert Springs like a Greene field. . . ."[18] To John Blakling and other Quakers he wrote in 1683 that the Assembly had passed eighty-three laws in its last session, and all but three had been passed unanimously, "the living word in testimony and prayer opening and closing our assemblies in a most heavenly manner, like to our general meetings." Later the same year he wrote: "Since mine to J. B. I have held two Generall Assemblies with precious Harmony, Scarce one Law that did not passe wth a *Nemine Contradicente*, and as our opening of them was deepe and wth heavenly Authority, So our Conclusions were wth the word and prayer and men fearing god in power are both loved and feared, And god is adding dayly to us."[19] In fact, the disharmony that before long was to plague the colony was already in evidence. Whatever the votes in the Assembly may have been, Penn was already running into opposition from colonists who doubted whether he was motivated by just—not to mention religious—concerns and who were themselves something less than holy

[17] "An Epistle to the People of God" (1684), *Works*, II, 707.

[18] Letter to John Blakling (Nov. 29, 1683), ACMC, XXIV, 476 (contemp. copy in FLL).

[19] Letter to John Blakling *et al.* (Apr. 16, 1683), PWP (copy in FLL); Letter to John Blakling (Nov. 29, 1683), ACMC, XXIV, 476 (contemp. copy in FLL).

experimenters. Penn's correspondence during this period, however, does indicate his vision and his continuing hopes for the new society.

Penn's colony incorporated also the socio-economic freedom that he considered requisite to a holy society. The colony did not begin with extremes of wealth and poverty, and there is little direct evidence of Penn's concern for the poor, the widowed, and the orphaned. However, his concern for the independence of the helpless was evident in the laws protecting defendants and criminals and in the laws against immoral and luxurious living, and in his general directives to the Council to deal kindly with the poor and oppressed. Moreover, such concerns were so deeply ingrained in the Quaker spirit that Penn did not have to emphasize the necessity of aiding those who needed it. In the earliest days the needs of the indigent and dependent were met by the Monthly Meeting more than by official government agencies, as nearly all of the colonists were Friends. At the Philadelphia Monthly Meeting in 1682 it was decided that "because some may through sickness, weakness, or Death of Relations be reduced to want or distress . . . care shall be taken to administer present supplies." Regular collections were then taken for the purposes of keeping a fund for the needy. In addition, the meeting undertook to provide food and employment for those in need and to underwrite their medical expenses. In 1684 the Meeting decided to provide the magistrates with regular contributions for the relief of all poor people, whether they were Friends or not.[20]

WHEN Penn discovered, by the late 1680's, that even supposedly regenerate men were more in need of coercion than he had hoped, he became more and more the feudal lord

[20] Philadelphia Yearly Meeting, Department of Records, Manuscript Minutes of the Philadelphia Yearly Meeting, i, 1, 21, 67, 98, 306, 14-15, 124, cited by Tolles, *Meeting House and Counting House*, 65-67, 70-71.

that Charles had no doubt intended him to be. However, even in his more optimistic days Penn had not conceived of Pennsylvania as a radically egalitarian society. Although his political theory was based on self-government and the rule of law, he believed throughout his life in hierarchical social relations, feared the "mob" or "rabble," and was at times filled with a nostalgia for the feudal past.[21] This aristocratic tendency was strongly reinforced by his belief in the rule of saints and especially his confidence in his own superior wisdom and righteousness. In a letter to Margaret Fox Penn wrote concerning Pennsylvania: "My life feels a work I have to do wth it for ye lord, yt his powr may be a top, but some are carnal, and others weak, and they would level all, and ye notion of freedom and commonweal that I fear it will leave Truth but little powr over ye bad in ye end."[22] Noncoercive ways in Pennsylvania were to operate within a strictly hierarchical conception of social relations. In society as in church, although the lower ranks were to be relieved of enough dependence so that they could accept some responsibility for their lives, when they became unruly and unwilling to accept advice and direction from their superiors, the principle of noncoercion had to give way to the principle of order.

The hierarchical view of social relations appeared early in Penn's works. In *No Cross, No Crown* he assured his readers that Quakers were not interested in eliminating social distinctions so much as in giving meaning to them. "The World's Respect is an empty Ceremony, no Soul or Substance in it: The Christian's is a solid Thing, whether by Obedience to Superiors, Love to Equals, or Help and Countenance to Inferiors."[23] The principle of hierarchy was solidly rooted in all parts of creation and in all human affairs. It was to be found in the relations among the heavenly bodies, in all life on land and sea and in the air, and in all human affairs.

[21] See Nash, *Quakers and Politics*, 31.
[22] To Margaret Fox (n.d.), PWP (A.L.S. in HSP).
[23] "No Cross, No Crown" (1682), *Works*, I, 324.

"Our Great Men, doubtless, were designed, by the Wise Framer of the World, for our Religious, Moral and Politic Planets, for Lights and Directions to the lower Ranks of the numerous Company of their own Kind, both in Precepts and Examples; and they were well paid for their Pains too, who have the Honour and Service of their Fellow-Creatures, and the Marrow and Fat of the Earth, for their Share."[24]

Although Penn warned the nobles and the well-born that virtues and merits, rather than birth, were the foundations of aristocracy, he not only condoned slavery but used slaves himself. For himself Penn preferred the gentleman's station in life, since it afforded him the power to do good and the opportunity to receive the affections of many people. It also provided him with time to observe other nations and to polish his passions and tempers with books and conversation.[25]

Despite his liberal emphases, Penn carried this view of men into his ideas of government. He was in harmony with the views of Fox and most other early Quaker leaders when he said that government had been set up by God; that it was to be obeyed "for conscience sake"; and that governors were to be respected as God's agents—men deserving a modest and awful distance and reasonable service.[26] But at times he seemed so concerned that government, both in England and Pennsylvania, be accorded the proper amount of respect by those less well educated that his aristocratic views conflicted with some of his basic social principles. From the beginning of his proprietorship, Penn's desire that the people remain subordinate to their natural leaders was evident. On his first visit to Pennsylvania he visited West

[24] "More Fruits of Solitude" (1699), *Works*, I, 856.
[25] "No Cross, No Crown" (1682), *Works*, I, 332-333; Letter to James Harrison (Oct. 25, 1685), PWP (A.L.S. in HSP); Letter to James Harrison (Dec. 4, 1685), PWP (A.L.S. in HSP).
[26] "His Second Speech to the Committee [of Parliament]" (Mar. 22, 1678), *Works*, I, 120; "Address to Protestants" (1679), *Works*, I, 801, 812; "Key Opening the Way" (1692), *Works*, II, 787-788.

Jersey, where he was, with several other Quakers, a proprietor. He reported back to his fellow proprietors: "I finde the people strict, and not easy to be enclined from the Point the[y] fix at; And having some pretence to Religion fastens the knott the more: So that men of greater Sight, patience and skill then themselves ought to have the management of them; for, believe me, they are a shrow'd People, and are not wth out Councell and helpe, that gives difficulty to those mostly concerned wth them."[27]

Enough of Penn's hierarchical approach to social relations was present in Pennsylvania's government from the beginning to elicit strong objections from several Quakers and from at least one of Penn's Whig friends. Although some mystery surrounds the question of the source and extent of the aid Penn received in framing the Pennsylvania government, drafts of constitutions which preceded the First Frame reveal that more democratic provisions were considered and rejected.[28] Presumably that is why the republican Algernon Sydney, one of Penn's advisors, was rumored to have called the Pennsylvania government, as Penn reported it, "the basest laws in the world, not to be endured or lived under, and that the Turk was not more absolute than I."[29] Sydney no doubt had in mind such provisions as Penn's aristocratic system of legislative power, his heavy-handed approach to the suppression of immorality and criticism of the government, and his failure to limit the property-holdings of large landowners.[30]

[27] Letter to the Proprietors of East Jersey (July 11, 1683), PWP (printed in N.J. Archives).
[28] The best discussion of this is in Nash, Quakers and Politics, 31-44.
[29] Letter, "To Algernon Sydney" (Oct. 13, 1681), Memoirs of the Historical Society of Pennsylvania, III, Pt. 1, 285-286.
[30] Regarding the first point, only the Provincial Council, composed of men of wealth and intellect, could propose and discuss legislation. The more democratic assembly was limited to voting on legislation proposed by the council. The suppression of immorality, gaming, and idle gossip was the end of several of the "Laws Agreed

More disturbing to Penn and more indicative of the relationship between Quaker thought and consensual political arrangements were the many criticisms leveled at Penn's government by Quakers, including Benjamin Furly, George Hutcheson, and Jasper Batt. Farther than Penn from the seat of power, they were unable to share his confidence in saintly rule. The most ferocious criticism came from Batt, who had hoped that Penn would frame a government that could serve as a pattern for future societies. When the First Frame became available, some Quakers in the West Country pointed out to Batt the conservatism it embodied, and he sent an expression of his concerns to Fox, George Whitehead, Alexander Parker, and William Gibson. Fox's only known response was to advise Batt to send his observations to Penn himself. This he did not hesitate to do.[31] Batt took Penn to task for "Entailment of the Government a negative voice and the unaccountableness of the Governour," the insignificance of the General Assembly, which could not introduce or discuss legislation, and the property requirement for citizenship, among several other things. In reply to the last charge, Penn asked "what civill Right hath any man in Government in these dayes besides property, at least without it," and cited the English practice

---

Upon in England." See *Pa. Archives*, 8th Ser., 1, lxiii. Penn's failure to limit the property-holdings of the wealthy was known by Sydney to be a deliberate omission of an important provision of James Harrington's *Oceana*, a work that had considerable influence on Penn in other respects. For discussions of Penn's relation to Harrington and of his attitude toward land-holdings, see Mary Maples (Dunn), "William Penn, Classical Republican," *Pennsylvania Magazine of History and Biography*, 81 (1957); Gary Nash, "The Free Society of Traders and the Early Politics of Pennsylvania," *PMHB*, 89 (1965), and "The Framing of Government in Pennsylvania: Ideas in Contact with Reality," *William and Mary Quarterly*, 3d Ser., 23 (1966); Tolles, *Meeting House and Counting House*, 114.

[31] I have not found Batt's letter to Penn, but in his reply Penn quoted extensively from it. (Feb. 5, 1683), ACMC, xxiv, 150-176 (contemp. copy of fragment in HSP).

as justification. In defense of the limited powers of the Assembly Penn also referred to the English practice, comparing Parliament to the Pennsylvania Council and the Knights of the Shire and the Burgesses to the Assembly. The practice was defensible "because ye Number of Knowing men is ever least in any Country" and in order that "ye confusion of a multitude might be avoided."[32]

Regarding the charge of "Entailment of the Government a negative voice and the unaccountableness of the Governour," Penn said that he retained the position of governor only so that he might "give no offence to some whose power, might crush all in ye Budd should I nominally have devolved all from me upon ye people. . . ." Moreover, he had no negative on the laws, he argued. The stipulation of the Frame that laws be made "By ye Governour with ye Assent and Approbation of the Freemen in Provinciall Councill and General Assembly" was necessary simply because "they are ye words of my Patent, and so a Legall Basis for our Lawes to stand upon."[33] Batt was especially skeptical of the truthfulness of this reply; he suspected Penn of harboring an absolute veto on all laws. His skepticism was well founded. Soon after the letter to Batt, Penn wrote in his commission to the Provincial Council to take over the government as deputy governor in his absence: "By the Por within Escpressed and mentioned I understand ye use of the Escecutive powr cheifly as chusing officers, etc. Intending yt all laws yt shall or may be made should receive and have my further determination Confirmation and Consent or else to be voyd in themselves."[34] Nor was this an isolated expres-

[32] Ibid., 156-157.   [33] Ibid., 154-155.

[34] Letter, "Commissioners, to Thomas Lloyd, President and the other Members of the Provincial Council, to the Deputy Governorship of Pennsylvania" (Aug. 6, 1684), PWP (contemp. copy in HSP). Although the Frame of Government of 1683 gave Penn a negative voice on Council—but not Assembly—proceedings, it is clear that Penn based his absolute veto on the charter. Second Frame of Government (1683), Pa. Archives, 8th Ser., I, 334-341. Letter to Thomas Lloyd (Sept. 21, 1686), PWP (A.L.S. in HSP).

sion of the proprietor's belief that he had a moral right to use the power he had been legally granted.

Penn's critics among the Quakers seem to have increased in number after the First Frame was replaced by that of 1683. Although the colonists themselves had asked for a new frame, and although they had debated it and in certain ways tied the governor more closely to the Council's will, there were parts of the new frame that were more conservative than the first. Now the Assembly as well as the Council was to include men "of most Note for their Virtue, Wisdom and Ability," and the governor was expressly granted a veto on the proceedings of the Council.[35] On his return to England after its promulgation, Penn found several Quakers criticizing him for the changes. In defense of himself he pointed out that what had been altered had been changed by the people themselves.[36]

The End of the Holy Experiment

In his advice to his children advocating the avoidance of public responsibilities, Penn made one exception. One had to forego the spiritual and physical benefits of a retired life if God called him to public service. This was Penn's justification for his own continued public activities, especially as proprietor of Pennsylvania and as a courtier and politician seeking toleration. But the fight for toleration had been largely won by 1688, and in any case Penn's difficulties over his relationship with James ended his welcome at court and much of his political usefulness. Apart from his work as a public Friend, from 1690 Penn's public activities centered on his attempt to retain Pennsylvania and to exercise his rights as proprietor over his colonists. But the evidence provided by his correspondence makes it difficult to believe

[35] *Pa. Archives*, 8th Ser., I, 334-341.
[36] Letter to Stephen Crisp (Feb. 28, 1685), PWP (A.L.S. in ACMC); 104-105; Letter to Margaret Fox (Oct. 29, 1684), PWP (copy in FLL).

that Penn was unwilling to follow his own advice and retire from the Pennsylvania venture because he still viewed his leadership of the colony as a religious calling. There is little evidence to suggest that he continued to see himself as sponsoring a model consensual society in the hope that his colony would be the vanguard of the kingdom. The same loss of confidence in transformationism that led to his developing sectarian outlook was reflected in the increasingly authoritarian way in which Penn tried to control Pennsylvania beginning in the late 1680's. Penn came to recognize that governing the colony required the time-worn coercive measures. His threats in this regard were much more prominent than his actions, however; for the most part the Pennsylvanians continued to operate as they saw fit.

The new society had turned out to be not so different after all. It was becoming evident already during Penn's first visit to the colony in 1683 and 1684 that the Quaker freemen, who constituted a large majority, either were not sufficiently motivated by religion to be model subjects for Penn's experiment, or disagreed with him about the nature of a Quaker social experiment. They struggled against Penn's land policy, ignored his demands for payment of quit-rents, and increasingly disregarded his wishes in their governing deliberations. Many of the colonists disobeyed the laws passed by their representatives as readily as they flouted Penn's wishes, and the colony experienced a steady growth of minor crime. In their relations among themselves the Friends succumbed to a petty factionalism in religion and politics. The divisiveness of social relations increased, as did the numerical and economic strength of non-Quakers. All these developments were intensified when the American colonies became the focus of the imperial struggle between England and France and the crown felt obliged to assert its rule more forcefully.[37]

[37] Nash has analyzed the socio-economic standing of the two sides in the ostensibly religious controversy instigated by George Keith and argued that the struggle had more of a social than a religious

As early as 1685 Penn was of the opinion that he had placed too high a premium on voluntary ways in his attitude toward the government of Pennsylvania. Exhorting the Council to punish vice strictly, he wrote, "I was apt my selfe to be but too mercifull; in yt follow not my example."[38] From that point on he gradually began to emphasize the need for the government to direct and control the people closely. Slackness of reins was recognized as one of the practices most harmful to good government. Moreover, Penn felt now that it was intolerable to have the people judging and accusing their rulers, who were to insure themselves against "vulgar censure." In *Fruits of Solitude* in 1693 he went so far as to argue that democracy held greater dangers than tyranny did. It was only prudent to let the people think that they governed themselves, for they were governable only when they were under such a delusion. But it was not necessary to worry continually about protecting them from a tyrannical government, since the people could invariably counteract oppressive measures, even if only through revolution. In addition, the remedy for tyranny, democracy, was often worse than the malady.[39]

Penn himself never became a tyrant. As late as 1700, when it became advisable to amend the laws and draw up a new frame of government, he gave the Council and even the Assembly much initiative in drawing it up. In 1701 he wrote to his appointees as justices in New Castle: "You are Trustees of ye peace, and are not called so much to serve me or any Interest of mine, as to serve the Publick, to whose Good

---

basis, although Keith himself was motivated in good part by theological interests. Nash's attempt to correlate university education and interest in theology represents an anachronistic imposition of twentieth-century patterns on the seventeenth, but his argument holds together nonetheless. *Quakers and Politics*, 145-160.

[38] Letter, "William Penn to the Council" (Aug. 19, 1685), *Pa. Archives*, 1st Ser., I, 93-94.

[39] "Fruits of Solitude" (1693), *Works*, I, 835-836.

each man is born a Debtor."[40] Nevertheless, Penn was constantly tempted to minimize democratic powers in Pennsylvania and was continually threatening to use the absolute power he held as proprietor of an essentially feudal state. He came gradually to the point of insisting that the executive powers should be held and exercised in independence of the Council.

On his departure from the colony in 1683, he had made the whole Council his deputy governor and reminded the colonists that their new governors were elected men. Within a few years he had appointed five men as a governing committee and then selected one man who was to have the full power Penn himself enjoyed as governor. Nor could he see any reason for the Council to oppose the election of men directly in his employ to the colony's representative bodies.[41] His attitude toward the Council and Assembly was reflected in his stern directives to them to pass particular proposals that he felt were needed. Not even the judicial branch of the government was seen as independent of his control. The man who had made his niche in English legal history by defending the right of a jury to freedom from control by the bench instructed his officers of government in 1687 to punish juries that decided against him in cases involving quit-rents owed to him.[42]

These actions were congruent with Penn's increasing insistence on his rights and powers as "Lord of the Soil" in Pennsylvania. The proprietary arrangement that had seemed an anachronism in light of Penn's earlier political beliefs became more and more useful to him in the 1690's. Writing

[40] Letter, "To the Justices of New Castle, Pa." (1701), *Pa. Archives*, 1st Ser., I, 143.

[41] Letter to James Harrison (Sept. 8, 1687), PWP (A.L.S. in HSP); Letter to Thomas Lloyd (Mar. 28, 1688), PWP (A.L.S. in HSP); Letter to Secretary of the Provincial Council (Apr. 13, 1689), in *Pennsylvania Colonial Records*, I (Philadelphia, 1852), 319-320.

[42] Instructions to officers of government in Pennsylvania (Sept. 17, 1687), PWP (A.L.S. in HSP).

to the newly appointed Governor Fletcher in 1692 after losing the colony, he cautioned "that I am an Englishman and that country and government of it inseparably my property, dearly purchased every way and much indebted to me and my children. . . ."[43] Similarly, to the English Secretary of State, James Vernon, he wrote in 1700 that he, "as Lord of the Soil erected into a Seignory, must needs have a Royalty and share herein, else I am in much meaner Circumstances than any Ld of a Manor upon the Seacoasts in England Ireland or Scotland."[44] Although he did not as strongly emphasize the feudal aspects of the situation when writing to the colonists, he clearly believed that not only the land but the right to govern was an essential part of the property granted him by the crown. This was so, he said, in "all Manors, Courts, Leets, and Barrows in England, in Palatines or Seignories," and so surely also in proprietary governments. Indeed, this "possession" of the government was the only encouragement and reward he had for his arduous undertaking, and he considered it much more valuable than the land itself.[45] Although Penn apparently believed from the beginning of the "holy experiment" that his charter empowered him to declare laws void at any time on his "property," it was only after he had become disillusioned with the colonists that he regularly threatened to do so.[46]

Penn often said that he wanted Pennsylvania's government to be as much like the English government as possible. But it appears that he came increasingly to view his own proprietary powers as more absolute than those he believed

[43] Letter to Benjamin Fletcher (Dec. 1692), PWP (printed in *N.Y. Col. Documents*, IV, 33).

[44] Letter to James Vernon (Mar. 10, 1700), PWP (contemp. copy in HSP).

[45] Letter, "To His Son" (c. 1704), *Pa. Archives*, 2d Ser., VII (Harrisburg, 1878), 11.

[46] Letter to the Provincial Council (Aug. 12, 1689), *Colonial Records*, I, 316. See also Frederick Tolles, "William Penn on Public and Private Affairs, 1686, an Important New Letter," *PMHB*, 80 (1956), 236-247.

the king possessed in England. Although he talked and wrote more about his powers than he used them, the very fact that he could think in this manner indicates the extent to which his hopes for a regenerate society of willing men had receded by the late 1680's and 1690's. His increasing respect for the staying power of the old order made him view his responsibilities as proprietor in a less religious and more worldly light.

PENN's colony was in many respects one of the more successful of the colonial attempts to build a new society, but as a holy experiment it was a failure. Rather than providing a model of a harmonious Christian society and proving the viability of Quakerism as a foundation for a Christian social order, Pennsylvania showed that Quakers were not "fitted to rule themselves or to be ruled by a Friend thats a Governor."[47] In the light of the amount of praise that has been heaped on Penn the "gentle founding father," it is tempting to argue that the self-righteous and increasingly authoritarian governor goaded the colonists into their factionalism and peevishness. Certainly even the early Penn appeared entirely too paternalistic and moralistic to Quakers who were, in his view as well as theirs, his fellow-saints. In addition, his heavy-handed letters were a poor substitute for his presence in the colony and indicated to the sensitive colonists that their society was not the foremost of Penn's concerns. And the proprietor's anachronistic—although understandable—insistence that the colonists pay him rent for the "personal property" they occupied and his land policies in general made the renters suspect that what interest he did have in the colony was "experimental" in a financial rather than a religious sense.

Penn, however, was in no sense a tyrannical or selfish proprietor. Although he early became doubtful of the Quakers' good sense in government, when the control or the well-being of Friends in Pennsylvania was threatened and they

[47] Thos. Holme to Penn (Nov. 25, 1686), *PMHB*, 15 (1966), 350.

turned to Penn for help, he responded to their pleas like a scorned lover being welcomed back—even when the tormentor, as in the case of Governor Blackwell, had been appointed by Penn himself. Penn's Quaker principles and some personal shortcomings may have contributed to the colony's difficulties, but surely it was the colonists more than Penn who lost sight of the religious ideals, if they had shared them at all. Virtually all who came into contact with the Pennsylvania Quakers in a governmental capacity found something in the Quaker personality that made them litigious, uncooperative, and almost ungovernable.[48]

Many explanations have been offered for the Quakers' behavior in Pennsylvania. Gary Nash in particular has pinpointed several factors of obvious import that were more or less operative in most of the American colonies. For one, Penn, as proprietor, had to be an enterprising propagandist, and he had created expectations regarding the colony that no wilderness home could fulfill. Psychologically conditioned to expect a New Jerusalem, many colonists had to learn that the effects of the Fall extended across the Atlantic, where it was necessary to work even harder than in Europe to earn bread. More important were the transforming effects of the wilderness on the colonists. Faced with open spaces, new opportunities for gain, and unlimited land, "settlers dispersed, quested individually after the economic security they had lacked in England, and vigorously opposed proprietary or royal policies issued in the name of community, whether that was defined as Pennsylvania or the empire at large."[49]

Again, in the new society there was little of the stability that is produced only by the slow development of the social organism with its hierarchy of classes and functions and its prescriptive authority. In Pennsylvania as in most colonies, the scrambling for money, position, and power caused by the lack of fixed institutions and settled patterns of political

[48] See esp. Nash, 174-175.   [49] Ibid., 339.

power was compounded by the fact that there was a rather narrow social base among the immigrants: the upper and lower classes were decidedly under-represented, and the middle classes had little experience in political, economic, and social leadership.[50]

The Pennsylvanians, however, seem to have been somewhat more litigious than other colonists, and surely the discrepancy between their religious ideals and their social and political factionalism was greater. This may have been in part because some of the factors mentioned above were more operative in Pennsylvania than elsewhere, but there are good reasons to assume that the Quakerism of the colonists was partly responsible as well. One suggestion that has appeared prominently in the literature about Pennsylvania is the belief that Penn expected "greater moral and political perfection for his colony, than a just estimate of human nature would warrant."[51] According to this view, the Quakers' confidence in the inner light and their belief that this was the eschatological era in which government and society could become more consensual was without foundation. To the extent that they expected voluntary ways to be made possible by an increase of divine power in themselves and all men, they were simply mistaken. Penn, to be sure, counted on a gradual transition, and he therefore provided laws and penalties and the means of enforcement to control human sinfulness. It could be argued, however, that a gradual transition toward less government interference with individual liberty necessitates making highly visible the laws that are retained and the government's determination to enforce them. Penn's government was barely visible. The proprietor himself was absent most of the time; the Council was often not in session for several months at a time; the

[50] See *ibid.*, 161-178.
[51] Thomas F. Gordon, *The History of Pennsylvania, from its Discovery by Europeans to the Declaration of Independence in 1776* (Phila., 1829), 54, quoted by Joseph E. Illick, "The Writing of Colonial Pennsylvania History," *PMHB*, 94 (1970), 10.

Assembly averaged between one and two weeks of meetings a year; and the courts met irregularly. Moreover, the criminal code that the law officers were to enforce was extremely mild by European and colonial standards.[52] Penn was writing as early as 1685 that his government was "too lenient," but when his appointee, the puritan John Blackwell, tried to act on that judgment, Penn did not support him.

Another factor stemming from the Friends' attitude toward government was their tendency to look upon their religious lives as somewhat distinct from their socio-political lives. In England the Friends had been largely excluded from political life and, because of their Restoration sectarianism, largely avoided political stands and did not relate their religious beliefs to the social and political questions that political power or even citizenship in a self-governing society thrusts upon one. Although politically conscious Friends knew the political implications of Quaker principles, such men were few. When Friends attempted to discuss political responsibilities at Quaker meetings, Fox warned them to keep "the world" out of the sanctuary. At the London Yearly Meeting in 1688 Stephen Crisp wanted some enlightenment on whether Friends could stand for Parliament and vote, but Fox warned that it was "not Safe to conclude Such things in Yearly Meeting But keep to the power of God, and discourse of Such things among themselves that are concerned." Fox even objected to Penn's suggestion that a committee be appointed to advise on such matters.[53]

The evidence indicates that the Pennsylvanians of the seventeenth and early eighteenth centuries were as deeply involved in their religion as English Friends of the same period, but Penn was asking them to operate in new territory when he sought to have them apply Quaker principles

[52] See Bronner, *Holy Experiment*, 91; Nash, *Quakers and Politics*, 165-167.

[53] FLL, MSS, London Yearly Meeting, I, 199-200, in ACMC, xxx, 20.

in their political lives. It was natural that some balked at the idea of mixing their religious and secular affairs and that others came to startlingly different conclusions about the implications of Quaker principles for political responsibilities. These differences were especially the result of the fact that the Quakers, like the sectarians of the Continent, had worked out a functional separation between their own role and that of governors and governmental enforcement authorities. Although unable to use physical coercion themselves, Friends granted the legitimacy of government's defense of its citizens and had underlined this legitimacy by performing duties of a semi-militaristic nature (such as reporting on enemy movements threatening to Quakers in the expectation of government defense in the Barbadoes), paying all taxes, and demanding government protection. When called on to assume governing responsibilities themselves, Friends had either to make government less coercive or split their personalities by assuming two conflicting roles as Quakers and as public citizens. It is not surprising that Pennsylvania Quakers disagreed among themselves, some stressing the acceptance of more coercive ways and others abiding by a purer witness. The disagreements surfaced in the Keith controversy and on many other occasions.[54]

The sectarianism of the Quakers helps to account for their inability to produce a harmonious saintly society; more directly relevant to the attempt to explain their "government-ishness" was the fact that English Friends, despite their disclaimers, had exhibited less respect for the authority of government and less of a sense of its necessary place in human affairs than had virtually all Anglicans and all other nonconformists. No doubt this was in part because they had been persecuted and had suffered at the hands of government more consistently and more intensively than other religious groups. They had been told—and presumably they tried hard to believe—that governments had been ordained of

[54] See Hermann Wellenreuther, "The Political Dilemma of the Quakers in Pennsylvania, 1681-1748," *PMHB*, 94 (1970), 135-172.

God; that God had created and deposed every single government that had appeared among men; that governing authority was the authority of God himself; and that it was to be obeyed "for conscience sake" when exercised justly and only passively disobeyed in a respectful way on other occasions. But from the beginning of their existence Friends had always found government in the position of the enemy—creating and enforcing laws that they knew were ungodly, twisting laws and acting where none existed, and depriving them of the goods and services that governments had been created to protect. They had difficulty believing that the governments that ruined them or left them to rot to death in jail were nevertheless agents of divine authority, and their disrespect for their tormentors is manifest in the records they have left behind.

The Quakers' instinctively negative attitude toward governmental authority, however, was more than simply a product of the persecution they had suffered. The radical rhetoric of the "sectaries" who had sprung to life in the apocalyptic excitement of the revolutionary period was intentionally destructive of the authority of present governments. Although few of them saw themselves as the agents of revolution, they knew that governments in general were fallen and corrupt and were the main agents of the rising forces of the Devil. They were to be destroyed by the heavenly hosts and replaced by the direct rule of God himself or Christ the King.

As I have indicated, the Quakers fully shared this testimony about the fallenness and the demonic quality of present human governments as well as the expectation that their power would shortly be ended. For this reason, as well as because of their perfect knowledge of and power to obey the law of God, the saints, according to Fox, were beyond the authority of human governments. They were to acknowledge only the authority of God through the inner light.[55] This position was in apparent conflict with the belief

[55] "Saul's Errand to Damascus," *Works*, III, 589.

372

that Friends were to be obedient "for conscience sake" and were to be "obedient" and respectful even in disobedience. The two directives can be harmonized only if it is assumed that Fox meant that governments were to be obeyed "for conscience sake" because Friends were bound to eschew the ways of carnal or coercive disobedience that would be necessary to replace human governments. On this understanding, just laws were to be obeyed by the saints because they were just, not because they were just laws of a divinely instituted government—or, in other words, Friends were incidentally to obey the just laws of men when these laws coincided with the divine laws that were the direct object of their allegiance. This understanding of the Quaker position on government is the most plausible way of harmonizing the two sides of their witness. In any case, it was clearer in Quaker thought that just government was to be obeyed than it was that the authority of its human agents was to be recognized by the saints.

Even if the Quakers were not impressed by the authority of human governments in general and that of the English Crown and Parliament in particular, it could be argued that they had every reason to assume that their public Friend, who had pledged himself to justice in government and whose laws were voted on by elected representatives, was heading a government that acted justly and therefore should be obeyed. Quakers had never stood for a complete leveling in religious or socio-political affairs and had been accustomed to accepting an informal religious hierarchy—of which Penn was a member—and hierarchical social and political relations. The fact that Penn's original laws had been voted on by elected representatives who were themselves saints and who then passed on all additional laws should have been seen as an additional safeguard.

Two factors, however, operated in such a way as to mitigate the force of these considerations. First, it was impossible for the colonists to separate Penn's government from England's and to view their allegiance to Penn as separable from their allegiance to the crown. As Penn himself pointed out every time he tried to defend his reservation of great powers for himself, his own governmental power had been created *ex nihilo* by the crown, and all power exercised by Pennsylvanians was delegated through the proprietor from the crown. Moreover, as Governor Blackwell had so bluntly insisted to the Council and Assembly, and as Penn increasingly claimed himself after 1688, his own position in the mixed government of Pennsylvania corresponded to that of the monarch in England, and his powers as feudal lord of both the land and the governing powers of Pennsylvania were greater than he or anyone else claimed for the English king. Penn's proprietary position inevitably linked him with the distrusted English authorities, and he himself did not hesitate to re-inforce the Friends' naturally negative attitude toward English authority on occasion by counseling the colonists to ignore and disobey the English government whenever he thought they could do so with impunity and by urging them to tamper with their legal codes temporarily merely to please the English authorities.

A second reason for Penn's difficulty was the fact that his authority as a public Friend and his reliance on "weighty" Friends for positions in the Council in Pennsylvania did not awe the rest of the Quaker colonists. On the matter of obeying and disobeying laws of governments, Friends had taken a completely egalitarian attitude. It was their belief that all men possessed knowledge of the law of God through their inner light and that regenerate men also were sufficiently sanctified that they would not deceive themselves about which human actions and laws were in accord with the divine law. Therefore when Friends in England spoke of the duty to disobey unjust laws, they set forth no firm lists of essential or central divine laws against which one was to judge human laws, and did not require Friends to seek the guidance of the meeting or Publick Friends or counsel them to disobey only when absolutely certain of the injustice of the law involved. They were certain that all Quakers could recognize an unjust law when they saw one and could act on their own authority—or, rather, on the authority of God mediated through each individual conscience. Every Pennsylvania Quaker had therefore been led to assume that injustice was a matter for him to decide. The Wilkinson-Story controversy had indicated that public Friends believed that when a man's testimony conflicted with that of most Friends and especially the leaders, he should bow to communal authority or the advice of the elders, but they had required no similar guidance by the religious leaders in the case of civil disobedience. In addition, just as they failed to distinguish in this regard between greater and lesser Friends, so also they made no attempt to distinguish between greater and lesser injustice. Friends had not been counseled to obey the government when the law involved related to an issue of minor importance on which unjust obedience was a lesser evil than the destruction of governmental authority involved in all acts of obedience.

The Quakers recognized that government was necessary to punish evil-doers, but they seem to have seen no particular need for saints to worry about preserving the authority of governments. Friends disobeyed governments as unhesitatingly over the registration of marriages and burials as over laws relating to the right to worship; they also disobeyed in instances where they were not forced to do so by an unjust law they could not escape, as when they went naked for a sign. The early Quaker position was that all issues relating to the law of God were equally important and that to disobey a particular spiritual directive to go naked was to place human above divine authority. The Quakers of Pennsylvania, however, lived in a world in which some laws were seen as more important than others, and particular leadings were rare. It seemed to them that the earlier Quaker witness had simply pitted the righteous individual against the tainted authority of government. In Pennsylvania as in England the righteous individual prevailed, but now the victim was not the governmental authority of Cromwell or

Charles but the Quakers' own attempt to provide a harmonious consensual social order as a guide for the rest of the world.

THE factionalism of Pennsylvania was a severe disappointment to Penn, but despite his irate letters and his threats regarding his "property," he learned to modify his hopes for the colony. He could take some solace in the fact that the increasing prominence of non-Quakers in the colony would shortly have diluted the experiment regardless of Quaker attitudes, although he also knew that a more "holy" community of Friends could have had an effect on other settlers. In any case, Penn never soured completely on the Pennsylvanians. As late as 1708 he could write to his Provincial Council in a public letter for all Pennsylvanians: "My ancient Love, if you can believe it, reaches to you as in times past and years that are gone, even in that divine rest and Principle of love and life yt made us near to one an other, above all worldly considerations; . . . that we may glorify God his and our everlasting ffather, in our body Soules and Spirits. . . ."[56]

No doubt Penn was able to escape complete embitterment toward the Pennsylvanians because other developments had already modified his hopes for setting up God's kingdom in the world. The failure of the holy experiment was simply one of a series of at least partial defeats for the major hopes of Penn's life. The Friends had not, in the late 1660's and 1670's, swept on to the ends of the earth as the vanguard of true spiritual religion. If Penn's feverish political activity in the late 1670's was a manifestation of his hope that at least England could be transformed, by 1680 even that modified goal seemed impossible to realize. A major, if less ambitious, goal was partly achieved in 1688 with the passing of the Toleration Act, but Penn was seen at the time more as a traitor than a hero, and he was too busy for the next few

[56] Letters to S.C., T.S., G.O. *et al.* (Provincial Council) (Sept. 28, 1708), PWP (A.L.S. in HSP).

years trying to defend his honor to savor the fruits of his efforts. Under the Toleration Act the Society of Friends, at least, seemed secure in its existence, and Penn could take pride in that accomplishment as a leading public Friend. But that was a modest victory indeed, and in certain respects a defeat, for the Friends in the light of their original aims, and in any case many Quakers, including George Fox's family, were suspicious of Penn and made him a source of minor controversy in the movement. Nor was Penn's success in his life any more evident when he restricted his vision even more and focused on personal and family affairs. In addition to his financial difficulties and the threats to his proprietary rights, he received little but disappointment from his offspring. Especially trying were the death at the age of twenty of his promising son Springett and the rakish pursuits of his oldest living son, William.

Penn's primary goal in life was to defend and spread the message of spiritual Christianity and to make its power operative in societies beset by sin. Despite his strenuous efforts God's kingdom did not come to Europe, England, or Pennsylvania, and his will was not done "on earth as it is in heaven." By the last years of his life Penn had come to realize that he would pass from the kingdom of "this world" to the kingdom of God only when he passed through the portals of death.

PRIMARY SOURCES

The Intellectual Background of Quakerism

Bibliographical guides to puritan sources are numerous, and their material need not be repeated here. I have found especially useful as guides to the sources Norman Pettit, *The Heart Prepared: Grace and Conversion in Puritan Spiritual Life* (New Haven, 1966), for Elizabethan and Stuart puritanism, and Geoffrey Nuttall, *The Holy Spirit in Puritan Faith and Experience* (Oxford, 1946), for late Stuart and Interregnum forerunners of Quakerism. A Stuart puritan mentioned prominently by Penn whose works show clearly the thrust in an experiential and spiritualist direction among certain puritans is Richard Sibbes. See his *Complete Works*, ed. A. B. Grosart (6 vols.; Edinburgh, 1862-1864). Two more prominent later puritans who had extensive theological discussions with Penn and whose works represent differing trends within the movement are Richard Baxter and John Owen. Baxter is an excellent representative of what I have called the rational side of puritanism in Interregnum and post-Restoration England. See especially the *Practical Works* (4 vols.; London, 1838). Owen is the theologian of the Interregnum and beyond who best demonstrates the conservative Calvinism of many puritans despite their developing emphasis on the Holy Spirit. See his *Works*, ed. William H. Goold (1850-1853; rpt., 16 vols.; London, 1965-1968).

Intermediary figures between puritanism and Quakerism are less well known than the above. I have traced the path to Quakerism through the works of several writers whom Penn and others designated as forerunners of Quakerism: John Saltmarsh, *Sparkles of Glory, or Some Beams of the Morning Star* (London, 1648), *Free-grace: or, the flowings* of *Christs blood freely to sinners* (London, 1645), *Smoke in the Temple* . . . (London, 1646), and *Some Drops of the Viall* . . . (London, 1646); William Dell, *Works* (New York, 1816); Richard Coppin, *Michael Opposing the Dragon* . . . (London, 1659); John Webster, *The Saints Guide: or, Christ the Rule* (1653; 3d edn., London, 1699) and *The Drawings of the Father* (n.d.; rpt., Glasgow, 1884); and Gerrard Winstanley, *Works,* ed. George Sabine (Ithaca, 1941), especially "The New Law of Righteousness" and "Truth Lifting Up Its Head."

Early rational or liberal Anglicans who were read by Penn and influenced him include John Hales, *Golden Remains of the Ever-Memorable Mr. John Hales* (London, 1659); and Jeremy Taylor, especially *The Liberty of Prophecying* (London, 1647), and *Ductor Dubitantium; or, The Rule of Conscience* (London, 1660). Contemporary Anglicans with whom Penn came into contact include Edward Stillingfleet, who got him to explain some of his phrases from *The Sandy Foundation Shaken,* and whose similarities to Penn can be seen in *Origines Sacrae* (London, 1663) and *A Rational Account of the Grounds of the Protestant Religion* (London, 1664), and John Tillotson, with whom he carried on a correspondence. See especially "The Rule of Faith" in his *Works* (3 vols.; London, 1752), and his *Sermons,* ed. Ralph Barker (14 vols.; London, 1695-1704). I have found interesting similarities and points of comparison also in Edward Fowler's *The Principles and Practices of Certain Moderate Divines of the Church of England, Abusively Called Latitudinarians* . . . (2nd edn., London, 1671).

Quaker Thought

George Fox may not have been the totally dominant and singularly creative founder and leader of Quakerism he has sometimes been made into, but he was a prolific theological writer and, as his correspondence with Penn shows, a strong leader and guide on theological issues even if his somewhat nonacademic phrases had to be explained at times by better-trained writers. In addition to the various editions of his *Journal*, of which the general reader will find most useful that edited by John Nickalls (Cambridge, 1952), his treatises and letters, collected in his *Works* (8 vols.; Philadelphia, 1831), are most representative of both the most orthodox and the most radical theological tendencies of the Quaker movement.

Other important first-generation Quaker spokesmen include James Nayler, *A Collection of Sundry Books, Epistles and Papers* . . . (London, 1716), possibly the clearest writer and the most orthodox among the earliest spokesmen; Edward Burrough, *Memorable Works* [London, 1672], an excellent controversialist and as radical as any Quaker in his depreciation of the historical Jesus; and Isaac Penington, *Works* (2 vols.; London, 1681), who developed the Quaker body-spirit dualism farther than most. A transitional figure who tried to systematize Quaker theology in his monumental *Rusticus ad Academicos in Exercitationibus Expostulatoris Apologeticis Quatuor; or The Rustic's Alarm to the Rabies* . . . (1660; rpt., London, 1672), whose Quaker theology clearly reflects his General Baptist anti-Calvinist background and contrasts in ways with the spiritualist divine-human dualism of Nayler and Burrough. Fisher appears to have influenced Penn strongly.

The contemporaries of Penn whose writings provide the best means of understanding Quaker thought between 1660 and 1700 are Robert Barclay, George Whitehead, and George Keith. Although Barclay and Keith tried to express the body-spirit dualism more philosophically than had earlier Friends, they were also highly knowledgeable about Christian doctrinal history and were articulate exponents of a Quaker theology that they saw as essentially in continuity with the best of historical Christian doctrine. The philosophical thrust can be seen in Barclay's "The Possibility and Necessity of the Inward and Immediate Revelation of the Spirit of God" (1676), in *Truth Triumphant* (London, 1692), and Keith's *The Way Caste Up* . . . (London, 1676) and *Immediate Revelation* . . . (Aberdeen, 1668). The most important systematic statement of Quaker theology and one that played down some of the more aberrant Quaker doctrines was Barclay's *Apology for the True Christian Divinity* . . . (Latin, 1676; English, 1678). After Keith left the movement, he wrote many attacks on what he then conceived as the heresies of Quaker doctrine. Keith's emotions sometimes overcame his fine theological mind, but his treatises give important insights into the relationship between Quaker and orthodox theology. See especially *The Deism of William Penn and His Brethren* . . . (London, 1699); *Gross Error and Hypocrisie Detected, in George Whitehead and Some of His Brethren* (London, 1695); *An Exact Narrative of the Proceedings at Turners-Hall* . . . (London, 1696); *Second Narrative* . . . (London, 1697); *Some of the Many Fallacies of William Penn Detected* (London, 1699); and *The Quakers Examined, or an Answer to the Apology of Robert Barclay* (London, 1702).

William Penn

Students of the life and work of William Penn have encountered difficulties because of the lack of a modern scholarly edition of Penn's published works and the widely scattered locations of unpublished Penn papers. The past situation and current efforts by the Papers of William Penn Committee to rectify it are described by Caroline Robbins in "The Papers of William Penn," *Pennsylvania Magazine of History and Biography*, 93 (1969). Penn's published works are most easily accessible in *The Collected Works of William Penn* (2 vols.; London, 1726), which was prepared under the direction of a committee of Friends and edited by Joseph Besse a few years after Penn's death. Selections from this nearly complete collection were reprinted in 1771, 1782, and 1825. In the seventeenth century Quaker committees such as this one sometimes took the opportunity provided by collected editions to omit or alter material the editors considered unfortunate. Such was not the case with the Penn

committee. Extensive comparison of the 1726 *Works* treatises with the first and later editions of individual tracts
reveals that Besse did not intentionally omit passages or
change the content of Penn's works, although a few sections
separated from the main text, such as appendices that later
appeared in expanded form as separate works by Penn, were
omitted as appendices and simply printed as they later appeared. The only extensive changes were the capitalization
of all nouns, in accordance with eighteenth-century practices, and the introduction of extensive use of italics. The
latter, apart from their use in Scriptural quotations, served
no apparent purpose and were clearly not for reasons of
emphasis. In addition to these alterations, very occasional
changes of punctuation and relocations of phrases can be
found in a few of the treatises because of the editor's desire
to clarify a few of Penn's ungrammatical or unclear sen-
tences. Printing errors led to the omission of a few phrases
and lines, although this is compensated for by the correction of the many more numerous omissions and errors in
the earlier editions of individual tracts. Finally, Besse's edition is somewhat careless on joint authorship and follows an
unusual dating practice. Works written by Penn in conjunc-
tion with other Friends are simply listed as Penn's, and it is
possible that the committee members and Besse were more
knowledgeable than we about the actual authorship of treatises signed by several Friends and knew that Penn was in
fact the main author of the treatises printed. On the matter
of dates, as Besse noted, he cited in *Works* the year in which
Penn originally published a work, whereas the edition
printed was the "last and best" in the case of works that
saw more than one edition.

Because the Besse edition makes no intentional substantive
changes in Penn's treatises, it has seemed appropriate to
make use of it rather than citing the individual treatises in
their separately published form except when I refer to editions other than those used in *Works* or to published documents or tracts not in that collection. Dating considerations

and other information correcting and elucidating *Works* citations have been provided in footnotes. I hope that my study can serve as a guide to Penn sources for students of colonial history, English religious thought, and Quakerism. It would be pedantic to bypass the more accessible and useful Besse collection in favor of rare individual tracts simply because it is not quite a *verbatim ac literatim* transcription, especially when it is realized that Penn was not careful about publishing details in his individual publications and that, in any case, a Quaker committee placed its *imprimatur* on Penn's individual tracts only after reviewing and, presumably, making changes in them. Not all of Penn's treatises are found in the *Works*, however, and, as I have noted in the text, it is necessary to check earlier editions than those used in the *Works* if one is interested in the development of Penn's thought. The most extensive collections of Penn tracts can be found at Haverford College, The Quaker Collection; The Albert Cook Myers Collection in the Chester County Historical Society, West Chester, Pa.; and Friends Library, London.

Unpublished Penn papers are located in many collections primarily in England and the United States, and some for which transcriptions exist cannot now be located. Nevertheless the vast majority of unpublished materials by Penn can be found at the Historical Society of Pennsylvania and the Friends Library, London. The Penn materials are scattered in a variety of collections in these depositories. Until recently the most extensive attempt to assemble and order the Penn papers (along with published works) was that of the Albert Cook Myers Collection. The fruit of several decades of labor from about 1900 to the 1930's in preparation for a complete edition of Penn papers and published works is available in this collection in chronologically ordered notebooks. Because the unpublished papers are neatly transcribed in chronological order and interspersed with the published works, this is a most useful collection, and I have used the whole of it. Nevertheless, although Myers used photocopying on occasion and was an excellent transcriber, the material was never made ready for publication, and there are the inevitable problems with transcriptions. Moreover, Penn papers have been found since Myers was at work.

A complete collection of Penn papers is currently being made at the Historical Society of Pennsylvania by Hannah Benner Roach under the direction of the Papers of William Penn Committee. This is a photo-reproduction collection of all known unpublished manuscripts relating to Penn. The project began in 1969, and in July 1972 the collection included more than 2600 items and was largely complete. I have worked through this collection, and most of my citations to unpublished materials are from it.

Secondary Sources

The Intellectual Background and Milieu of Quakerism

It is not necessary to become involved here in the extensive debates among the various schools of interpretation on the puritans. I can best indicate my own approach to the movement by listing a guide or two for each of several facets of the phenomenon. Despite all the controversy about puritanism and the specific advances in knowledge since 1938, as well as the author's simplistic attitude toward the political implications of the movement, I have found William Haller's *The Rise of Puritanism* (New York, 1938) the best general guide to the background, participants, and general character of Stuart puritanism for the purposes of my study. Everett Emerson, ed., *English Puritanism from John Hooper to John Milton* (Durham, North Carolina, 1968), provides a useful classification of the kinds and periods of puritanism to 1640. Alan Simpson, *Puritanism in Old and New England* (Chicago, 1955), and Sydney Ahlstrom, ed., *Theology in America: The Major Protestant Voices from Puritanism to Neo-Orthodoxy* (New York, 1967), Introduction, define succinctly the essence and *differentia* of the movement.

Especially important for my study is Norman Pettit's *The Heart Prepared*, which backs Haller's categories and discusses theological developments in a way that prepares one for an understanding of Interregnum theological developments. The theology of the covenant is also presented in illuminating fashion by John von Rohr, "Covenant and Assurance in Early English Puritanism," *Church History*, 34 (1965), and C. Conrad Cherry, "The Puritan Notion of the Covenant in Jonathan Edwards' Doctrine of Faith," *Church History*, 34 (1965).

Christopher Hill delineates the significance of the movement within English society in several studies, especially *Society and Puritanism in Pre-Revolutionary England* (New York, 1964). The political and economic implications of puritanism are discussed from opposing but equally necessary points of view by David Little, *Religious Conflict, Law, and Order: a Study in Pre-Revolutionary England* (New York, 1969), and Michael Walzer, *The Revolution of the Saints* (Cambridge, Mass., 1965).

For a very different approach to English religious history from 1600 to 1640, see Charles H. and Katherine George, *The Protestant Mind of the English Reformation: 1570-1640* (Princeton, 1961), Charles H. George, "A Social Interpretation of English Puritanism," *Journal of Modern History*, 25 (1953), and "Puritanism as History and Historiography," *Past and Present*, No. 41 (Dec. 1968). Michael Walzer provides a perceptive response to the Georges in a review essay on *The Protestant Mind* in *History and Theory*, 2 (1962).

The transition from Stuart to Interregnum puritanism and especially the increase in eschatological ferment is discussed by John Wilson, *Pulpit in Parliament: Puritanism During the English Civil Wars, 1640-1648* (Princeton, 1969), and William M. Lamont, *Godly Rule: Politics and Religion, 1603-1660* (London, 1969). The splintering of the movement into several sects is adequately recounted by Wilbur Jordan, *The Development of Religious Toleration in England, From the Convention of the Long Parliament to the*

Restoration, 1640-1660 (Cambridge, Mass., 1938); A.S.P. Woodhouse, ed., *Puritanism and Liberty: Being the Army Debates (1647-9) from the Clarke Manuscripts with Supplementary Documents* (London, 1938); Robert Barclay, *The Inner Life of the Religious Societies of the Commonwealth* (3d edn.; London, 1879); and William Haller, *Liberty and Reformation in the Puritan Revolution* (New York, 1955). The best guides to the developing spiritualist tendency in puritanism of the period and a natural sequel to Pettit are the works of Geoffrey Nuttall, especially *The Holy Spirit in Puritan Faith and Experience* (Oxford, 1946), and *The Puritan Spirit: Essays and Addresses* (London, 1967). Several articles by J. F. Maclear emphasize the same developments. See especially " 'The Heart of New England Piety Rent': The Mystical Element in Early Puritan History," *Mississippi Valley Historical Review*, 42 (1956), and "The Making of the Lay Tradition," *Journal of Religion*, 33 (1953). Richard Greaves, "John Bunyan and Covenant Thought in the Seventeenth Century," *Church History*, 36 (1967), enables us to see how developments in the 1640's led to divergences over the covenant, grace, and free will. The intellectual implications of puritan thought, especially in its relationship to the rise of empirical science, are thoroughly discussed in Robert Merton, "Science, Technology, and Society in Seventeenth-Century England," *Osiris*, 4, ed. George Sarton (1938).

The social, political, and economic developments in Interregnum puritanism are discussed by Hill, *Puritanism and Revolution* (London, 1958); Margaret James, *Social Problems and Policy during the Puritan Revolution* (London, 1930); Wilhelm Schenk, *The Concern for Social Justice in the Puritan Revolution* (London, 1948); Eduard Bernstein, *Cromwell and Communism: Socialism and Democracy in the Great English Revolution*, transl. H. J. Stenning (London, 1930); and A.S.P. Woodhouse, *Puritanism and Liberty*, among many others. Millennial tendencies among both puritans and spiritualists are discussed by Leo Solt, "The Fifth

Monarchy Men: Politics and the Millennium," *Church History*, 30 (1961); Alfred Cohen, "Two Roads to the Puritan Millennium: William Erbury and Vavasor Powell," *Church History*, 32 (1963); and John Wilson, "Comments on 'Two Roads to the Puritan Millennium,'" *Church History*, 32 (1963). The issue of consensualism versus coercion is handled in a most balanced manner by Woodhouse in *Puritanism and Liberty*. Geoffrey Nuttall, *Visible Saints: The Congregational Way 1640-1660* (Oxford, 1957) and William Haller, *Liberty and Reformation*, on the one hand, and Leo Solt, *Saints in Arms* (Stanford, 1959), on the other, argue for consensualism and coercion, respectively.

Although studies of individual spiritualists exist, there is no fully adequate study linking spiritual puritans, "waiting" and spiritualizing Seekers, Ranters, and Quakers. Geoffrey Nuttall is probably the most knowledgeable student of the groups to the left of the puritans, but he emphasizes too strongly their continuity with puritanism, especially in *The Holy Spirit*. Rufus Jones, *Spiritual Reformers in the Sixteenth and Seventeenth Centuries* (New York, 1914), and *Studies in Mystical Religion* (New York, 1909), has studied these groups as fully as anyone, but Jones wrote with an inadequate understanding of English religious thought, especially puritanism, and he stressed the Continental links of Quakerism unduly. George Sabine's Introduction to *The Works of Gerrard Winstanley* and J. F. Maclear's articles are most useful introductions to spiritualist thought. Several works by Theodor Sippell, especially *Werdendes Quäkertum* (Stuttgart, 1937), analyze certain spiritual puritans as forerunners of Quakerism. The intellectual, and particularly the "liberal" or rationalistic, implications of spiritualist thought are discussed by Jerald Brauer, "Puritanism, Mysticism, and the Development of Liberalism," *Church History*, 19 (1950); Roger L. Emerson, "Heresy, the Social Order, and English Deism," *Church History*, 37 (1968); and Rufus Jones and J. F. Maclear in works already cited. Rufus Jones in *Spiritual Reformers* and *Studies in Mystical*

Religion and Robert Barclay in *The Inner Life of the Religious Societies of the Commonwealth* identify all of the spiritualist groups. Rewarding individual studies include Leo Solt, *Saints in Arms*, on the theology of the spiritual puritans; George A. Johnson, "From Seeker to Finder: A Study in Seventeenth Century English Spiritualism Before the Quakers," *Church History*, 17 (1948); Champlin Burrage, "The Antecedents of Quakerism," *English Historical Review*, 30 (1915), on some Seekers; George Sabine's Introduction to *The Works of Gerrard Winstanley*; Charles Wellborn, "Gerrard Winstanley: A Case Study in the Relation of Religion and Culture," *Union Seminary Quarterly Review*, 25 (1970); Richard T. Vann, "From Radicalism to Quakerism: Gerrard Winstanley and Friends," *Journal of the Friends Historical Society*, 49 (1959); and on the Ranters, Norman Cohn, *Pursuit of the Millennium* (1957; rpt., New York, 1961), and G.F.S. Ellens, "The Ranters Ranting: Reflections on a Ranting Counter Culture," *Church History*, 40 (1971).

Useful introductions to the nonconformist sects after the Restoration include Geoffrey Nuttall and Owen Chadwick, eds., *From Uniformity to Unity: 1662-1962* (London, 1962), Gerald R. Cragg, *Puritanism in the Period of the Great Persecution 1660-1688* (Cambridge, 1957), and C. E. Whiting, *Studies in English Puritanism from the Restoration to the Revolution, 1660-1688* (London, 1931), with Nuttall and Chadwick discussing the effects of the Restoration, Cragg emphasizing the situation of nonconformists in Restoration England, and Whiting identifying the doctrines and intellectual developments. The development of "liberal" or rational theology and particularly the search for a more universal and reasonable kind of "inward certitude" than church, Scripture, or the Spirit could provide is discussed well in Basil Willey, *The Seventeenth-Century Background* (1934; rpt., New York, 1953), Gerald Cragg, *From Puritanism to the Age of Reason* (Cambridge, 1950), Louis Bredvold, *The Intellectual Milieu of John Dryden* (Ann Arbor,

1934), and the first few chapters of Roland Stromberg, *Religious Liberalism in Eighteenth Century England* (London, 1954). The reaction against creedal and Calvinist emphases in Anglicanism has been discussed by many writers. William Tulloch's *Rational Theology and Christian Philosophy in England in the Seventeenth Century* (2 vols.; Edinburgh, 1872) is still an extraordinarily useful guide to the Falkland Circle and the Cambridge Platonists. Herbert J. McLachlan's discussion of anti-Trinitarian, anti-orthodox, and rational thought in *Socinianism in Seventeenth-Century England* (London, 1951) makes its greatest contribution by showing the links between radical sectarians of the Interregnum and developing liberal Anglican thought. The best discussion of the intellectual assumptions and theology of the Latitudinarians is Martin I. J. Griffin's doctoral dissertation, "Latitudinarianism in the Seventeenth-Century Church of England" (Yale University, 1962).

Quakerism

The best general introduction to the Quaker movement—its history, social relations, theology, and socio-political implications—is Hugh Barbour, *The Quakers in Puritan England* (New Haven, 1964), although I believe that Barbour stresses unduly the puritan and "orthodox" nature of the movement and errs in setting Penn off sharply from the first generation. William Braithwaite's monumental two-volume history, especially in the revised version with notes by Henry J. Cadbury, *The Beginnings of Quakerism* (Cambridge, 1955) and *The Second Period of Quakerism* (Cambridge, 1961), is still very useful. A brilliant monograph that tells the reader more about early Quakerism than its title promises is Richard T. Vann, *The Social Development of English Quakerism: 1655-1755* (Cambridge, Mass., 1969).

The question of the immediate prehistory of Quakerism and its relationships with other sects will probably never be settled to the satisfaction of most scholars. Two earlier interpreters, Robert Barclay of Reigate in *The Inner Life of the Religious Societies of the Commonwealth* and Rufus Jones in *Spiritual Reformers* and *Studies in Mystical Religion* and other works, overemphasize the Quakers' debt to Continental Anabaptists and Spiritualists, although these studies are decidedly more useful than many recent Quaker scholars have recognized. Barclay's stress on the affinities between General Baptists and Quakers—an emphasis also found in William Tallack, *George Fox, the Friends, and the Early Baptists* (London, 1868)—predates certain ecclesiological developments in Quakerism but is still very convincing. A more accurate account of Quaker organizational developments is found in Arnold Lloyd, *Quaker Social History: 1669-1738* (London, 1950). Geoffrey Nuttall, especially in *Holy Spirit*, and Theodor Sippell, notably in *Werdendes Quäkertum* and *Zur Vorgeschichte des Quäkertums*, stress the relationship between Friends and what I have called spiritual puritans. The similarities and differences between Quakers and Seekers are discussed in George A. Johnson, "From Seeker to Finder." Winthrop Hudson has tried to show that Fox's major mentor was Gerrard Winstanley in "A Suppressed Chapter in Quaker History," *Journal of Religion*, 24 (1944) and "Gerrard Winstanley and the Early Quakers," *Church History*, 12 (1943), but to my mind his claim for direct influence by Winstanley and its suppression by Quaker historians is effectively refuted by Henry Cadbury, "An Obscure Chapter of Quaker History," *Journal of Religion*, 24 (1944). Nevertheless, the early Quakers' silence about a man whose thought was virtually identical with theirs and who probably later became a Friend is intriguing.

The theology of seventeenth-century Quakerism is discussed in Barbour, *Quakers in Puritan England*, and in Nuttall's *Holy Spirit* and his *Studies in Christian Enthusiasm* (Wallingford, Pa., 1948). Edward Grubb, *The Historic and the Inward Christ* (London, 1914), is a useful attempt to relate Quaker Christology to orthodox Christian doctrine. Maurice Creasey's doctoral dissertation, "Early Quaker Christology with Special Reference to the Teaching and

Significance of Isaac Penington, 1616-1679" (Univ. of Leeds, 1956), is an illuminating analysis of Quaker doctrines, although it overemphasizes the differences between first generation Quakers and Penn, Barclay, and Keith. Creasey's *"Inward" and "Outward": A Study in Early Quaker Language* (London, 1962) and "The Quaker Interpretation of Religion," *Quaker Religious Thought*, 1 (1959), and Christine R. Downing, "Quakerism and the Historical Interpretation of Religion," *Quaker Religious Thought*, 3 (1961), are also insightful and representative studies by Quaker scholars since the revival of puritan studies, but to my mind they oversimplify the early Quakers' spiritualism by denying its tendency toward a body-spirit dualism. Other articles in *Quaker Religious Thought*, especially those by Lewis Benson, T. Canby Jones, and Wilmer Cooper, are most useful. J. William Frost has elucidated post-Restoration Quaker theology in its relation to orthodoxy in "The Dry Bones of Quaker Theology," *Church History*, 39 (1970).

George Fox's thought has been presented adequately by Rachel King in a pioneering, if narrow, study, *George Fox and the Light Within* (Philadelphia, 1940), and by T. Canby Jones in "George Fox's Teaching on Redemption and Salvation" (unpubl. Ph.D. diss., Yale Univ., 1955)—another very "puritan" treatment. Lewis Benson is probably the most important Fox scholar writing today. See his several contributions to *Quaker Religious Thought*. The only other early Quaker theologian who has been the subject of several major studies is Robert Barclay. Leif Eeg-Olofsson obscured as well as elucidated Barclay's thought by trying to analyze it with Anders Nygren's Swedish Lutheran categories in *The Conception of the Inner Light in Robert Barclay's Theology: A Study in Quakerism* (Lund, Sweden, 1954). Useful studies by Quakers include Francis Hall, "The Thought of Robert Barclay: An Evaluation," *Quaker Religious Thought*, 7 (1965) and Elton Trueblood, *Robert Barclay* (New York, 1968).

The question of the social origins of seventeenth-century

Quakers is of interest to students of Penn's life and thought because of the distinction customarily made between Penn the gentleman and courtier and the lowly Friends. Alan Cole in "The Social Origins of Early Friends," *Journal of the Friends Historical Society*, 48 (1957) and "Quakerism and the Social Structure of the Interregnum," *Past and Present*, 44 (1969) defines the early Quakers as largely "petty bourgeoisie," whereas Vann, *Social Development*, has found more of the upper bourgeoisie and lesser gentry, especially among public Friends. Judith Jones Hurwich, "The Social Origins of the Early Quakers," *Past and Present*, 48 (1970) enters an objection to Vann's generalizations on the basis of limited data. Quaker social and political thought and activities are discussed by Alan Cole in "The Quakers and Politics, 1652-1660" (unpubl. Ph.D. diss., Cambridge Univ., 1955) and by Barbour in *Quakers in Puritan England*. Both studies play down the Quaker thrust toward self-government and social equality in favor of "the rule of the saints." J. F. Maclear's article on Quaker activities in 1659, "Quakerism and the End of the Interregnum: A Chapter in the Domestication of Radical Puritanism," *Church History*, 19 (1950), is an illuminating discussion of the Quaker temptation to assume political power and of the shift toward passivity and sectarianism. Quaker social attitudes after 1660 are handled well by Arnold Lloyd, *Quaker Social History*.

The significance of Quakerism to the Pennsylvania colony has been dealt with many times, although there is still much work to be done, especially on the relationship between the Quaker colonists' religion and their social, political, and economic activities and attitudes. Edwin B. Bronner, *William Penn's Holy Experiment: the Founding of Pennsylvania, 1681-1701* (New York, 1962), has related the history of Pennsylvania as a Quaker utopia. The socio-political, economic, cultural, and ethical attitudes of the leading Quaker colonists have been surveyed well by Frederick Tolles in *Meetinghouse and Countinghouse: the Quaker Merchants of Colonial Philadelphia, 1682-1763* (Chapel Hill, 1948).

Guy Hershberger, "The Pennsylvania Quaker Experiment in Politics, 1682-1756," *Mennonite Quarterly Review*, 10 (1936), has seen the colony as a testing ground for the Quakers' hope for the political institutionalization of their noncoercive ways. Quaker pacifism in Pennsylvania has been admirably presented by Peter Brock, *Pacifism in the United States From the Colonial Era to the First World War* (Princeton, 1968), chapter two, and by Hermann Wellenreuther, "The Political Dilemma of the Quakers in Pennsylvania, 1681-1748," *Pennsylvania Magazine of History and Biography*, 94 (1970), and will be analyzed in a forthcoming study by Guy Hershberger. The best recent study of the colony is Gary Nash's *Quakers and Politics: Pennsylvania, 1681-1726* (Princeton, 1968), which examines the economic interests in the early colony and the relationship between social and economic structure and political power.

William Penn

Penn has been the subject of as many published studies as any major colonial figure has, but until recently many facets of his life and thought were inadequately understood. More than forty biographers have tried to bring Penn back to life, but it is generally recognized that a definitive scholarly biography has yet to be written. Catherine Owens Peare's popular *William Penn: A Biography* (1956; rpt., Ann Arbor, 1966) is a highly informative and readable account of his life. The most useful biography for students of particular aspects of Penn's life and work, including the religious, is William I. Hull, *William Penn: A Topical Approach* (New York, 1937). Mabel Brailsford has written a comprehensive study of the young Penn, *The Making of William Penn* (London, 1930). The older biographies that provide the most information on Penn's religious life and interests are Samuel Janney, *The Life of William Penn: With Selections from his Correspondence and Autobiography* (Philadelphia, 1852), and John W. Graham, *William*

Penn: Founder of Pennsylvania (2nd edn.; Philadelphia, 1918).

Monographs on Penn have dealt with all aspects of his mind and life, but the only truly satisfactory ones relate his political and economic thought and activities. In *William Penn, 1644-1718: A Tercentenary Estimate* (Philadelphia, 1944), William Wistar Comfort devoted a large chapter to Penn as "the defender of Quakerism," but Comfort's grasp of seventeenth-century religious thought was limited. Penn's ethical thought has been analyzed in Irvin Goldman, "Deviations Toward Ideas of Natural Ethics in the Thought of William Penn," *Philological Quarterly*, 18 (1939), and Jay T. Allen, "The Guide for Ethics in the Thought of William Penn" (unpubl. Ph.D. diss., Syracuse Univ., 1967). Herbert Wood has pointed perceptively to Penn's denigration of the doctrine of means and to his easy confidence in the universality of true religion in "William Penn's 'Christian Quaker,'" in Howard H. Brinton, ed., *The Children of Light* (New York, 1938). Penn's views on religious liberty and their significance for political theory have been expounded by Hans Joachim Dummer, *Die Toleranzidee in William Penns Schriften* (Lengerich, Westfallen, Germany, 1940), and, less successfully, in Richard J. Oman's doctoral dissertation, "William Penn: A Study in the Quaker Doctrine of Political Authority" (Univ. of Edinburgh, 1958).

Frederick Tolles' *Meetinghouse and Countinghouse* quotes extensively from Penn and provides much insight into his political, economic, and social views. Less rewarding but useful is Edward C. O. Beatty, *William Penn as Social Philosopher* (New York, 1939), a presentation of Penn's views on social, political, and economic matters. Several recent students of aspects of Penn's political and economic life have provided solid monographs of great use. Mary Maples Dunn's narrow but sound *William Penn: Politics and Conscience* (Princeton, 1967) presents Penn's political theory and its relationship to his zeal for religious toleration. Joseph Illick's *William Penn the Politician* (Ithaca, 1965) goes be-

yond the biographies to show how Penn utilized political
influence and how his political abilities affected colonial and
other endeavors. Edwin B. Bronner's *William Penn's Holy
Experiment* emphasizes Penn's religious vision and goals in
Pennsylvania. The relationship between these visions and
the reality of Pennsylvania life and the effects that the discrepancy had on Penn are discussed in Bronner and in Gary
Nash's *Quakers and Politics.*

INDEX

Nayler, James, 10, 54, 57, 63n, 65n, 67n; on conversion, 69-75; epistemology of, 76; on Jesus Christ, 83n, 84n, 294; millennialism of, 86; physical-spiritual dualism of, 76; political and social views of, 86ff; procession to Bristol, 311; and Restoration Quaker writers, 7; theological rationalism of, 237

Negroes, 294

neo-Platonism, 174, 183

Nestorianism, 276-77, 281

New Jersey, 133, 140, 329n, 338n, 358-59

Nicholas, Henry, 49, 50, 53

Nickalls, John L., 13n

Nicolson, Marjorie Hope, 78n

nonconformists, 158, 218-22, 231, 235-36, 241, 260, 316, 325, 371. *See also* puritanism

Norton, Mrs., 104n

Nuttall, Geoffrey, 9n, 12n, 13n, 17n, 29-30, 33n, 47n, 53n, 61n, 71n, 87n, 182, 216, 218n, 228, 237, 305-06

Oldmixon, John, 95n, 97

Origen, 284

Orme, William, 27n, 167n

Ormonde, Duke of, 101

Owen, John, 28, 53, 96, 121n, 129, 167n, 262, 274, 293; and Penn, 97-98, 98n

Oxford University, 96-98, 101, 102-103

Pagitt, Ephraim, *A Discovery of 29 Sects . . .* , 8

Paracelsians, 52n

Parker, Alexander, 360

Patrick, Simon, 121n, 163n, 226n

Paul of Samosata, 285

Peare, Catherine Owens, 100n, 101n, 106n

Pelagians, 160, 161, 162

Penington, Isaac, 7, 60, 63n, 231, 281, 291; on conversion, 69-75; on Jesus Christ, 83n, 279-80; millennialism of, 85n; and Penn, 128; physical-spiritual dualism of, 183, 279-80; political and social views of, 319, 320; as Quaker theological writer, 6; on salvation history, 68

Penn, Gulielma Springett, 128, 199

Penn, Margaret, 94, 94n, 136n

Penn, Springett, 377

Penn, William, 63n, 92; arrested or in jail, 106, 107-09; on atonement of Christ, 107, 109, 147, 296-304; and Christian orthodoxy, 146-48, 269-74; on civil disobedience, 138-39, 327, 328, 342; on coercion and consensualism, 322-46, 350-67; colonial activities of, 140-42, 348-77; on conscience, 243ff, 247-48, 324, 333; on conversion and regeneration, 103-09, 148-49, 154-59, 168-82; conversion of, 101-09; divine-human dualism of, 169-75; doctrine of God, 283-87; on ecclesiology, 330-36; on England, 120-21, 124-25, 127; epistemology of, 77, 77n, 153-58, 199-215, 303; on faith, 180; family of, 94-95, 362, 377; on Fox, 335; in France, 98, 99, 100; on fundamental rights, 340-42, 351-52; on grace and free will, 169-75, 255-61; on the heavenly flesh of Christ, 290-91; on the Holy Spirit, 154-57; influenced by

Fisher on Scripture, 207; on the inner light, 153-58, 169-75, 207-08, 239ff, 330n; in Ireland, 101, 103-04; on Jesus Christ, 281-92, 296-304; on justification, 107, 109, 175-80; on means of grace, 202-15; millennialism of, 118, 121-26, 138-46; at Oxford, 96-98, 101; on Pennsylvania, 140-46, 348-67; perfectionism of, 181-82; physical-spiritual dualism of, 194-215, 287-88; political theories of, 3, 336-56, 358-59, 364-67; as politician, 3-4, 137-41; puritanical outlook toward world and society, 110-12; as Quaker leader, 4, 93-94, 126-41, 143; as Quaker writer and theologian, 4-6, 129-33, 143; on Quakers' peculiar customs, 114-16; on Quakers' relations with the world, 116-18, 142-46; on reason, 110, 147, 153, 158, 239-61, 271-72, 324, 338, 339; relations with Barclay, 128, 133, 135, 136-37, 137n; relations with Fox, 128, 131, 134-36, 136n; religious development of, 95-103; on religious liberty, 3, 272, 323-30, 340-42, 352; on Restoration era, 112-13, 124-25; on resurrection, 195-97; on Roman Catholicism, 139, 326-30; on the sacraments, 205-06; on salvation history, 118-26, 127, 138-46, 334-35; at Saumur, 98, 99, 100; on Scripture, 154-55, 207-15, 249-50; social theories and activities of, 344-46, 356-58; theological anthropology of, 197-99; theological relationship to liberal thought, 153, 174-75, 239-61, 269-74;

on times of visitation, 173; on the Trinity, 107, 109, 147, 283-87; on universalism, 257-61, 300-04

works mentioned by title in text:
An Address to Protestants . . . , 131; *A Brief Account of the Rise and Progress of the . . . Quakers . . .* , 131, 143, 148; *A Brief Examination . . .* , 134; *The Christian Quaker . . .* , 132, 147; *England's Great Interest . . .* , 139; *England's Present Interest . . .* , 131; *The Great Case of Liberty of Conscience . . .* , 131; *The Guide Mistaken . . .* , 107; *Innocency with Her Open Face . . .* , 109; *Judas and the Jews . . .* , 134; *Just Measures . . .* , 134; *A Key Opening a Way . . .* , 132, 133, 147; *A Letter of Love . . .* , 131; *More Work for George Keith . . .* , 134; *No Cross, No Crown . . .* , 107, 131; *One Project for the Good of England . . .* , 328; *The People's Ancient and Just Liberties . . .* , 339n, 340; *A Persuasive to Moderation . . .* , 131; *Primitive Christianity Revived . . .* , 147, 206, 254; *Quakerism a New Nickname . . .* , 132; *A Relation and Description of . . . Two Kingdoms . . .* , 107-08; *A Reply to a Pretended Answer . . .* , 147; *The Sandy Foundation . . .* , 107, 129, 272, 284, 297-98; *A Serious Apology . . .* , 132; *Some Fruits of Solitude . . .* , 147, 364; *The Spirit of Alexander the Coppersmith . . .* ,

Penn, William (*cont.*)
134; *A Testimony to the Truth
of God* . . . , 147, 148; *A Treatise of Oaths* . . . , 131; *Truth
Exalted* . . . , 107, 129, 327; *A
Visitation to the Jews* . . . ,
200
Penn, William, Sir Admiral, 95,
95n, 99, 106, 108, 114, 127,
136n, 348
Penn, William III, 377
Penney, Norman, 56n, 58n, 320n
Pennsylvania colony, 3, 87, 133,
136; charter of, 352; failure of
as holy experiment, 367-76;
Fox's warning against world-
liness of, 231; frames of government of, 321-22, 337, 337-
38n, 351-53, 354, 359-60, 361n,
362, 364; General Assembly of,
146n, 328, 351, 355, 360, 361,
361n, 362, 364, 365, 370, 374;
Penn's attitude toward, 140-
46, 243, 348-50, 362-67; Provincial Council of, 351, 356,
359-60n, 361, 361n, 362, 364-65,
366n, 369, 374, 376; Quakers'
attitude toward, 321-22, 359-
62; and religious liberty, 328,
329-30, 352
Pennyman, Mary, 96n, 97n
Pepys, Samuel, 98, 100, 101-102
perfectionism, Familists on, 50;
Penn on, 181-82; Quakers on,
64-66, 67-68, 168, 310
Perin, Matthew, 282n
Perkins, William, 14, 17n, 26,
26n, 121n; Penn's dependence
on his faculty psychology, 247
Perrot, John, 131, 134
Peters, Hugh, 47
Petition of Right, 340, 353
Pettit, Norman, 13n, 16n, 17n,
25n, 26n

Philadelphians, 52n
Philpot, John, 212
physical-spiritual dualism, of
Penn, 194-215, 287-88; of
Quakers, 75-84, 183-94, 276ff;
of spiritualists, 41-43
plague, 101, 103
Plato, 259
Platonic philosophy, 183, 193-94,
199, 222, 223ff, 228, 232, 239,
246, 251ff
Plomer, Henry R., 53n
Plotinus, 237, 259
Plutarch, 259
political and social thought, of
Penn, 3, 336-356, 358-59, 364-
67; of puritans, 19-20, 305-10,
338, 343; of Quakers, 86-89,
318-22; of spiritualists, 308-10
Popish Plot, 140, 327
Popple, William, 113-14n
Powicke, Frederick J., 167n
predestination, doctrine of, 16,
25-29, 213
preparation, doctrine of, 17, 25-
28, 73-74, 160-64, 312
Presbyterianism, Presbyterians,
10, 12, 13, 15, 16, 30-32, 32n,
35-36, 60, 64, 65, 91, 107, 130,
264, 273; Penn's view of, 120;
political and social tendencies
of, 308; relations with Penn,
132
Preston, John, 14, 17n, 23, 26n,
218-19
Provincial Council, *see* Pennsylvania colony
puritanism, 127, 183, 220, 290,
316; on coercion and consensualism, 305-10; on conversion,
16-19; on covenants, 18, 18n,
25-29, 307; definition of, 9-20;
divisions in, 9; emphasis on
Holy Spirit, 17, 18, 29-30;

Sprigge, Joshua, 47, 121n
Stafford, Earl of, 23
Stillingfleet, Edward, 109, 121n, 226n, 268n; cited by Whitehead on atonement, 293; cited by Whitehead on justification, 167
Stoicism, 174, 223f, 226, 232, 251ff
Story, John, 131, 134, 318, 333, 334, 335, 375
Story, Thomas, 205n
Stromberg, Roland, 194n, 268n
Sweden, 120
Sydney, Algernon, 139, 359, 360n
Sylvester, M., 12n
Symonds, Richard, 47

Tallack, William, 34n
Taylor, Jeremy, 99, 121n, 243, 268n
Tertullian, 252, 284
Tillotson, John, 121n, 223, 226-27, 268n
Timaeus, 259
Tindal, John, 121n
Tolles, Frederick, 216n, 353n, 356n, 360n, 366n
Tory party, 140
Tower of London, 107, 129
traducianism, 198n
Travers, Rebecca, 145n, 198n
Troeltsch, Ernst, 6, 237
Tulloch, John, 164n, 165n, 224n, 267n
Turner, Robert, 141n, 349n
Tyndale, William, 331
Tyrrell, George, 216

Ulmorum Acherons, 104n
Unitarianism, Unitarians, 165, 267-69, 276
universalism, Anglicans on, 223-27, 267; Penn on, 257-61, 300-04; Quakers on, 63-64, 70-74,

235-37; spiritualists on, 44-45. *See also* chapters 2, 5, and 6, *passim*

Vane, Sir Harry, 47, 222, 230
Vann, Richard, 9, 23n, 58n, 62n, 66, 67n, 127, 135
Vernon, James, 366
Vincent, Thomas, 107, 129
Vittells, Christopher, 50
Voltaire, 216, 228
von Rohr, John, 18n
Vulliamy, C. E., 104n

Waldenses, 120
Walwyn, William, 230
Walzer, Michael, 10, 15, 15n, 20n, 305ff
Weber, Max, 305
Webster, John, 40-41, 44, 47, 53, 90
Weigel, Valentin, 53, 91, 277
Weigelians, 52n
Wellenreuther, Hermann, 371n
West, Benjamin, 3n
Westminster Assembly, Confession, 28n, 32, 164, 165
Whichcote, Benjamin, 225n
Whig party, 139-40, 339, 342, 346, 359
Whitehead, George, 134, 360; co-author of *The Christian Quaker* . . . , 113n; co-author of *A Serious Apology* . . . , 115n; on Jesus Christ, 293; on justification, 167; and Penn, 135, 137; on perfectionism, 168; physical-spiritual dualism of, 77, 183
Whiteman, Anne, 13n, 16n
Whiting, C. E., 32n, 34n, 35n, 36n, 52n
Wilkinson, John, 131, 134, 318, 334, 375